ENGLISH LITERARY CRITICISM:
17TH AND 18TH CENTURIES

It is the prerogative of the ancients in all things to do neither too much nor too little. But we moderns have considered that in many matters we have advanced far beyond them when we changed their pleasant by-paths into highways, even though in consequence the shorter and safer highways should shrink again into paths that lead us through wild places.

Lessing, *Preface to Laokoon*

The eighteenth century was a century of experiments in a new aesthetic.

Anon.

ENGLISH LITERARY CRITICISM: 17th AND 18th CENTURIES

by

J. W. H. ATKINS

M.A., HON. LITT.D., MANCHESTER

FORMERLY FELLOW OF ST. JOHN'S COLLEGE, CAMBRIDGE;
EMERITUS PROFESSOR OF ENGLISH LANGUAGE AND LITERATURE,
UNIVERSITY COLLEGE OF WALES, ABERYSTWYTH

BARNES & NOBLE INC.

New York

PRINTED IN GREAT BRITAIN

PREFACE

IN the following survey of English literary criticism in the 17th and 18th Centuries—more correctly from 1650 to *c.* 1800—my primary object has been, as in my earlier works on critical history, to recall the actual theories and judgments of the various critics and their bearing on literary appreciation as it slowly developed. For, it seems to me, it is only in the light of such data that speculation of a general kind may be profitably indulged in. The period under review marks a fairly definite, if complicated, phase of English critical history. It forms as it were the bridge between the early strivings of the Renascence period and the great achievements of the 19th Century: and no apology is therefore needed for its detailed and separate study. With the fading of Renascence influences and the distraction of new and conflicting doctrines from France, a fresh course was now set in critical matters, a course which, modified by philosophical and other considerations, was ultimately determined by the independent native genius. And this course which in a large measure prepared the way for later critical adventures I have endeavoured to trace.

Owing to the large increase in the critical output at this stage some economy in the selection of material was inevitable. At the same time some account of French doctrines of the 17th Century was found to be essential as the necessary background of English critical activities for the best part of two centuries: and the opening chapter has been devoted to that particular purpose. Apart from this, the main lines of the development and the more significant critics have been considered: and the actuating motive throughout would seem to have been a conscious and prolonged desire to arrive at sound standards and methods of evaluating literature.

Some of the results of course will be familiar: the ultimate rejection of the neo-classical creed, for instance, or the more enlightened estimates of medieval and Elizabethan literatures. Less familiar, however, may be the marked influence of 'Longinus', of art-critics and others in fostering a new aesthetic outlook: while the importance of the Shakespeare studies and the valuable works of Kames and Morgann has been stressed anew. Moreover, corrected estimates have occasionally been submitted. Was

Pope's *Essay on Criticism*, for example, merely his version of the neo-classical creed? or again, was Johnson anything more than a 'hanging judge' and the dogmatic 'high priest of classicism'? The main finding however is that the period was essentially the seed-time of the later 19th-Century harvest: from critics great and small came hints that something more than common sense was needed for the critical business. And, for the rest, in the writings of critics ranging from Dryden to Cowper will be found much good reading along with critical doctrines of more than historical interest and abundant judgments that have since commended themselves to later generations.

With much gratitude I must record my indebtedness to scholars who by their earlier contributions in this same field have lightened my task to a considerable degree. Guidance of a general kind was afforded by Saintsbury's valuable sketch of the whole period: but even yet more helpful were the scholarly editions of various scattered texts. Of these the more notable were Spingarn's *Critical Essays of the 17th Century*, W. P. Ker's *Essays of John Dryden*, D. Nichol Smith's *Eighteenth Century Essays on Shakespeare*, and G. Birkbeck Hill's edition of *Johnson's Lives of the Poets*; and to them and others references are made throughout the pages that follow. Finally, my best thanks are due to a friend and former student, Mrs. David Evans of Aberystwyth, for her most generous assistance in putting together the Index.

J. W. H. A.

Aberystwyth
   23rd February 1950

CONTENTS

vii

ironical remarks on poetry. Farquhar, earlier native tradition of comedy upheld. Welsted, *Dissertation*: remarks on the rules, on 'taste', 'poetical reason' and original genius: defective judgments. Hughes, appreciation of Spenser. Blackwell, historical criticism applied to Homer. Bentley, masterly *Dissertation*: reckless treatment of *Paradise Lost*

Intellectual conditions (1740–65).

I. *Influence of 'Longinus'*: William Smith, translation: Lowth, on Hebrew poetry: attempt at classifying: its unique verse and style: 'sublimity'. Young, *On Original Composition*: neo-classicism attacked: Longinian 'imitation' commended: plea for original genius: comments on contemporaries

II. *Antiquarian interests:* Studies in non-classical literature. Gray, his critical works: literary theory: poetic style and diction: Greek chorus: essence of poetry: lyric poetry: comments on Pindarics, descriptive poetry and the caesura: critical judgments: Chaucer's verse, Lydgate and medieval literature. Joseph Warton: Pope as a poet: neo-classicism condemned: general terms rejected: blank verse and 'romantic' themes commended: critical standards and judgments. Thomas Warton: defence of the *Faërie Queene*: historical approach needed: its sources and medieval chivalry: verse and diction: Chaucer and allegory: *History of English Poetry* (13th–16th Centuries): historical and comparative survey. Hurd, early neo-classical leanings: corrected estimate of the age of chivalry and Elizabethan times: value of medieval romances: their influence on Shakespeare, Spenser and Milton: defence of the *Faërie Queene*: form determined by subject-matter: unity of design: attack on neo-classical doctrine: defence of 'romantic' literature and 'fine fabling': Hurd as a critic.

17th-Century judgments: 18th-Century editors and essayists.

I. *Work of editors:* Rowe, biography and emendations. Pope, Quartos and Folios: collation but arbitrary tests: censure and praise. Theobald, corrected estimates of Quartos and Folios: enlightened textual criticism. Johnson, comprehensive treatment: corruption of texts and means of remedying them: Shakespeare's art: universality

CHAPTER I

THE BREAK WITH RENASCENCE TRADITION:
NEW FRENCH INFLUENCES

IN the long development of literary criticism in England the period covered by the second half of the 17th Century and the century that followed is one of the first importance. It is a phase that represents an integral and indispensable chapter in English critical history, an advance on the performance of the Renascence period, and a preparation leading up to the achievements of the 19th Century; and in it a host of fresh influences were brought to bear from various quarters, making the story one of many complications that call for detailed and careful inquiry. Not without justice the criticism of this period has been described as one long attempt to escape from a false position adopted at the opening of the period. But the actual performance is something more than a negative and retreating action. It embodies positive efforts to reach the light in which definite progress was made in critical insight and judgment, while such efforts were shared by an ever-increasing number of contributors among whom were some of the great masters, Dryden and Johnson for example. To some minds the period is apt to seem the least significant and inspiring, lacking alike in the freshness and initiative of Renascence writers who preceded, and in the illumination provided by 19th-Century critics. To such readers the net performance is largely one of frustration and of promise that was never quite realized. But such an estimate is mainly the result of superficial reading and of judgment formed in the light of the later 19th-Century triumphs. For these two centuries, despite many shortcomings, represent, primarily and above all, strivings that led ultimately to the light. They stand for a coherent and unbroken movement with a character and significance of its own, in which new problems were faced, new critical methods devised, many acute appreciations made, and in which a wider outlook and much of positive and enduring value were actually achieved.

The beginnings of this new phase are therefore of considerable interest in critical history; and they may be traced to the period round about the middle of the 17th Century, when a definite break was made with that Renascence culture which,

throughout the 16th Century and the opening decades of the
17th, had furnished the main guidance. At that date English
criticism was diverted into fresh channels under the influence of
French doctrine which was destined to affect critical efforts
throughout the then literary world. Earlier English critics had
rendered valuable service in improving on the sporadic criticism
of medieval times, and in giving rise to a critical consciousness
which resulted in efforts to lay the foundations of a national
literature in the light that had dawned at the Renascence. In
their theorizing they had elaborated no system. The doctrines
they submitted were drawn indiscriminately from classical, post-
classical and medieval sources; but as yet no authority was regarded as final. Earlier teaching was in general submitted to the
tests of Nature or reason; and in discussing new developments
weight was attached to the demands of native genius and experience. This freedom of inquiry and this reliance on first principles
were among the distinguishing features of Renascence criticism
and they account for the enlightenment displayed at this early
stage, in the occasional recognition of such matters as the value
of the Middle Ages scorned by Humanists, the possibilities of
progress in literature, the occasional use of the historical method
in forming judgment, and, not least, the fact that the appeal of
literature was not confined to scholars and coteries but was
directed to men and human nature in general. Such then was the
critical tradition in England that was interrupted about the
middle of the 17th Century by certain French influences. And as
these influences were to be more or less active for the best part
of two centuries, they therefore call for careful consideration at
this stage.

The causes, in the first place, which led to this break with
Renascence culture in England were of various kinds. But the
main influence undoubtedly came from the ever-increasing
contacts with France, that country which, under Richelieu and
Louis XIV, had won unchallenged prestige, having become the
first power in Europe, supreme in politics and in all spheres of
intellectual activity, the *arbiter elegantiarum*, moreover, in all
social and literary arts, and the seed-plot of ideas for the rest
of Europe. Many of these contacts were of a personal kind.
French influence, for instance, had begun soon after the
marriage of Charles I with Henrietta Maria of France (1625), with
whom had come to England a colony of courtiers and wits. Then
as a result of civil conflict in England (1642–8) many Royalist
men of letters had sought refuge in France. They included

Hobbes, Waller and Denham, Davenant, Cowley and Evelyn—
a significant list—along with Charles himself; and they returned
at intervals after a stay of four years or more, imbued with the
charm of French culture centred at Paris. Nor was the prolonged
residence in England of Saint-Evremond, together with other
men of letters and ladies of society, without its effect. Exiled
from France, Saint-Evremond made England his home (1662-5,
1670-1703), at first within the circle of the Duchess of Mazarin;
and there as the intimate friend of Hobbes, Waller, Cowley,
Buckingham and others he brought fresh ideas to literary
circles and added liveliness to conversations at Will's.

Apart from this, English life after the Restoration (1660) was
permeated through and through with French influences, influences on manners, morals, fashions and dress; and in the literary sphere a like transformation became visible. Never before
nor since have the production of literature and the interest
in literature been more widely diffused among the upper and
educated classes in England than at this date, and it was to
France with its array of genius that all looked for guidance.
French literature was translated, imitated and freely pillaged;
French critical essays and treatises, hot from the press, were
translated and discussed in social circles; French literary ideals
and standards were accepted as authoritative. And the results
are seen in the rapid metamorphosis which took place in English
literature at this date, as reflected not only in the drama, the
verse and prose style of the Restoration period, but also, and not
least, in the critical thought of the time.

Of greater importance, however, is the need for a clear understanding of the nature of those French doctrines which exercised so potent an influence in critical history. And first to be
considered is that body of theory which ultimately constituted
a literary creed and to which the term 'neo-classical' has latterly been applied, a term, it might be added, which has the
merit of distinguishing such theory from the actual doctrines of
classical antiquity. For the new creed after all was but an imperfect adaptation of ancient, and more especially of Aristotle's,
teaching; so that there was something to be said for the description 'pseudo-classical', a term however that failed to be generally accepted. Attempts have since been made to trace the
beginnings of some such system in earlier English theorizing,
notably in occasional injunctions to follow the ancients and to
adopt their literary 'kinds'; but with greater justice it has
been maintained that the doctrine embodied in this French

neo-classical system was ultimately derived from 16th-Century Italian critics. A considerable debt was indeed owed to 16th-Century Italians. Yet it is to France, and France alone, that the crystallizing of this Italian theory, and the formulation of a definite system, were ultimately due; and in the process much of what was valuable in Italian theorizing was unfortunately lost. In England fragments of classical doctrine had been set forth from time to time; but no systematic exposition had been attempted. As late as 1632 Henry Reynolds, in his *Mythomystes*, was still enamoured with the Neo-Platonic doctrines of the 15th-Century Italian Humanist, Pico della Mirandola.

For the origin of this neo-classical theory in France we must look to the work of no one man or generation. It was the outcome of a widespread movement which gathered strength as time went on, and which had originated, strangely enough, as a reaction against the literary tradition set up by Ronsard, who, at the time of his death (1585), was one of the most famous men of letters in Europe. For this *volte-face* political considerations were in some measure responsible. Already by 1590, after a protracted period of religious troubles in France, a general longing for peace had ensued, accompanied by a sense of the urgent need for disciplined order in all spheres of life. And in this chastened atmosphere the literary doctrines and achievements of Ronsard were called in question. His free and enthusiastic imitation of the ancients, for instance, the importance he attached to the *furor poeticus*, and the liberties he allowed to imaginative genius, all these were being challenged at the close of the 16th Century. Such doctrines, it was said, in less gifted hands would lead to abuse and licence; and of these dangers the false grandeurs of Du Bartas were held to furnish ample illustration. The real significance and charm of the Ronsard tradition, in short, were being ignored. The reputation of the poet, subsequently shaken by Malherbe, was treated with increasing contumely throughout the 17th Century, until Boileau finally declared him to be an outmoded poet without any readers, thus completing the triumph of neo-classical ideals and standards.

Nor was this all. Another factor which contributed to the same end was the confusion which prevailed in the early decades of the century in matters of literary theory and practice. Apart from the Ronsard tradition, for instance, there were in the air at the time conflicting theories derived from antiquity, from 16th-Century Italy and from Spain; there were also the different dramatic practices of Jodelle, Hardy and others; and the result was a perplexing clash of poetic and dramatic doctrines. It was a situation that called for some amount of clarification. And the discord was in part resolved by Malherbe (1555–1628), who, by his severely rational and dogmatic teaching, laid the foundations of the new creed, and voiced the longings of his generation for order and system in literature as in other departments of life. The movement thus begun was developed by men and events that followed. National thought continued to move in disciplined channels under the regimes of Richelieu and Louis XIV; and the new creed developed gradually between 1630 and 1660, was crystallized after 1660, and established in its final form by Boileau and others.

Of the foundations laid by Malherbe, in the first place, that *grammairien à lunettes*, who, according to Chapelain, knew but little of poetry, there is this to be said. His work was of a limited character; though he impressed on his countrymen the need for form and correctness in literature. He reformed language and verse, the instruments of literature; but his real influence lay in making a fresh start with poetry necessary. To him poetry was an art rather than an inspiration; yet he has nothing to say about the several 'kinds'. He condemned the earlier poetic technique, demanding clarity and rational form in expression; and whereas he propounded no specific theory of poetry his influence was nevertheless considerable, especially in *salons* and other literary circles. In short, what he did was to give new direction to the study and cultivation of the poetic art; and this was generally recognized by the generations that followed, as was suggested by Boileau's familiar and resounding remark, '*Enfin Malherbe vint*,' wherein he is hailed as a sort of literary Messiah.

It was after the death of Malherbe (1628), however, that neo-classicism entered on the first stage of its actual development and began to take definite shape. Poetry now became the main concern; and the need for artistic discipline was emphasized by the affectations and contortions of the Précieux school. Malherbe had affected to ignore the teaching of antiquity; but theorists now turned for guidance to later authority, to those 16th-Century Italians by whom the doctrines of the ancients, and of Aristotle in particular, had been discussed and expounded. As a result, between 1630 and 1660 there emerged as the compilation of various hands the first rough draft of what is known as the neo-classical system. According to that draft poetry was, briefly, to be reformed by imitation of the ancients; such imitation was to be effected by submission to a code of rules based on ancient authority; and since epic and drama were the most important of the 'kinds', they were to receive the main attention. At this early stage the development of the theory was largely due to the influence of the French Academy, founded by Richelieu in 1635, together with the teaching of Chapelain, La Mesnardière, and the Abbé D'Aubignac, though minor contributions came also from Balzac, Scudéry, Sarrasin, Segrais and others. Altogether the new system was visibly forming; and in *salons* and elsewhere authority was triumphing over independence, discipline over freedom.

The first *pronunciamento* by exponents of the new doctrine was made in the course of the attack, engineered by Richelieu, on Corneille's *Cid* (1636), in the course of which the battle for the Unities was fought and won. Conceived in Italy, that doctrine in France had already become a much-vexed question, vigorously opposed by Ogier (1628), advocated by Mairet (1631), and fiercely discussed on all sides in treatise and Preface. The culmination of the controversy however came in the assault by Scudéry and Chapelain under the auspices of the Academy, when the *Cid* was condemned for breaches not only of the Unities, but of the rules of decorum and probability as well—all rules which were to be part and parcel of the neo-classical creed. By 1640 the battle was over; and as a result, not only was a new formula established for French dramatic art, but the future of literary theory was also roughly determined.

Meanwhile Chapelain (1595-1674) was emerging as the leading exponent of the new creed. A scholar, well-read in Italian literature, a minor poet, and a man of society besides, his influence was spread abroad more by his correspondence than by his actual writings; though characteristic even of his early Preface to Marino's *Adone* (*c.* 1620) were certain features of the new system, notably a respect for the rules with their divisions and sub-divisions. At the same time an exposition of the new code was being attempted by La Mesnardière, a medical man in Richelieu's service; and this code appeared in his *Poétique* (1639), in which the influences of Scaliger and Heinsius are evident, though but one volume, that on dramatic poetry, was completed. Still more important was the *Pratique du Théâtre* (1657) of the Abbé D'Aubignac, in which the rules were presented as being in accordance with reason, while a keen sense of stage requirements is revealed throughout. In addition further

contributions to the new doctrine were made in the Dialogues
and Essays of Sarrasin, and in the Prefaces of Scudéry; while in
1633 had also appeared Godeau's *Discours de la Poésie chréti-
enne*, which, based on Tasso's teaching, forestalled the short-
lived triumph of Christian epics (1650–60).

Up to 1660, therefore, the main ideas of neo-classicism had
emerged in detached and somewhat irregular fashion. The cult
of ancient literary forms had been laid down as a fundamental
dogma, and sundry efforts had been made to elaborate the new
doctrine. So far, however, a systematic exposition had been
lacking; and it was during the reign of Louis XIV (1661–1715)
that the neo-classical creed was set forth in something like final
and coherent form. Under the absolute government of that
monarch had come a new unity of thought and feeling, in which
the ideals and standards of court life were predominant. Moreover, the revolt against the extravagances of the Précieux
school having culminated in the comedies of Molière and the
trenchant *Satires* (1666) of Boileau, the demand for positive
guidance had become even yet more insistent. And, in the
meantime, the effects of earlier influences were now beginning
to be felt—the rationalism of Descartes, for instance, or again,
the encouragement given to systematic and authoritative teaching by the earlier Catholic reaction and by the organizing ability
of the Jesuits in particular. On the other hand, classical scholarship had meanwhile deteriorated, being regarded as mere pedantry; and efforts were now made to defer to the spirit of polite
society by popularizing learning, *en la dépaysant des collèges et
la délivrant des mains des pédants*—the aim which Balzac had
previously declared to be his. These then were the conditions
under which the neo-classical doctrine finally emerged. It was
a new creed; in form systematic, in spirit dogmatic, though
couched in a style suitable for courtly readers.

It was by Boileau (1636–1711), however, that the new orthodoxy was duly established; though associated with him in the
task were other less gifted writers, notably, le père Rapin, Le
Bossu and others. Already in 1674 Boileau's *Art poétique* and
Rapin's *Réflexions sur la Poétique et les Poètes* had appeared,
and they were followed by Le Bossu's *Traité du Poème épique*
(1675); all works of the first importance in critical history, if
of varying intrinsic values. In these works were formulated the
literary precepts which were to survive throughout the 18th
Century; and since all three were forthwith translated into
English, their influence on English criticism was considerable.

By Boileau, in the first place, the general principles of neo-classicism were laid down in memorable form, but in terms which differed vitally from those of earlier theorists. Starting from a firm belief in the existence of absolute and unvarying standards of excellence in literature, he held that such standards were attainable in each of the 'kinds' by following rules drawn from the ancients. The ancients, however, he accepted as guides, not because of their antiquity, but because they conformed with the dictates of Nature or reason; and in thus basing his system on rational grounds, rather than on an unreasoning following of the ancients, he transformed in significant fashion the current theory.

Rapin's contribution was of a more detailed and systematic kind; though, like Boileau, he set out the neo-classical canon at large, and adopted as his basis Boileau's new doctrine. In his *Réflexions sur la Poétique*, a treatise on poetry in general, his guide throughout is Aristotle; and he accepts Aristotle's rules on the ground that they *ne sont faites que pour réduire la nature en méthode*.[1] Apart from this he expounds in lucid fashion the rules for both tragedy and the epic; and his influence for the time being, in England at least, was greater that that of Boileau owing to the direct nature of his treatment. Of less intrinsic value, but important historically, was Bossu's treatise on the epic, which became at once the standard work on the subject, superseding Mambrun's *De poemate epico* (1652), and maintaining its authority throughout the 18th Century. Bossu's treatment, like that of Rapin, is of a detailed and logical kind; and his definition of the epic, together with his analysis of its structure, are his main contributions to literary theory. They were elements, however, which gave an unfortunate direction to the development of neo-classicism, in narrowing its outlook and reducing the epic to something like an ingenious mechanism, thus giving rise to epic formulas and recipes in later generations.

Such then were the main stages in the development of neo-classicism in France; and it now becomes necessary to consider, briefly, the actual nature of the new orthodoxy, first, its sources, then its chief doctrines, and finally, its significance in critical history. It has been already stated that the literary atmosphere of the early 17th Century was one of revolt against the Ronsard tradition, and that in the search for more stable foundations guidance was sought in the ancients. In the teaching of Aristotle were found elements which by common consent supplied

---

[1] i. xii: cf. Pope's 'nature methodized'.

abroad a significant treatment of the moral law. The epic poet, he explained, first decides on the moral he wishes to teach, and then clothes it in an allegory in a manner *vraisemblable et divertissante*. He further analysed the parts of an epic and describes them as made up of fable, characters, machinery, episodes, sentiment and expression. But while this conception was generally approved, by Boileau as well, various other precepts were prescribed from time to time. Thus Rapin (following Aristotle) demands that the action should be one, simple and entire, in extent neither too vast nor yet too limited, but with episodes related to the main theme to give variety. Elsewhere it was held (in accordance with Tasso's doctrine) that historical subjects were best suited for epic treatment, provided that such themes dealt with periods neither too modern nor too remote, in order to facilitate freedom of treatment.

Then, too, specific injunctions were issued concerning the more detailed treatment of the epic. A quiet beginning, for instance, was required; the story was not to be related *ab ovo*: a perfect hero was necessary; and the action was to be developed by the intervention of the gods. To the use of this divine machinery considerable importance was attached; and Le Bossu urges that an early invocation to the gods was essential, since it was not only an act of piety but also a means of adding verisimilitude to the later participation of the gods in the action. And in this connexion a further pronouncement was made. Influenced by Tasso, who had recommended Christian themes for epic purposes, attempts had been made in France (1650–60) to dispense with ancient mythology and to produce a number of Christian epics. The experiments of Le Moyne, Scudéry, Chapelain and Desmarets, however, were all unsuccessful, though previously advocated by Godeau (1633) and later on defended by Desmarets (1674). And Boileau in consequence condemned the use of Christian themes and machinery in the epic. Such a treatment of Christian mysteries, he argued, could but detract from simple faith and reverence, while pagan mythology he regarded as the life and ornament of epic poetry.

Similarly, in connexion with tragedy certain definite rules were laid down. In general, its appropriate themes were held to be historical in character, the dignity of tragedy requiring subjects that involved great interests of state. Verisimilitude, decorum and the three Unities were moreover to be observed throughout; the treatment was to be illuminated by great thoughts and noble expressions; and the tragic hero was to be of exalted rank. Then, too, its structure was also defined. There was to be a protasis in which the characters revealed themselves; and this was to be followed by the main intrigue, the *reconnaissance* and *dénouement*. The play was to consist of five acts; three or four actors alone were to appear simultaneously on the stage; and the tragic effects for the most part were described as those of pity and fear. Of the Aristotelian 'catharsis', however, but little is said; though Rapin gives an interesting version of that ancient doctrine. In tragedy, he explains, human passions are rectified by the passions themselves. The emotions of pity and fear, he states, are enfeebling in their effects; and they are duly regulated by tragedy. In the agitation of the soul, he adds, consists the tragic pleasure; and here he parts company with Aristotle, for whom the calm and balance resulting from the regulation of the passions constituted the particular pleasure conferred by tragedy.

With regard to comedy, many of the rules for tragedy were held to apply here as well; though its plots were in general to be invented, not drawn from history. No tragic elements (*tragiques douleurs*) however were to be allowed to intrude; the plot was to consist of a neat intrigue ending happily, and with characters drawn from the ranks of lowly life. Special attention, however, was to be devoted to characterization, which was to be in accordance with recognized types and the demands of decorum. Here Nature was to be the guide, providing bizarre personalities represented in contemporary life, in *la cour* and *la ville*. Moreover, reason or good sense was to animate the action throughout. There was to be no foolish or irrational doings; and one of the graces of comedy was refined *badinage* (*badiner noblement*).

These then, in brief, were the main lines along which the neo-classical creed was formulated in 17th-Century France; and what now can be said of its significance in critical history, and its value as a permanent contribution to critical theory? That the system was primarily the outcome of a reaction against earlier excesses, some apparent, some real, that it was fostered by contemporary political and social influences which made for the recognition of authority in all walks of life, and that, further, it resulted in a code specially congenial to the French genius with its demands for order, lucidity and concentration; these facts establish its claim to be regarded as a provisional orthodoxy, of value to French writers at this particular date. At the same time it obviously aimed at something more than this, at providing none other than permanent rules for literary creation and judgment. And at first sight it had not a little to commend it to future generations. It was for instance a sound instinct that had directed critics in their search for effective methods and standards to resort for guidance to ancient classical literature, the greatest literary achievement then available, and further, to recommend an imitation of those earlier master-pieces. The procedure was one that had been suggested by great critics of antiquity; it was one, moreover, that had since been found effective in practice, and not by Virgil alone. Then, too, in adopting Aristotle as their main guide there was much to be commended; for had he not analysed and expounded with mar-vellous insight some of the guiding principles of that ancient literature at its best? Nor were Aristotle's doctrines accepted on his authority alone. They were claimed to be in accordance with the fundamental laws of Nature or reason; so that the system was ostensibly based on sure foundations. In addition, the system had the further merit of being easily intelligible with its neat classifications and its definite rules; it was also set forth in effective fashion by Boileau and others; and altogether it is no wonder that it became more or less authoritative for the best part of a century or more.

It was in the development of the creed, however, that defects in the system became apparent, despite the admirable governing principles with which critics had entered on their task. For one thing, a radically wrong conception had been formed of the process of 'imitation', which was taken to mean a more or less mechanical reproduction of ancient technique, of external and structural details that constituted the ancient formal character-istics of epic, tragedy and the rest. Yet such a procedure could only lead to indifferent results; and it was far from the minds of those 1st-Century critics at Rome—Cicero, Horace, 'Longinus' and others—who had advocated an imitation of Greek models. To them it stood rather for a process of the spirit, an imagina-tive stimulus derived from contact with works of genius; or again, for a process of re-creation, in which were assimilated, not the mere forms, but the spirit and methods, of ancient workmanship, with a view to the production of something new out of the old, something adapted to changes of medium and environment. And Ascham in England together with Du Bellay in France had preserved something of this conception when the former had declared imitation to be, not the indiscriminate borrowing of verbal or structural details, but a process of

assimilation in which artistic instincts and artistic judgment
were constantly at work, freely adapting and refashioning the
methods of earlier models.

Then, too, an unfortunate result of this mechanical conception of imitation was the importance attached to rules as guides
ensuring correct methods and standards in the work of literary
creation. As Rapin frankly and confidently declared, 'the only
way to please is by the rules'. Yet rules as such could have but
a crippling and restricting effect, as opposed to the freedom
required for literary activities. And, apart from this, the rules
that were laid down were derived, not from a first-hand examination of ancient masterpieces themselves, but from theories
of earlier and fallible critics. Moreover, there was one further
defect of considerable importance in that the rules submitted
were regarded as fixed and final, admitting of no modification
in either time or place. Boileau, for one, shared in the belief that
there existed absolute and unvarying standards of literary perfection; and this lack of historical sense, this failure to recognize
the possibility of relative standards, was characteristic of neo-
classical teaching as a whole, and it led astray Boileau's own
and later generations.

Again, the use made of Aristotle was inaccurate and misleading. The truth was that his *Poetics* was but superficially
read, owing not only to difficulties in the text itself and to the
decline of Greek scholarship at this date, but also to the fact that
acquaintance with the text was in consequence almost wholly
second-hand, being derived through the media of earlier Latin
translations and commentaries. Hence the misunderstanding of
his teaching, with its esoteric doctrines, its ambiguities and its
strange terminology. To begin with, the principles he enunciated
were taken for rules binding on all ages; whereas his attitude
throughout had been merely retrospective, his object being to
seek the laws underlying earlier Greek literature, and he makes
no claim to legislate for the future. In one place [1] indeed he stated
that such a claim lay outside his purpose; and here he hints at
the possibility of relativity in literary standards.

Nor was it only that his more recondite doctrines, such as
those of 'ideal imitation' and 'catharsis', were either ignored or
but rarely expounded. Many of the characteristic elements of
the neo-classical creed were none other than distortions of his
actual teaching. The 'kinds', for instance, which to Aristotle
were but a convenient classification of the practice of Greek

---

[1] *Poetics*, 1449 a, 7.

poets, now became a system of fixed types of poetry with definite qualities and fixed rules. His law of 'probability', which related not to subject-matter but to dramatic structure, was also misrepresented. He had admitted the use of impossible incidents when rendered probable by artistic treatment; but the neo-classical 'verisimilitude' related to subject-matter alone, so that the 'probable impossible', or 'the world of fine fabling', was ruled out of poetic treatment. Then, too, the rules relating to the Unities, 'decorum', and the use of types in characterization, all were propounded in a sense and with an absoluteness that were non-Aristotelian. For, as is well-known, Aristotle had prescribed the Unity of action alone, the Unities of time and place being added by Castelvetro and others. With Aristotle, again, 'decorum' had stood for fitness or seemliness in general; whereas it now became narrowed to the conventions of a sophisticated society, a test which long ago, under another absolute political regime, had characterized the judgments passed on Homer by Hellenistic critics. Moreover, nowhere in the *Poetics* is to be found the special importance attached to social rank as such in the characters of tragedy.

At the same time it would seem at first sight that sound foundations had been provided for neo-classicism when it was claimed that the rules, like the teaching of Aristotle, were no arbitrary decrees but were firmly based on Nature or reason. Yet here again something vital was wanting. Earlier Humanists, followed by English critics, had adopted as their guide in intellectual matters the test of Nature or reason; but hitherto that test had been somewhat vaguely and loosely defined. Now, however, attempts were made to explain 'reason' in more philosophical terms. It was explicitly described as the master-faculty in man which regulated all other faculties, being endowed with the power of restraining the fancy and of distinguishing the false from the true. The control of the fancy and the exposition of truth were, however, not the prime functions of the poet; and the part played by the imaginative and emotional sides of men was for the most part ignored. Ostensibly based on the nature of the human mind, neo-classicism after all rested on imperfect philosophical foundations. That basis, it is true, was something other than the prosaic 'reason' of the logician; yet it embodied but an imperfect conception of the human mind, and its limitations were increased when humanity was confined to the artificial and sophisticated society of the day.

Such then was the main characteristic of the neo-classical

system as expounded in 17th-Century France; and despite its manifold deficiencies it was destined to exercise considerable influence on contemporary criticism in England and to evoke a prolonged challenge in the century following. That it acted as a purifying factor for the time being in France, more especially in counteracting earlier extravagances, this much must be granted. The institution of such rules as the Unities also doubtless responded to an innate tendency of the French genius towards concentration and to a desire for an exact representation of life. Moreover, commended in rational and persuasive fashion by leading authorities in France at a time when that country had attained intellectual hegemony in Europe, it is not strange that its doctrines were accepted by wider circles and that it became recognized as a sort of international creed.

Yet the system contained within itself the seeds of its own decay. The antiquity it imitated was not the living world of ancient Greece and Rome, but a faded, bookish and limited antiquity, viewed at second-hand through the pages of divers authorities. The imitation it involved was not an attempt to recapture the soul and methods of antiquity, but an imitation superficial and pedantic, which copied external details and laid down rigid rules which stifled originality, condemned flights of fancy, and in general ignored all ideas of progress and development. And the result was a narrow creed, crippling the creative spirit and condemning the poet to the observance of lifeless formulas and sterile practice. The truth was that a system founded on a shallow knowledge of Aristotle, and arrived at deductively, could form no lasting guide to either the creation or the appreciation of great poetry. The emotional and imaginative effects of great art could not be attained by following rules of composition, by ordered structure and the like; the reason alone would not suffice for aesthetic discernment in art; nor could finality be assumed in the standards of artistic values. Something more was needed than this rationalistic simplification of what after all was a complicated and an elusive subject; and later generations were gradually to learn in their literary theorizing the value of the means actually employed by Aristotle, namely, the use of inductive, historical and psychological methods.

While, however, the emergence of the neo-classical system was undoubtedly the main result of French critical activities during the 17th Century, it would be wrong and misleading to regard the period as wholly dominated by the tenets of that creed. From the first there were signs of protest and of other and more liberal views concerning literature. Early in the century the basis of neo-classicism had been challenged in France by dramatists opposed to a servile copying of the ancients and to an observance of the Unities. Later on the challenge was renewed, and now in more effective fashion, by two influential personalities, namely, Corneille and Saint-Evremond; and at the same time fresh light on literature generally had come from antiquity by way of Boileau's translation of 'Longinus', however imperfect, as well as from certain passages of Petronius' *Satyricon* which now became current coin. Nor was this all; for a reaction against the rules and all that they stood for in both creation and judgment became visible in the works of Chevalier de Méré and La Bruyère, and with them appeared the promise of a new aesthetic. All alike witnessed to a growing discontent which threatened the foundations of neo-classicism and went to modify the system by lessening its narrowness and rigidity. The way was thus prepared for a wider outlook on literature; and if the earlier protests had passed unheeded, the later activities were of definite influence in later critical history.

Of interest, in the first place, were the early sporadic attempts to foster independence in art, influenced possibly by the Spaniards, Tirso de Molina and Lope de Vega, though Montaigne had previously maintained that the moderns were free to correct and modify the works of the ancients. Thus Deimier in his *Art poétique* (1610) had held that the poet should be as free as Nature in her production of roses and carnations; that he should therefore adapt his art to his own particular genius; and elsewhere ridicule is poured on attempts to make use of classical metres in poetry. D'Urfé, again, in his Preface *to Sylvanire* (1627) had claimed that French poetry ought necessarily to differ from that of the ancients, seeing that music, architecture, and all arts had undergone change. It was from Ogier, however, in his Preface to Schelandre's tragicomedy *Tyr et Sidon* (1628) that the most striking pronouncements came, when he protested against the restrictions imposed by the Unities, objected to clear-cut distinctions of the 'kinds', and in general denied the necessity for rigid rules to guide the poet. And the reasons he gives for his attitude are eminently sound. He points out, for example, that a blind imitation of the ancients was out of place in modern times. All had since changed, he urges, and modern writers could not escape the law of progress. Thus tastes were said to differ in accordance with nationality, age and manners;

so that the business of the poet was to adapt his work to the
'intellectual climate' of his country and generation.[1] And in this
connexion he recalls the 12th-Century dictum of Bernard of
Chartres, that the moderns were 'as dwarfs on the shoulders of
giants', and therefore saw farther than the ancients.[2] Yet something, he allows, could still be gleaned from antiquity, though a
meticulous copying of Greek tragedy, for instance, a religious
performance governed by ancient conditions, was both ill-timed
and futile. 'We shall imitate the Greeks much better', he acutely
adds,[3] 'by paying heed to our national genius and language, and
by selecting what may be fitted to the humour of our nation.'
In short, judgment in imitation was essential, as Sturm and
Ascham had previously noted. His advice is therefore 'to add
and omit, avoiding faults and adopting only what is excellent';
and by this free treatment, it was argued, the spirit of antiquity
would be more nearly attained than by the literal methods of
'grammarians' and others.

Such theories, however, were set forth only to be silenced by
the official pronouncements of Chapelain and Scudéry in connexion with the *Cid*. But their animating spirit was subsequently
kept alive by Corneille and Saint-Evremond, who fought, not
without success, against the prevailing tyranny of the rules,
and who were to influence in particular contemporary English
thought. At first the impression made on Corneille (1606–84)
by the strictures of the Academy was profound; and in his
later plays he adopted methods more in accordance with the
conventional theory. When, however, D'Aubignac's *Pratique du
Théâtre* appeared in 1657 he attempted to justify that faith
which he had cherished from the first; and in 1660 he wrote his
three *Discours* on the dramatic art, as well as three *Examens*
of his own tragedies. His theorizing is mostly concerned with
tragedy; but after a keen and lengthy study of Aristotle's
Poetics, together with Italian commentaries, he arrives not only
at certain laws of tragedy itself, but also at certain guiding
principles of the literary art in general, all of which gave
evidence of reasoned and original thinking.

As his chief guide he takes the *Poetics* of Aristotle; but that
work he approaches in a spirit different from that of his contemporaries. Recognizing the need for reading it in a historical
light and recalling that Aristotle's remarks were limited to plays
of his own time, Corneille notes that there were obvious gaps and
obscurities in his treatment; and he therefore considers the

[1] *Préface*, p. 18.   [2] *ibid.* p. 19.   [3] *ibid.*

spirit, rather than the letter, of the work, while claiming the right to interpret it in accordance with his own good sense and experience. And the results are seen in his free and reasoned treatment of ancient doctrine, recalling in some measure the Ronsard tradition. In Aristotle he found confirmation for not a few of his own cherished ideas; but elsewhere he does not hesitate to suggest other precepts where necessary. Thus in opposition to many of his contemporaries he follows Aristotle in describing the primary function of art as that of giving pleasure, that is, the pleasure afforded by a faithful representation of human nature. Or again, he perceives that Aristotle had laid down general principles, but no absolute rules binding on all ages and peoples; and as a stout opponent of all rules himself, he therefore advocates freedom for the activities of genius.

Then, too, further evidence of his critical reading of Aristotle is provided by his remarks on tragedy in particular. His demand for a *liaison des scènes*, for instance, is none other than Aristotle's 'law of probability', according to which the various incidents in a plot should develop in a 'probable or necessary sequence'. Moreover, the relative position he adopts with regard to the Unities is also that of Aristotle, for he sees that some subjects lend themselves more easily than others to a strict observance of the rules. On the other hand equally significant are those places where he departs from Aristotle's teaching, influenced possibly by some Italian comment, but also assuredly by his own dramatic experience. Aristotle's description of the tragic effects as 'pity and fear', for example, was generally accepted by neo-classical critics; but Corneille notes also, as Minturno had done, the further effect of 'admiration', aroused by the grandeur and dignity of the tragic theme. Again, whereas Aristotle had required in the tragic hero but a moderate virtue, Corneille holds, less certainly, that the central character might be either saint or criminal, provided it was represented in lifelike and sympathetic fashion. The result of such discussions in the main was to justify his own dramatic practice in the light of Aristotle's teaching; and that justification formed a valuable commentary on the reigning system, suggesting a more liberal treatment of ancient doctrine than that characteristic of neo-classical theorists. Apart from this the methods he employed were not without their later influence; for with him began, as distinct from formal treatises, those reasoned inquiries into basic literary matters, as well as those detailed judgments on literature in the concrete illustrated by Dryden and others.

3

Of this spirit which militated against the rigours of neo-classicism an equally effective use was made by Saint-Evremond (1613–1703), that *grand seigneur*, soldier and wit, a disciple of Montaigne, who wrote to amuse himself, and who proved to be not only one of the most suggestive of critics by reason of his independent spirit, his fine taste and charm of style, but also one of the most influential of them all as a result of wide circles of friendship formed in France and England alike. Concerning his attitude to the neo-classical system he leaves us in no doubt in the course of those miscellaneous Essays and Discourses which constitute his critical works. He condemns outright the basic principles of that system, its rules in general, as well as certain precepts relating to the 'kinds', thus suggesting views of a wider, less constricting, character.

In the first place he objects to that principle which inculcated a close imitation of the ancients; his main point being that in such imitation poets were adopting methods that had since become obsolete. He could conceive of certain laws of art founded on good sense or reason which would always remain; but the methods of the ancients, he contended, had had their day, and the prevailing mixture of ancient and modern had proved a failure.[1] Hence Homer's poems, confessedly master-pieces, were nevertheless no fit models for modern poets. Indeed, had Homer lived then, he would have adapted his poetry to modern conditions. The true use of Homer's works, he main-tained, was to help in forming artistic judgment, that judgment which should everywhere regulate modern poetry. And else-where he adds that even Aristotle could not be accepted as an infallible guide. That his *Poetics* was 'a fine work', he readily concedes; 'but then there is nothing so perfect', he states, 'as to rule all ages and nations';[2] and, moreover, 'Corneille had revealed new beauties for the stage not known to Aristotle'.

Then, too, he refuses outright to recognize a system based on rules, whether derived from the ancients or founded on reason. Rules, he allowed, might be useful 'to avoid confusion', and good sense might 'moderate the ardour of inflamed fancy'.[3] But then, he states, 'it is necessary to remove from the rules all troublesome constraint and to banish too scrupulous a reason which leaves nothing to freedom and Nature'. In comedy especi-ally, he notes, it would be 'folly to subject ourselves to too austere an order or to torture ourselves in matters intended only

---

[1] *Oeuvres*, ed. Des Maizeaux (1739 ed.), iv. 335–7.
[2] *ibid*. iii. 171.   [3] *ibid*. iii. 280.

for pleasure'. Apart from this he comments with amazement on the superabundance of rules for tragedy current in his day; and he ridicules in characteristic fashion D'Aubignac's failure in his tragedy, *Zénobie*, quoting for that purpose the caustic remark of Monsieur le Prince. 'I am grateful to Mr. D'Aubignac', stated that worthy,[1] 'for having followed so closely the rules of Aristotle; but I cannot forgive the rules of Aristotle for having made Mr. D'Aubignac write so poor a tragedy.' The truth was, as Saint-Evremond pointed out in another place, that poetry demanded a special kind of genius 'which does not accommodate itself too closely to good sense. Sometimes it is the language of the gods, sometimes the language of fools, and rarely that of the *honnête-homme*.'[2] And moreover he held that 'the cult of the clear idea is incompatible with the care for beauty. Carried too far it dries up the fancy, which is, with sensibility, the most abundant source of poetry.'

Similar emancipating tendencies are also revealed in his comments on tragedy, the poetic 'kind' that was receiving most attention at the time; and here, once again, he points out the unsuitability of ancient guidance, particularly in the use made of gods and goddesses in the action. By the ancients, he recalls,[3] all-powerful but capricious gods were held to control the deeds of men; and this then formed part of the common belief. Since that time, however, things had changed; and this element of the supernatural had come to be regarded as fabulous and incredible. Nor could its place be fitly or convincingly taken by saints and angels; for the introduction of such characters on to the stage would shock good people and be ridiculed by the irreligious. And indeed, argued Saint-Evremond, were an adaptation of ancient methods possible and Christian machinery invented, such an innovation would still be ineffective, for the spirit of Christianity was directly opposed to that of tragedy. 'Saintly humility and patience, as opposed to ardour and force' were said to be quite contrary to the virtues of tragic heroes. He therefore maintains that the action of modern tragedy should be great and wholly human throughout. Its theme should be the greatness of the human soul, exciting not only 'pity and fear' but 'admiration' and 'transport' (*ravissement*) as well. And with this pronouncement (implicit in Aristotle) modern theorists would generally agree, as when it is nowadays stated that in its essential form tragedy represents not human misery but human nobility and greatness.

[1] *Oeuvres*, iii. 171.   [2] *ibid*. iii. 97–8.   [3] *ibid*. iii. 170 ff.

Not content, however, with decrying the use of supernatural elements in modern tragedy, Saint-Evremond ventures further and suggests that ancient tragedy itself would have been better without the gods and goddesses,[1] since they made the theatre a school of superstitious terror and compassion, weakening the morale of men and making them prone to bewail misfortunes instead of seeking for remedies. And this view leads to an attack on the doctrine of 'catharsis', a theory devised by Aristotle, according to Saint-Evremond, in order to mitigate the harm done to Athenian minds of which he was fully conscious. That a soul should be agitated in order to calm it by later reflexion he described as a strange proceeding; for few spectators would be capable of returning to tranquillity by later meditation and thought. Aristotle's theory of 'catharsis' is therefore brusquely dismissed as absurd; a theory, added Saint-Evremond, 'which no-one hitherto has understood and which Aristotle himself did not understand'.

Nor was it only in questioning the main principles of neo-classicism that Saint-Evremond rendered service to his generation. His approach to critical matters was also something new; for he makes, practically for the first time, a notable use of historical, comparative and psychological methods of criticism. His sense of the historical factor, for instance, is seen in his frequent references to social conditions; as when he suggests that increased refinement had rendered distasteful the fierce and passionate heroes of antiquity, or again, when he points out that the more rational society of modern days viewed external Nature in a different light from that of the ancients, so that ancient similes relating to heaven, the sun, and the like, had since become meaningless. Then, too, he makes use of comparison and contrast in bringing out the specific qualities of literature; as when, for example, he contrasts ancient and modern drama, or discusses the relative merits of French and English plays. And, besides, his psychological approach is visible throughout. Thus emotional effects, he explains, should not be overdone. 'Better too little than an excess of passion', he urges,[2] 'for too little leaves to our imagination the pleasure of adding, . . . the other gives the trouble of pruning—always difficult and annoying.' Or again, he ridicules that unreal emotion which indulges in elaborate expression. 'A soul deeply touched', he explains,[3] 'does not have the power of thinking much or of diverting itself with the variety of its conceptions.' And in

[1] *Oeuvres*, iii. 178 ff.   [2] *ibid*. iii. 190.   [3] *ibid*. iii. 191–2.

general he calls for restraint in emotional passages, reminding his readers of Cicero's dictum: *cito enim arescit lacryma praesertim in aliena miseria.*[1] Such views and treatment were worlds away from the pedantic and dogmatic methods of most of his contemporaries; and together with his wide culture, his easy and courtly manner, and above all his delightful style, they opened up new possibilities in the field of critical activities.

Meanwhile, apart from the efforts of Corneille and Saint-Evremond to inculcate more liberal views concerning literature, other agencies were making for the same end; and of these, highly significant, in the first place, were the attempts to revive acquaintance with certain critical works of antiquity, other than those of Aristotle and Horace. It was Boileau who first restored to modern readers some knowledge of the difficult treatise of 'Longinus', *On the Sublime,* 'one of the most precious relics of antiquity', as Boileau himself described it, 'a book of gold', according to Casaubon; and the revival was one of first-rate importance in critical history. Certain editions and Latin translations had previously appeared. In the year 1554 Robortello had already unearthed and edited the text, remarking that it was an *opus redivivum antea ignotum a tenebris in lucem editum.* Later on a Latin translation was prepared by Pétra, which was reproduced in Langbaine's edition of the Greek text (1635), and in Le Fèvre's edition of 1663; then in 1674 appeared Boileau's *Traité du Sublime, ou du Merveilleux dans le Discours,* a version which for the first time gave the work a wide publicity; and this was followed by his *Réflexions critiques sur quelques passages du rheteur Longin* (1694), a work fit to be read by *'tout le monde et même des femmes'.* Both works however had unfortunately serious limitations which prevented a real understanding of what 'Longinus' had written. The translation, for instance, was based on the imperfect rendering of Pétra, helped out by comments of Langbaine and Le Fèvre; for Boileau himself was but ill-equipped to cope with the actual Greek text. In his second-hand version, moreover, the free methods of D'Ablancourt as a translator were followed, so that what was presented was little more than a rough translation of selected passages; and in his Preface he explains that his aim had been, not to offer a complete or accurate version, but only to put together a treatise on the 'sublime'. And the same free treatment is present in his *Réflexions,* which consists of critical remarks, suggested by passages in 'Longinus', but with a bearing primarily on French

[1] *Oeuvres,* iii. 190; cf. Cic. *Part. orat.* § 17.

literature, and particularly on the attacks made by Perrault and others on the ancients. Neither of the works can therefore be said to have done full justice to 'Longinus'; and yet, in spite of all shortcomings, something of 'Longinus's' unique quality came through in the passages selected.

What was achieved was the revelation of a number of great simple truths calculated to transform the critical outlook and to correct the current idea that literature was simply a matter of rules and the 'kinds'. To begin with, there was the discussion of the term 'sublime' in the Preface to his *Traité*.[1] Described as something more than the 'high' (*grandis*) style of ancient oratory, with its imposing vocabulary and its dignified movement, it was said to be rather that more subtle 'element of the marvellous and extraordinary in discourse which carries us away, ravishes and transports us'. A given passage, so Boileau explains, could be in the 'high' style and yet not be 'sublime'. Such a statement, for instance, as 'the sovereign arbiter of Nature from a single utterance formed the light' was said to be in the 'high' style; but it was not 'sublime', since it contained no element of the marvellous or surprising in its expression. On the other hand, the famous pronouncement in *Genesis* (quoted by 'Longinus') beginning 'God said let there be light', he maintained, was truly 'sublime', with even something of the divine in it, owing to the grandeur and immensity of the thought expressed in utter simplicity.

And Boileau further enlarges on the point when, later on, Huet, the learned Bishop of Avranches, demurred to his judgment, declaring the biblical passage to embody a great thought but one barely and inadequately expressed. To this Boileau in his *Réflexions* (X)[2] replied that here was surely something that was awe-inspiring and irresistible in its appeal—the tremendous idea of God moving on the face of the waters, with light breaking through on primitive Chaos, and that idea surprisingly couched in terms simple and obscure—though the effect, he allows, could not be proved but only felt. Boileau was here noting a subtle aesthetic effect hitherto unappreciated by critics; and his contention that the 'sublime' consisted in the arresting combination of great thought and the simplest of language was of considerable interest in critical history. It gave, for one thing, a new interpretation to the term ὕψος (elevation) of 'Longinus', which has since been generally adopted; also to the term *sublimis* (or *grandis*) employed by earlier editors and translators.

[1] *Oeuvres*, ed. Gidel, iii. 435 ff.   [2] *ibid*. iii. 399 ff.

What was more, in recognizing imaginative and emotional appeals as valid tests of literary value, it prepared the way for a revolution in the use of critical terms and in methods of critical appreciation; and its influence may be detected in the later illuminating discussions of Lowth, Burke and others.

Apart from this, Boileau also succeeds in conveying to his readers certain *dicta* culled from 'Longinus's' treatise, some of which are of importance. He recalls, for instance, that the 'sublime' out of place becomes sheer bathos;[1] that the poet in his descriptions should deal, not with petty or irrelevant, but with characteristic, details;[2] that the works of great poets are not necessarily faultless, since even in Pindar and Sophocles occur passages uninspired;[3] or again, that the audacity of bold metaphors might be moderated by the use of disparaging phrases, such as 'so to speak' or 'as it were'.[4] Of greatest significance, however, was his striking pronouncement on the final test of literary value, which ran counter to neo-classical standards. From 'Longinus' he had learnt that it was only 'the approbation of posterity that could establish the true merit of literary works';[5] and with this assertion of the need for permanence of appeal, for *quod semper, quod ubique, quod ab omnibus* was found to be pleasing, one of the great fundamental laws of literary judgment was promulgated anew.

Of lesser importance, but significant also of a widening approach to the teaching of antiquity, were the references now made to Petronius by Saint-Evremond, Rapin and others, references relating to certain passages in his *Satyricon* which seemed to convey more than one message for the times. To Petronius attention had been drawn by the interest shown by Saint-Evremond in that *arbiter elegantiarum*, whom he had praised for his style, his characterization, and above all, his sound literary taste; for had he not ridiculed the 'new-fangled' prose style of his day, the *vanus sententiarum strepitus*, as well as the false judgments which preferred Lucan to Virgil? On the other hand, Rapin is less enthusiastic in his estimate. Petronius he describes as one 'whom no man of modesty dares to name unless on account of the directions he gave for writing'; and yet 'among the ordures of his *Satyricon*' he too finds certain admirable precepts for poetry, while Petronius's attacks on contemporary prose affectations he regards as highly 'judicious'.

It was therefore upon two passages alone of Petronius's work

---

[1] *Réflex*, ii. [2] *ibid*. vi. [3] *ibid*. viii.
[4] *Réflexions critiques* xi. [5] *ibid*. vii.

that interest was concentrated at the time, the first relating to Encolpius's strictures on contemporary oratory,[1] the second to Eumolpus's comment on epic theory.[2] The former, with its attack on the alleged tricks and extravagances of 1st-Century orators and prose-writers, was welcomed as a precedent for the censures passed by Boileau and others on the Précieux school. The other, which implied the necessity for the intervention of the gods (*deorum ministeria*) in epic poetry, a passage in which Petronius was more definite than Aristotle, was also paraded, in support of the contemporary view that dignity and uplift were acquired by the use of this epic machinery.[3] At a later date Coleridge was to find greater significance in the rest of Petronius's pronouncement.[4] But, for the time being, comments were confined to this one point of minor interest, the need for epic machinery. And yet it was on the strength of such limited teaching that Pope later on placed Petronius alongside 'Longinus' and Quintilian as a critic—a puzzling and surprising assignment which suggests but a superficial acquaintance on the part of Pope with ancient critical history.

But the emancipatory ideas submitted by Corneille and Saint-Evremond and the new leaven supplied by 'Longinus' were not the only influences which tended to counteract the rigidity of the neo-classical system at this date. In the latter half of the century a growing reliance on the instinctive perception of literary qualities became apparent, particularly in the writings of Chevalier de Méré and La Bruyère; and pleas for the recognition of 'taste' as a criterion of literary values, irrespective of all rules, marked not only a departure from the reigning system ˙ ˙˙ the beginning of a new phase in the critical develop-ment. ˙˙ ˙ ˙ Spaniard Gracián (1584–1658), in the first place, was attributed the introduction of the term into the critical sphere. In his *Oráculo Manual*[5] he had conceived of 'taste' as a special sense which operated in contact with literature and art; and his work, translated first into French, and later on into English as *The Courtier's Manual Oracle* (1685), had considerable influence on later criticism. The term itself was welcomed as supplying something that had hitherto been lacking; though what it stood for was by no means new. The special sense implied had already been exercised, if unconsciously, by all who had protested against the restrictions of the neo-classical creed; by the Précieuses in some measure despite their vagaries, and by

---

[1] *Satyricon*, § 1.　　[2] *ibid*. § 118.　　[3] cf. Rapin, *Réflex*. ii. xi.
[4] *Biog. Lit*. ch. xiv (ed. Shawcross, ii. 11).　　[5] ch. lxv (on 'taste').

Corneille, Saint-Evremond and others, in the insight displayed in their appreciation of qualities not accounted for by the rules.

At first the appeal to *le bon goût* was made in a tentative and apologetic fashion, as to something irregular and unauthorized, representing little more than instinctive feeling. And this phase is illustrated by Méré's comment on Virgil (1669), when, refusing to be influenced by Scaliger's praise of that poet, he asserts that he judged only by his own taste, and that the only true test was to examine without bias how works affected one's own self. There were many verses, he stated, that proved distasteful, though written in accordance with the rules; and indeed, it was good taste alone which could create sound rules in all that concerned what was proper and fitting.

I only say what I feel [he added][1] and what effects . . . things produce on my heart and my mind. . . . For sentiment (i.e. feeling) acting without reflexion is usually the best judge of what is decent and pleasing; and the best proof that a thing ought to please is that in fact it does please.

That the concept of 'taste' could however imply something more than mere impressionism was subsequently suggested by La Bruyère in his *Caractères* (1688). With Méré the appeal of literature, it is true, had been to the mind (*esprit*) as well as to the heart. But La Bruyère definitely stresses the rational element in 'good taste' when he states that 'between good sense and good taste there is the difference between cause and effect', and that 'good taste is only good sense in its critical function'.[2] Moreover, he insisted that the judgments resulting were not necessarily the product of mere individual whim, since there existed an absolute standard of values independent of rules and authority of all kinds. 'There is a point of perfection', he writes,[3] 'as of excellence or maturity in Nature. He who is sensible of it and loves it has perfect taste.' And La Bruyère's appreciation of verbal perfection is shown by his demand for the employment of *le mot propre*, on the ground that for every idea there was one, and only one, adequate expression.[4] That he was also conscious of qualities in literature not easily defined is likewise clear; and from now on, the expression *je ne sais quoi* was to be freely used—a term familiar to the Précieuses and one which Gombauld had discussed before the Academy in 1635.

---

[1] *Oeuvres*, ii. 76.   [2] *Caractères*, § 56.
[3] *ibid*. § 31.   [4] *ibid*. § 17.

Nevertheless, his final commendation of judgment by 'good taste' is as heart-warming as it is illuminating:

When the reading of a book [he states][1] elevates the mind and inspires brave and noble sentiments seek no other rule by which to judge it; it is good and made by the hand of a true workman.

With him in short began a more effective method of aesthetic appreciation; and 'taste' after all is no Philistine test, for the ultimate (and 'Longinian') test of all great literature is none other than a consensus of tastes.

Then, too, from other sources came further evidence of the growing conviction that there was more in literature than could be explained or appreciated by the rules. And this was supplied by sporadic utterances, sometimes from unexpected quarters. Not without its significance, for instance, was Molière's comment in *La Critique de l'École des Femmes*[2] (1663) deriding the rules and rejecting them as tests of literary value. A dramatic utterance, it is true; but it also represented views that were being expressed at the time. Thus the rules of art, it is stated, were made out to be 'great mysteries'; yet they were nothing more than observations to which good sense had arrived without the aid of Aristotle or Horace. And as for their worth as tests of dramatic value it is added that

If plays written in accordance with the rules do not please, whereas those which please are not in accordance with the rules, then it necessarily follows that the rules were badly made. Let us therefore disregard this quibbling (*chicane*) whereby public taste is restricted, and let us consider in a comedy merely the effect it has upon us.

Then, again, already in 1674 Rapin had incidentally censured the jejuneness bound up with mere 'correctness';[3] he had also asserted that a greater penetration was needed to discover what was excellent in a work of art than to point to what was defective. Most significant of all however was his contention that 'there are no precepts to teach the hidden graces (*grâces secrètes*), the insensible charms (*charmes imperceptibles*), and all that secret power of poetry that passes to the heart';[4] and here was obviously something outside the range of the orthodox theory. Apart from this it is worth noting that the presence of mysterious effects in poetry was incidentally suggested by Boileau in his comments on the 'sublime'. And besides, there

[1] *Caractères*, § 31.　　　　　　　　　[2] Sc. vi.
[3] *Réflexions sur la Poétique*, I. xxxi.　　[4] *ibid*. I. xxxv.

was Saint-Evremond's acute commentary on the term *vaste*, as 'relating to the great and frightful';[1] for, as he explains, 'part of our thought is apt to remain unexpressed', and much was therefore left to suggestion.

And to these might be added further hints and performances which all witnessed to a covert unrest and a groping for a wider outlook in literary matters. Doubts, for instance, were being expressed concerning the static idea of literature bound up with neo-classicism, when Bouhours in his *Entretiens d'Ariste et d'Eugene* (1671) suggests the influence of climate and environment on literary creation, and wonders whether in the cold regions of the north *un Allemand peut être bel-esprit*. The old hostility to Ronsard, again (*pace* Boileau), no longer held the field unchallenged; since Méré for one had recalled Montaigne's praise of that poet in that he had 'raised poetry to its zenith'. At the same time a beginning, however tame, had been made with the investigation of a sister art by Du Fresnoy in his *De Arte Graphica* (1668), a work discussed by Dryden and soon to be followed by Roger de Piles's *Cours de Peinture par Principes* (1708). Fénelon (1651–1715), too, in his early work, *Dialogues sur l'Eloquence*, had called attention to the magnificence of Biblical literature, and was later to complain of the dire effects of the rigid regularity of contemporary style, which, he asserted, had excluded all surprise, variety and rhythmical effects. And meanwhile, though respect for the ancients was in general maintained, there were signs of revolt against the tyranny of their rule. The infallibility of Aristotle, for instance, had been challenged by Cartesian doctrine; ancient poets had been burlesqued by Scarron and others; Biblical themes for the epic had been sought to displace the old classical stories; and, finally, the Quarrel between the Ancients and the Moderns was not without its significance in this respect.

Concerning the heated clash of opinions evoked by the famous Quarrel, however, this much might here be added, that whereas it seems at first sight to be nothing more than an ill-conceived and ill-mannered reaction against the earlier slavish admiration of antiquity, it nevertheless has its place in the critical development. Spirited replies to the abuse of Perrault and Fontenelle came from Huet, La Fontaine and La Bruyère, and by them and others the ignorance and arrogance of the Moderns were faithfully dealt with. Yet the Moderns had also called attention to matters of some substance. By them, for

---

[1] Dissertation *On the 'vaste'*.

instance, the rights of the native French genius in matters of literary creation were asserted, while the claims of educated readers to form literary judgments, as opposed to those of pedants and theorists, were also upheld. Moreover the law of progress they held to constitute a law of the human spirit; and since the attack had embraced not literature alone but the sister arts as well, the way was thus prepared for a wider consideration of aesthetic problems. On the whole, however, no great positive results can be said to have ensued. Ancient prejudices were merely countered by modern prejudices; though the actuating spirit was one that threatened the foundations of the reigning system.

For a proper understanding of those French influences which gave new direction to English criticism at this date some appreciation of the main currents of French thought is therefore essential. It is not enough to note the crystallizing of literary theory into a neat and coherent form since known as neoclassicism; though that system was what specially commended itself to contemporary readers and to the 'age of reason' that followed. What was handed on, however, was no agreed scheme of pure and unadulterated neo-classical theory. From the first, conflicting voices had been raised propounding doctrines that ran counter to the orthodox theory. Such views, as with Corneille, Saint-Evremond and La Bruyère, were the result of keen insight on the part of individuals, or, as with Boileau, the outcome of the timely revival of one of the most inspiring of the ancients. But what is beyond all doubt is that in the air at the time, along with the fixed tenets of the neo-classical school were suggestions, tentative as yet, that the secrets of literatur were not wholly explained by that school, that literary creation was not simply a matter of observing the 'kinds' and the rules, and that in sound literary judgments relative standards and the historical method, the heart as well as the head, all played their parts. These ideas were seeds that bore fruit in a later generation, and led ultimately to the disintegration of neoclassicism. The errors inherent in the orthodox creed had at least this virtue. They proved to be an incitement to future inquiry; and here, as in other fields of thought, truth from error was finally to emerge.

CHAPTER II

THE TRANSITIONAL STAGE: DAVENANT, HOBBES, COWLEY,
SPRAT AND DRYDEN

W H E N we turn to consider the critical activities which marked
the second half of the 17th Century in England it becomes evident that amidst the confusion of many voices a new chapter
was being opened in critical history, revealing fresh interests,
new problems, changed methods and a wider outlook, all differing from those of the earlier period (1500–1650), during which
Renascence influences had prevailed. With the Restoration
(1660) something like a new literature, as well as a new society,
had come into being. The first half of the century had witnessed
a moderating of Elizabethan raptures and enthusiasms as well
as a growing tendency towards more serious thought and more
complicated emotions, developments which for the time being
were fostered in part by the Puritan regime. And now, with
government, social life and manners being visibly transformed,
and with new influences active as well, fresh literary ambitions
were cherished, giving rise to new literary adventures and to
inquiries into literary principles themselves. In the critical discussions that followed, Dryden already stands out as the domin-
ating figure, though his efforts were shared by many of his
contemporaries. And in attempting to review the main critical
achievements of this second half of the 17th Century attention
will be directed to two main stages in the development. Thus
consideration will first be given to a transitional period (1650–
74), engaged chiefly with immediate problems suggested by
current difficulties, as well as with early influences from France
including those of Godeau, Chapelain and Corneille; and, secondly,
to a stage of further critical developments (1674–1700) in which
problems of a more general character were considered, under the
influence of a fresh influx of French theory, drawn from the
works of Boileau, Rapin, Le Bossu and others, though native
interests continued to claim their share of attention.

It is therefore with the transitional stage (1650–74) that the
present chapter is concerned. And for the causes that led to
changes in the critical sphere at this date we have but to recall
something of the intellectual conditions which then prevailed.
Apart from the reaction which followed Puritan austerities and

the increased zest for literature which resulted in cultured circles, of significance, in the first place, was the growing interest in scientific and philosophical thought represented in the founding of the Royal Society (1660), and more especially in the writings of Hobbes. Still more important, however, was the confusion then current concerning literary forms and ideals. Were Elizabethan dramatic methods and standards, for instance, to be adopted in spite of their clash with those of the ancients and the modern French school? Were the poems of Quarles and Heywood or the loose romances of Chamberlayne and others to take the place of the ancient epic, long regarded as the highest form of poetry? Or again, were the 'metaphysical' style in poetry and the florid long-winded manner in prose to be the characteristic forms of literary expression? But while the urgency of immediate problems was the main driving force behind the critical movement at this date, hardly less compelling was the impetus derived from those earlier contacts with French thought, of which something has already been said, though as yet French influence was mainly confined to the teaching of Chapelain and Corneille. Such then were the conditions which gave new direction to critical effort at this date. And the results are seen not only in the proposals for a religious epic, in the suggestions for stylistic reform, and in important discussions of dramatic matters, but also in the new approach to literature heralded by Hobbes's psychological teaching.

The earliest signs that a new phase of criticism was being inaugurated about the middle of the 17th Century came from a group of writers including Sir William Davenant (1605–68), Thomas Hobbes (1588–1679) and Abraham Cowley (1618–67), all exiled Royalists who had previously sought refuge in France, and whose works gave evidence not only of French influence, but also of that independent spirit in matters of poetry which was to characterize English thought throughout most of the century. And in due course they were followed by Sprat and Dryden, whose earlier works also belong to this transitional period and thus treat of matters that were engaging attention at the time.

Of interest, in the first place, is Davenant's *Preface to Gondibert* (1650), the work of a prolific playwright who was the first to introduce scene-shifting and operatic music on the stage, and who now claimed to have invented a new kind of epic, doubtless inspired by similar efforts in contemporary France. His newly developed zeal for poetry, and for the epic in particular, he is at

some pains to explain and defend. Poetry, for instance, he describes as 'the clearest light by which they find the soul who seek
it'; and this, despite the abuse showered on it by those whose
'conscientious melancholy had amazed and discouraged others'
devotion'. Nor, he added, was Plato's ban to be taken too seriously; for elsewhere that philosopher had honoured the poet
with garlands, while Aristotle had subsequently 'silenced his
master'.[1] In short, poetry, he held, was a valuable agency for
'guiding the people' in an age of distraction. It was contrary to
neither religion, Nature, nor reason; though, strangely enough,
it had hitherto lacked the support of divines and statesmen
alike.

It is with the epic, however, that Davenant is mainly concerned. To dramatic poetry, he recognizes, objections had been
raised on the ground that it conduced to levity and frivolity,
though that, he retorts, was not the whole story. Nevertheless,
he concedes that the epic was generally regarded as the most
beautiful form of poetry, especially when treating of sacred
themes; and following (with some difference) Godeau, Chapelain
and others, he proceeds to expound his idea of a modern epic
as represented in his own *Gondibert*. He is convinced, to begin
with, that a blind following of the ancients was not enough.
Faults had been found in all earlier epic poets from Homer down
to Spenser; and concerning Spenser in particular he refers to his
use of 'many exploded words', and to his wild fancies, which he
likens to 'extraordinary dreams such as . . . poets and painters
. . . may have in the beginnings of fevers'.[2] Mere imitation he
therefore discards, though Nature, he allows, inclines us to
imitate, and imitation might minimize defects. On the other
hand he maintains that it tended to hinder progress; for 'sailing
by others' maps no new discovery could be made'.

What he therefore advocates is a new epic form, mainly
based on Tasso, 'the first modern to revive the heroic flame'.
It was to embody a Christian theme as being most conducive to
virtue;[3] a story treating of a former age as permitting greater
liberty of treatment; and while the scene might be placed in
Italy, 'once the stage of the world', the subjects dealt with
should be love and ambition, 'the raging fevers of great minds'.
In such an epic, he adds, there would be no need to employ the
pagan machinery of the ancients, or to follow Homer 'where
Nature never comes, even into Heaven and Hell'. At the same

---

[1] Spingarn, *Critical Essays of the 17th Century*, ii. 51.
[2] *ibid.*, ii. 7.   [3] *ibid.* ii. 9 ff.

time the whole work should be seasoned with 'wit',[1] which he
defines as something more than refined speech or fanciful conceits, and as a new and vivid presentation of truth, with Nature
represented in an unusual, though not an affected, dress. Nor
is this all; for he has yet an original suggestion of his own to
make. Arguing that nowhere were great actions depicted more
effectively than in earlier English plays, he recommends that
their dramatic structure should be adopted for epic purposes;[2]
so that an epic poem should consist of five Books (i.e. acts),
with various cantos (i.e. scenes), and with the action developed
on dramatic lines. These suggestions, he claims, had been illustrated in his *Gondibert*, in which, he notes, he had also adopted
the four-line stanza with alternate rhymes, as being less 'breath-
less' than the heroic couplet.

Such is the first of the *Prefaces* imitated from the French
which now became a feature of critical activities in England. In
its frequent appeals to Nature, its defence of poetry, and its
occasional euphuisms it forms a link with earlier English
theorizing; but it lacks the charm of earlier discourses, as well
as the directness and clarity of later writers, by reason of its
discursiveness, its long and unwieldy parentheses. At the same
time it gives evidence of some original thinking and a free treatment of French doctrine; while it also contains some pregnant
sayings, such as, 'Fame is the first, though but a little, taste of
eternity,' or again, 'Learning is not knowledge but a continued
sailing by fantastic and uncertain ways towards it.' Its chief
interest, however, lies in its reflexion of new influences from
France and in its attempt to establish in England a modified
form of the ancient epic.

Of greater significance are the contributions of the philosopher Hobbes, which consist of *An Answer to Davenant's
Preface* (1650) and a later *Preface to a Translation of Homer*
(1675), both of which are concerned primarily with epic poetry,
though their importance lies not so much in the light thrown
on that particular 'kind', as in the new direction given to
literary studies by his psychological methods in dealing with
the relation existing between the creative mind and poetry in
general. In the first place, having been asked by Davenant for
his opinion on *Gondibert* Hobbes frankly disclaims his compet-
ence for that task; and if we may judge from his extravagance
in assigning something like immortality to Davenant's poem, it
would seem that his reluctance was not ill-founded. He there-

[1] Spingarn, *op. cit.* ii. 20 ff.   [2] *ibid.* ii. 17.

fore proposes to submit his views on poetry in the abstract; and, like Bacon before him, he approaches his subject anew and from a purely rational standpoint, treating first of the different 'kinds'.[1] As his starting-point he recalls the old doctrine that the universe was made up of three separate regions, the celestial, the aerial and the terrestrial; and he therefore argues that poets in imitating human life had treated of the corresponding divisions of mankind—those connected with the court, the city and the country—and that heroic themes had been created for the court, less serious themes for the restless and inconstant city, and themes uninspiring but not unwholesome for humble country-dwellers. Hence poetry heroic, comic (*scommatic*) and pastoral. But each of these primary 'kinds' might assume either narrative or dramatic form; so that the ultimate 'kinds', he states, were six in number, namely, epic and tragedy, satire and comedy, pastoral and pastoral comedy. Sonnets and other lyrical forms he briefly dismisses as mere 'essays' and but parts of a poem.

This attempt at classification, however, is mainly of academic interest; and more to the point is his analysis of the poetic process by which, in accordance with his mechanistic philosophy, the raw materials of experience are woven into works of art—an analysis reminiscent in part of medieval psychology. Thus 'Time and Education', he explains,[2] 'begets experience; Experience begets memory; Memory begets Judgment and Fancy; Judgment begets the strength and structure, and Fancy begets the ornaments, of a Poem.' And it is in this connexion that he conveys his chief message to his age. According to his theory both 'fancy' and 'judgment' are essential agencies in poetic creation. 'Fancy' he defines[3] as the faculty which discerns resemblances between different objects, whereas 'judgment' detects differences between objects apparently similar; and his distinction became a commonplace in later criticism. What however is chiefly notable is that not only is Hobbes the first to define the two terms, but he is also the first to insist on the essential part played by 'judgment' in all artistic creation. 'Fancy' in a poem, he notes,[4] was apt to be more admired than 'judgment or reason'; in it was said to consist the 'sublimity' of a poet; and to it was commonly given the name of 'wit'. Yet in all poetry, he maintains, discretion or 'judgment' was indispensable; and

---

[1] Spingarn, *op. cit.* ii. 54.   [2] *ibid.* ii. 59.
[3] cf. *Human Nature*, x. 4; *Leviathan*, i. 8.
[4] Spingarn, *op. cit.* ii. 70.

'judgment' consisted in seeing that 'fancy' should be controlled and that every part of a poem should be effectively arranged. Hence the later conventional antithesis between 'judgment' and 'fancy' or 'wit'. Nor was this all; for involved in his theory was an important change in critical terminology. To the Elizabethans 'wit' had stood for 'intelligence', and later, for 'ingenuity' or 'fancy'; whereas, from now on, 'wit' in poetry was to suggest an element of 'judgment' or 'propriety' as well. This new connotation of 'wit' was generally accepted in view of the extravagances of much of the earlier poetry; and with it the way was prepared for a new aesthetic.

In keeping with this analysis of the poetic process are sundry remarks of his in attempts to read a more definite meaning into terms that had hitherto been vaguely used. In one place, for instance, he stresses the importance of language as 'securing permanence for the results of previous thought, and therefore economy in the actual process of thinking'. Elsewhere, as opposed to the earlier conception of 'reason', he maintains that 'reason is not, as sense and memory, born with us, nor gotten by experience only, . . . but attained by industry'.[1] Or, again, there is his well-known definition of laughter as 'nothing else but sudden glory arising from some sudden conception of some eminence in ourselves by comparison with the infirmity of others or with our own formerly'.[2] Based as this definition was, on his view of the utter selfishness of human nature, it fails to account for all the facts; and Wilson had dealt more happily with this elusive subject when he declared that 'to tell in plain words what laughter is . . . passeth my cunning'.[3]

Of interest, again, are his occasional remarks on poetry in general, all revealing his rationalistic and psychological methods of approach. Thus while he regards verse as an integral part of poetry, though all in verse was not necessarily poetry, he already notes with approval the current vogue of the rhyming decasyllabic line in serious poetry, adding that 'a longer line is not far from ill prose while a shorter line is a kind of whisking'.[4] At the same time he allows that in lesser forms, such as the sonnet or epigram, a more intricate rhyming system might be employed, where a display of virtuosity was the primary aim; as with those who sought fame in difficulties overcome, by verses devised in

[1] *Leviathan*, I. iv.
[2] *Human Nature*, ch. ix.: *Leviathan*, I. vi.
[3] *Arte of Rhetorique* (1553), ed. Mair, p. 135.
[4] Spingarn, *op. cit.* ii. 57.

the form of an egg, an altar, or a pair of wings. Such devices, however, he regards as 'needless difficulties' and distracting 'toys', unsuitable for epic purposes. Then, too, fiction he describes as an essential element in poetry; though he utters a warning concerning its permissible limits. In view of the earlier fondness for 'enchanted castles, . . . iron men, flying horses' and the like, he maintains that the beauty of a poem does not reside in far-fetched elements of that kind, but that an observance of verisimilitude above all things was necessary. 'Beyond the actual works of Nature', he states,[1] 'a poet may now go, but beyond the conceived possibilities of Nature, never.'

Elsewhere he comments on the conventional invocation in the epic. His common sense rebels against the use of what after all was but a heathen custom; and he holds that the principles of Nature are a sufficient guide for the poet, instead of claiming to speak by inspiration 'like a bag-pipe'. Or again he decries the use of technical terms in epic poetry, and recommends the employment of general expressions as being more in keeping with epic dignity. And, lastly, he urges the need for a clear and natural style and for a discarding of artifices prescribed by text-books, 'the ordinary boxes of counterfeit complexion',[2] as he calls them. He therefore derides for instance the current use of rhetorical and inflated expressions, 'the windy blisters of a troubled water'; also the obscurity that resulted from ambitious attempts at expressing more than was perfectly conceived. Such passages, he remarks, were sometimes called 'strong lines', whereas in reality they were nothing more than 'riddles dark and troublesome'.

The general trend of Hobbes's theorizing on literature therefore becomes plain; and more important than his detailed theories is the fact that with him began a new approach to literature and a more inward treatment of literary problems. By him philosophy was brought to bear on aesthetic matters; and his rationalistic outlook not only led to a bridling of poetic fancy and to a discrediting of works of pure romance, it also suggested a simpler and more lucid expression in verse and prose alike. It was as a pioneer in psychological inquiries, however, that his main influence was ultimately felt. Regardless of ancient, as of French neo-classical, theorists, he applied a keen and logical mind to literary problems; and despite all limitations, his great prestige as a philosopher added weight to his teaching while also commending his methods to later Restoration critics.

[1] Spingarn, *op. cit.* ii. 61.   [2] *ibid.* ii. 62.

Less weighty, but of definite interest, is Cowley's[1] Preface to his *Poems* (1656), in which the most popular poet of the day revealed not only his estimate of his own poetic achievement but also something of his views on poetry in general. Of his early poems, it is true, he has not much to say; they are but 'the little foot-steps of a child'. The poems relating to the Civil War, again, he would consign to oblivion as being 'unprofitable'; though he defended his treatment of love in *The Mistress* as being 'a seemingly necessary preparation for all poetry'. As with Davenant, his main interest is concentrated on his attempt at a religious epic represented in *Davideis*, of which only four of the twelve Books planned were completed. Designed as it was to treat of a single theme, namely, the troubles of David, his story, he points out, had dealt with selected details only, in accordance with epic rules; and that, moreover, in the narrative were embodied many noble and illuminating episodes, also in accordance with epic requirements.

Of greater importance, however, are, first, his comments on poetry in general, and, secondly, his advocacy of the religious epic and the Pindaric ode in particular. Significant, in the first place, of the growing interest in the relation between the creative mind and poetry itself are his comments on those conditions which conduce to the most fruitful poetic activities. Doubtless drawing on his own experiences, he suggests (as 'Longinus' and Tacitus before him had done) that 'a warlike, various, and a tragical age is the best to write of, but worst to write in',[2] that a serene and cheerful spirit is needed for 'the Muse to breed in'. And recalling the numbing effects of Ovid's exile he urges that the soul must be at ease if it is 'to communicate delight to others', which, as he significantly states, 'is the main end of poetry'. Then, too, he has a word to say on the much-debated theme of 'wit'; and like most of his contemporaries he protests against the use of 'false wit' in poetry. This he describes as excessive fancy unregulated by reason, while he also condemns frequent playing on words. Thus he states, in terms reminiscent of Sidney, that

> Jewels at nose and lips but ill appear,
> Rather than all things wit, let none be there.[3]

---

[1] It is noteworthy that the spelling 'Cooley' occurs more than once in the records of Trinity College, Cambridge (see *Cowley's Prose Works* ed. Lumly, Intro. x. (f.n). Does this represent the 17th-Century pronunciation of 'Cowley'? cf. 'Cowper'.

[2] Spingarn, *op. cit.* ii. 80–1.   [3] *Ode to Wit.*

But in decrying the use of ingenious and subtle images he himself is guilty of the evil he deplores. From this 'false wit', however, his prose is entirely free; and among the merits of his critical Preface is the effortless, conversational style which makes it everywhere good reading.

Of special value, however, are his remarks on the religious epic. In his Preface to *The Cutter of Coleman Street* (1663), written towards the close of his life, he claimed to have endeavoured 'to root out the ordinary weeds of poetry and to plant it almost wholly with divinity'; and this claim is supported by his spirited argument in favour of Christian poetry in the earlier Preface. Contemporary poets, he there complains,[1] were immersed in flattering the great, in 'unmanly idolizing of foolish women', or at best in relating 'senseless fables'; so that it was true to say that 'the Devil had captured poetry and that it was time to restore it to the kingdom of God'. His effort is therefore 'to baptise poetry in Jordan'; for, he added, 'it will never become clean by bathing in the waters of Damascus'. It was not, he explained, that a loss would be involved in turning to religious themes; for the Bible was full of poetic material and even of poetry itself. Moreover there was no future in serving up 'new-heated the cold meats of the ancients' to readers already surfeited with such fare. The field of antiquity had long been exhausted; and nothing was left thus late in the day for those who 'came a-gleaning, not after the first reapers, but after the very beggars'. It was true, he added, that in their day these 'mad stories of gods and heroes' had served a laudable purpose; but to modern readers they should seem no more edifying than their worthy successors, the Knights Errant'—a rather ungrateful reference when his boyhood's debt to Spenser is recalled. That difficulties were presented by a Christian epic he does not deny; and Quarles in his *Job Militant* (1624) and Thomas Heywood in his *Hierarchy of the Blessed Angels* (1635), he notes, had only succeeded in 'abasing divinity'. Yet the rules for the Christian epic were those prescribed for the secular epic. What was needed was a fruitful theme, a fitting arrangement, an observance of *decorum*, an 'illustrious' style and majestic verse; and hitherto, he laments, nothing worthy of the kind had appeared in English.

Then there are his remarks on the Pindaric ode, which as one of 'the lost inventions of antiquity' he claimed to introduce to English readers.[2] Already in 1584, however, Southern had

---

[1] Spingarn, *op. cit.* ii. 88 ff.   [2] *ibid.* ii. 86.

adapted some of Ronsard's versions of Pindar; and, claiming to
be the first 'to touch Pindar's string', was curtly reproved by
Puttenham and charged with 'pilfering'.[1] Later on Ben Jonson
had attempted the Pindaric form in his *Underwoods*,[2] and had
there reproduced correctly the proper arrangement of strophe,
antistrophe and epode. And now Cowley, apparently unaware
of these earlier ventures, expounds his views on Pindar's 'way
and manner of speaking', which he describes as 'the noblest and
highest kind of writing in verse'. The essence of such verse, he
held, consisted in the use of long and sudden digressions,
accompanied by bold figures and couched in varied and irregular
measures, in which sound echoed sense, thus giving expression
to varying moods and unbridled passion. As he stated elsewhere,
this Pindaric form was

> An unruly and a hard-mouthed horse
>   Fierce and unbroken yet,
>   Impatient of the spur or bit,
> Now praunces stately and anon flies o'er the plain.[3]

Yet this was to ignore the true form and nature of the Pindaric
ode and to prescribe what was little more than free and impassioned verse, in which broken lines and other irregularities
were the main factors. In an age when Latin, rather than Greek,
sources were the chief inspiration, this reference of Cowley's to
Pindar was not without its interest; nor was it without its later
influence, as was seen for instance in Dryden's *Song for Saint
Cecilia's Day* (1687). It was nevertheless a misleading pronouncement which led also to much formless and uninspired verse-
writing; and it remained for Edward Phillips, then Congreve,
and later on Gray, to make the necessary correction.

Meanwhile other important matters were engaging the attention at this date, notably, the disordered state of the literary
language and the false ideas of style which then prevailed.
References have already been made to casual censures of 'false
wit' in poetry; but now serious attempts were also made to
stay the plague of corrupt rhetoric, which, with its abuse of
figures, its indulgence in conceits, its puns and unwieldy parentheses, had distorted all forms of prose-writing. The protest, it
is true, was not confined to England alone. A similar movement
was also active in France, a movement which had found expression in Furetière's elaborate allegory of 1658,[4] depicting the

---

[1] G. Smith, *Eliz. Critical Essays*, ii. 171–2.   [2] lxxxviii.
[3] *Pindarique Odes*, p. 22.   [4] Spingarn, *op. cit.* I. xxxvii (f.n.).

perversions of style current in his day. In England, however, a consciousness of the need for some check to similar abuses had already been independently felt, particularly in connexion with pulpit oratory. And, judging from statements made by Fuller (1640), James Howell (1643) and others, or again, from John Wilkins's *Ecclesiastes* (1646), with its positive injunctions for reform in style, it would seem tolerably clear that a general awareness of the stylistic evils then current was widespread in England about the middle of the century. Then in 1670 a fierce attack on the corrupt artifices of the pulpit came from John Eachard, a Cambridge scholar, in his *Grounds and Occasions of the Contempt of the Clergy*; and Dryden, two years later, ascribed the general corruption of eloquence to divines of Jonson's day, among whom, he added, this vicious oratory was still rife.[1]

Under such conditions it is not surprising that efforts were now made to bring about reform under the aegis of the newly-formed Royal Society, though the interests of that Society were mainly those of philosophy and natural science. In 1664 it had appointed a Committee for 'improving the English tongue', with Evelyn, Waller and Dryden among its members; and a plea was made for an Academy of letters which should act as an arbiter in language and style. Nothing much however came of their deliberations, though Evelyn's 'indigested thoughts' expressed in a letter (1665)[2] afford some indication of what they had in mind. Thus he suggests that definite rules of grammar, orthography and punctuation should be established; and that a check should be placed on coinages 'minted by our *Logodaedali*'. He notes further that 'such as have lived long in Universities do greatly affect words and expressions nowhere in use besides'; and recommends that inquiry should be made into dialect forms and that a collection of courtly expressions should be made to give grace to expression. On the other hand he urges that while archaisms should be discarded, foreign words, particularly French words, for which there existed no equivalents in English, should be welcomed; and among such words, it is perhaps worth noting, were *naïveté, ennui, bizarre, emotion, chicaneries, effort* and the like. In this rough sketch Evelyn's main object was to introduce order where chaos prevailed; for in such matters, he maintained, 'there ought to be a law as well as a liberty'.

It was in connexion with these activities that Thomas Sprat

---

[1] Ker, *Essays of J. Dryden*, i. 173.
[2] Spingarn, *op. cit.* ii. 310.

(1635–1713) first figures in critical history; though even more notable, being the first of its kind in English, was his appreciation of Cowley and his works. In his early years Sprat, who subsequently became Bishop of Rochester, had interested himself in secular matters; and in his *History of the Royal Society* (1667) he makes an interesting contribution by way of digression to the contemporary debate on style.[1] He holds, to begin with, that the time was ripe for the establishment of an English Academy, which should give much-needed guidance in linguistic matters and should also pass judgment on literary works as they appeared. Hitherto, he notes, little enough had been done by way of regulating the language; and meanwhile a flood of 'fantastic' terms had been introduced by Puritan zealots, while from other quarters had come a host of 'outlandish' words.

It is however with the larger question of contemporary style that he is mainly concerned; and here his suggestions are of considerable significance. The root of the trouble, he explains, was that 'superfluity of talking'[2] with its specious tropes and figures which characterized most forms of writing in his day, and which resulted in nothing but 'misty uncertainties'. Nothing, he adds, is easier than this way of writing which 'makes so great noise in the world' and was tacitly accepted by all. Yet the true remedy, he maintains, had been prescribed by the formal resolution of the Royal Society in connexion with works on natural philosophy. It had decreed 'a rejection of all amplifications, digressions and swellings of style, and a return back to the primitive purity and shortness'. And in so doing it had exacted from all its members 'a close, naked, natural way of speaking, positive expressions, clear sense, a natural easiness, bringing all things as near to the Mathematical plainness as they can'. This, then, was the bold remedy suggested by Sprat for correcting the defects of contemporary literary style in general; and Aristotle, in opposing in his *Rhetoric* the false splendours of Gorgianic prose, had also been thinking along much the same lines.

Nor, it might be added, were the reasons given for this advice any less suggestive than the advice itself; for Sprat's argument is based on the idea that literary standards and methods, so far from being fixed for all peoples and times, necessarily varied in accordance with national character, national genius and the *milieu* generally. Englishmen, he states, preferred to have 'reason set out in plain, undeceiving expressions', whereas the French would have it 'delivered with colour and beauty'; and

[1] Spingarn, *op. cit.* ii. 112 ff.   [2] *ibid.* ii. 116 ff.

verse or rhyme the more appropriate medium for dramatic expression? Or again, what about comedy, and what was to be said for the recent introduction of scenery on to the stage? To the discussion of these and other problems Flecknoe, Howard, Shadwell and Dryden each made his contribution; and with them a new phase of dramatic criticism was inaugurated.

Of minor importance was the contribution of Richard Flecknoe, an Irish priest who had already written for the theatre when his *Short Discourse of the English Stage* (1664) opened up some of the problems that were exercising men's minds at the time. Its author, as is well known, was subsequently ridiculed by Dryden in his *MacFlecknoe* (1682). But his remarks concerning the stage provide no evidence that he was in reality 'through all the realms of Nonsense, absolute'. Slight those remarks may be, but at least they are sensible and of historical interest. To begin with, he maintains that 'of all arts that of the dramatic poet is the most difficult'; and in recalling the earlier English tradition it is significant that out of the long roll-call of dramatists from Marlowe to Ford he already selects Shakespeare, Jonson, Beaumont and Fletcher as the most representative.[1] He claims however that their works were faulty, quotes with approval the remark of a contemporary that 'Shakespeare's writings were a fine garden, but it needed weeding'; and then suggests that whereas Jonson was too grave and ponderous, Beaumont and Fletcher were much given to 'witty obscenity' and overdrawn characters. The chief fault common to all, however, was said to be 'the huddling too much matter together', thus making the plays 'too long and intricate'; and it becomes evident that his preference is for the French type of play, 'closely and evenly wrought, without any breaks, thrums or loose ends', though he enlarges no further on the necessary rules.

At the same time he commends the recent introduction of scenery on the English stage as an improvement on the bare effects of tapestry and rushes; and he gives credit to the Italians and then to the French for their pioneer work in this field.[2] Such scenery, he maintains, assisted the imagination of the spectator, transporting him as if by magic from place to place; though on the other hand, he wisely notes that it had also its drawbacks, since spectacular devices tended to appeal more to the sight than to the hearing, so that 'what makes our stage the better makes our plays the worse'. Nor must we overlook his comment on the much-abused term 'wit'. This he describes as

[1] Spingarn, *op. cit.* ii. 92. [2] *ibid.* ii. 95–6.

'the spirit and quintessence of speech', having nothing to do with puns or word-jingles, but consisting rather of that 'pleasant and facetious discourse', taught by no precepts of art but acquired only by Nature and social intercourse. ' 'Tis vain', he adds, 'to say any more of it; for if I could tell you what it were, it would not be what it is.'[1]

In the meantime views of a different kind relating to the English drama were being submitted by Sir Robert Howard (1626–98), the brother-in-law of Dryden, in his *Preface to Four New Plays* (1665) and subsequently in the *Preface to the Great Favourite* (1668). His main contention is that the future of the English drama lay not in following French methods, though he is conscious that to many of his countrymen 'what the French do ought to be the fashion'. On the contrary he asserts the superiority of earlier English plays,[2] despite their mixture of mirth and sadness which he regards as distracting and confusing, though not untrue to life; and then he proceeds to give reasons for his judgment. Noting, to begin with, that dramatic form had varied throughout the ages, he holds that the best Roman plays, those of Seneca, Plautus and Terence, would fail, even if translated, to attract any sort of modern audience. And yet, he points out, these were the plays, with their excessive use of narrative, necessitated, it is true, by the grim nature of many of their stories, that were accepted as models by the French; and this, in spite of the truth enunciated by Horace[3] that deeds enacted were more effective than deeds merely related.

Then, too, he questions the propriety of rhyming verse as used by the French for dramatic purposes; and here he is replying to Dryden's defence of rhyme characteristic of that critic's early days.[4] Howard's preference is for the blank verse (to him still a 'hard expression') of earlier English dramatists, on the ground that it was less artificial, and therefore approximated more closely to the natural expression of men in actual life. In non-dramatic poetry, consisting of a 'premeditated form of thought', rhyme, he concedes, had its place along with other devices. But in the drama, with its apparently *ex tempore* interchange of thought, such artifices, he maintains, seemed unnatural, and tended as well to shackle the fancy. Nor does he refrain from attacking the three Unities.[5] He ridicules, for instance, the idea that by limiting the time-duration of a play to twenty-four

---

[1] Spingarn, *op. cit.* ii. 94. [2] *ibid.* ii. 98 ff.
[3] *Ars Poetica*, 272–3. [4] Spingarn, *op. cit.* ii. 101: see p. 60 *infra*.
[5] *ibid.* ii. 108.

hours the action might be more convincingly presented within the space of two and a half hours. Such a procedure, he argued, was ineffective, whether twenty-four hours or a thousand years was the period concerned. In either case complete verisimilitude was impossible; and, as he added, 'impossibilities are all equal and admit of no degree'. The truth was that Howard was utterly opposed to those neo-classical theorists who 'laboured to give strict rules to things that were not mathematical'. In the creation and appreciation of the dramatic art, he held, taste alone should decide[1]—a striking assertion at this early date. And for a man to 'like or dislike by the rules of others', he added, 'was like believing, not what he must, but what others directed him to believe'.

These views of Flecknoe and Howard, however, were not the only contributions to dramatic theory at this date. Likewise illustrative of the unsettlement at the time was the doctrine put forward by Thomas Shadwell (1642–92) at the outset of his dramatic career in his Prefaces to *The Sullen Lovers* (1668) and *The Humorists* (1671). Unlike Howard he is prepared to accept the French neo-classical rules relating to the Unities and the like. On the other hand he advocates a following of the earlier English tradition, particularly in the field of comedy;[2] and what he inculcates above all is a development of comedy on Jonsonian lines. In the comedy of his day he detected a marked tendency towards 'bawdy, profaneness and brisk writing', an indulgence, too, in 'wild romantic tales wherein they strain love and honour to that ridiculous height that it becomes burlesque'. Such conceptions of comedy, however, he deliberately discards, since they contributed nothing to what he regarded as the primary function of the comic art, namely, that of instructing. That purpose, he held, was best served by the delineation of 'humours', whereby the common extravagances of human conduct, 'affected vanities and artificial fopperies' were held up to ridicule and laughed out of court.[3] Mere jesting, brisk repartee or neat intrigue would not suffice, any more than the 'exploded barbarisms' of devil, giant or monster. Comedy as an intrument of social and ethical reform could be created only by a satirical treatment of real characters drawn from ordinary life. And, in this respect, he notes, comedy was more useful than tragedy; for while tragedy dealt with the vices of high life which touched but the few, comedy depicted the cheats and follies of everyday life.

[1] Spingarn, *op. cit.* ii. 106.   [2] *ibid.* ii. 150 ff.   [3] *ibid.*, ii. 153 ff.

It was therefore in the realistic representation of human characters with satirical intent that Shadwell held the essence of comedy to consist. And apart from Jonson's 'humours', Shakespeare's Falstaff alone seemed to him to have fulfilled the comic purpose.[1] Nor, he maintained, were such creations devoid of 'wit', as was so often stated. For the delineation of 'humour' called for keen observation and for judgment in selecting; and this, according to Hobbes, was of the essence of 'wit'. As Shadwell himself explains, 'judgment does indeed comprehend wit; for fancy rough-draws, but judgment smooths and finishes'.

Interesting however as were the remarks of Howard and others on dramatic standards and methods, yet more important were the efforts made by John Dryden (1631–1700) during these same transitional years to pronounce judgment on some of the problems with which contemporary dramatists were faced. Already in 1664 had appeared the Epistle Dedicatory of his tragicomedy *The Rival Ladies*; and from now on to 1674 he deals in Prefaces, Prologues, Essays and the like with questions relating mainly to the drama. With him, it becomes evident, a new force had entered the critical field. Encouraged no doubt by Corneille's method and manner of dealing with the situation in France, he applies to current problems an open mind and a keen judgment, refusing to be bound by pedantic formulas or by earlier native tradition; while equally characteristic from the first is the easy conversational manner in which he communicates his judgments. He endeavoured, as he explains, 'to write English as near as he could distinguish it from the tongue of pedants and that of affected travellers'; and, dispensing with all false rhetoric, he develops a style, masculine, vivid and pliant, eminently suitable for critical discussion and everywhere readable by reason of its liveliness and charm.

In the Epistle Dedicatory of *The Rival Ladies*, to begin with, he notes the basic difficulty that beset the dramatist in the matter of plotting, and the need for attaining what Aristotle had called 'a probable or necessary sequence'. The plot, in short, was to be of an organic character, logically developed from beginning to end; and for this, he adds, the exercise of 'fancy, memory and judgment' was indispensable. It is however with the question of the verse most suitable for dramatic purposes that he is for the moment concerned. And his conviction is that the example of Italian, French and Spanish dramatists in employing rhyming verse was one to be followed by English

---

[1] Spingarn, *op. cit.* ii. 150.

writers, more especially as Waller, followed by Denham and Davenant, had shown the possibilities of the rhyming couplet in English. This meant of course a discarding of the native tradition illustrated by Shakespeare in his use of blank verse; though already, it is worth noting, Dryden credits him with 'a larger soul of poetry than ever any of our nation'.[1] Yet Shakespeare, he rashly assumes, had first 'invented' that form of verse in order 'to shun the pains of continual rhyming'; and, recalling that to the French such verse was merely *prose mesurée*, he remarks that blank verse after all was but little removed from mere prose.

On the other hand the advantages of rhyming verse, he held, were considerable. Besides being a help to the memory and giving point to repartee, it was above all effective in curbing the poet's fancy, that 'lawless faculty that like a high-ranging spaniel must have clogs tied to it lest it outrun the judgment';[2] whereas blank verse, being more easily written, gave to the poet free licence to indulge in unbounded fancies. Rhyming verse was therefore no mere 'embroidery of sense'; the effort imposed in the business of rhyming brought judgment to bear and gave leisure for regulating the fancy, thus giving clear expression to thought. So far Dryden obviously fails to appreciate the subtler qualities of blank verse, concerning which he was to learn much by later experience. Meanwhile he was doubtless influenced by the new vogue for the heroic couplet; and his lavish tribute to Waller, who 'first made writing easily an art, and . . . showed us to conclude the sense most commonly in distichs',[3] became later one of the most familiar of the critical commonplaces of the period.

With the publication of the poem *Annus Mirabilis* (1666) treating of the Dutch War and the Fire of London, Dryden takes the opportunity in the accompanying Preface of expounding his views on certain aspects of poetry in general. And, first, he points out that whereas *Annus Mirabilis* had treated generously of heroic action it was nevertheless no epic, but rather a historical poem, being 'tied severely to the laws of history' throughout. More significant are his comments on the verseform employed; for they suggest a certain fluidity in his ideas at this stage. He had previously extolled the rhyming couplet of Waller; but now he describes the four-line stanza with alternate rhymes as the more noble and dignified form.[4] The rhyming

---

[1] W. P. Ker, *Essays of J. Dryden*, i. 6.   [2] *ibid*. i. 7 ff.
[3] *ibid*. i. 7.   [4] *ibid*. i. 12.

couplet, he allows, presented fewer difficulties, since 'every two lines concluded the labour of the poet'. The quatrain, however, offered greater scope and freedom, inasmuch as the sense was not confined within the limits of the couplet. As with those who wrote in Alexandrines or in 'Chapman's old measure', so poets who wrote in quatrains, Dryden maintained, 'by lengthening of their chain make the sphere of their activity the larger'; so that, it is worth noting, the heroic couplet was becoming established not without some critical doubts and comments.

A similar openness of mind is revealed when he decries the use of general terms in poetry, despite the teaching of Hobbes. On this matter, it is true, he was also to change his mind; but his first thoughts, embodying a plea for the use of particular terms, are not without their interest. Then, too, he has some suggestions to make on the subject of 'wit', hitherto variously described as intelligence, fancy or judgment. And his analysis of the term marks an attempt to dissipate something of the vagueness of the critical terminology then in use. Thus he distinguishes between 'wit active' or the poetic faculty and 'wit written' or the poetic product.[1] To the poetic faculty he assigns a new and comprehensive term, namely, the 'imagination'; and the 'imagination' he regards as many-sided, a faculty responsible for the invention, the fancy and the judgment that went to the making of a poem. On the other hand, 'wit' in a poem consisted in the 'delightful imagining of persons, actions, passions or things'; it was not the result of epigrams, antitheses, puns or grave *sententiae*. The whole problem, it is true, was not cleared up; but new light had been shed on the confusion that prevailed, and his particular use of the term 'imagination' is not without its interest.

In 1668, however, appeared the most elaborate and one of the most attractive and lively of Dryden's critical works. It was the *Essay of Dramatic Poesy*, written three years previously, at a time when, having fled from the Plague in London, he had sought refuge at the country residence of his father-in-law at Charlton in Wiltshire. In this work he reveals once again his unsettled views regarding the drama; though he also promises to deal later with epic and lyric poetry, a promise that was only partly fulfilled in connexion with the epic. And the method he adopts for voicing his perplexities is that of the dialogue, a device doubtless suggested by earlier conventional discussions in the works of Chapelain, Sarrasin, Desmarets, and the Spaniard

---

[1] W. P. Ker, *op. cit.* i. 14.

Tirso de Molina. It was a form which permitted of a full discussion of conflicting views, without requiring any definite finding in conclusion. Such a finding, after the fashion of the old *débat*, was left to the judgment of the reader; and Dryden from the first makes it plain that his purpose was to debate, not to dogmatize. In other words, the work was an essay in which all was frankly said to be 'problematical'. To his dialogue, moreover, Dryden gives a picturesque setting reminiscent of the Platonic tradition or of Cicero's *De Oratore*. The scene is placed on the Thames, with swallows darting around and within hearing of the Dutch guns engaged in the battle of June 1665; and as their thunder diminishes the dialogue is carried on by three noble patrons, Sir Robert Howard (Crites), Sir Charles Sedley (Lisideius), Lord Buckhurst (Eugenius) and Dryden (Neander) himself. The main theme—a vindication of English plays—is introduced by light gossip about lost glories, in which Wither, Cleveland, and other 'levellers of poetry' come in for drastic treatment; and then in more serious vein the interlocutors restrict their discussion to the drama, and proceed to consider the respective merits of ancient and modern achievements, of French and English plays, while a final inquiry is made into the burning question of the proper verse-form for dramatic purposes.

Crites, to begin with, undertakes to present the case for the ancients.[1] He points out, for instance, that the dramatic art had been indigenous to ancient Greece, since 'every age', he explains, 'has a kind of universal genius which inclines those who live in it to some particular studies'. Moreover, the drama there had attained an early maturity, whereas, natural science rather than the arts being latterly the main preoccupation, less progress had consequently been made in dramatic affairs. Then, too, he claims that dramatists had become less highly esteemed than in ancient Greece, and that the desire to excel had therefore vanished. Yet emulation, he adds, as Velleius Paterculus[2] had long ago pointed out, was a necessary factor in artistic development; and this, too, accounted in some measure for the decline in the drama. Apart from this he recalls that men in his day looked mainly to the ancients for their rules of the drama; and he discusses in some detail the merits of the Unities and the like. Finally he urges that the ancients had possessed the power of expression in a superlative degree. This, he argued, was shown by the deference paid to them by 'the greatest man of the last age, Ben Jonson'. For, as Crites added,

[1] W. P. Ker, *op. cit.* i. 36 ff. [2] *Hist. Rom.* i. 17.

he 'was not only a professed imitator of Horace, but a learned plagiary of all the others; you may track him everywhere in their snow'.

To these arguments Eugenius replies by claiming that modern dramatists had actually improved on the work of the ancients;[1] though, as Paterculus[2] had urged, it was always difficult to assess fairly the value of contemporary writings. Apart from this, however, there were many defects in the ancient drama, defects in structure, plot and characterization. Thus the division of a play into *protasis*, *epitasis* and the rest,[3] he held, was ineffective; tragic plots were mostly based on hackneyed tales of Thebes and Troy; while, in comedy, characters were limited to certain stock types. Then, too, argued Eugenius, the ancients did not always observe their own rules of the Unities; though, as he points out, apart from the Unity of action, those rules were not Aristotelian but French in origin. And if their technique was faulty, so also was their moral teaching. Instead of 'punishing vice and rewarding virtue' they often displayed 'a prosperous vice and an unhappy piety'; while their themes of lust, revenge and ambition gave rise to horror rather than pity in an audience. Finally, he hesitates to apply to their plays the modern test of 'wit' in view of differences in language and conditions. Yet 'wit', he asserts, consists of 'deep thought in common language'; and 'a thing well said will be wit in all languages'. With this the discussion is brought to a close by Crites's concession that whether the moderns surpassed, or merely differed from, the ancients, yet the ancients had they lived in later times would doubtless have made many changes.

The debate now takes a new turn, and Lisideius and Neander enter on a discussion of the respective merits of French and English plays.[4] Lisideius grants, to begin with, that English plays of forty years previously had clearly surpassed those of the French. On the other hand he held that political troubles at home had since hampered progress; that 'the Muses who ever follow peace went to plant in a new country'; and that the French, aided by Richelieu and Corneille, had latterly reformed their stage so that it had become unrivalled in Europe. In the first place, he remarks, contemporary French dramatists had scrupulously observed the three Unities. They had discarded absurd tragicomedies—an English invention—with their mingled

---

[1] W. P. Ker, *op. cit.* i. 43 ff. 　　[2] *Hist. Rom.* ii. 92.
[3] Due to Scaliger and not to Aristotle, as Eugenius asserted.
[4] W. P. Ker, *op. cit.* i. 56 ff.

passions, running 'through all the fits of Bedlam in two hours and a half'; and yet at the same time they had provided variety in plenty. Then, too, he claimed, their plots were founded on familiar history, modified and transformed for dramatic purposes; whereas Shakespeare's historical plays were nothing more than bare chronicles of kings, cramming years into hours in unnatural fashion. Again, another notable feature in which the French surpassed the dramatists of both England and Spain was their economy in plotting, their selection of significant details, which, while constituting a great and complete action, yet allowed for a more searching treatment of emotions and passions. Nor less notable was their skill in narrative; though too much explanation, he confessed, was apt to be tedious. On the other hand there were many incidents in a story which could not well be represented on the stage, such as duels, battles, and scenes of cruelty, and these were best related, not acted. Such narratives, he maintained, could be both impressive and convincing; whereas to represent 'an army with a drum and five men behind it' was merely ridiculous, while a death-scene in an English tragedy was often the most comic part of the play. These then were the main points in which French plays were held to excel; and to these were also added effective characterization, a logical development of the plot, and the use of rhyme in preference to blank verse.

Neander now takes up the challenge and with the skill of a great advocate attempts what after all was the main object of the *Essay*, namely, a vindication of the English drama.[1] To begin with, he freely concedes the regularity of French plays, their observance of *decorum* and the like, for what they were worth; but on appealing from the rules to the laws of Nature as the ultimate test, he finds them defective in many particulars. For one thing he claims that they lacked touch with actual life, that their 'humours' were 'thin-sown', Molière, who here followed the English tradition, being the chief exception. Then, too, he disapproves of their rigid separation of tragic and comic elements. The English practice of mingling those elements had in his opinion provided a better way, since 'contraries . . . set off each other, and a continued gravity keeps the spirit too much bent', and therefore called for relief. Nor could he admire the bareness and severity of French plays in excluding underplots and minor episodes. Provided such details contributed to the main design, he held that they added a pleasing variety, the

[1] W. P. Ker, *op. cit.* i. 67 ff.

effect being similar (as he puts it) to that of the twofold movements of planets in the *Primum Mobile*.

Furthermore, the argument that a rigid observance of the
Unity of action gave opportunity for impassioned appeals left
him unconvinced, since such appeals consisted mostly of long-
winded declamations, boring to English audiences who looked
to the stage primarily for amusement. And, apart from this,
such long-drawn utterances were surely untrue to life; for, as he
added, it was 'unnatural for any one in a gust of passion to
speak long together'. On the contrary, brief utterances were
more likely to stir the emotions; and as for comedy, repartee,
he stated, was 'one of its chief graces'. Rather more, he confessed, was to be said for the French use of narrative in order to
dispense with scenes of violence. Yet such scenes, he notes, were
part of the English tradition, being a concession to the native
temperament which somehow delighted in these things. And it
might at least be said that if English playwrights indulged in
too much action, the French also fell short in employing too
little.

So far, it will have been noticed, Neander has been testing
French standards in the light of Nature; and his finding is that
whereas the French had more strictly observed the rules, yet
English plays had qualities of their own which rendered them
still more effective. And then in concluding his inquiry, he
boldly challenges the whole French system by means of an
argument drawn from Corneille himself, to the effect that experience had shown that French dramatists had suffered from
too strict an observance of the rules, and had thereby banished
from the stage many artistic beauties. Regular English plays,
Neander maintained, were not entirely wanting, and of these he
selects Jonson's *Silent Woman* as an example. For the rest, however, English plays, he contended, were more original, more
varied and spirited; and these qualities he illustrates from the
works of outstanding English dramatists.

Then follow Neander's illuminating appreciations of Shakespeare, Beaumont and Fletcher, and Jonson, which opened up
fresh possibilities in the critical sphere, possibilities previously
realized only by Jonson in his remarks on Shakespeare and by
Carew in his elegy on Donne. Neander's well-known judgment
on Shakespeare,[1] to begin with, has since attained classic rank;
and this by reason of its keen insight, its suggestive and happy
expression. That Shakespeare was no discovery of the 18th

---

[1] W. P. Ker, *op. cit.* i. 79.

Century is shown by the fact that he is already hailed by Neander as 'the largest and most comprehensive soul of all modern, and perhaps ancient, poets'. Moreover reference is made to his unlaboured art, his inborn genius, his lifelike characterization, though he is also said at times to stumble into bombast and punning. But the final judgment is unequivocal. 'He is always great when some great occasion is presented to him; no man could say he ever had a fit subject for his wit and did not then raise himself high above the rest of poets.' And this, it is added, was the judgment, not only of his own contemporaries, but also of Caroline courtiers at a time when Jonson's reputation stood at its highest.

Hardly less interesting are the remarks on Beaumont and Fletcher,[1] whose popularity is evidenced by the fact that two of their plays were then being performed for one of Shakespeare's or Jonson's. The two dramatists are credited with gaiety and 'wit', with skill in intrigue and a lively display of the passions, while they are also said to have excelled in their 'imitation of the conversation of gentlemen'. Concerning Jonson Neander has more to say; and he describes him above all as 'the most learned and judicious of dramatists'. Of 'a sullen and saturnine nature', he is said to have been frugal of 'wit', self-critical, apt to be concise and laboured in expression, and lacking in the lighter graces; whereas 'humour' being his sphere, he treated mainly of ordinary life. What distinguished his tragedies is said to have been their vast learning, the faithful pictures of ancient Rome drawn from classical sources. Yet with him, declared Neander, there could be no question of plagiarism; for 'he invades authors like a monarch, and what would be theft in other poets is only victory in him'. And in general it is suggested, 'something of art was wanting to the drama till he came'. The judgment finally closes with a comparison between Jonson and Shakespeare, in which the former is described as the more correct poet, the Virgil or pattern of art, the latter as the greater wit, the Homer or father of English dramatists. Most significant of all, however, is Neander's last word on their respective merits. 'Jonson', he declares, 'I admire, but I love Shakespeare'; and here judgment is pronounced, not in accordance with rules of technical excellence, but in the light of the general impression and of the emotional appeal to the whole man.

The main object of the *Essay*—the vindication of English plays—has now been achieved; though, in support of the main

[1] W. P. Ker, *op. cit.* i. 80.

thesis, an *Examen* of *The Silent Woman* is also attempted in
the course of which occur some notable remarks on Falstaff.[1] He
is, for instance, described as a bundle of frailties, and therefore
in current terminology, 'a miscellany of humours'. More significant, however, is the explanation of the mirth he provokes, which
is ascribed to the elements of unexpectedness and contrast.
'His quick evasions', it is asserted, 'are amusing in themselves,
but they also receive a great addition from his person'; and
here, not only is some aid afforded towards the understanding
of that complicated personality, but a hint is also given of new
methods in the elucidation of character.

Yet Dryden is unable to close the *Essay* without some reference to the vexed question of the verse most suitable for
dramatic purposes.[2] And Crites, who is allowed to broach the
matter anew, notes, to begin with, in his defence of blank verse,
that it had established itself in popular favour since Shakespeare and others had written; that rhyming verse was essentially an artificial form of expression, since 'no man without
premeditation speaks in rhyme'; while Aristotle had held that
tragedy was best written in verse nearest prose. Nor could he
accept the argument that rhyme was instrumental in curbing
wild fancies, for the poet who was unable to restrain his flights
in blank verse would be equally culpable in verse of a rhyming
character.

To this Neander replies by marshalling his arguments in
favour of rhyming verse,[3] boldly asserting that 'in serious plays
rhyme is more natural and more effectual than blank verse'.
In the first place he points out that blank verse could be as
stiff and unnatural as rhyming verse was sometimes said to be;
that, significantly enough, it was rhyming verse, not blank
verse, that had been universally adopted abroad. And, if Aristotle's 'nearness to prose' was a point to be considered, then
rhyming verse could be made to resemble prose by varying the
cadences, by running the sense on from one line to another, or
by irregular devices after the 'Pindaric' fashion; whereas blank
verse was none other than prose itself, a *sermo pedestris*, even if
at its best a 'poetic prose'. Nor was any weight to be attached
to the argument that the populace, dazzled by past glories, then
favoured blank verse as a dramatic medium; or again, that
Shakespeare and others had employed it with excellent results.
The truth was, so Neander urged, that the possibilities of that
way of writing had been exhausted by those earlier dramatists;

---

[1] W. P. Ker, *op. cit.* i. 84.   [2] *ibid.* i. 90 ff.   [3] *ibid.* i. 94 ff.

and all that was left for a later age with its different genius was
to employ that rhyming verse in which excellences unknown to
an earlier age had latterly been attained. More important than
all, however, was the claim that rhyming verse—according to
Neander, 'the noblest kind of modern verse'—was the only
adequate verse-form for tragedy. Tragedy he defined as 'a representation of Nature, but Nature wrought up to a higher pitch,
. . . just as statues which are placed on high are made greater
than the life, that they may descend to the sight in their just
proportion'.[1] And for such a treatment of Nature, he urged,
rhyming verse was the only verse-form. Blank verse, on the
other hand, which was 'too low' for an ordinary poem, was said
to be altogether unsuitable for tragic purposes. A tragic poet
employing blank verse, so Neander explains, 'might indeed follow
Nature, but he must do it on foot; you have dismounted him
from his Pegasus'. With this the case for rhyming verse is
practically complete; and Dryden's own predilection at this
date is plainly manifest. Whereupon the *Essay* concludes in
picturesque fashion, with the moonlight playing on the Thames
as the noble disputants land and disperse on their several
occasions.

Such then is the famous *Essay*, which in its liveliness, its
shrewd reasoning and urbanity represents a foretaste of what
was to be best in Dryden's later critical work. In its pages
French influence may definitely be traced, particularly that
of Corneille, whose free play of intellect in his *Discours* and
Examens found in Dryden a ready response; and this was to
remain a distinguishing feature of his criticism right on to the
end. As yet his ideas were obviously in a fluid condition. He was
'sailing', as he explained later,[2] 'in a vast ocean without other
help than the pole-star of the ancients and the rules of the
French stage'; but the guidance of neither does he wholly accept.
On the other hand, his test of literary value is an inborn sensibility, not so very different from the Nature or reason of the
earlier Renascence period; and it is to that particular test that
we owe the acute and masterly appreciations of Shakespeare
and Jonson.

While the *Essay* thus constitutes Dryden's most formal contribution during this transitional period, he is still much concerned with immediate dramatic problems; and in his *Defence
of an Essay of Dramatic Poesy* (1668), his *Preface to the Mock
Astrologer* (1671) and his *Essay of Heroic Plays* (1672) these

[1] W. P. Ker, *op. cit.* i. 100–2.   [2] *ibid.* ii. 17.

problems are submitted to further scrutiny. His views on rhyming verse and the Unities had in the meantime been challenged by Howard; he himself was entertaining fresh ideas concerning comedy, as well as the possibilities of a new dramatic type, the heroic play; and these matters he discusses freely and informally as occasion arose.

On the question of rhyming verse, in the first place, Dryden still maintains his position in the *Defence of an Essay*, where he reiterates with some additions his earlier reasoning. His chief argument here however is that rhyme pre-eminently causes delight, and thus discharges the real function of poetry. For, as he adds in noteworthy fashion, 'delight is the chief, if not the only, end of poesy; instruction can be admitted, but in the second place, for poesy only instructs as it delights'.[1] This argument based on a modification of the Horatian formula, however true in itself, is nevertheless by no means convincing. As Howard pointed out, Dryden had not here faced up to the real issue, which was the suitability of rhyming verse for specific dramatic purposes. Again, Dryden now replies to Howard's attack on the Unities;[2] and he rests his defence, not on an appeal to the authority of Aristotle and others, but on rational and psychological grounds, his main point being that an observance of the Unities conduces to the credibility of a plot. Employing the term 'imagination' in his new and comprehensive sense,[3] he explains that 'imagination participates of reason', and that where fiction is concerned, 'reason suffers itself to be hoodwinked that it may better enjoy the pleasures of fiction'. And here, it might be noted, he is hinting at that 'willing suspension of disbelief', suggested long ago by Gorgias and repeated by Plutarch,[4] which made illusion acceptable. There was one condition, however, and that was that the fiction should not be too wildly improbable. 'There are degrees in impossibilities', so Dryden reminds his readers; and since the limitations imposed by the Unities of time and place laid less strain on the reason, they were therefore to be commended in dramatic works.

Meanwhile his views on comedy were undergoing change. He had already realized that he was not 'fitted by Nature to write comedy', being, so he confesses, of 'a saturnine and reserved temperament,[5] and thus lacking the qualities needed for that

---

[1] W. P. Ker, *op. cit.* i. 113.   [2] *ibid.* i. 125 ff.
[3] *ibid.* i. 27: see p. 54 *supra*.
[4] See Atkins, *Lit. Crit. in Antiquity*, i. 18; ii. 314.
[5] W. P. Ker, *op. cit.* i. 116.

sort of work. And now, in his *Preface to the Mock Astrologer*, dissatisfied with his own achievements, he suggests something like a new conception of the comic art. The prevailing tendency, he notes, had been in the direction of farce with its overdrawn characters and absurd situations—due partly to French influence, partly also to popular tastes—though he recognizes that Jonson's comedy of humours had hitherto provided acceptable models. Now however he doubts whether even Jonson's example was wholly adequate.[1] His art had consisted mainly in the imitation of folly, in making men 'pleasantly ridiculous' on the stage; and this had called merely for the exercise of observation and judgment. Moreover, to deal with nothing but 'humours' was to avoid 'the conversation of gentlemen', and to treat only of 'the follies and extravagancies of Bedlam'. What was wanting was the salt of 'wit' or 'sharpness of conceit'; and in this connexion Dryden recalls Quintilian's teaching that 'to make fun of folly is easy, for folly is laughable in itself. It is what we supply of our own that gives rise to refined laughter.'[2] And therefore he states that in comedy he would have more of the *'urbana* (elegant), *venusta* (charming), *salsus* (witty), *faceta* (laughable)[3] and the rest which Quintilian reckons up as the ornaments of wit' —all qualities which he maintained were wanting in Jonsonian comedy. Such elements, he notes, were specially effective in repartee, which he regarded as 'the greatest grace of comedy'. Yet discretion, he adds, was everywhere needed; and he quotes Cowley's injunction, to the effect that 'rather than all wit let there be none'. For a superfluity of wit, which he finds in Shakespeare and Fletcher, was after all the greatest of follies.

Then, too, he has a word or two to say on other aspects of the comic art, as when, for instance, he defends his own frequent treatment of 'debauched persons' in comedy,[4] on the ground that since 'the first end of comedy is delight, and instruction only the second', therefore 'comedy is not so much obliged to the punishment of faults as tragedy'. This doctrine he supports by reference to the practice of Plautus, Terence and Jonson. And in maintaining that considerations of morality and justice are of minor importance in comedy he argues on lines similar to those of Martial, who in defending his own audacities had asserted *Iocosa carmina* to be ineffective without prurience.[5] Moreover, in adopting this position and in his demand for a plentiful supply of the salt of wit, he was obviously preparing

---

[1] W. P. Ker, *op. cit.* i. 138 ff.   [2] *Inst. orat.* vi. 3. 71.
[3] *ibid.* vi. 3. 17.   [4] W. P. Ker, *op. cit.* i. 141.   [5] *Epig.* i. 35.

the way for Congreve's later achievements. Nor, again, without its interest is his comment on the borrowing with which he was charged, and which had been condemned as so much plagiarism.[1] Recalling Shakespeare's indebtedness to the Italians for his plots and that of Beaumont and Fletcher to Spanish sources, he justifies such procedure by explaining that what was borrowed was merely the poet's raw material, whereas the life-giving touches and the secret graces were said to come from the poet himself. 'The price (or value) of a work of art', he therefore asserts, 'lies wholly in the workmanship';[2] and here was formulated a new and valuable principle in critical history.

Equally significant, however, are Dryden's remarks on yet another species of drama, namely, the heroic play, which was at the height of its popularity about 1670. Already Dryden, together with Howard, Settle and Crowne, had achieved a fashionable success in that dramatic form; and now, with the publication of *The Conquest of Granada* (1672), there appeared also *The Rehearsal*, that famous burlesque concocted by Buckingham, Sprat and others, in which the defects of the whole species were ridiculed, and which drew from Dryden his defence of heroic plays in the same year. The burlesque, it is true, was not directed against Dryden alone; but in the running commentary provided by Bayes and the two 'languishing gentlemen', Messrs. Smith and Johnson (the prototypes of Puff, Sneer and Dangle in the *Critic*), it is Bayes who plays the leading part; and the reference to Dryden was too obvious to be missed, in view of his recent appointment to the poet laureateship in 1670.

In the play itself, which represents biting criticism in dramatic form, the standards and methods of heroic plays are brought to the test of common sense. By means of travesty and grotesque exaggeration the unreason and artificiality of such plays are cunningly revealed—the rant and bombast, the mechanical structures and motiveless actions, the clumsy efforts to convey necessary information, the subordination of an incoherent plot to grandiose speeches, and the constant harping on the conflict between honour and love. At the same time the satire is made more pointed by the naïve comments of the complacent Bayes as the action develops. He glories, for instance, in that unspeakable character, Drawcansir, who can

> Make proud Jove, with all his thunders, see
> This single arm more dreadful than is he;

---

[1] W. P. Ker, *op. cit.* i. 144 ff.   [2] *ibid.* i. 147.

and whom he frankly admires as 'a fierce hero that . . . snubs up kings, baffles armies, and does what he will without regard to good manners, justice or numbers'.[1] Elsewhere the same acute critic calls attention to the agonizing struggle between love and honour that goes on in the mind of Prince Volscius when engaged in the homely task of pulling on his boots; and this struggle, adds the admiring Bayes, is artfully comprised in a single scene.[2] Then, too, he reveals occasionally, in his artless fashion, odd secrets of the craft; as when he notes that 'you must ever make a simile when you are surprised',[3] that 'spirits must not be confined to talk sense', or again, that the two kings of Brentford had perforce 'to speak in French to show their breeding'.[4] To this attack Dryden does not deign to reply in kind; nor was the burlesque all at once successful in laughing heroic plays out of court. Of its stage success, however, there can be no doubt. It is referred to with approval by later critics; according to Rymer, 'we want a law for acting *The Rehearsal* once a week to keep us in sense'.[5] And if common sense was to prove defective as the ultimate criterion of literary values, yet for the time being the play doubtless opened men's eyes to the absurdities that ran riot in heroic plays.

It was under these conditions that Dryden put forward his reasoned defence of heroic plays in an essay prefixed to *The Conquest of Granada*; and this he supplements with some remarks in the *Epilogue* to the second part of that play, enlarging further on the matter in a *Defence of the Epilogue* (1672). His main plea is that the heroic play in general was an enterprising attempt to realize on the stage a new form of drama more in keeping with contemporary conditions than were the tragedies and comedies of Elizabethan and Jacobean times. Its origin he traces to Davenant's *Siege of Rhodes*[6] (1656), which he describes as an innovation occasioned by the Puritan ban on tragedies and comedies. In that play, he notes, moral virtues had been treated in imperfect fashion; and upon that model Dryden now claims to have improved by embodying qualities of what was then regarded as the noblest form of literature, namely, the heroic poem. In this way he was following, as it were in reverse, the procedure of Davenant, who for his epic *Gondibert* had adopted certain formal features of the drama,[7] thereby illustrating the unsettled condition of literary theory at this date; so that

---

[1] *Rehearsal*, IV. i.   [2] *ibid*. III. ii.   [3] *ibid*. II. iii.
[4] *ibid*. II. ii.   [5] *Short View of Tragedy*, p. 158.
[6] W. P. Ker. *op. cit*. i. 149.   [7] See p. 36 *supra*.

Dryden's resultant doctrine was that the heroic play was none
other than 'an imitation in little of a heroic poem in which love
and valour were the main themes'.[1]

Such an innovation, he further points out, was made possible
since the epic or heroic poem (as Aristotle had stated) had
structural features in common with the drama. At the same
time in heroic plays all things were to be represented on a more
majestic scale than that of ordinary life;[2] and this deliberate
enhancing of effects he made an essential feature of his experi-
ment. Here, however, he was at variance with Davenant who
had recommended for the heroic poem a more familiar treatment of everyday life; and Dryden therefore recalls in his
support the stock passage of Petronius, quoted by most critics
of the epic at this date, to the effect that the epic dealt not with
actual facts, but with all the flights of an 'enthusiastic' fancy,
including actions involving the intervention of the gods (*deorum
ministeria*).[3] It was in vain, added Dryden, that 'your phleg-
matic heavy gownsman' denounced these 'enthusiastic' elements
as unnatural; for the heroic poet was 'not tied to a bare representation of what is true or exceeding probable', but might
treat of things supra-natural which would give 'a freer scope
for imagination'.[4] This then was Dryden's main argument in
defence of his heroic plays. It was in keeping with his definition
of tragedy as 'a representation of Nature wrought up to a
higher pitch', also with his reminder of the analogous effect of
statues placed aloft.[5] And on this he rested his apology for all
exaggerations and extravagances; though he claims further that
his use of 'drums and trumpets', previously countenanced by
Shakespeare, was also intended to 'raise the imagination of the
audience', while his extravagant heroes, modelled on those of
Homer, Tasso and Calprenède, were free from the meticulous
French treatment, in which 'love and honour were weighed by
drachms and scruples'.

With this explanation of the nature of the heroic play, however, Dryden was not content. He was conscious that he had
yet to show that it was a form of drama in closer conformity to
the genius of his age than were the earlier tragedies and comedies.
And this is the task he undertakes in the *Epilogue* to *The Conquest
of Granada*, Part II, and in *The Defence of the Epilogue*. In the
former his main contention is but briefly suggested; and it is

[1] W. P. Ker, *op. cit.* i. 150.   [2] *ibid.* i. 151.
[3] See Atkins, *Lit. Crit. in Antiquity*, ii. 163–5.
[4] W. P. Ker, *op. cit.* i. 153.   [5] See p. 61 *supra*.

in the *Defence*, a sort of postscript, that his case is more fully presented. There he prepares the way for his censures of earlier plays by stating that his own age was one that accepted nothing from earlier ages 'on trust', and by referring also to the just but censorious remarks of Horace on the earlier work of Lucilius. And then, despite his reiterated assurances of reverence for Shakespeare, Jonson and Fletcher, he proceeds with his main thesis, that 'the language, wit and conversation of our age are improved . . . above the last, . . . and that our plays have received some part of those advantages'.[1]

First, in connexion with language, he refuses to regard the preceding period as the Golden Age of poetry.[2] In the plays of Fletcher and Shakespeare, he states, would be found solecisms and obscurities on every page, apart from impossible plots and clumsy expressions. The truth was, so he maintains, that 'the well-placing of words for sweetness of pronunciation was not known till Mr. Waller introduced it'; and since then, new words had been imported and fresh meanings given to old and familiar terms. Then, too, he held, the preceding age had been deficient in 'wit', by which he meant 'propriety of language', or else 'sharpness of conceit'. In the former sense Shakespeare had been a great offender.[3] He is stated in places 'to have written better than any poet in any language'; yet elsewhere, it is added, he had written 'below the dullest writer of ours or any precedent age'. In short, he was said to be 'the very Janus of poets'. Fletcher, again, was too luxuriant; 'a true Englishman, he knows not when to give over'. And, as for Jonson, he was lacking in sharpness of conceit, much given to puns, to playing with words —a vice of the age, seen, according to Dryden, in Sidney, though attributed originally to pulpit-orators, who, added Dryden, 'are commonly the first corruptors of eloquence'.

But most significant of all was said to be the lack of courtliness and gallantry in those earlier plays,[4] in contrast with the refined manners and conversation of contemporary works. This element of refinement Dryden regarded as the outstanding characteristic of the new age which therefore called for a modification of dramatic ideals. Jonson in particular was allowed to be correct and judicious; yet he had dealt mostly with scenes of low life. Whereas 'gentlemen', added Dryden, 'will now be entertained with the follies of each other; and though they allow Cobb and Tib to speak properly, yet they are not much pleased with

---

[1] W. P. Ker, *op. cit.* i. 163.   [2] *ibid.* i. 164 ff.
[3] *ibid.* i. 171 ff.   [4] *ibid.* i. 174 ff.

their tankards or with their rags'. Such, then, was Dryden's
defence of the heroic play; and it is obviously a piece of special
pleading, a biased and hostile review of Elizabethan and Jacobean drama, in which, for the time being, he discards his better
judgment, to bolster up his argument in deference to the
sophisticated tastes of his day.

A few years later, however, *Aureng-Zebe* (1676), the last of
the rhyming heroic plays, appeared; and in the *Prologue* he
renounces his earlier position, declaring that

> Passion's too fierce to be in fetters bound,
> And Nature flies him like enchanted ground.

Moreover, by now he had 'grown weary of his long-loved mistress, rhyme'; and he yielded precedence to an earlier age 'less
polished, more unskilled'. These saner views are subsequently
developed in the *Preface to All for Love* (1678), where, in abandoning finally his attempt at innovation, he claims to have
reverted to the practice of the ancients, not only in observing
the Unities, but also in representing his tragic hero as neither
perfect nor yet wholly evil.[1] At the same time he holds that some
modifications were necessary, since English tragedy demanded
'a larger compass' and greater freedom than that of the ancient
models.[2] He also 'disencumbers' himself from rhyme, reluc-
tantly acknowledging blank verse to be better suited for his
tragic purpose. And in matters of style, despite his previous
censures, he claims to have followed 'the divine Shakespeare',
whose purity of language and miraculous achievements, he now
confesses, had exhausted all praise. Nor does he find in French
tragedy models wholly satisfactory; for French dramatists, he
maintains, observed too strictly that false *decorum*, those trifling
punctilios dictated by courtly etiquette and artificial codes of
honour. Such attention to 'nicety of manners', he held, dealt
with non-essentials; it resulted in characterization neither natural
nor convincing. And he recalls honest Montaigne's statement
that *la cérémonie nous défend d'exprimer par paroles les choses
licites et naturelles*,[3] adding that he, for his part, was content to
have 'kept himself within the bounds of modesty'. It was a
timely comment, and one of considerable importance, especially
in view of the later imbecilities of Rymer and others in literary
judgment. And with such thoughts in mind he condemns those
chedreux critics, who formed their judgments wholly by French
standards, while he incidentally states his own conception of

---

[1] W. P. Ker, *op. cit.* i. 191.   [2] *ibid.* i. 200.   [3] *Essais*, I. ii. c. 17.

the critical business. 'Poets themselves', he suggests,[1] 'are the most proper though not the only critics'; or again, 'the judgment of an artificer in his own art should be preferable to the opinion of another man.' And, in any case, he for his part would 'desire to be tried by the laws of his own country'.

Such then were the varied critical activities of this third quarter of the 17th Century (1650–74), in which a distinct break with the work of earlier English critics becomes perceptible. As before, the test generally applied was that of Nature or reason; and while use was made of ancient and French doctrine, little deference was paid to rules as such, the independent earlier attitude towards authority being still retained. Now, however, attempts were already being made in the light of Hobbes's philosophy to treat literary problems in psychological fashion. Wit, judgment, fancy and the like were variously defined, increased importance being attached to judgment in literary creation; and by Dryden a more comprehensive meaning was tentatively given to 'imagination' as distinct from mere 'fancy'. As yet, it might be noted, current problems monopolized the attention; and the future possibilities of the epic, comedy, and the heroic play were freely canvassed. Moreover, the heroic couplet was generally accepted as the verse-form of the new age, but not without challenge; for the freer, more irregular form of 'Pindaric' verse, together with the four-line stanza with alternate rhymes, and blank verse also found their advocates. At the same time a demand was being made for a simplified prose style. Nor were there wanting some interesting appreciations of literature in the concrete. Shakespeare and Jonson, as well as Cowley, come in for illuminating comments; and some sense is occasionally shown of the importance of historical and biographical factors in forming judgments. Altogether this transitional stage is one of controversy, of confused efforts to develop contemporary literature along sound lines. Yet it reveals much that is new and interesting; and not least, the earliest groping pronouncements of Dryden on the literary art. With him, then as later, will be found no doctrinaire consistency; as yet, so he explains, he was but feeling his way and attempting to 'draw the outlines' of a new art.

[1] W. P. Ker, *op. cit.* i. 195.

CHAPTER III

NEW FRENCH INFLUENCES: RYMER, MULGRAVE, TEMPLE, WOTTON, PHILLIPS, WOLSELEY AND COLLIER

D U R I N G the last quarter of the 17th Century English criticism entered on a new phase, a phase confused and varied as before, but notable also for marked changes, as a result of which questions of a more fundamental and general kind were discussed, though immediate problems still claimed some amount of attention. This extension of interests was due primarily to French activities already outlined; and notably to the crystallizing in France of neo-classical doctrines previously developed there in detached and irregular fashion. In this connexion particular interest is attached to the year 1674, the year in which there appeared not only Boileau's *Art Poétique* and his translation of 'Longinus', but also Rapin's *Réflexions sur la Poétique*. And the effects in England were instantaneous and widespread, more especially as those works were soon followed by Le Bossu's *Traité du Poème épique* (1675), by numerous versions of Saint-Evremond's *Essays* (after 1684), by Bouhours's *Manière de bien penser* (1687), Dacier's *Préface sur les Satires d'Horace* (1687) and his translation of Aristotle's *Poetics* (1692), as well as by Perrault's *Parallèle des Anciens et des Modernes* (1688). As a result a new field of literary inquiry was opened up in England; a new direction was given to critical studies; and currency was also given to fresh doctrines relating to the epic, tragedy and satire, as well as to new standards of literary judgment. Of the reality of the impression thus made on English critics there can be no doubt. Frequent acknowledgements, for one thing, are made to the French sources; and, what is more, most of the French works were rendered more accessible by means of translation,[1] a process now applied, practically for the first time, to foreign critical works in England. Nor, it might be added,

---

[1] e.g. Rapin's *Réflexions*, tr. by Rymer, 1674; Le Bossu's *Traité*, tr. 1695; Saint-Evremond's *Mixed Essays*, tr. 1686; and Dacier's *Essay on Satire*, tr. 1692. Many translations also appeared under new titles: thus D'Aubignac's *Pratique* became *The Whole Art of the Stage* (1684). Boileau's *Art Poétique* appeared as Soames's *Art of Poetry* (1680) with English analogues added by Dryden, and Boileau's tr. of 'Longinus', as Pulteney's *Treatise on Loftiness and Elegance of Speech* (1680).

and use made of improbabilities, an ill-fitting stanza, and of particular instead of general terms. For Cowley, on the other hand, rather more was to be said; but he too had chosen to ignore epic rules in his *Davideis*. His theme, for instance, had consisted of no one complete action, but of certain episodes relating to sufferings in David's life. Moreover, the theme, contrary to Aristotle's teaching, was based on history, and on sacred history at that, which therefore contained many improbabilities in keeping with 'an extraordinary and unaccountable dispensation'. 'Poetry', added Rymer, 'has no life . . . without probability';[1] and in general he maintains that English poetry in its more ambitious forms had hitherto failed through neglect of those rational principles now expounded by Rapin.

Yet he is not prepared to admit that English poetry was inferior to that of other nations; and in order to vindicate the quality of the native poetry, despite its manifold defects, he compares (here following the lead of Scaliger[2] and Rapin[3]) the various treatments of a set theme by poets both ancient and modern, and shows to his own satisfaction that Dryden more than held his own with them all.[4] With a pedantic display of learning he submits to his test certain descriptions of 'night' by Apollonius Rhodius and Virgil, Ariosto, Tasso, Marino, Chapelain, Le Moyne and Dryden; and thus makes use, to all appearances, of the comparative method of criticism. Yet his treatment can only be described as of the most superficial and puerile kind. In submitting to analysis literature in the concrete and in attempting to treat of the 'niceties of poetry' rather than the grammatical trifles of his predecessors he was anticipating later and more fruitful critical methods. But his judgment was vitiated throughout by the limitations of his test, which was the conformity of the poet's treatment with a prosaic common sense; and this was to account for his later and even more disastrous judgments.

His main judgments followed later in his remarks on earlier English tragedy in the two works already mentioned. Much concerned, as he explains, about the decline of English tragedy, in his *Tragedies of the Last Age* (1678) he gives, first, his views on the subject generally, and then submits three of Beaumont and Fletcher's plays to detailed examination. As before he requires an observance of Aristotle's rules and the dictates of

---

[1] Spingarn, *op. cit.* ii. 171.   [2] cf. *Poetice*, Bk. v.
[3] cf. *Les Comparaisons des grands Hommes de l'Antiquité*.
[4] Spingarn, *op. cit.* ii. 174–81.

reason. Thus for tragic themes, he states something more philosophical than history was needed, since 'yesterday-truths' were unable to illustrate truths 'universal and eternal'.[1] There should also be a 'purging of the passions', as well as an observance of a non-Aristotelian 'poetic justice',[2] the latter requirement, derived possibly from Scaliger,[3] being one of the earliest uses of the term in English. In forming his judgments, however, he neglects entirely such requirements as these, along with the 'mechanical parts' of tragedy, structural qualities and the like. And, concentrating solely on the plot, 'the soul of tragedy', he maintains that common sense, and common sense alone, was a sufficient test of literary merit. Moreover, those who adopted other standards he attacks in heated fashion. To judge by taste alone or to deny the validity of ancient standards was for him the mark of mere 'stage-quacks'; while those who refused to recognize 'reason' as the ultimate over-riding test of literary merit were none other than the 'fanatics of poetry'. 'Reason', he adds,[4] 'must ratify whatever by fancy is attempted, . . . or else 'tis all null and void'; and 'reason', loosely interpreted and standing for Nature, common sense or probability, becomes for him in practice the sole critical test.

And the results are seen in his comments on *The Maid's Tragedy*, which he ridicules on account of the unnatural quality of its plot and characters. Common sense, for instance, required an observance of Nature, which, according to views then current, he took to mean the code of conduct recognized in civilized society; and with a narrow court etiquette as his criterion he shows up what he regards as the absurdities of the play.[5] Thus Evadne is obviously shameless; yet according to Nature the distinguishing quality of woman should be her modesty. Again, she slays the king; yet 'in poetry no woman is to kill a man, . . . much less a king'. Aspatia's violent handling of Amintor is also highly indecorous; in Rymer's opinion, 'it may be romance, but not Nature'. Moreover, the king is clearly a monster; but Rymer doubts whether in poetry a king could be accessory to a crime. Amintor, again, presumably a man of honour, nevertheless betrays his mistress and tamely endures affronts; whereas Melanthius offends nice feelings by breaking off a duel, though, as was well known, 'when the sword is once drawn in tragedy the scabbard may be thrown away'. Such then are Rymer's common-sense findings, submitted with the arrogant

---

[1] Spingarn, *op. cit.* ii. 188.   [2] *ibid.*   [3] cf. *Poetice*, iii. 97.
[4] Spingarn, *op. cit.* ii. 185.   [5] *ibid.* ii. 194 ff.

conviction that 'poets would grow negligent if the critics had not a strict eye on their miscarriages'.[1]

Some fourteen years later he returns to the attack in his *Short View of Tragedy*, which he introduces with substantial remarks on the drama and its history, revealing wide and unusual learning that doubtless accounts for the deference paid to him by his contemporaries, Dryden among the number. And notable in this connexion is his reference to Provençal poetry and its influence on Chaucer.[2] In his main treatment, however, he pays, as before, lip-service to Aristotle and the rules; but only in so far as they accorded with his idea of common sense. Thus the Chorus he holds to be 'the most necessary part of tragedy', since it kept the poet from 'rambling'.[3] He also refers casually to the Unities as a necessary deduction from common sense, insists again on the need for 'poetic justice'; and sketching a plot for a new play, *The Invincible Armado*, to be based on Aeschylus's *Persians*, he blandly invites Dryden to attempt its completion.[4]

At the same time his ultimate test is no longer confined to Nature interpreted in the narrow sense of court etiquette. His conception had apparently widened so as to include matters of expression, probability and the like. And in his comments on *Othello*, which he selects as the most popular of Shakespeare's plays, common sense is applied to something other than lapses or irregularities of social conduct. Thus to common sense many of Shakespeare's poetic utterances were said to be sheer nonsense. 'A rap at the door', he suggests, for instance, would have been more effective than Iago's picturesque summons for admission.[5] In fact, added Rymer, many of his scenes 'would be better without words'; and, in any event, 'in a play one should speak like a man of business'. Then, too, his verse was said to outrage common sense; or as Rymer puts it, 'in the neighing of a horse or the growling of a mastiff there was . . . more humanity'.[6] Elsewhere he derisively notes that 'Desdemona drops her handkerchief, therefore she must be stifled'.[7] 'Yet', he adds, 'no pagan poet but would have found some machine for her deliverance'; and this Rymer happily supplies, to his own satisfaction.

But it is on the element of unreason, the glaring improbabilities which he detects throughout the play, that he concentrates his keenest vision. It was absurd, in his opinion, to

[1] Spingarn, *op. cit.* ii. 163.   [2] See W. P. Ker. *op. cit.* ii. 307–8.
[3] Spingarn, *op. cit.* ii, 209.   [4] *ibid.* ii. 215–19.
[5] *ibid.* ii. 211.   [6] *ibid.* ii. 225.   [7] *ibid.* ii. 253.

suppose that Othello's talk was the charm that inveigled Desdemona, that Othello, a 'blackamoor', could be a lieutenant-general, or the 'dissembling, false, insinuating' Iago a typical soldier. Besides, in almost every scene there were said to be palpable absurdities that caused the audience to 'deny their senses in order to reconcile them with reason'. So that his judgment is that Shakespeare in this play 'against all law, humanity and reason has made havoc of his theme'. In it Rymer is able to detect 'some burlesque, some humour, . . . but the tragical part is plainly none other than a bloody farce without salt or favour'.[1]

All this of course is the very madness of criticism; and Macaulay's description of Rymer as 'the worst critic that ever lived' is fairly well justified. From his man-handling of Shakespeare it becomes plain that in aesthetic sensibilities he was entirely lacking; that for literary appreciation something more than a barren scholarship is essential; and that his interpretation of the terms 'Nature or reason' as nothing more than an unimaginative common sense led inevitably to ludicrous findings. What he brought to bear in his critical efforts was none other than the *petite raison*, which concerns itself with 'peddling improbabilities' and insists on a close representation of actual commonplace facts; whereas a less superficial acquaintance with Aristotle would have shown him that irrational, improbable and even impossible details might be made plausible by the poet's art. Reasonableness, it is true, he places before rules and theories; and his interest lies not in abstract doctrines but in a detailed examination of literature in the concrete. But to dramaturgic skill and poetic flights he is both blind and deaf; while 'romance' and 'Fairyland' are to him mere terms of abuse. In his attacks on Shakespeare he may have been influenced by *The Rehearsal*, and possibly by Dryden's lapse in defence of heroic plays; but nothing can excuse his senseless and worthless comments. Nor does he commend what he has to say by his manner of saying it. For his views are presented in an offensive, overbearing and colloquial style reminiscent of the most truculent of Humanistic pedants; and he prides himself on his incoherent, unsystematic treatment, possibly in supposed imitation of the more lucid Rapin, whose *Réflexions* were however designed merely to avoid the necessary connexions in continuous discourse. In matter, as in manner, Rymer may be said to represent the nadir of criticism.

[1] Spingarn, *op. cit.* ii. 255.

Yet after all in critical history Rymer cannot finally be dismissed in this summary fashion; for his critical works, intrinsically worthless, have a certain historical interest for modern readers. He was not the first, for instance, to require a false *decorum* in literature, a tendency to which sophisticated ages had apparently been liable. Hellenistic critics of Homer, for example, including the great Aristarchus[1] (2nd Century B.C.) had fallen into the same absurdities; and the tradition was carried on by later scholars. Thus Scaliger[2] dilates at some length on Homeric improbabilities and breaches of *decorum*; how the goddess Venus was wounded by mortal hand, how Mars, for all his divinity, groaned aloud, while Ulysses slays boars at short range with his bow. And Rapin,[3] too, is unhappy about much the same things. How, he asks, could Ulysses with an excellent wife waste time with Circe and Calypso? Was it quite nice of Priam to wish his children dead provided Hector lived? Or again, how undignified of Mercury to act as Priam's coachman, and of Nausicaa to be gracious to men in Ulysses's condition. Of like nature were the crude impertinences of Perrault and Fontenelle; and the learned Rymer's contribution is the English counterpart of this contemporary tendency. It was the result, in short, of no personal and eccentric perversion, but of a long tradition revived by Scaliger and uncritically adopted at this date. Then, too, apart from reflecting what men were thinking about literature in his day, Rymer's work has also the negative interest of revealing once for all what aesthetic criticism is not, and that an unimaginative common sense is not the key to sound literary appreciation. With his contemporaries, it is true, he carried weight; but the reaction was not long delayed and was seen in the censures that came from Dryden, Butler, Dennis and others. A positive result of his tirades was the increased and more enlightened study of Shakespeare's works in the days that followed. For the rest, his critical work is little more than the result of knowledge ill-housed, the reaction of a pedantic mentality and a coarse-grained personality that found delight in vulgar and insolent abuse.

Meanwhile, if Rymer's introduction to French neo-classical theory was overshadowed by his astounding judgments, a more effective exposition of that theory came from the influence of Boileau's *Art Poétique*, which inspired forthwith an output of

---

[1] See Atkins, *Lit. Crit. in Antiquity*, i. 190.
[2] *Poetice*, v. ch. 2.
[3] cf. his *Comparaison d'Homere et de Virgile, passim*.

translations and adaptations of that work, as well as of Horace's
works, thus giving rise to a new form of critical treatise in verse,
dealing with general principles and with English analogues for
French and Roman poets. Already before 1680 there had come
from one admirer of Boileau, the dissolute but brilliant Earl of
Rochester (1647-80), *An Allusion to Horace*, the earliest example
in English of those Imitations that translated Roman into modern instances; and this was followed by Roscommon's translation of Horace's *Ars Poetica* (1680) and Oldham's version of the
same work (1681). To Rochester, it might be noted, is ascribed
A Trial of Poets for the Bays, an adaptation of Suckling's *Session
of the Poets* (1637);[1] and now he gives an English colouring to
one of Horace's *Satires*,[2] in which that poet had defended his
earlier strictures on Lucilius's verse. In similar fashion Rochester repeats his earlier censure of Dryden's rhyming verse,
though he concedes that otherwise with him 'excellencies more
than faults abound'. Dryden's verse, however, he maintains,
was not so very different from that of tedious Crowne, blunder-
ing Settle, hasty Shadwell and the laboured Wycherley, Waller
alone being the accepted model. At the same time he has some
characteristic precepts to give. He urges, for instance, the use of
the file, that poets should write 'to please the few who know',
that epithets should not be overdone, and with reference to
current satires and lampoons he shrewdly notes (here following
Horace[3]) that

> A jest in scorn points out and hits the thing
> More home than the morosest satires sting.

—a hint which Dryden illustrates in his *Absalom and Achitophel*.
   The influence of Boileau, however, was more directly revealed
in Sir William Soames's *Art of Poetry* (1680), which represented a
translation of the *Art Poétique*, revised and adapted by Dryden.
Its main interest lies in the references to English poetry made by
Dryden in adapting Boileau's sketch, in the course of which
English parallels to French poets were sought and judicial
estimates suggested. Thus Spenser (like Marot) is credited with
'a richer vein of poetry'; while with Davenant (as with Ronsard)
is associated 'a new-found art, which changed all, spoilt all'. In
the reaction that followed, English poets are said to have taken

---

[1] For the influence of Boccalini in these works, see Atkins, *Eng. Lit.
Crit.: the Renascence*, p. 301. f.n.
[2] I. x.   [3] *Sat.* I. x. 14–15.

fewer liberties, until 'at last came Waller',[1] who (like Malherbe) was

> the first whose art
> Just weight and measure did to verse impart.

It was an artificial and inadequate attempt at tracing literary development; but, together with other pronouncements of Dryden, it helped to establish Waller's reputation for later writers.

Of yet greater interest was the attempt made by the Earl of Mulgrave (1648-1721) in his *Essay upon Poetry* (1682) to commend Boileau's neo-classical doctrine to English readers; and his poem, closely modelled on that of Boileau, treats of the subject with special reference to English conditions and needs. The parts played by genius and art, and the value of judgment, without which 'fancy is but mad', are his first and governing principles; after which he treats first of the minor 'kinds' and then of the drama and epic. For songs, to begin with, he demands a natural and unaffected utterance, as well as a freedom from bawdry, that 'poor pretence to wit'; and his incidental reference here to 'such nauseous songs as the late convert (i.e. Rochester) made' involved him later in a clash with Wolseley.[2] For the elegy, however, devoted to eulogies and love-complaints, he requires coherent thought and no undue use of epigrams; for the higher flights of the ode an exercise of that judgment which Cowley is said to have lacked; while satire, he insists, despite an earlier tradition, called for no rugged treatment, since 'a satire's smile is sharper than its frown'[3]—a truth, he asserts, that had recently been illustrated in Dryden's *MacFlecknoe*.

Turning then to the drama he avoids the more technical remarks of Boileau, his aim being merely to deal with defects of the English stage. In tragedy, for instance, he decries the use of long and dull soliloquies, also of figures of speech, 'art's needless varnish', except in descriptive and emotional passages; while skill in dialogue, he complains, apart from Shakespeare and Fletcher, had been entirely lost, his own age being cloyed with 'sheer wit', when 'wit so overflowed as to be none at all'. As for the tragic plot, that, he demanded, should be coherently developed, with no 'faultless monsters', but with characters whose faults led to disaster, thus calling for pity. Moreover, all speeches should be in character; there should be no irrelevant

---

[1] cf. Boileau's *enfin Malherbe vint* (i. 131).
[2] Spingarn, *op. cit.* ii. 288.   [3] *ibid.* ii. 290.

'beauties', no extraneous wit. And in comedy, more especially, general, not individual, eccentricities should be derided, the aim being 'to spread folly broad'; and in this respect, he adds, 'Falstaff seems unimitable yet'.[1] Finally, regarding the epic he has little to say. For guidance he refers his readers, not to Le Bossu, but to Homer and Virgil; to Homer, who had shown 'where all the mighty magic lies', to Virgil, who had never said 'too little or too much'. And not without its significance is the fact that in the second edition of the poem (1691) Mulgrave places Milton at the head of epic poets, above even Tasso and Spenser.

Yet another of these treatises in verse, dealing however not with neo-classical doctrine but with the much-vexed doctrine of translation, came from the Earl of Roscommon (1633-85), and in his *Essay on Translated Verse* (1684) French influence once again may be detected. In England previously the method of free translation had for the most part been instinctively followed in practice; and Chapman (1616) had discussed briefly the merits of that method. Jonson, on the other hand, has sometimes been described as 'the recognized exponent of the literal theory'. But for this there seems but little justification, apart, that is, from his translation of Horace's *Ars Poetica*; whereas his treatment of Latin passages in his *Discoveries* is far from being literal. Meanwhile in France the question had been vigorously debated; and Perrot d'Ablancourt became the leading advocate of a free translation (1649), which, concentrating on the sense rather than the words of an original, won general approval by the grace and charm of his translations of Tacitus and others, his *belles infidèles* as they were called. Already in 1647 Sir John Denham was apparently affected by the movement, when he commended Sir William Fanshawe for his version of *Pastor Fido*, praising the translator for abandoning 'the servile path' of a literal rendering. 'Transplanted wit', so Denham explains,[2] 'all the defects of air and soil doth share'; but

> A new and nobler way thou dost pursue,
> . . . .
> They but preserve the ashes, thou the flame.

And his theory was more fully developed in a well-known passage of the Preface to his *Destruction of Troy* (1656).

It is a vulgar error in translating Poets [he writes] to affect being *Fidus Interpres*, . . . for it is not his business alone to translate

---

[1] Spingarn, *op. cit.* ii. 293.
[2] Verses prefixed to Fanshawe's version of *Pastor Fido*.

Language into Language, but Poesie into Poesie; and Poesie is of so subtile a spirit, that in pouring out of one Language into another, it will all evaporate; and if a new spirit be not added in the trans-fusion, there will remain nothing but a *Caput mortuum*.

In the same year, moreover, Cowley made use of the method in his *Pindarique Odes*; and in 1680 Dryden discussed the whole question in his *Preface to the Translation of Ovid's Epistles*.

Of interest, however, is Roscommon's contribution to the dis-cussion in his *Essay on Translated Verse* (1684), in which he calls attention to what he regards as some of the finer points in this business of free translation. Claiming, to begin with, that in translating ancient verse Englishmen had been more successful than the French owing to the genius of the language, he sug-gests that, in translating generally, judgment was more essential than 'invention' (i.e. originality), and then insists that pedantry should be avoided, that 'good breeding' was necessary, that all 'pompous nonsense' was out of place, and that immodest words were unpardonable, since 'want of decency is want of sense'.[1] He further recommends that a congenial author should be chosen, so that the translator might identify himself with the poet and become 'no longer his interpreter but he'; that, more-over, no effort should be spared to arrive at the meaning of the original; and here, it is worth noting, he reminds his readers, as Aristarchus long ago had done, that a poet was best interpreted by himself.[2] At the same time, the meaning, when arrived at, should be clearly expressed since

> He only proves he understands a text
> Whose exposition leaves it unperplexed.

And, in general, the translator, he maintains, should 'write with fury but correct with phlegm'.

Then with a reminder that 'the sound is still a comment of the sense',[3] he utters certain caveats: that words admired in ancient Rome 'may neither suit our genius nor our clime'; that in view of the liberties taken by way of digression, it was 'safer to leave out than to add'; and in one place he warns his readers against what he regarded as Homer's use of false *decorum*. Finally noting that the exigencies of rhyme had hitherto tended to cramp the style of translators, he boldly suggests that the 'numerous prose', the blank verse, of Milton might

---

[1] Spingarn, *op. cit.* ii. 300.
[2] *ibid.* ii. 302: see Atkins, *Lit. Crit. in Antiquity*, i. 188.
[3] Spingarn, *op. cit.* ii. 307 ff.

with advantage be adopted, and submits in support a specimen
of such verse, recalling both in matter and manner *Paradise
Lost* (Bk. VI). He asserts that rhyme, of which antiquity had
been ignorant, had been cultivated by Old Norse bards and
unlearned monks in former ages; but what he now advocated
was the employment of unrhymed verse in the work of translation. Rymer in 1678 had proposed to defend rhyme against
Milton's theory and practice in *Paradise Lost*, which 'some',
he characteristically added,[1] 'are pleased to call a poem'. From
Roscommon, however, came now a striking appreciation of
Miltonic blank verse, in which, he held, something of the old
'Roman majesty' once more appeared; and his remarks are
among the earliest tributes to Milton's fame.

Apart from these signs, revealed mainly by Court poets, that
the influences of Boileau and Rapin were beginning to be felt
in England, yet another aspect of contemporary French thought
—the Quarrel between the Ancients and the Moderns—gave
rise at this time to further critical activities, which, while they
throw but little light on the question at issue, are nevertheless
of interest in the critical development. The quarrel, as is well-
known, was no new thing. Questionings by Cinthio, Castelvetro
and others had been heard in 16th-Century Italy: the problem
had been casually raised in England by Bacon and Hakewill;[2]
and towards the end of the 17th Century in France the debate
became still more heated, being fanned into flame by the
provocative methods of Perrault and Fontenelle. The question
thus raised was in reality of a fundamental character. It was a
direct and disturbing challenge to the neo-classical theory then
forming, based as that theory was on an unquestioning reverence for the ancient classics. In France, however, the whole
business was badly handled, with ignorance on the one side
and pedantry on the other; while all disputants alike indulged
in personal polemics and in the crude controversial methods of
Rymer. Nevertheless it became the occasion which gave rise to
certain critical works by English writers; to Temple's *Essay
upon Ancient and Modern Learning* (1690) and his essay *On
Poetry* (1690), as well as to Wotton's *Reflections upon Ancient
and Modern Learning* (1694), which represent the English
contribution to the current controversy.

To that controversy the attention of the eminent but cautious
statesman Sir William Temple (1628–99) had been drawn by

---

[1] Spingarn, *op. cit.* ii. 208.
[2] See Atkins, *Eng. Lit. Crit.: the Renascence*, p. 316.

his reading of Fontenelle's *Digression sur les Anciens et les Modernes* (1688); and, as the title of his work suggests, it proposed to deal, not with literary values, but with the abstract problem of the relationship between ancient and modern learning. It was in fact a laudable attempt to raise the debate to a higher plane by considering the intellectual progress made in those respective ages; and his verdict is definitely given in favour of the ancients. In one place, it is worth recalling, he discriminates between learning and knowledge. Learning he defines as an acquaintance with 'the different and contested opinions of men in former ages, about which they have perhaps never agreed',[1] knowledge as consisting 'of things that are generally agreed to be true'; and this accounts, he shrewdly adds, for 'so much of the one and so little of the other in the world'. After which he proceeds, in the light of much uncritical learning, but with the help of reason and experience, to examine the question anew, reserving poetry for further consideration, which he supplies in his essay *On Poetry* of the same year.

The first claim made by the moderns, he notes, was based on the old argument of Bernard of Chartres,[2] handed down by Vives and recalled by Hakewill,[3] to the effect that the moderns were as dwarfs standing on the shoulders of giants and thus capable of seeing farther than the giants themselves. The second claim, likewise made by Vives and cited by Jonson,[4] was that Nature being ever the same, the moderns were therefore not intellectually inferior to the ancients. To these claims Temple replies by suggesting, in the first place, that valuable as was the learning enshrined in the comparatively few Greek volumes that had come down, yet more substantial was the Egyptian and Chaldean lore that in times still more remote had furnished guidance to the early Greeks, to Thales, Pythagoras and others. Apart from this, the ancient Greeks, as compared with the moderns, were rightly regarded as 'the first mighty conquerors of ignorance'; whereas modern knowledge was mainly of a derivative kind, and knowledge thus acquired tended to cripple initiative. 'Strength of mind,' added Temple,[5] 'as well as of body, grows more from the warmth of exercise than of clothes'; so that 'if we are dwarfs we are still so, though we stand upon a giant's shoulders.'

---

[1] Spingarn, *op. cit.* iii. 36.
[2] *ibid.* iii. 33: see Atkins, *Eng. Lit. Crit.: Medieval*, p. 70.
[3] See Atkins, *Eng. Lit. Crit.: the Renascence*, pp. 45, 316.
[4] *ibid.* p. 315.   [5] Spingarn, *op. cit.* iii. 48.

At the same time he is aware of the argument that conditions varied, and that modern conditions might be specially conducive to development in the intellectual sphere. That an advance had been made since the Dark Ages he is ready to concede; yet it did not follow that modern learning had outgrown that of the ancients. No advance in his opinion was visible in philosophy, architecture or science, while poetry had palpably suffered through the 'ignorance of the friars and the barbarousness of the Goths'. The truth was, he asserted, that it was modern self-complacency that had lauded modern achievement, a self-complacency that was without justification in view of actual results; and this was plainly seen when French philosophers were compared with Plato and Aristotle, Boileau with Virgil, or Harvey with Hippocrates.[1] But apart from this there was the language disability; for if the mental powers of the moderns were even greater than those of the ancients, yet their languages were unstable, changing every hundred years, whereas Latin had been framed by 'the thoughts of . . . the noblest nation . . . enriched by the spoils of Greece'.

Moreover there were other hindrances to the advancement of modern learning;[2] religious and political quarrels, for instance, the loss of patronage, or again, the scorn of serious learning revealed in the modern craze for ridicule and burlesque. From this last charge, added Temple, even the 'inimitable wit and humour' of *Don Quixote* was not exempt, since that work had turned 'romantic honour and love into ridicule'[3]—a comment repeated during the following century and echoed by Byron in his well-known judgment that 'Cervantes had smiled Spain's chivalry away'.[4] Temple's position in the quarrel is therefore clear; he is for the ancients. 'Whoever converses much among the old books', he writes,[5] 'will be something hard to please among the new'; and he ventures to describe one of these ancient works, the *Letters of Phalaris*, as the greatest of the epistolary kind[6]—an unlucky judgment that was shattered by Bentley's masterly *Dissertation* of 1692. It was a glaring instance of that unsifted learning characteristic of Temple's treatment: and it is evident that his attitude throughout is that of a gifted amateur whose views were dictated not by an informed and impartial judgment, but by an ardent sympathy with the past which found charming expression in his concluding statement that 'all the rest are baubles, besides old wood

---

[1] Spingarn, *op. cit.* iii. 63.   [2] *ibid.* iii. 66 ff.   [3] *ibid.* iii. 71.
[4] *Don Juan*, xiii. 11.   [5] Spingarn, *op. cit.* iii. 32.   [6] *ibid.* iii. 65.

to burn, old wine to drink, old friends to converse with and old books to read'.

Rather more substantial is his essay *Of Poetry* in which he submits his views not only on earlier Humanistic literary doctrine but also on French neo-classical theory, while he attempts in conclusion a survey of poetry down through the ages. First, with regard to earlier doctrine, he alludes briefly to the age-long question of the function of poetry, which, as he stated, had been much discussed but to little purpose, having become 'an exercise of wit rather than an inquiry after truth'. 'Few things however', he adds, 'will bear too much refining'; and a happy mixture of pleasure and profit was in his opinion the sensible solution. Then there was the matter of 'poetic inspiration', long associated with supernatural causes and effects, with the workings of divine emanations, celestial fire and the like. To this conception, however, he is unable to subscribe, regarding it as a delusion happily corrected by Meric Casaubon's *Treatise concerning Enthusiasm* (1655), in which the term had been defined as 'an effect of Nature, not of divine inspiration or diabolical possession'.[1] And this common-sense view is shared by Temple, with whom 'poetic inspiration' stood for no supernatural or mysterious influences, but was in fact none other than the workings of human genius, 'a natural process with natural effects'; or again, 'the free gift of heaven or Nature', conferring power to raise or modify the passions. In poetry, he significantly added, were united all the effects of eloquence, music and painting; and for its creation were required 'a great agitation of mind to invent, a great calm to judge and correct'[2] —an anticipation in some sense of Wordsworth's later account of its origin as 'emotion recollected in tranquillity'.[3] On the nature of poetry he has little more to say, though he explains that by poetry he meant, not Boileau's minor forms—the song, the elegy and the rest—but 'a just poem', that is, the epic, as illustrated in the incomparable works of Homer and Virgil.

It is in his comments on French neo-classical theory, however, that Temple reveals most clearly his insight and judgment. In spite of the lucid expositions of Boileau, Rapin and Le Bossu, backed as they were with all the weight of authority, he refuses to accept the rules bound up with their system; and further complains that 'so much paper had been blotted' in commending their theories that their teaching had grown

---

[1] Spingarn, *op. cit.* iii. 76.   [2] *ibid.* iii. 81.
[3] *Preface to Lyrical Ballads* (1800): cf. Dennis, p. 152 *infra*.

tedious by mere repetition. French wits, he remarked, not content with Aristotle and Horace, had been 'exact in their rules but to little purpose', for poetry was 'too libertine to be confined to so many rules', and such constraint involved the loss of both spirit and grace.

'Tis as if [he adds][1] to make excellent honey, you should cut off the wings of your bees, confine them to their hive, . . . and lay flowers before them such as you think the sweetest and like to yield the finest extraction; you had as good pull out their stings and make arrant drones of them. They must range through fields as well as gardens, choose such flowers as they please, and by proprieties and scents they only know and distinguish. They must work up their cells with admirable art, extract their honey with infinite labour, and sever it from the wax with such distinction and choice as belongs to none but themselves to perform and judge.

With this illuminating conception of the poet in mind Temple courteously refrains from commenting on the poetic productions that had resulted from an observance of the much-advertised neo-classical rules. He merely remarks that no great poet had appeared in either Greece or Rome who had profited by the rules of Aristotle or Horace; and in his opinion, all that could be claimed for rules of any sort was the ability 'to hinder some men from being very ill poets, but not to make any man a very good one'. The real test of poetry, in short, lay in its spiritual power, its emotional effects, without which no man, however formally correct and pleasing, could be judged a poet; and here was a definite challenge to the restricting influence of the French neo-classical system.

Of less importance is his historical sketch of the development of poetry,[2] though in spite of much uncritical learning as before, it gives evidence of a growing sense of the value of an historical approach to the subject, and is not without its suggestive remarks in places. In treating of poetry as the first sort of writing among the Greeks and Hebrews he merely follows 'beaten paths', and travelling in them, as he puts it, 'only raises dust'. Nor is he more enlightening in tracing the change from poetry into prose, when he describes the romance as the last kind of poetry in prose, attributing its origin to the Gothic genius, and incidentally commending Sidney as the greatest of modern poets in virtue of his *Arcadia*. Next follows an account of the decline of poetry in the Dark Ages, ascribed again to the Goths and Vandals, whose runic measures are said to have led to the

---

[1] Spingarn, *op. cit.* iii. 84.   [2] *ibid.* iii. 85 ff.

adoption of rhyme and to have been the quarry from which
came 'the visionary tribe of fairies, elves and goblins',[1]—fanciful and misty information derived from the pioneer work of two
earlier Danish scholars.[2] The survey is then completed by the
story of the revival from Petrarch onwards, in which, Temple
now on safer ground is more judicial and suggestive. He notes
the attempts of Ariosto and Tasso to revive 'the just poem',
the ancient epic. But he comments as well on the general failure
to produce other than 'scraps' of poetry, i.e. songs and sonnets,
odes and elegies, satires and occasional verse; also on the efforts
made to commend such 'scraps or splinters' by an indiscriminate
infusion of epigrams and conceits; and, latterly, by the cultivation of a vein of ridicule and smoothness of verse and style.
Such ingredients, he added, were designed 'to give taste to
compositions which had little of themselves'. They were
specious and futile devices; for it was 'as if a building should
be nothing but ornament or clothes nothing but trimming'.

At the same time he holds that in one form of poetry, that is,
the dramatic, Englishmen had surpassed, not only the ancient,
but modern, dramatists as well.[3] And here he is possibly influenced by Saint-Evremond's generous tribute to English
comedy,[4] and by Rapin's judgment[5] that the English had a
greater genius for tragedy than other nations, as a result of
their hardy national spirit, and the character of their language
which was 'proper for great expressions'. Temple's claim, however, is that English dramatists had excelled above all in
'humour', that is, in the variety of uncommon but not unnatural characters. It was a feature, he stated, originated by
Shakespeare, in marked contrast to the limited and stock
characters of the ancient stage; and here it is plain that he is
making use of Jonsonian terminology, and that 'humour' as
yet had not acquired its later meaning of a special quality
of mind and art. Moreover, this rich variety of uncommon
dramatic characters he explains as arising out of the peculiar
conditions of English life, from the enjoyment of political
liberty, a marked freedom of speech, and even from the capricious climate, which had won for England the description of 'the

[1] Spingarn, *op. cit.* iii. 96.
[2] i.e. Olaus Wormius (*Literatura Runica,* 1636) and Thomas Bartholin
(*Antiquitates Danicae,* 1689), see Spingarn, *op. cit.* iii. 309.
[3] Spingarn, *op. cit.* iii. 103.
[4] cf. *de la Comédie angloise* (1677).
[5] cf. *Réflexions sur la Poétique,* ii. xxiii.

region of spleen'.[1] Such conditions, he maintained, were conducive to the cultivation of individuality, to the formation of an
infinite variety of 'originals', which were duly reflected in the
national literature. And here was indicated a widening critical
vision, a growing appreciation of the influence of contemporary
conditions on literary creation. It was a matter that had been
voiced in France by Saint-Evremond and others: and it militated
against the fixed standards prescribed by the neo-classical
school.

In Temple's contribution to literary criticism there is much
discursiveness, much dead wood gathered in the course of his
wide reading, but also not a few seminal ideas and much that
marks an advance in the critical development. Earlier theories
of poetry, for instance, as well as the new French system, he
discusses in an independent spirit and with shrewd common
sense; while he also insists on the free activity necessary for the
poet, the relative standards imposed by varying social conditions, and, in addition, he calls attention to early forms of
poetry apart from those of the Graeco-Roman tradition, and
to the relations existing between poetry, music and painting.
Such testimony was of significance at this date; yet of more
enduring value is the spirit that animates his work. In concluding his essay *On Poetry* he returns once again to the Ancient
and Modern controversy, and holds that whereas modern
achievements in both poetry and music had fallen short of those
of the ancients, yet they were by no means without their merit.
Both, he maintained, gave lasting and innocent pleasure to
quiet minds, and

When all is done [he added] human life is, at the greatest and the
best, but like a froward child that must be played with and humoured
a little to keep it quiet till it falls asleep, and then the care is over.

This passage is one of the happy utterances, reminiscent of
Sidney, but his work throughout is characterized by a gracious
and picturesque style; and it is this fragrant quality that has
kept his work sweet and commended it to later ages.

Of the remaining contributions at this date to the current
controversy, the *Reflections* (1694) of William Wotton (1666–
1726) was the most notable, being a reasoned commentary on
Temple's superficial treatment, though lacking in the grace of
the earlier work. Wotton's attitude, in the first place, is of a
judicial kind. He is no blind advocate of the moderns: and in

---

[1] Spingarn, *op. cit.* iii. 105.

Perrault's attack on the ancients he finds much to deprecate and condemn. He rejects outright, for instance, Perrault's arguments that progress in poetry and oratory had been made inevitable by the mere passing of time;[1] that new rules had been discovered, old rules more carefully scanned, and that Cicero had necessarily surpassed Demosthenes, and French orators, Cicero. All this, Wotton held, was not easy to prove; nor could he allow Perrault's claim that the modern mind had acquired an inexhaustible fund of new thoughts and that later ages had become more polished. What Perrault called 'politeness', he maintained, was none other than French gallantry, an artificial 'straining of Nature'; whereas the artistic simplicity of the ancients had lacked appreciation, though 'nearer to Nature'. Moreover, Perrault's judgments on the ancients, he pointed out, had been based solely on translations which failed to reproduce the quality of the original works, for, as Denham[2] had stated, 'in pouring the spirit of ancient poetry from one bottle into another the most volatile parts had been lost'. 'Sense', added Wotton,[3] 'is sense in every tongue, yet all languages have a peculiar way of expressing the same things, which is lost in translation.' And he cannot accept even the much-admired free translations of d'Ablancourt, who, in his opinion, had failed in trying to do two different things at once, namely, to translate the ancients and to produce works in elegant French.

But while Wotton cannot approve of Perrault's handling of the problem, he is likewise dissatisfied with Temple's line of argument; and this he attempts to modify in certain particulars. He concedes, to begin with, that a profound respect for the works of the ancients was only to be expected, since, remote in time, they excited no envy, and, besides, men from childhood's days were wont to hear them spoken of with the utmost reverence. Nor could this reverence be dismissed as mere prejudice; for those works had supplied a very real pleasure and were the accredited guides in literary matters. Yet, added Wotton, some amount of blind admiration was still present, superstition which could only be dispelled by a reasoned explanation of their greatness; and this he endeavours to supply by recalling the conditions under which they appeared.

In the first place, much, he held, was due to the great artistic merits of the Greek and Latin languages, Greek unrivalled in beauty and musical effects, Latin grave and majestic; and in

[1] Spingarn, *op. cit.* iii. 217 ff. [2] See p. 81 *supra*.
[3] Spingarn, *op. cit.* iii. 222.

all these qualities modern languages were said to be comparatively deficient. Nor could it be said that the ancient effects
might be recaptured by later imitators, as Buchanan had
clearly shown; for, as Wotton explained, 'copying nauseates
more in poetry than anything',[1] and the future lay with writers
in the vernacular. Then, in the second place, not a little was due
(especially in oratory) to the political liberties enjoyed by those
ancient commonwealths; for, stated Wotton (here echoing Tacitus in his *Dialogus*), 'it is liberty alone which inspires men with
lofty thoughts and elevates their souls to a higher pitch than
the rules of art can direct'.[2] These, then, according to Wotton,
were the conditions which had rendered possible the literary
achievements of the ancients; and he therefore agrees with
Temple, though for different reasons, in assigning superiority
to the ancients. At the same time he maintains that modern
writers under similar conditions might attain equal success,
and this, he states, 'for anything hitherto said to the contrary,
seems to be very probable'. His position is therefore not unreasonable; and his treatment illustrates the growing concern
with the effects of prevailing conditions on the work of creation.

Such then were the main channels along which French influences affected critical discussion at this date; and in general
a growing acquaintance with French doctrine and with the
theories of Boileau and Rapin in particular becomes perceptible, thereby extending the range of critical activities.
As yet, however, despite the efforts of Rymer, Mulgrave and
others, French theories were only partially and tentatively
accepted, while definite objections to their adoption were being
raised by Dryden and Temple. And this attitude was further
represented by Samuel Butler (1612–80), who, in his essay
Upon Critics (*c.* 1678), with Rymer's outrageous *Tragedies of
the Last Age* primarily in mind, fiercely derided those who
judged modern plays by neo-classical standards.[3] He denounces, for instance, all attempts to reduce 'tragedy by rules
of art back to its antique theatre', and the demands made for
a strict observance of Aristotle's laws; for 'an English poet',
he held, 'should be tried by his peers', and not by pedants and
philosophers. Moreover, Aristotle's rules, he pointed out, had
been modified by Italian and French commentators; and yet
these were the rules employed by 'our English plagiaries' for
inveighing against the poetry and wit of Beaumont and
Fletcher, whose 'worst miscarriages' were said to give greater

[1] Spingarn, *op. cit.* iii. 206.   [2] *ibid.* iii. 211.   [3] *ibid.* ii. 278 ff.

delight than all that pedants ever wrote. The essay is more
remarkable for its crude strength than for accurate learning,
and is couched in language that Rymer would understand.
But it gave expression to what was undoubtedly a wide-spread
feeling at the time; and not without their interest are Butler's
further comments on contemporary literary failings in his
Characters, and notably in his pungent descriptions of 'a small
poet', a critic, an imitator, a plagiary and the rest.

In the meantime, during this last quarter of the 17th Century,
apart from attempts to expound neo-classical principles, apart
also from the discussion evoked by the Quarrel in France,
there were other critical activities concerned, not so much with
general principles, as with problems of the native literature,
thereby revealing a consciousness of certain defects in contemporary prose style, an awakening of interest in earlier
literary developments, and an uneasiness concerning that most
striking of contemporary achievements, the Restoration drama.
Least productive, in contrast with the critical activities of
earlier generations, was the attention now given to matters of
prose style; though Glanvill's *Essay concerning Preaching* (1678)
is of interest as representing a contemporary movement of
some importance. On the other hand the renewed interest in
the past is evidenced by more than one work; and the *Theatrum
Poetarum* (1675) of Edward Phillips, which was followed by
Gerard Langbaine's *Account of the English Dramatic Poets*
(1691), prepared the way for a better understanding of the
native literature. Meanwhile the licentiousness which characterized much of the current literature was arousing fierce
protest; and while Robert Wolseley, it is true, in his *Preface to
Valentinian* (1685) defended Rochester against the charge of
immorality, the full force of the storm directed against the
Restoration drama was felt in Jeremy Collier's *Short View of
the Immorality and Profaneness of the English Stage* (1698),
though his general position had previously been maintained by
Blackmore in his *Preface to King Arthur* (1695). As with the
attempt at recalling literary history, this plea for morality was
not without its sequel in the years that followed, even if its
immediate effect, owing to its very violence, was apparently
slight.

With regard to the efforts now made, in the first place, to
improve prose style, the chief feature was the renewed attention
given to pulpit oratory. Protests had previously been raised
against the pedantry, the conceits, the elaborate metaphors and

illustrations that had disfigured earlier preaching; but the most effective demand for a more simple and natural form of utterance had come from Sprat, though it had applied merely to secular writings. With the later Caroline divines, however, less florid methods of pulpit oratory, different from those of Donne and Jeremy Taylor, were being cultivated; and these changes had been accompanied by remarks from Wilkins, Eachard and others. At the same time attacks were being launched in France against 'metaphysical' preaching. Rapin, for one, in his *Réflexions sur l'Usage de l'Eloquence de ce Temps*[1] (1672) had discussed pulpit oratory at some length, and had held that 'sacred eloquence ought to support itself by simplicity and good sense, without too much studied artifice'.[2] His influence, as has been shown, was considerable at this date; and he may well have given fresh impetus to what was otherwise a national movement, which led at this stage to a special consideration of pulpit oratory.

Of this movement Joseph Glanvill (1636–86) was the chief exponent; and in his *Essay concerning Preaching* his prescription is 'the close, naked, natural way of speaking' recommended by Sprat, with however some differences. Thus clearness throughout is the one indispensable quality demanded.[3] And this is said to require, first, an avoidance of all hard and obscure words. Not that he would condemn outright all borrowings from classical or foreign sources, seeing that English was a mixed language and had been enriched in the past with many borrowed terms. Indeed, a meticulous avoidance of all Latinisms he regarded as sheer vanity and affectation; as when attempts were made to substitute for 'eternity' so grotesque a form as 'all-timeness', or 'all-placeness' for 'immensity'. What, however, he did condemn was the use of unfamiliar foreign expressions, for which there already existed in English adequate equivalents. Moreover he would not banish all words and ideas unfamiliar to the unlettered; for many of such terms, he recognized, were essential to any treatment of divinity. But they were at all times to be sparingly used and used with discretion. Equally important was the avoidance of that 'bastard rhetoric' which had crept into the pulpit, and which consisted of 'affectations of wit and finery, flourishes, metaphors and cadencies', calculated merely to tickle the fancy. Such false eloquence, he maintained, with its 'starchedness of affected speaking' was

---

[1] English translation (1672).   [2] ch. xxxii.
[3] Spingarn, *op. cit.* ii. 273 ff.

ineffective and scorned by the judicious; and 'plainness', he reiterates, 'is ever the best eloquence and 'tis the most forcible'. Yet another common practice condemned was the use by 'popular' preachers of modish, familiar and colloquial phrasing, intended to appeal to the plain man. Such expression was sometimes advocated as being 'savoury and precious'; whereas in reality, he held, it was vulgar, degrading and even blasphemous. And Glanvill ends as he had begun, with his demand for 'plainness', incidentally bearing witness to the changing standards of prose that were preparing the way for Addison and Swift.

More considerable were the attempts to attain in literary matters 'a firmer perspective of the past'; and of these, the *Theatrum Poetarum* (1675) of Edward Phillips (1630–96), nephew of Milton, calls for notice in the first place. The work itself, it is true, is nothing more than a rather formidable collection of biographical notes relating to earlier poets, curiously arranged; but its Preface is of critical interest, as throwing light on the beginnings of the historical movement, the aim being, as Phillips states, to call to memory poets who 'slept inglorious in the crowd of forgotten vulgar, . . . scarce known to the learned themselves'. Of English literature prior to 1630, he rightly complains, little was known except the works of a few dramatists; and what was known was dismissed as antiquated, compared with the smooth, refined style affected in his day. That earlier writings should appear strange and even uncouth to the fastidious he is prepared to admit; but if read with understanding, he maintained, they would be found to possess excellences of their own. Chaucer, he reminds his readers, had still his admirers, on account of his 'facetious' way and his quaint old English. But among those who followed him, the Elizabethans in particular, there was, he held, no lack of literary quality; and he further points out that if the passing taste of the day was to be the criterion of literary value, then the time would come when to a later age the admired productions of contemporaries would appear out of date and would be discarded as obsolete. He does not presume to question contemporary standards of taste; at the same time he asserts that 'what was *verum et bonum* once continues to be so always'. It was a hint that reigning fashions were not the final tests in literary matters;[1] and it constituted a plea for the historical approach in forming literary judgments.

[1] Spingarn, *op. cit.* ii. 263 f.

Less significant, though still of interest, are his remarks on
poetry generally, wherein he submits his views on current
questions. What he has to say, for instance, on metrical affairs
is both suggestive and timely. Conscious of a reaction against
certain earlier verse-forms, namely, the Spenserian stanza and
the sonnet, he found no valid reason for discarding them. They
had been derived, he points out, from the Italian, since classical
measures were found unsuitable for English verse; and in view
of their effective use by the Elizabethans he now strongly
advocates their revival. Thus Spenser's stanza, he suggests, an
improvement on Tasso's *ottava rima*, was better suited for epic
purposes than either the heroic couplet or Davenant's four-
line stanza with alternate rhymes;[1] and again, there was more to
be said for the sonnet than for Cowley's innovations in his so-
called Pindaric odes. On that particular verse-form, moreover,
he has a further comment to make; and he is the first to point
out that in structure it had little in common with the odes of
Pindar.[2] Wanting the strophe, antistrophe and epode which
gave form to the ancient Greek verse, Cowley's Pindarics, he
justly states, had a nearer affinity with that free kind of verse
called monostrophic or apolelymenon, employed by Aeschylus
in his Choruses and referred to by Milton in his Preface to
Samson Agonistes. And equally noteworthy is his final judgment on the verse best fitted for epic purposes, when he declares
that 'measure alone, without any rhyme at all, would give far
more ample scope and liberty both to style and fancy than can
possibly be observed in rhyme'.[3] It was a declaration in favour
of blank verse, that verse-form which was so slowly and reluc-
tantly being appreciated; and his judgment he supports by a
reference to *Paradise Lost*, which, as he states, 'had come forth
not many years ago'.

Rather more conventional are his remaining remarks on the
various 'kinds' of poetry which he duly recalls, noting that
they were fixed and final, since no new form could possibly be
devised. His main attention is given to epic poetry and tragedy;
and he expounds roughly the accepted doctrine of the time.
Thus the epic, he states,[4] should treat of remote history, embodying at the same time probable episodes and an allegory.

---

[1] Spingarn, *op. cit.* ii. 265 ff.

[2] Johnson's claim that Congreve 'first taught English writers that
Pindar's odes were regular' (*Lives*, ii. 234) was unfounded, since his
Discourse on the Pindaric Ode appears only in 1705.

[3] Spingarn, *op. cit.* ii. 266.   [4] *ibid.* ii. 267.

In it there should be no far-fetched or 'romantic' incidents, no assigning of modern manners to old-world characters, but the main effort should be devoted to the noble expression of noble thoughts. Tragedy, he continued,[1] should treat of the falls of illustrious persons, and that in a style 'not ramping but . . . sedate and moving'. He is doubtful about the use of the chorus and the observance of the Unity of time; but condemns outright the 'linsey-woolsey mixture' of comic and tragic elements, while he also finds irksome 'the continued rhapsody of rhyming couplets'. At the same time, he observes, your perfect poem was not achieved by the mere observance of laws. For this, poetic 'energy' or genius was required in order to make the work live. And this, he states, had been shown by Spenser, in spite of his obsolete diction, or again, by Shakespeare, for all his 'unfiled expressions, his rambling and indigested fancies', which had made him 'the laughter of the critical'. Such then is Phillips's contribution to the critical development; and while for him no great claim as a critic can be made, yet his Preface, though written in a laboured style, gives evidence at least of some independent thinking.

Illustrative also of the reviving interest in the past betrayed at this date was *An Account of English Dramatic Poets* (1691) by Gerard Langbaine (1656–92), son of Gerard Langbaine the elder, Provost of Queen's College, Oxford, and editor of 'Longinus' (1636). The work is primarily a contribution to literary history and biography, compiled by one possessed of a wide acquaintance with English and continental literature. But it has also a certain critical interest, inasmuch as its author, posing as a 'champion in the dead poets' cause', attacks Dryden for his earlier censures of Shakespeare, Fletcher and Jonson, and more particularly for his references to their various borrowings, which Langbaine interprets as charges of plagiarism.[2] His reply is that Dryden himself had been yet more guilty of the same charge, and that he, 'more than all men living, had no reason to throw the first stone'. And this Langbaine proceeds to demonstrate by a detailed *examen* of that dramatist's plays, in the course of which, giving chapter and verse in meticulous fashion, he points out what he calls Dryden's 'petty larcenies', his unacknowledged plunderings of Italian, Spanish and French sources. He is aware that Virgil, Terence and others had likewise been great borrowers, and that the great Scaliger had approved of such procedure. But whereas the ancients, he noted, had

---

[1] Spingarn, *op. cit.* ii. 269.　　　　[2] *ibid.* iii. 110 ff.

justified themselves by their treatment of the borrowed material, he refuses to justify Dryden on the same grounds. That claim of Dryden, indeed, he dismisses as merely 'a sophisticated truth with an alloy of lie in it'.

As a literary judgment this pronouncement of Langbaine is of no account; for nowadays it is clear that Dryden's use of plots and suggestions culled from various sources implied no real diminution of his worth, since he too gave new life to what he had appropriated. Moreover, the judgment is obviously the result of fierce animus and prejudice, and is coloured throughout by an arrogance, a disorderliness and a display of pedantry all alike suggestive of Rymer's influence and methods. What, however, is of critical interest is the fact that in making for the first time a serious study of the sources of literary works Langbaine was unconsciously inaugurating an extension of critical activities which was to prove of value in later times. As yet, and for some time to come, such investigations were made in the spirit of literary sleuths avidly unmasking the pilferings and deceits of authors. A later generation was to realize that all borrowings were not necessarily plagiarisms, that they were often none other than the raw material on which the poet worked, and that a clear estimate of their nature would enable the poet's artistic achievement to be more justly appreciated. And Langbaine's detailed inquiry into Dryden's sources was the first step toward the development of this useful critical process.

It was not only in contemporary prose and the earlier native literature, however, that critical interest was now being shown. Contemporary poetry and drama also gave rise to some amount of discussion in which more than one matter of significance was raised; though of the exposition of dramatic theory there was less than might have been expected, especially in view of the vital changes seen in the development of Restoration comedy, from the earlier fashion of Jonsonian 'humours' to the daring pictures of the roystering life of the time depicted by Etherege, Wycherley, and Congreve. From William Congreve (1670–1729), however, came certain hints regarding his practice, and they are worth recalling. Thus in one place he states (in line with epic theorists) that he designed his moral first and then invented the plot;[1] that he observed the Unities to avoid confusion; and elsewhere he defends his use of soliloquy, explaining that 'a man in a soliloquy is only thinking aloud',[2] and that it was a means of communicating necessary information.

[1] Ded. to *Double Dealer*.   [2] Maskwell in *Double Dealer*.

Apart from this he explains that in his latest artificial comedy he had renounced the old satirical, didactic function of comedy for that of mere pleasure.

> Satire, he thinks, you ought not to expect,
> For so reformed a town who dare correct?
> To please, this time, has been his sole pretence,
> He'll not instruct lest it should give offence.[1]

At the same time he claims to have achieved a new turn of style, the wit and sparkle of which he ascribes to his contact with 'the quality';[2] though elsewhere he is conscious that an artistic selection of their conversation was necessary, since the mere reproduction of 'the extempore discourse of the two wittiest men on earth' would of itself prove ineffective.[3] Moreover, his characters, he states, were designed 'to appear ridiculous, not so much through a natural folly (which is incorrigible and therefore not proper for the stage) as through an affected wit, a wit, which at the same time that it is affected, is also false'.

These, however, are but stray remarks let fall for the most part by the dramatist at work, and when Congreve gives more formal consideration to matters of theory it is by way of reply to an earlier request of Dennis that he writes his letter *Concerning Humour in Comedy* (1695). Here, however, he is content to refine on the Jonsonian term, though in practice he had already abandoned the conventional formula for comedy. Thus 'humour', he explains,[4] is neither folly nor wit, nor personal defect, nor mere affectation, not even the grotesque manners of a class, but rather 'a singular manner of doing or saying any thing peculiar and natural to one man only'. In addition, he distinguishes between 'wit' and 'humour',[5] when he holds that although humorous characters need not be devoid of 'wit', yet such 'wit' should not be indiscriminate; and in order that characters might be consistently drawn he suggests that 'the manner of wit should be adapted to the humour'. Apart from this, 'humour', he maintains, is a phenomenon that is lacking in women, whether owing to an excess, or a deficiency, of passion; though, on the other hand, he would agree that there was more 'humour' in English comedy than in any other.[6] In fact he would describe it as 'almost of English growth'; and this he held was due to the

---

[1] Prol. to *The Way of the World*.   [2] Ded. to *The Way of the World*.
[3] Spingarn, *op. cit.* iii. 247.   [4] *ibid.* iii. 248.
[5] *ibid.* iii. 243–4.   [6] *ibid.* iii. 252.

greater freedom enjoyed by Englishmen, a truth amply illustrated, he adds, by the old saying that 'he that will have a
May-pole shall have a May-pole'. It thus becomes plain that
where 'humour' was concerned, Jonsonian terminology still
held the field; that as yet there was no definite approach to its
modern meaning; and that Congreve here does little more than
follow Temple's lead.

Meanwhile the shameless picture of the profligacy of the age,
reflected alike in the licentious Court poetry and in Restoration comedy, had been exciting comment; and before the close
of the century the intermittent remarks of Evelyn, Mulgrave,
Roscommon and others developed into a storm of protest
which culminated in the work of Collier. But matters had
already come to a head with the publication of the spirited
Preface to Valentinian (1685) of Robert Wolseley (1649–97),
the main substance of which was a defence of Rochester's
'nauseous songs', as described by Mulgrave; whereupon the
age-long question of art *versus* morality was broached once
again, and now in no uncertain fashion. The immediate
occasion of the *Preface* was a desire to explain the imperfections of Rochester's revision of Fletcher's tragedy, *Valentinian*, from which, Wolseley held, certain defects had been
removed, while an air of good breeding had also been infused.
This task completed, a glowing eulogy of Rochester followed.
His wit, his magnanimity and his personal charm are all recalled; 'never', stated Wolseley, 'did men stay in his company
unentertained or leave it uninstructed'. As for his poetry, it had
the stamp of originality and an unaccountable charm, with
lapses perhaps, though the extremes of a 'slovenly looseness'
and a 'too nice correctness' were alike avoided; and after all,
as Wolseley reminded his readers, 'the loosest negligence of a
great genius is infinitely preferable to that *obscura diligentia* of
which Terence speaks'.[1] Moreover, his wit was used 'to nip in
the very bud the growing fopperies of the time'; and, it was
added, 'there never was any time or country that wanted satire
so much, that could bear it so little as ours'.

With this estimate of Rochester as a man and a poet in mind,
Wolseley makes a frontal attack on Mulgrave as one who 'with
scraps of Bossu, Rapin, Boileau and Dryden' had compiled an
Art of poetry and had ventured to censure Rochester after his
death. In scathing terms he is denounced as one of the irrespon-
sible detractors and 'bully-writers' so common at a time when

---

[1] Spingarn, *op. cit.* iii. 1: cf. Terence *Andria*, prol. 21.

'satire like a sword in the hands of a madman ran tilt at all manner of persons', and when 'none were so forward to teach others
as those who could not write themselves'. The attack, in short,
is conducted with violence, but not without a certain piquancy
and skill; and recalling Mulgrave's charge that 'bawdry cannot
be wit', Wolseley turns finally to deal with the general question.

Dismissing forthwith the conventional claims of morality in
poetry, he states categorically that a poet's excellence was to
be measured, not by the worth of his subject, but by his treatment of that subject;[1] and on this doctrine he founds his whole
argument. Some of Virgil's best strokes, for instance, he points
out, are his descriptions of bees, ants and snakes, things little
or unlovely in themselves, but rendered noble and beautiful by
his treatment. Horace, again, had exempted from artistic treatment nothing that was natural: while Dryden had declared that
there was 'as much art . . . in a lazar as in a Venus'.[2] And this
principle held good, continued Wolseley, not in poetry alone,
but in the sister arts of painting and sculpture as well, governed
as they were by the same rules as poetry. Thus many of the
greatest achievements of Pheidias, Titian and others had dealt
with subjects likely to offend your moral purists; and yet they
had been immortalized by great creative geniuses.

Were such triumphs, it was then asked, to be condemned on
account of their realistic treatment of the human form? And
what was to be said of the works of Martial, Catullus, Tibullus
and Ovid, with their elements of bawdry? All, he contended,
had the saving grace of 'wit', that term of 'doubtful and unsettled signification', which he now ventured to define as 'a true
and lively expression of Nature'. Besides, all had conformed
with the principles of Aristotle and Horace; and what was more,
they had successfully survived the Longinian test of time.[3] In
this same category, therefore, he would include the songs of
Rochester; for it was the 'wit', the workmanship, of the poems
that he defended, not their 'obscene manners', since bawdry in
itself, he confessed, was 'but a poor pretence to wit'. His suggestion was therefore that Rochester's poems should be regarded as the fruit of youthful extravagance when the poet 'was
carried away with the precipitancy of that *liber spiritus*, as
Petronius called it, by the too great fervour of his universal
genius and the overfruitfulness of an unbounded fancy'.[4] And
if, added Wolseley, such poetry could not be justified in point

---

[1] Spingarn, *op. cit.* iii. 15.　　[2] Preface to *Tyrannic Love.*
[3] Spingarn, *op. cit.* iii. 20–21.　　[4] *ibid.* iii. 25; cf. *Satyricon,* § 118.

of decency, it might well be excused in view of those for whom it was intended, namely, the gay and frivolous society attached to the Court. This, then, is the main substance of Wolseley's argument; but before concluding he cannot refrain from a passing shot at Mulgrave's verse, and more particularly, his employment of diction which by then had become antiquated.[1] Ridiculing Mulgrave's use of the form *undeservèd*, he remarks that 'the final *eds* had vanished from common usage along with the *for-to's*, the *thereons*, and such forms as *'midst*, *'twixt*, and the rest'—a remark that incidentally throws light on the changing conception of the literary language.

In this Preface of Wolseley we have without doubt one of the more striking and readable of the critical works of the period. A youthful admirer of the versatile Rochester, he is perhaps unduly severe on the more orthodox Mulgrave; but for the rest his case is presented in considered and judicial fashion, with an effective marshalling of arguments drawn from no less authorities than Aristotle, Horace, 'Longinus' and Petronius, with principles of the sister arts in mind, and the whole lit up with a rare liveliness that gives grace to his manner of expression. Apart from this, the work is notable as being the first serious attempt in English to face up to the abstract problem of the relation of art to morality: for the plea of the 15th-Century Italian Humanist, Battista Guarino,[2] for aesthetic rather than moral judgments of literature, had hitherto passed practically unnoticed. And in demanding due recognition of the art enshrined in Rochester's poems, despite their unedifying and offensive themes, Wolseley was calling attention to what was in reality an important critical principle. It was what Aristotle, and following him Plutarch, had apparently recommended in dealing with the ugly and morally harmful in art. Yet the doctrine thus expounded by Wolseley was after all but a half-truth. For Aristotle had also implied that for normal and healthy minds the proper aesthetic pleasure was possible only when the requirements of morality were satisfied,[3] and that the presence of immoral elements detracted from the aesthetic effect—a judgment that has commended itself to most modern readers. Among Wolseley's contemporaries, it is true, his bold contention found but little acceptance; and moral tests continued to be regarded as final and decisive. Yet his protest was not

---

[1] Spingarn, *op. cit.* iii. 27.
[2] See Atkins, *Eng. Lit. Crit: the Renascence*, p. 27.
[3] cf. Butcher, *Aristotle's Theory of Poetry and Fine Art*, pp. 211 ff.

altogether in vain. His demand for other than purely moral-istic standards in literature represented a timely, if imperfect, plea for criticism of a purely aesthetic kind.

Views of another kind were however forthcoming from other quarters. Apart from old and deep-seated prejudices instilled by the early Fathers and handed on by Gosson, Prynne and others, a growing concern had latterly been felt regarding the immor-ality of the contemporary stage and its effects on the national life and character. In France, for instance, as a result of the Catholic reaction, the subject had also received attention, first, from the Prince de Conti in his *Traité de la Comédie* (1666), and later on, from Bossuet in his *Maximes et Réflexions sur la Comédie* (1694). In England, however, the matter became one of the first importance; and numerous works devoted to the improvement of manners had been published between the appearance of Sir George Mackenzie's *Moral Gallantry* (1669) and the anonymous *Reformed Gentleman* (1693). After the Revolution of 1688, it is true, the zest for the unbridled licence of Charles II's days was gradually subsiding under the influ-ence of the new Court; and already in 1687 Sedley had remarked on the fickleness of public taste, which he compared to the 'sudden whims of English weather'. But these changed condi-tions merely fired the reformers to renewed efforts; and the ancient controversy now came to a head. In 1694 Joseph Wright denounced the evil influence of the stage in his *Country Conver-sations*. A further protest by Sir Richard Blackmore in 1695 was followed by the pamphlet, *Immorality, Debauchery and Profane-ness Exposed* (1698), of George Merriton, a literary lawyer; and in the same year there appeared the formidable treatise of the non-juring clergyman, Jeremy Collier (1650–1726), namely, *The Short View of the Immorality and Profaneness of the English Stage*, which constituted the representative pronouncement on the subject.

From the uninspired and uninspiring Blackmore, in the first place, came attempts to reform the public taste by means of moral epics, including *Prince Arthur* (1695), *King Arthur* (1697), *Job* (1700) and *Creation* (1712); while in his *Satire upon Wit* (1700) he directly attacks contemporary poets and plays. His chief pronouncement, however, is in his *Preface to King Arthur*, and there he maintains, to begin with, that in ancient Greece all literature was designed to moral ends, pleasure being but a minor consideration, whereas in his own day there was abroad a conspiracy calculated to undermine all religion and virtue.

8

Your fine gentleman, he complains, is represented on the stage as 'a finished libertine', Court ladies as immodest and profane; the clergy are caricatured, virtuous citizens' wives derided and worthy aldermen badly handled. Such treatment he attributes to the general corruption of manners and religion; and he refuses to accept the current excuse that such plays were dictated by the taste of playgoers, and that dramatists would starve unless they humoured their audiences. Nor was the evil confined to the stage alone; the same strain is said to run through the other kinds of poetry. Hence, he explains, his efforts in his epics to 'rescue the Muses out of the hands of these ravishers and to restore them to their sweet and chaste mansions'. And lest his epics should fail in their reforming purpose he proceeds to expound the true nature of that poetic 'kind', reproducing to that end the teaching of Le Bossu.[1] According to that theory the epic was a narrative of one complete and illustrious action, with suitable episodes, related in allegorical and metrical fashion, with the help of Christian machinery, and in a manner probable, delightful and likely to cause wonder, the object throughout being 'to cultivate the mind with instruction of virtue'.

This formal protest of Blackmore, however, can hardly have been more effective than the epics themselves; and a sterner note was sounded with the appearance of Collier's *Short View*;[2] for into the reforming movement Collier flung himself with frenzied zeal and with a concentrated force that compelled attention. The main charges of his indictment were those previously levelled by Blackmore, though now elaborated; and to each he assigns a chapter of his work. Those charges consisted of the indecency of the stage, its profanity, its abuse of the clergy and its undue rewarding of vice; and these chapters he supplements with a detailed examination of certain plays of Dryden, D'Urfey and Vanbrugh, together with a sort of appendix consisting of a summary of ancient and medieval arguments against stage-plays. The work is therefore something more than a collection of trite commonplaces drawn from earlier authorities. To those ancient stock arguments on which previous controversialists had relied he attached but secondary importance; and he deals in the main with literature in the concrete, with specific plays and dramatists, and not only with those already mentioned. And well equipped as he was with a wide and detailed knowledge of contemporary plays, he has little

---

[1] Spingarn, *op. cit.* iii. 235 ff.   [2] *ibid.* iii. 253 ff.

difficulty in exposing, what was plain to all, the immoral and degrading elements in Restoration drama.

Yet while there was substance in Collier's censure, there was also much that invalidated his argument as a serious contribution to critical literature. He was not without some acquaintance with earlier critical authorities, with Aristotle and Horace, Heinsius, Jonson and others; and in places he fortified his judgments by an appeal to conventional principles and rules. He holds, for instance, that no precedent for the prevailing licentiousness was to be found in the plays of Aristophanes, Plautus or Terence. He derides Dryden's assertion that the chief end of comedy was to amuse and to make men laugh; for as he triumphantly retorts, Jonson was clearly of a different opinion. Elsewhere, again, he condemns Vanbrugh's *Relapse* for its non-observance of the Unities, its faulty structure and its lack of *decorum* in the matter of characters.

At the same time his main guide and inspiration was undoubtedly Rymer, whose doctrine, methods and manner he had thoroughly assimilated. Like Rymer, it is true, he has the merit of dealing with actual works of literature. But then he also approaches those works in the same arrogant spirit as Rymer had dealt with the Elizabethans; he makes abundant use of Rymer's offensive colloquial style; and there is also on occasion the same pedantic display of learning, as when, for instance, in claiming respect for the clergy he recalls their treatment at the hands of writers from Homer down to Corneille and Molière. More than this, however, his main arguments against the immorality he deplores are based on Rymer's doubtful teaching, when indeed they are not due to his own blindness to dramatic values or else to Puritan prejudices. Thus in charging the Restoration drama with representing vice as triumphant, he objects in particular to 'the fine time lewd people had on the stage'; and this he does on the ground that such treatment was not in accord with Rymer's demand for 'poetic justice'. He notes that Dryden had defended himself by stating that he knew of no such law; but this apology Collier ridicules in the light of Jonson's theory and practice. Or again, there was the scandalous treatment of persons of quality on the stage. 'What necessity is there', he asks, 'to kick coronets about on the stage and to make a lord only in order to make him a coxcomb.' And here his objection is based on the failure to observe Rymer's 'false decorum', that narrow Court etiquette which was held to represent truth to Nature. Apart from this, many of his censures were due to sheer inability to appreciate dramatic values. In Ophelia's pathetic ravings, for instance, he can see little more than 'lewd frenzy'; Falstaff, again, is said to be 'thrown out of favour for being a rake and dies like a rat behind the hangings'; while he condemns outright, and under any circumstances, all Biblical allusions on the stage.

It is therefore not strange to find that Collier's remedy for the state of affairs he deplores was, as Dryden pointed out, to abolish the stage, not to reform it. And as a reasoned appreciation of an aesthetic kind this treatise of Collier is consequently worthless. With a single eye for garbage throughout he ignores entirely the artistic merits of Restoration comedy at its best, its ingenious situations, its sparkling wit, its vivid characterization and its faithful reflexion of the artificial Court life of the time. His judgment, in fact, is of a purely ethical kind, bolstered up by false critical doctrine; and he writes regardless of the important half-truth voiced by Wolseley. On the vexed question of art *versus* morality, he adheres rigidly to the old tradition; and altogether it was a judicious estimate of his performance that came from Dryden, who, while confessing that Collier had 'taxed him justly' on the score of immorality, was nevertheless constrained to add that

It were not difficult to prove, that in many places he has perverted my meaning by his glosses, and interpreted my words into blasphemy and bawdry, of which they were not guilty. Besides that, he is too much given to horse-play in his raillery, and comes to battle like a dictator from the plough. I will not say 'the zeal of God's house has eaten him up'; but I am sure it has devoured some part of his good manners and civility.[1]

On the other hand it must be conceded that the violence of Collier's attack was successful in calling attention to what was a serious defect in the literature of the time, a defect that detracted from the delight it otherwise afforded. That the treatise shook up the social conscience to some purpose cannot be doubted. A proclamation against immorality was forthwith issued; fines were imposed on playwrights and actors; and D'Urfey, Congreve, Dennis and Vanbrugh all attempted, perhaps unwisely, to reply. Moreover, it has since been claimed that the work was further responsible for those later changes by which the stage became a school of morality in the hands of Steele and others. It has in fact been hailed as 'a most important

[1] W. P. Ker, *op. cit.* ii. 272.

document in the history of criticism', and as 'the earliest instance in our history where a piece of criticism has apparently changed to a very great extent the face of an important department of literature'. Such claims, however, seem excessive in view of the character of the work, and more especially since earlier plays continued to be acted. The truth would seem to be that Collier's negative appeal attained little more than the momentary success of a sensational tirade; and that the gradual recovery of national good sense after 1688, together with the healthy influence of the new Court in social matters, are sufficient to account for the reform that in due course followed.

CHAPTER IV

'THE FATHER OF ENGLISH CRITICISM': DRYDEN

MEANWHILE the new direction thus given to critical activities in England by French influences of 1674 and after was not confined to writers already mentioned. The last quarter of the 17th Century witnessed also the maturing of the critical genius of Dryden, who now developed a wider outlook, which resulted in work that overshadowed the sporadic efforts of his contemporaries and confirmed his position as the most vital critic of his generation, while it also represents the most significant part of his critical output. During the transitional stage he had concerned himself mainly with immediate problems, with matters of verse-form and the future of the English stage; whether for instance French or native models were to be adopted and whether changed conditions did not call for a new form of comedy as well as for a new type of play known as the heroic drama. Moreover, as yet his criticism had been subject to an uncertain and unsettled judgment. After 1674, however, his critical pronouncements assumed a more general and a firmer character, as a result of his assimilation of what was most valuable in the new French teaching. Through the works of Rapin, Boileau, Le Bossu and Dacier he had become acquainted with the newly organized neo-classical doctrine, and he has something to say on the rules and the 'kinds'. What however was more important was his assimilation of more fruitful ideas gathered with a shrewd instinct from the same and other sources, ideas which represented the less familiar part of French theory. As we have seen, his contemporaries had expounded some amount of neo-classical doctrine, often in verse-form after Boileau's fashion, and had replied directly to Perrault and others. The effects on Dryden, however, were of a different order. From Rapin and Dacier, for instance, he derived a closer acquaintance with Aristotle, from Boileau a shrewd idea of 'Longinus's' illuminating doctrine, and from Saint-Evremond a sense of the need for an active and open mind in all critical inquiries. Such influences found a ready response in his own nature; for free speculation, fostered by Corneille, had marked his earlier critical efforts. And from now on, they modified and enriched his critical work, giving to it a wider range, a more inward treatment and a finer judgment.

Nor were these the only influences that gave fresh impetus and a new direction to his critical work during this last quarter of the 17th Century. It was not without its significance, for example, that the period witnessed the first formation of a large literary society in London, a society of wits eager for some acquaintance with literature and literary doctrine; and an exposition of literary principles became from now on Dryden's chief preoccupation. Among the chief questions that were agitating men's minds at the time was that which had been raised in France by Perrault and others. And by way of an indirect reply to the attacks of the moderns Dryden devoted his latter years to the work of translation, thus introducing to his readers in modernized form not a few of the ancient classics. The task was one that had been imposed upon him primarily by financial stress, though partly inspired, as he would have us believe, by Roscommon's *Essay* of 1685. And to most of these translations he attached a critical Preface, defending and appraising the work of the ancient writers, while he also compiled, in separate form, *Lives* of certain of their number, Plutarch and Lucian, for example. The result was a marked expansion of Dryden's critical horizon, fresh literatures being brought under examination and further opportunities afforded for viewing native achievements in the light of ancient standards. Apart from this, however, among the influences on his critical work at this stage was also the appearance of *Paradise Lost* (1667, 2nd ed., 1674), which accounted in part for his increased concern with the epic from now on; whereas the popularity of a French work on painting (1668) provided the occasion for an attempt at inculcating a wider aesthetic. Moreover, those were the days of Lely and Kneller; and by Dryden an interest in the sister arts was thus inaugurated, an interest that was to be a marked feature of later criticism.

When we turn to his critical works produced during this period we find that they consist of Prefaces and Dedications, in accordance with his earlier practice. No attempt is made at a systematic exposition of either theory or judgments; but as this or that work appeared it was accompanied by an effort to improve the occasion by discussing literary principles or matters otherwise suggested by the work in hand. Up to 1685 he was still experimenting; and his first Prefaces are concerned as before with matters of current interest and procedure. Thus

the immediate occasion of his *Apology for Heroic Poetry* (1677)
was the publication of his opera, *The State of Innocence*, a
dramatic version of *Paradise Lost*. Hitherto Milton's epic had
met with a mixed reception, and Dryden first endeavours to get
justice done. Condemning outright all censorious and captious
critics, he recalls 'Longinus's' views of what true criticism was;
after which he proceeds to his main business, that of explaining
wherein the greatness of epic style, such as Milton's, really lay.
Interest of a different kind is attached to *The Grounds of Criticism in Tragedy*, which forms the Preface to his *Troilus and
Cressida* (1679), an adaptation of Shakespeare's play of the
same name. Modernization of earlier drama played a great part
in current activities; and Dryden now raises the whole question.
Justifying the process generally by an appeal to Greek precedents, he calls attention to 'Longinus's' conception of 'imitation'; and then discusses to what extent earlier English writers
of tragedy should be thus 'imitated'. His contention is that the
traditions of Shakespeare and Fletcher should be followed in
so far as they were consistent with the principles laid down by
Aristotle, 'Longinus' and Horace. And with this in view he
submits a fairly detailed account of Aristotle's theory of tragedy
—one of the first of its kind in English—after which he treats
of the achievements of both Shakespeare and Fletcher. Of
lesser importance is the Preface to his *Translation of Ovid's
Epistles* (1680) in which he gives some account of the poet's life
and works, and then expounds the current theories of translation. More lively and vigorous, however, is the Dedication of
The Spanish Friar (1681), a tragicomedy of the Elizabethan
kind. He here defends the liberties of that type of play, the
double plot and the mixture of tragedy and comedy, and distinguishes between dramatic 'beauties' of the meretricious and
genuine kinds.

After 1685 his critical Prefaces are nearly all occasioned by
the business of translation. And already in that year appeared
his Preface to *Sylvae*, the second part of his *Miscellany Poems*,
which consisted of translations of various ancient poets. Writing
in his most spirited fashion he discourses once again on methods
of translation, gives some interesting appreciations of Virgil,
Ovid, Lucretius, Theocritus and Horace, and in addition throws
light on the real character of what was known as 'Pindaric'
verse. Of the Preface to his opera *Albion and Albanius* (1685)
but little need here be said; whereas considerable interest is
attached to the Dedication of his *Examen Poeticum* (1693), the

third part of his *Miscellany Poems*. Here he continues his earlier crusade against contemporary critics, defends the English drama against the ancients and moderns alike, comments on Ovid and Homer, and adds brief notes on his own principles of versification. A more ambitious venture is represented in his *Preface to Juvenal* (1693), otherwise known as *A Discourse concerning the Original and Progress of Satire*. It is a lengthy and discursive essay based largely on Dacier's *Préface sur les Satires d'Horace* (1687), though the works of Casaubon, Heinsius and others are consulted as well; and the result is an erudite, if somewhat tedious, disquisition on ancient satire, happily relieved however by comparisons drawn between Persius, Horace and Juvenal, and what is more, by some interesting remarks on modern satire and on epic poetry as well. A different field is next invaded in his *Parallel of Poetry and Painting* (1695), which formed a Preface to the translation of Du Fresnoy's Latin poem, *De Arte Graphica* (1668). In it an attempt is made to promote interest in a wider aesthetic; and while the main contention is that both poetry and painting were in different degrees representations of the ideal, the general principles common to both arts are also discussed. Then, reverting once again to more familiar tracks, he treats in his *Dedication of the Aeneis* (1697) of epic poetry, and Virgil in particular. For his material he draws freely on Segrais's Preface to his translation of the *Aeneid* (1668); and in the course of a lengthy disquisition he discusses the comparative values of epic and tragedy, submits a defence of Virgil against his detractors, and adds some remarks on the verse and style of his own translation of the *Aeneid*. Last of all comes his *Preface to the Fables* (1700), prefixed to a volume of translations from Homer, Ovid, Boccaccio and Chaucer. Its main feature is a masterly appreciation of Chaucer, whose claim to recognition he establishes by comparisons with Ovid and Boccaccio, and by a penetrating analysis of his artistic achievement. Long acclaimed as a masterpiece in judgment, method and style, the Preface is otherwise full of good things and thus fitly marks the culmination of Dryden's work in the field of criticism.

These, then, were Dryden's critical contributions during the last quarter of the century; and it is seen at once that his field of inquiry has visibly broadened, and that here are something more than discussions of immediate problems or laboured and conventional expositions of cut-and-dried theory. They are works intended, as he himself explains, not for mere scholars, but for cultured circles, for *viris bonis et non inlitteratis*; and he further confesses, 'I have not engaged myself to any perfect pattern, neither am I loaded with a full cargo';[1] thereby eschewing both system and pedantry. The method was possessed of obvious advantages; and it was one that commended itself to his courtly readers, enlivened as it was by his easy and picturesque style, and by intimate revelations concerning his decaying fortunes or his ill-treatment at the hands of hostile critics. At the same time equally clear is the fact that owing to the multifarious themes of these Prefaces and their informal and inconsequent character, any attempt at forming a clear estimate of his actual achievement is by no means easy. His views emerge, it is true, with tolerable clarity; but in a careless, unregulated fashion, so that his exposition is littered with repetitions, inconsistencies, digressions and the like. And of this desultory manner of writing and its attendant disabilities he is fully conscious. 'I have taken up, laid down, and resumed as often as I pleased the same subject', he confesses;[2] while elsewhere he has scruples concerning his 'hasty and loose writing', suggesting that there was probably 'more spirit than judgment'[3] in the unconsidered thoughts thus submitted. Hence his attempts to defend his choice of methods. 'A loose epistolary way of writing', he notes,[4] had been adopted by Horace in his *Ars Poetica*; a few years later he suggests that it was from 'honest Montaigne' that he had learnt that 'the nature of a Preface was rambling';[5] whereas the truth probably was that his 'loose and rambling' method was dictated from the first by none other than his own native inclination (fostered by Corneille), by that active mind to which, as he states, 'thoughts came crowding in so fast that the only difficulty was to choose or reject'. Yet whatever may have been the decisive factor, the choice of method was a good one, providing as it did, in spite of some confusion, abundant scope for spirited writing and for judgments of a sincere and spontaneous kind.

In view of these facts the critical achievement of Dryden at this later stage is probably best appreciated, not by examining his works *seriatim*, but by considering his general contribution to literary theory and judgment; and this is the plan adopted in the following pages. In these Prefaces will be found a host of scattered utterances that throw new light on literature and literary criticism as well. There are, for instance, his remarks on the nature and art of poetry, as well as on the forms that poetry

---

[1] W. P. Ker, *op. cit.* ii. 124.   [2] *ibid.* ii. 164.
[3] *ibid.* i. 269.   [4] *ibid.* ii. 164.   [5] *ibid.* ii. 255.

may assume; there is also his more liberal conception of the
critical function, together with a host of fresh and striking
appreciations of literature in the concrete. The light thus thrown
is mostly intermittent and incomplete, but it is always illuminating; and it marks something new in the sphere of critical
activities.

Of interest, to begin with, are his remarks on the nature of
poetry, a subject less frequently discussed in his day than in
the Renascence period, though Hobbes in the meantime had
opened up a new and fruitful line of inquiry. What Dryden does,
however, is to call attention to certain aspects of Aristotle's
theory, and notably to his conception of what constituted the
possible subject-matter of poetry. Aristotle's statement had
been that the poet might imitate 'things as they were or are',
or 'things as they are said or thought to be', or again 'things as
they ought to be'.[1] The first of these clauses was at the time
generally accepted; and Dryden now attempts to extend the
prevailing notion by dealing with the ideas embodied in the
rest of Aristotle's definition. In the first place he therefore
claims that the poet was not confined to 'things as they were or
are', that is, to mere verisimilitude; he might imitate 'things as
they were said or thought to be', that is, things bound up with
legends of the people. Thus

Poets [he states] [2] may be allowed the liberty for describing things
which really exist not, if they are founded on popular beliefs. Of
this nature are fairies, pigmies and the extraordinary effects of magic;
for 'tis still an imitation, though of other men's fancies; and thus are
Shakespeare's *Tempest* and his *Midsummer Night's Dream* . . . to be
defended.

By Hobbes a strict verisimilitude had been described as the
utmost limit of poetic liberty. 'Beyond the conceived possibilities of Nature', he had insisted,[3] 'a poet may never go'; and
here, Dryden utters a timely warning against the restriction of
poetry within the confines of factual truth, while commending
supra-natural themes, including 'the fairy way of writing',[4] to
which coherent and convincing form had been successfully
given.

Equally important, however, is his exposition of Aristotle's
remaining clause, namely, that the poet might imitate things as
they ought to be; and this he does in his *Parallel of Poetry and*

[1] *Poetics*, 1460 b, 10–11.　　　[2] W. P. Ker, *op. cit.* i. 187.
[3] See p. 39 *supra*.
[4] cf. Dryden, Ded. to *King Arthur* (1691), for origin of this expression.

Painting, drawing upon Bellori's *Vite de' Pittori* (1672) for that purpose.[1] Thus poetry in general is described as essentially an imitation of things in their ideal form, of things, that is, as they were first created and as they ought to be. The phenomena of Nature, it is explained, are necessarily imperfect, being subject to change and decay. Yet Nature ever strives to correct these defects by aiming at perfection in all her creations; and art in like manner imitates the creative processes of Nature in also striving to represent things in that same ideal form. Hence in poetry (as also in painting) an idealized form of life and humanity is depicted; we see therein 'the scattered beauties of Nature united by a happy chemistry, without its deformities or faults'.[2] This was none other than Aristotle's 'ideal imitation', concerning which Sidney alone had previously furnished an adequate idea; and while specially true of ancient classical literature, it is not without its bearing on modern literary art.

At the same time Dryden suggests that in actual practice some modification of this general principle was necessarily involved.[3] In portrait-painting, for instance, the idea of perfection is said not to apply; and similarly in both comedy and tragedy, so Dryden contended, human nature is represented with certain defects, whereas in the epic alone are ideal characters possible. Here, however, he fails to convey the true meaning of Aristotle's doctrine; for with Aristotle the idealizing process consists in presenting characters, not of flawless virtue, but characters consistently drawn.[4] And it might further be added that a like misrepresentation of Aristotle's meaning occurs elsewhere[5] when he fails to grasp the distinction of the two types of poet implied by Aristotle in contrasting the conscious (εὐφυής) poet, who works under the control of a higher reason, with the 'enthusiastic' (μανικός) poet, who, dominated by his emotions, wrote in a transport of frenzy.[6] Dryden in this place follows Rapin's reading of Aristotle's text,[7] and there suggests that poetry was the outcome of conscious art and never of unbridled frenzy, thus freeing Aristotle from the charge of countenancing 'the madness of poetry'.

Apart, however, from these efforts to extend the range of poetry beyond the domain of mere verisimilitude, Dryden is

---

[1] W. P. Ker, *op. cit.* ii. 117 ff.   [2] *ibid.* ii. 137.   [3] *ibid.* ii. 125 ff.
[4] See Butcher, *Aristotle's Theory of Poetry and Fine Art*, p. 232. Elsewhere Aristotle's idea is correctly given, see p. 118 *infra*.
[5] W. P. Ker, *op. cit.* i. 221–2.   [6] *Poetics*, 1455 a, 31.
[7] cf. Rapin, *Réflexions sur la Poétique*, I, ch. v.

not greatly concerned with abstract questions relating to the nature of poetry, whereas his remarks on the poetic art are both extensive and practical. From the first he had felt the need for guidance in art derived from earlier masters; and more than once he discusses whether classical, French, or native models were to be utilized for that purpose. Meanwhile from Boileau's *Longinus* he had gathered a new conception of how best to imitate great masterpieces, and this conception of 'imitation' he explains in his *Preface to Troilus and Cressida*. That idea was something different from the earlier crude notion of a slavish copying of formal characteristics, or an indiscriminate borrowing of incidents, phrases or diction. It differed also from the more reasoned and effective process suggested by Ascham, in which literary methods were studied, the general ordering of an author's material, his omissions, his additions and the rest. It was rather a process of the spirit which aimed at recapturing something of that vital force which had gone to the making of the earlier masterpiece. As Dryden explains[1] (here closely following 'Longinus'[2])

> Those great men whom we propose to ourselves as patterns of our imitation, serve us as a torch . . . to enlighten our passage, and often elevate our thoughts as high as the conception we have of our author's genius.

The effect of such imitation was therefore that of inspiration and illumination, an imaginative stimulus derived from earlier models; and this pronouncement of Dryden is of significance in his critical development. It suggests a process vastly different from that of the neo-classical school, with their concentration on the formal aspects of ancient classical literature.

At the same time Dryden maintains that in poetry, as in all arts, certain rules were necessary, in order 'to inform our judgment and reform our taste'. All arts, he argued,[3] were imitations of Nature; and since Nature was constant throughout the ages, the rules of Aristotle, based on experience and confirmed by practice, still retained their validity, and were not lightly to be discarded, as Lope de Vega had done. Moreover, in reply to those who flouted all rules he endorses Rapin's dictum that 'the rules were made only to reduce Nature into method';[4] and that therefore they were no 'magisterial prescriptions' of Aristotle or others, but rational principles founded on good sense and reason.

---

[1] W. P. Ker, *op. cit.* i. 206. [2] *On the Sublime*, c. 13. 1.
[3] W. P. Ker, *op. cit.* ii. 134. [4] *ibid.* i. 228.

As an illustration of what he has in mind he then discusses certain general rules under the conventional headings of *inventio*, *dispositio*, and *elocutio*. For the invention of subject-matter, in the first place, he concedes that no rules were possible; a happy genius alone would suffice, and that was a gift of Nature. With regard to *dispositio* (arrangement or design), however, many rules were available. Each poem or play, for instance, should be all of a piece, free from irrelevancies or trifling ornaments. The main character of a play should be placed in the foreground with minor characters (or episodes) in support; the passions, besides, should be discreetly handled; while the use of contrast was also said to be effective, since *contraria juxta ac posita magis elucescunt*.[1] Then, too, on *elocutio* (or expression) he has something to say, an element in poetry which he frequently compares to the colouring in a picture. Thus style, he urges, should be skilfully varied. Certain passages in a work required strong and glaring colours, provided by tropes and figures, together with gracious sound-effects and neat turns of thought, whereas others called for less forceful and elegant treatment, and were to be couched in a quieter vein. And, finally, comes a shrewd warning against too meticulous care, along with a reminder of the commonplace ascribed by the elder Pliny[2] to the poet Apelles, who is said to have censured Protogenes for not knowing when 'to give over'.[3]

A work [wrote Dryden] [4] may be over-wrought as well as under-wrought; too much labour often takes away the spirit by adding to the polishing, so that there remains nothing but a dull correctness, a piece without any considerable faults but with few beauties; for when the spirits are drawn off there is nothing left but a *caput mortuum*.

And here was a warning against excessive 'filing', and against the adoption of an uninspired correctness as an all-sufficient aim.

Besides these general remarks on poetic technique, however, Dryden has some specific comments to make on diction and versification, all worthy of note. To begin with, he refuses to accept Hobbes's dictum that 'the choice of words and harmony of numbers' are of the first importance in a poem. That venerable philosopher, he suggests, 'had studied poetry as he did mathematics, when it was too late';[5] and verbal and metrical

---

[1] W. P. Ker, *op. cit.* ii. 147.   [2] *Hist. Nat.* xxxv. 10.
[3] cf. Rapin, *Réflexions sur la Poétique*, 1. ch. xvi.
[4] W. P. Ker, *op. cit.* ii. 152.   [5] *ibid.* ii. 252.

effects, Dryden repeats, provide but the colouring of poetry, though such effects are the first qualities that strike the reader. Yet 'if the draught be false,' he adds, 'the figures ill-disposed, the characters obscure or inconsistent, or the thought unnatural, then the finest colours are but daubing and the piece a beautiful monster at the best'.

At the same time he recognizes that both diction and verse play their parts in the poetic process; and his views on diction, in the first place, give evidence of a mind playing freely on verbal effects in poetry. Thus he maintains, for one thing, that English, encumbered with consonants and hosts of monosyllables, has certain defects as a poetic medium compared with Italian, that 'softest, sweetest and most harmonious of languages';[1] for 'monosyllabic lines', he suggests (rather hastily), 'generally turn verse into prose and even that prose is rugged and unharmonious'.[2] The main task in English was therefore to give sweetness to poetic diction by choosing words not only for elegance but also for sound; while the varying quality of English vowels should be carefully studied and vocalic effects skilfully arranged.[3] Then, too, he pronounces on certain questions that had been subjects of earlier controversy. For dialect forms, for instance, he has no liking. The Doric dialect of Theocritus, he confesses, 'has an incomparable sweetness in its clownishness, like a fair shepherdess in her country russet talking in a Yorkshire tone';[4] but then, he adds, Theocritus wrote for Sicilians who used that dialect. In similar fashion he objects to the use of archaic forms. Antiquated words, he states,[5] are never to be revived but when sound or significance is wanting in the current language; and then they are best accompanied by other words which remove their obscurity. Concerning foreign borrowings, however, he betrays a more open mind. He himself had been accused of excessive latinizing in his translations, and his retort is that 'what I want at home I must seek abroad'.[6] The native language, he held, sufficed for ordinary purposes, but poetry called for a heightened expression, often beyond the reach of 'our old Teuton monosyllables'. And in such cases he defends the use of Latin expressions which commended themselves by their beauty or splendour; though this liberty, he allowed, should be sparingly employed, since not everyone could distinguish between pedantry and poetry.

Furthermore, he states his dislike for compound words,[7]

---

[1] W. P. Ker, *op. cit.* i. 273.   [2] *ibid.* ii. 227.   [3] *ibid.* ii. 216.
[4] *ibid.* i. 265.   [5] *ibid.* ii. 29. 241.   [6] *ibid.* ii. 234.   [7] *ibid.* i. 189.

which, though elegant in Greek, had been disastrously employed by Sidney and others. And again, he now objects to the use of technical terms in poetry, thus reversing his earlier judgment.[1] At this later date he recommends the use of general terms as employed by Virgil; and this he does on the grounds that they were more dignified and better suited for cultured readers, while they also relieved the poet from the affectation of 'being thought learned in all things'. Finally, to one particular form of expression he attached great importance, namely, the turns of words and thoughts in which Ovid and Virgil were said to have excelled, and which had been introduced into English by Waller and Denham.[2] Such expressions he regarded as among the most beautiful, and he quotes from Denham's *Cooper's Hill* a well-known example of their effect; though the device, he recognizes, was unsuitable for impassioned utterance, since 'passions are serious and will admit of no playing'.[3] Already, however, the merits of the device were being questioned in some quarters; and Butler in his *Characters* ridicules these turns as a species of quibbling, which had 'nothing in it but easiness, and being never used by any lasting wit would in wiser times fall to nothing of itself'.[4]

Less frequent are the remarks on versification, though he claims to have collected material for a treatise on English prosody. Of definite interest, however, is his realization of the possibilities of blank verse at this later date, that verse-form so slowly appreciated; though both Phillips and Roscommon, it is true, had already recognized its value. In his earlier period Dryden had finally allowed that blank verse was more suitable than rhyme for dramatic purposes; yet for a time he remained unconvinced by Milton's choice of verse for his great epic.[5] Towards the end, however, he is reconciled to its use even for epic purposes; and he states that 'he who can write well in rhyme can write better in blank verse'.[6] Moreover, 'rhyme', he adds, 'is certainly a constraint to the best poets; . . . what it adds to sweetness it takes away from sense'; and in translation it often makes us 'swerve from an author's meaning'.

Then, too, he has something to say on Cowley's 'Pindaric' verse, the verse-form which Phillips had already shown to differ in structure from the real Pindaric form. At the time it was being employed as a sort of free verse, which, as Dryden explained,

---

[1] W. P. Ker, *op. cit.* ii. 236: see p. 54 *supra.*   [2] *ibid.* ii. 108.
[3] *ibid.* ii. 257.   [4] *ibid.* ii. 288 (n).
[5] *ibid.* ii. 29.   [6] *ibid.* ii. 220–1.

'allowed more latitude than any other verse-form'; but while its 'seeming easiness' had invited many practitioners, it had not been studied with sufficient care to make it a success. And now he suggests the secret of its effective use. It was something more, he states, than a chance grouping of lines of varying length; it was rather an artistic arrangement over which the ear presided directing the poet's judgment, and with each line depending on the line preceding. 'The cadency of one line', he asserted,[1] must be the rule to that of the next, and the sound of the former must slide gently into that which follows.' And for its successful treatment, he added, a musical ear and a great genius were needed. Concerning the heroic couplet, on the other hand, he has but few comments to make; and they are mainly suggestions for giving variety to that measure. Thus he approves of the occasional use of an Alexandrine,[2] to add majesty to the verse and to bring the thought to an effective close; or again, he commends a judicious use of triplet rhymes to bind and emphasize the sense[3]—both of which devices he himself employed. The latter, he held, were licences that gave to expression a masculine vigour which was wanting in French verse. 'Strength and elevation', he claims, 'are our standards; whereas the affected purity of the French has unsinewed their heroic verse.' At the same time he cannot approve of such irregularities as hemistichs or half-verses,[4] when the sense is broken off in the middle of the line; these he describes as 'imperfect products of a hasty Muse'. Nor, again, does he care for the use of the so-called 'caesura'[5] (i.e. synaloepha or elision of vowels) to prevent the clash of vowels. Such treatment, he held, gave a roughness to the verse and was not suitable for English, since the language was already overstocked with discordant consonants.

Such then were Dryden's theories concerning the nature and art of poetry in general; and these he supplements with comments on the more notable forms of poetry, namely, the epic, drama and satire. The epic or heroic poem, in the first place, he regards as 'the greatest work of human nature';[6] and this, despite Aristotle's preference for tragedy as a form more direct and concentrated in its effects. But this, argued Dryden, was 'to prefer a mushroom before a peach'; and he contends not only that the epic held pride of place, since tragedy was historically a development of the earlier epic, but that its action was also more extensive, its methods more deliberate, its effects

(margin note: forms of poetry)

---

[1] W. P. Ker, op. cit. i. 267–8.   [2] ibid. ii. 218–19.   [3] ibid. ii. 228–9.
[4] ibid. ii. 230.   [5] ibid. ii. 215.   [6] ibid. ii. 42, 158 ff.

more lasting, and its heroes more perfect, while its style besides
was more lofty and ornate, since the dramatist could not speak
too plainly, seeing that his sense had to be 'taken flying' (*volat
irrevocabile verbum*). The sole advantage of tragedy was said to
lie in its appeal to the eye; yet the manifold beauties of the epic,
he asserted, could be duly appreciated by leisured and careful
reading. At the same time he maintains that little had been
accomplished in this form of poetry since ancient times, and
that 'the file of heroic poets was very short'.[1] Tasso he des-
scribes, with some reservations, as a not unworthy follower of
Homer and Virgil; but, for the rest, he briefly dismisses all
modern epics as defective. Hence his attempts to point to a
better way, and to inculcate a truer appreciation of epic
qualities.

Least inspiring are his efforts when he is content to reproduce
the main features of Le Bossu's doctrine. Thus the epic story,
he states, should be 'one, entire and great',[2] with episodes of a
dignified character, the aim being to teach heroic virtue by
means of moral example. To this end the epic hero should be
invested with qualities that excite admiration, namely, magnanimity, courage, patience and the like. And although, by
general agreement, a perfect hero was not essential, in view
of Aristotle's teaching that a character was poetically good if
consistently drawn, nevertheless Dryden's conclusion is that
your perfect hero after all is best,[3] for then the hero as a whole
is to be imitated. Apart from this, care was to be exercised in
the choice of episodes, which should contain no elements of a
discordant kind. All episodes were to be organically related to
the main theme, and conducing to virtue; whereas trifling narratives, such as the 'novels' (i.e. love-stories) introduced by Ariosto
and others, would merely detract from the general effect and
distract the reader, 'locking him up,' as Dryden put it,[4] 'like a
knight-errant in an enchanted castle, when he should be pursu-
ing his first adventure.' In view of these requirements, Le
Bossu's practical rule for intending epic poets is further quoted
by Dryden. Since moral teaching, it is said, is the chief business
of the poet, his first task was to decide on the moral to be conveyed.[5] This would direct the whole action to one centre; after
which a suitable theme would suggest itself, together with
characters, thoughts and style in keeping with the theme.

Dryden, however, is no slavish follower of Le Bossu or any

---

[1] W. P. Ker, *op. cit.* ii. 164 ff.   [2] *ibid.* ii. 154.   [3] *ibid.* ii. 159.
[4] *ibid.* ii. 155.   [5] *ibid.* i. 213; ii. 127–8.

other authority. Elsewhere, for instance, he draws on Segrais for epic theory; but, as he there explains, he also endeavours to submit 'something of his own'. And this he does when he tries to solve the question raised in France by Desmarets, Boileau and others, whether a Christian epic was possible in a modern age. One line of argument had been that the Christian religion from its very nature hindered the creation of a great modern epic.[1] The Christian virtues, it was pointed out, were patience, humility and resignation, spiritual qualities and virtues of a passive kind; whereas the epic required active and masterful qualities, which, often the result of pride and ambition, yet led to great actions and heroic deeds. In reply to this Dryden suggests that whereas patience, submission and the like were private virtues, there were nevertheless the public virtues (those of a ruler or a king), which included for instance prudence, magnanimity and fortitude, and that these might well form the subject of a modern epic, relating the story of some heroic deed performed for the common good and in honour of Christianity.

More serious, however, were the objections raised owing to difficulties in providing epic machinery for a Christian poem. Desmarets in his *Clovis* had rejected the old pagan gods as his supernatural agents and had substituted for them the Deity as well as angels and devils bound up with the Christian faith. This *merveilleux chrétien*, however, had been denounced by Boileau[2] as being likely to degrade the Christian mysteries; and in addition it was held to be less effective than the machinery of the ancients. As Boileau (in Dryden's words) had put it, a conflict with an almighty God meant but 'an unequal match for the poor devils who were sure to come by the worst of it'.[3] So 'what pleasure', he asked, 'could be raised from so pitiful a machine where we see the success of the battle from the beginning?' In reply to this Dryden has a suggestion of his own to make. In the employment of supernatural agencies in poetry he found no difficulty; and already in his earlier period he had defended 'enthusiastic' (i.e. supernatural) episodes in which gods and spirits figured,[4] quoting in support Petronius's *deorumque ministeria*, and recalling that men in all ages had believed in spirits, which, he declared (following Aristotle), was 'foundation enough for poetry'. Now however at this later date he puts forward a specific proposition,[5] namely, that the proper Christian

---

[1] W. P. Ker, *op. cit.* ii. 30 ff. [2] *Art Poétique*, iii. 198 ff.
[3] W. P. Ker, *op. cit.* ii. 33. [4] *ibid.* i. 152. [5] *ibid.* ii. 34–5.

machinery would be found in the ministry of angels alluded
to in the Bible and hinted at in Plato's philosophy. 'Guardian
angels', he stated, 'had been appointed by God as his vice-
regents for the protection of cities, provinces,' and the like. But
since they were neither all-knowing nor all-powerful, it therefore followed that a conflict between the good and evil forces
would not be one-sided; and in this way Boileau's objection
would be met. It was an erudite suggestion, tentatively submitted, though not without some amount of pardonable pride;
and if to-day the whole matter seems little more than ingenious
trifling, it is at least of historical interest as reflecting the
troubles of the *littérateurs* of that age.

Ingenious trifling, however, cannot be the term applied to
Dryden's further remarks on epic theory when in his *Apology
for Heroic Poetry*[1] (1677) he treats of those qualities that had
caused the epic to be generally regarded as the supreme kind
of poetry. Fresh from his reading of Milton and Boileau's
Longinus, conscious, too, of the fact that Milton was decried
because he was not understood, he undertakes to explain that
distinction of style which made the epic not only a great story,
but also a great story greatly told. By many of his contemporaries, he notes, epic poetry was regarded as so much bombast,
all that was 'dull, insipid, . . . and without sinews in a poem'
being held to be 'an imitation of Nature'; whereas the truth
was that 'the boldest strokes of poetry when they are managed
artfully are those which most delight the reader'. This, he maintains, was true of Homer and Virgil, Tasso and Milton; and
'generally to have pleased, and through all ages, must bear the
force of universal tradition'. Moreover, these bold emotional
effects, he added, had been obtained by a heightening of the
normal expression, with the help of tropes and figures, which,
so far from being arbitrary tricks invented by rhetoricians,
were devices based on Nature and thus responsive to the artistic
sense of man. They were in fact the natural accompaniments of
emotional utterance, when 'a man is not cool enough to reason
rightly or to talk calmly'; and, used with discretion, they were
as 'heightenings and shadows are in painting', to make things
stand out more clearly. Hence the use of metaphor, hyperbole,
exclamations, disordered narrative and the like—all poetic
licences indulged in by great poets in speaking of things in verse
which were beyond the severity of prose. They were liberties
that varied with different ages and languages; but they were

[1] W. P. Ker, *op. cit.* i. 182–4.

also those elements that gave to poetry its dynamic power, its imaginative and emotional effects. Thus does Dryden claim for epic poetry a style and diction from which ordinary convention shrank, adding further that his claim was in accord with his idea of 'wit' as 'thoughts and words elegantly adapted to the subject'. And when he sums up with the statement that 'sublime subjects ought to be adorned with the sublimest . . . expression', the Longinian source of his exposition is clear.

Along with epic theory, however, Dryden frequently comments on dramatic principles, in the course of which he summarizes Aristotle's conception of tragedy, and discusses in practical fashion the principles of characterization, as well as other matters suggested by his own experiences as a dramatist. To begin with, he is the first, after Jonson, to supply in English the more essential details of Aristotle's definition of tragedy, according to which tragedy is said to be 'an imitation of one, entire, great and probable action; not told but represented; which by moving in us fear and pity is conducive to the purging of those two emotions in our minds'.[1] Thus a single action, he explains, is necessary, since two independent stories would distract the attention; and he condemns in passing Shakespeare's historical plays as being chronicles not tragedies. Moreover, the action should be complete, with a natural beginning, middle and end; and this ruled out all episodic plots in which incident followed incident without logical sequence. Again the action should be a great one with great characters, to distinguish it from comedy with its trivial action and less exalted characters. And once again the action should have an air of actuality, though he allows that to invent something probable and to make it wonderful was not at all easy.

Having dealt with the plot, which, he adds, should be enacted, not related as in the epic, he then treats of the function of tragedy,[2] which is described as the Aristotelian catharsis, with however some notable differences. Thus tragedy, he states, in accordance with Aristotle's doctrine, aims at purging the passions of fear and pity by depicting examples of human misery; but for his explanation of the process he adopts a non-Aristotelian theory. According to Rapin[3] the chief vices in man were pride and hardness of heart. Pride was to be abated by exciting fear, hardness of heart to be softened by arousing pity; while the tragic pleasure was derived from the agitation of soul

[1] W. P. Ker, *op. cit.* i. 207.   [2] *ibid.* i. 209 ff.
[3] *Réflexions sur la Poétique*, ii. chs. xxvii and xviii.

thus caused. And this was the explanation adopted by Dryden, thus presenting Aristotle's doctrine in a modified form. For one thing, it was a correction of vices, a moral cure, that was held to be involved, and not the emotional adjustment suggested by Aristotle. Then, too, the tragic pleasure was attributed to mental disturbances, and not to the state of calm and balance brought about by the regulation of the emotions. At a later date however Dryden expresses some doubts about the whole theory, when he asks whether radical diseases could really be cured in the three hours' duration of a play. The effects of tragedy, he suggests,[1] were too violent to be lasting. Like 'chemical' (i.e. strong) medicines they were better calculated to relieve than to cure; and the cathartic process, in his opinion, was more effectually wrought by means of the epic.

With regard to the principles of characterization he has also something of interest to say; and here, he is guided by both Aristotle and Horace.[2] Thus dramatic characters, he states, should emerge clearly from action and discourse, from what the individuals do and say; they should be true to Nature, in accordance with age, sex, rank and the like; they should more-ever be consistently drawn; while traditional characters, like Achilles or Ulysses, should be represented in conformity with earlier tradition. To the tragic hero,[3] however, he gives special consideration as being the chief agent for inspiring pity and terror, a fact which necessarily determined his character. For pity to be excited, it was argued, the tragic hero had to be virtuous, since a villainous character would alienate all sympathy; he had also to be of exalted rank, in order to suggest that no condition was exempt from the turns of Fortune. On the other hand he was to be no immaculate figure, for 'such', added Dryden, 'was never in Nature'. Some frailty, some taint of nature was to be present in his make-up; but the good should outweigh the bad, thus leaving room for pity. And here in its essentials was the conception of the tragic hero shared by Aristotle and Shakespeare alike.

Equally interesting however are Dryden's remarks on matters suggested, not by earlier authorities, but by his own practical experience as a dramatist; for here he reveals not only his keen insight into stage effects, but also the changes which latterly came over his views concerning the drama. In the first place he emphasizes the importance of character-drawing, and strongly

---

[1] W. P. Ker, *op. cit.* ii. 158.
[2] *ibid.* i. 214–15; cf. Horace, *A.P.* 119, 126, 156.   [3] *ibid.* i. 210, 216.

condemns all colourless, ill-drawn characters. Most farces, he notes, failed grievously in this respect.[1] Their characters, he states, were unconvincing, surprising situations being the main feature, while the sole interest lay in what happened to a man rather than in what he was. At the same time he has no use for caricature,[2] for characters made up of single qualities. Your dramatic characters, he demands, should be drawn in the round; each should consist of a blend of qualities, provided they were not incompatible. Thus a man might not be both liberal and covetous, though he might be both liberal and valiant. And Falstaff, 'liar, coward, glutton and buffoon', is for this reason recalled as a character effectively drawn.

Hence he regards it as essential to be able to 'describe the passions naturally and to move them artfully'.[3] And such skill in handling the emotions he ascribes primarily (here following 'Longinus') to inborn genius and judgment; though it might also be attained by an acquired psychological knowledge which would prevent emotional scenes from being ill-timed, overdone or improperly developed. His advice is therefore to work up an emotional scene gradually, not to rush headlong into it, but to prepare the audience for it beforehand, and to remember that mere noise was not passion. Moreover emotional tension was not to be 'perpetually maintained at the same height'. This, he recalls, 'Longinus' had pointed out as having been the defect of Aeschylus,[4] who had everywhere written at 'high-flood of passion', in either rapture or fury. Besides, there should be some discrimination in these matters; for excessive passion should not be associated with every character in a play, so that all were represented as 'ranting, swaggering, and exclaiming'. In addition, all irrelevant matter should be excluded from a scene of passion, since 'he who treats of joy and grief together is in a fair way of causing neither of these effects'.[5] And among such irrelevant matter he included pointed wit, untimely epigrams and mere fustian, since 'no man', he states, 'is at leisure to make sentences and similes when his soul is in agony'.

Of this particular fault Dryden was himself conscious, and he gives instances of such lapses from his own *Indian Emperor*. The use of metaphors, however, he would not exclude from tragedy, seeing that 'Longinus' had considered them necessary for impassioned utterance;[6] yet 'to say nothing without a metaphor, a simile or description', he declared, was altogether too

---

[1] W. P. Ker, *op. cit.* i. 217.   [2] *ibid.* i. 215.   [3] *ibid.* i. 220 ff.
[4] *On the Sublime*, ch. v.   [5] W. P. Ker, *op. cit.* i. 223.   [6] *ibid.* i. 224.

stagy. Here Dryden has obviously in mind the defects of contemporary playwrights; and later on he frankly decries the
bombast and extravagances—those 'Delilahs of the theatre'—
that had disfigured his plays *Maximin* and *Almanzor*, though
he adds, characteristically enough, that 'when he wrote them
he knew that they were bad enough to please'.[1] Such 'false
beauties', however, he states, give no lasting value to a play,
any more than Sylvester's fustian in his translation of Du
Bartas where Winter is said

> To glaze the Lakes, to bridle up the Floods,
> And periwig with Snow the bald-pate Woods.

Such utterances, he allows, would win the applause of callow
playgoers; but then they were 'monstrous, . . . out of Nature,
an excrescence'. In the swiftness of performance purity of
phrase, clearness and majesty of style were often imperfectly
appreciated; but without these and other 'hidden beauties', he
added, 'a play might win immediate applause but not a lasting
admiration'.

Among his other pronouncements on dramatic theory are
those that witness to the development of his views concerning
the stage. In one place, for instance, he had suggested that
Le Bossu's epic rule should apply to the drama, and that the
first business of the dramatist was to decide on the moral and
then on the plot.[2] But this deference to neo-classical doctrine is
not characteristic of his remarks at a later date, which thus
point to a maturing and firmer judgment. Already in his earlier
period he had rightly remarked that the Unity of place had
formed no part of Aristotle's teaching;[3] and now he asserts that
there was no 'absolute necessity' for an observance of the Unity of
time.[4] The English stage, he stated, required a greater variety of
incidents than was possible under such restrictions; and whereas
Corneille had found one day too short for the development of a
great action, he himself was of opinion that 'better a mechanic
rule were stretched or broken than a great beauty were omitted'.
Then, too, at this later date, he has resolved his doubts about
the respective values of ancient and modern drama. 'The
Greeks', he asserted,[5] 'only gave us the rudiments of a stage
which they never finished, . . . and if we or our greater fathers
have not yet brought the drama to absolute perfection, yet at
least we have carried it much further than the ancient Greeks'.

---

[1] W. P. Ker, *op. cit*. i. 246.   [2] *ibid*. i. 213.   [3] *ibid*. i. 48.
[4] *ibid*. ii. 157.   [5] *ibid*. ii. 5.

And on one particular feature of the ancient drama, which was to be much debated later on, his views are quite definite. 'A good tragedy', he stated,[1] 'may subsist without a chorus'; and in the Chorus he sees merely an encumbrance of no entertainment value, which, besides, would be impracticable on the English stage. Moreover, he is now satisfied that French models were no sufficient guides for English dramatists, since English playgoers would not rest content with their thin plots, their few characters, and their servile adherence to the mechanic rules.[2] The truth was that he rediscovered that important principle, to the observance of which the Elizabethans had owed much of their success, namely, that the aim of the dramatist was to please his audience, 'not the cook's taste but the guests''.[3] He therefore ventures to reassert the principle anew, that in the dramatic business 'we are bound to please those whom we pretend to entertain, and that at any price, religion and good manners only excepted'.[4]

At the same time he remains undecided as to the merits of English tragicomedy. He defends it at first on the grounds that contemporary playgoers were sated with melancholy scenes, that a mixture of mirth was needed, 'the feast being too dull and solemn without the fiddles',[5] and that to threaten tragedy and then to avert it called for the exercise of both skill and judgment. Besides, this type of play, he suggested, was not necessarily an inartistic creation, 'a monster with two heads', for the underplot might well contribute to the main design.[6] Nevertheless, still later, he continues to harbour some of the old doubts. 'Our English tragicomedy' he describes 'as 'wholly Gothic'[7] (i.e. barbarous, uncouth), despite its undoubted success on the stage. He can no longer defend his *Spanish Friar*, with its 'unnatural mixture' of moving and amusing incidents; and his final judgment is that 'mirth and gravity destroy each other and are no more to be allowed for decent than a gay widow laughing in a mourning habit'.

Along with this theorizing on the nature and art of poetry in general and on the epic and drama in particular, there yet remain for notice certain pronouncements of his on those literary activities to which he devoted himself after 1680, namely, satire and translation. With regard to satire, in the first place, he

---

[1] W. P. Ker, *op. cit.* ii. 6, 144.   [2] *ibid.* ii. 7.
[3] See Atkins, *Eng. Lit. Crit. the Renascence*, p. 244.
[4] W. P. Ker. *op. cit.* ii. 7.   [5] *ibid.* i. 249.
[6] *ibid.* ii. 102.   [7] *ibid.* ii. 146–7.

attempts a critical study of its origin and development in antiquity, based mainly on the teachings of Scaliger, Casaubon,
Heinsius and Dacier.[1] Thus he takes his readers through the
long and tangled dispute, between Scaliger and Heinsius on the
one hand and Casaubon and Dacier on the other, concerning the
origin of this form of literature; and finally pronounces in favour
of the latter who, along with Quintilian,[2] had claimed that
honour, not for Greece but for Rome. He further traces the
growth of satire at Rome from Andronicus onwards; notes the
development of Varronian or Menippean satire, with its mixture
of verse and prose, mirth and sense; and explains that ancient
satire not only decried vice and exposed folly, but also commended virtue, and in this way differered from modern satire
which confined itself to invective alone.

So far Dryden had relied mainly on earlier scholars; and of
greater interest are his own pronouncements on satire in general,
as when, for instance, he gives his views on the respective merits
of the different methods pursued by Horace and Juvenal. It had
been stated somewhat arrogantly by Barten Holyday, the
learned Archdeacon of Oxford and editor of *Juvenal* (1673), that
Juvenal in discarding Horatian methods had greatly improved
satire, in that 'the business being to reform great vices, chastisement goes further than admonition, whereas a perpetual
grin, like that of Horace, does rather anger than amend a man'.[3]
To this 'perpetual grin' Dryden replies in spirited fashion, 'Let
the chastisement of Juvenal', he states, 'be never so necessary,
. . . let him declaim as sharply and wittily as he pleases, yet
still the nicest and most delicate touches of satire consist in
fine raillery'; and this point he drives home by a penetrating
psychological explanation and an illuminating reference to
Absalom and Achitophel.

How easy is it [he writes] [4] to call rogue and villain and that
wittily. But how hard to make a man appear a fool, a blockhead, or
a knave without using any of those opprobrious terms! . . . Neither
is it true that this fineness of raillery is offensive. A witty man is
tickled while he is hurt in this manner, and a fool feels it not. The
occasion of an offence may possibly be given but he cannot take
it. . . . The character of Zimri in my *Absalom* is, in my opinion,
worth the whole poem; it is not bloody, but it is ridiculous enough;
and he for whom it was intended, was too witty to resent it as an
injury. . . . I avoided the mention of great crimes and applied myself

[1] W. P. Ker, *op. cit.* ii. 15 ff.   [2] *Inst. Orat.* x. 1, 93.
[3] W. P. Ker, *op. cit.* ii. 92.   [4] *ibid.*

to the representing of blindsides and little extravagancies; to which, the wittier a man is, he is generally the more obnoxious (i.e. liable).

Such then is Dryden's defence of the Horatian method of satire. Juvenal's method he describes as that of *ense rescindendum* (i.e. a slashing sword), that of Horace as a pleasant cure; but the latter, he asserts, is the more difficult, a method requiring genius, yet after all the best for improving manners. It was a conception previously entertained by the 12th-Century Nigel Wireker in his *Speculum Stultorum*, when he stated that 'many are the diseases that yield more readily to unguents than to caustic'; and the theory, supported by more than one 17th-Century writer, was well illustrated by Dryden in his delightful strictures on Milbourne and Blackmore in his *Preface to the Fables*.

To this general advice Dryden adds further details concerning the most effective methods of modern satire; and, coming as they did from the master-satirist of the period, they are of some significance. In the first place he regards satire as 'a species of heroic poetry',[1] the models for which were to be found among the ancients. A satirical poem, he states, should in general treat of one main theme, with one particular moral, a rule observed by Persius and later on by Boileau;[2] otherwise, the most effective method was that of Horace, 'the sharp, well-mannered way of laughing a folly out of countenance'. On the most suitable verse-form he has rather more to say. He rejects, for instance, the burlesque eight-syllabled verse of Butler's *Hudibras* as 'a little instrument, though used by a great master'. But its quick returns of rhyme, he maintains, had certain disadvantages. They detracted from the dignity of the style, made the poet giddy with turning in too small a compass, and distracted the reader's attention 'from the thought to the close'. Moreover, its double rhyme also was out of keeping with serious satire; for it raised 'a grin with the excrescence of a word of two or three syllables in the close', thus[3] supplying but 'a boyish kind of pleasure'. On the other hand the appropriate line for satire was undoubtedly the English heroic, in which thought found ample room, and which allowed of those admirable turns of words and thoughts characteristic of the noblest verse. In short, what he desires for satire are the majesty of heroic poetry, the venom of the burlesque, and the dignity and delicacy seen in Boileau's satires.

Not less significant are his remarks on methods of translation, a subject to which attention had previously been drawn by

[1] W. P. Ker. *op. cit.* ii. 108.   [2] *ibid.* ii. 102 ff.   [3] *ibid.* ii. 106.

d'Ablancourt and others in France, and by Denham and Roscommon in England. In his *Preface to the Translation of Ovid's Epistles* (1680) Dryden presented his main ideas on the problem, though he also alluded to the matter elsewhere in later critical writings. To begin with, he distinguishes between three methods of translating an ancient author.[1] First, there was metaphrase, which stood for a literal rendering as seen in Jonson's version of Horace's *Ars Poetica*; there was also paraphrase, a freer rendering in which the sense of the original was faithfully retained, as in Waller's version of the *Aeneid*; and again, there was 'imitation', in which an original was freely adapted, with words and sense changed, as in Cowley's translation of Pindar's *Odes*. With metaphrase, in the first place, Dryden will have nothing to do. 'Too faithfully', he remarks, 'is too pedantically'; and he quotes Denham[2] in his support. Moreover, he adds, Latin, with its own particular idioms, often expresses compendiously in a single word what modern languages cannot convey in several; and he therefore refuses to recognize this word-for-word treatment, since it resulted in obscurity and lack of grace, and was like 'dancing on ropes with fettered legs'. Nor again has he any use for 'imitation', by which an ancient work was completely transformed, with modern equivalents substituted for ancient names, manners and the like. 'This', he remarks, 'is to create something new, not to represent the original.' What he thus recommends is the method of paraphrase as the only way of translating poetry from one language into another, retaining at the same time the substance and spirit of the original.

But this method, Dryden confesses, makes considerable demands on the translator; and he enlarges further on the art of translating poetry.[3] For one thing, the translator, he states, must have a keen sense of words, a mastery of his own, as well as the poet's, language. He must also possess a poet's sensibility, the power of appreciating the music of verse and beauties of expression. For it was only by such aids that his real task could be performed, that of faithfully reproducing not only the meaning but also the distinctive qualities of the original. And in this process, added Dryden, many difficulties presented themselves. Every language, for instance, had its own qualities, and what was beautiful in one was often 'barbarous' in another. Similarly, every poet had his peculiar characteristics—Virgil his compendiousness, Ovid his luxuriant fancy—and these qualities had

---

[1] W. P. Ker, *op. cit.* i. 237 ff.   [2] see pp. 80-1 *supra*.
[3] W. P. Ker, *op. cit.* i. 252 ff.

to be transferred from a synthetic language like Latin into English, a language of an analytical kind. The true aim of an English translator should therefore be to reproduce a poet's works so that 'if he were living, and an Englishman, the result would be such as he himself would probably have written'. His business, in short, was to reveal beauties hitherto unheeded by 'pedants or botching interpreters'. And here Dryden was denouncing those worthy but uninspired and uninspiring translators—the Holydays, the Ogilbys and others—who 'neither knew good verse nor loved it', and thus misrepresented ancient poetry to modern readers.

These then are the main aspects of literature and literary forms on which Dryden commented during this latter period; and many of his comments are of lasting value, thus marking a notable advance on his earlier theorizing. Equally notable however is the light he throws on the principles of literary judgment and the practice of the same. By his enlightened doctrine, his literary appreciations and his critical methods he enabled readers not only to perceive fresh beauties in literature, but also to understand more clearly excellences which they had hitherto but vaguely valued; and these after all are the supreme tasks of criticism in all the ages.

Not least valuable, to begin with, was his inculcation of a larger and more generous conception of the judicial side of criticism, and of the principles which should govern its most fruitful exercise. This was occasioned primarily by the glaring shortcomings and delinquencies of contemporary critics, but also by his reading of Boileau's *Longinus* as well. Again and again he refers with feeling to the 'illiterate, censorious detractors' of his day; and reminds his readers that 'ill writers are generally the sharpest censors', and that 'the corruption of a poet is the generation of a critic'.[1] He also recalls that in antiquity critics had defended poets against the assaults of Zoilus; whereas in his own day poets had become the butts of critical ignorance, prejudice and jealousy. Some there were, he stated, who commended Shakespeare in order to disparage contemporary poets, while others condemned outright all English writers. There were also the lay bishops or reformers of the stage, 'incompetent judges of character, religion, poetry and good sense';[2] or again *les petits esprits*, who appealed to the populace with their outrageous tastes;[3] as well as a galaxy of 'warm young men', with knowledge but no adequate judgment,

[1] W. P. Ker, *op. cit.* ii. 2.   [2] *ibid.* ii. 6.   [3] *ibid.* ii. 223 ff.

who preferred Statius, for instance, to Virgil. Such then is
Dryden's estimate of the reigning critics; though he also recognizes the existence of some of the better sort, the judicious
critics, gifted with true understanding and with 'a certain
magnetism in their judgment which attracted others to their
sense'.[1] It was to improve this situation that Dryden remon-
strated; and if he was not the first (nor yet the last) to complain
of critical abuses, he was at any rate the first to comment
constructively and to point to a better way.

Of the general principles expounded by Dryden in this connexion none was more fundamental than that which laid it down
that the business of criticism was not mainly that of finding
fault, despite the policing duties so arrogantly prescribed by
Rymer. Fresh from his reading of Boileau's *Longinus*, with its
revelation of the positive merits of Homer and others, Dryden
boldly declares that 'criticism, as first instituted by Aristotle,
was a process . . . of noting those excellencies which should
delight a reasonable reader',[2] and that these matters should be
the first concern of the critic. Then, too, from the same source
he had learnt that it was these excellences that ultimately determined the value of a literary work; and that flawless mediocrity
or mere correctness was not enough. The sublime genius, he
explains,[3] that soars to great heights but sometimes errs was
to be preferred to 'the middling or indifferent one that makes
few faults but seldom or never rises to any excellence'. 'Longinus', he recalls, had dilated at some length on the supreme
grandeur of Homer as against the uninspired correctness of
Apollonius;[4] and Homer, he reminded his readers, had nodded
at times, while Virgil was not exempt from occasional lapses.
Still more far-reaching perhaps was yet another basic truth
derived from 'Longinus', when he prescribes as the final criterion
of all great literature the test of time,[5] namely, *quod semper,
quod ubique, quod ab omnibus.* 'Generally to have pleased and
through all ages', he writes, 'must bear the force of universal
tradition'; and from the unanimity of that tribunal, he argues,
there could be no appeal, since 'those things which delight all
ages must have been an imitation of Nature'. It was an important pronouncement to which he refers incidentally elsewhere

---

[1] W. P. Ker, *op. cit.* ii. 225.
[2] *ibid.* i. 179: cf. Horace, *A.P.* 351, and Rapin, *Comparaisons*, i.
p. 145.
[3] *ibid.* i. 180.   [4] *On the Sublime*, c. 33.
[5] W. P. Ker, *op. cit.* i, 183–4; cf. *On the Sublime* c. 7. 4.

in his works; and this permanence of appeal still remains the final test of all great literature.

Apart from this Dryden has some illuminating suggestions of his own to offer. In one place, for instance, he notes the value of an acquaintance with earlier masterpieces of art[1] in any attempt at forming literary judgment; while elsewhere he states with greater emphasis that some amount of psychological insight into 'the causes and resorts of that which moves pleasure in a reader'[2] was also helpful. It was therefore necessary 'to sound the depths of all the passions, what they are in themselves and how they are to be provoked'; and this, he adds, was the method employed by Aristotle who in his *Poetics* had considered how the great Greek dramatists had appealed to the emotions. Equally significant, however, was his warning that hasty judgments in connexion with the best poetry were misleading.

A judicious poem [he states],[3] which at its first appearance gains no more upon the world than to be just received, . . . insinuates itself by insensible degrees into the liking of the reader; the more he studies it the more it grows upon him; every time he takes it up he discovers some new graces in it. And whereas poems, which are produced by the vigour of imagination (i.e. fancy) only, have a gloss upon them at the first, which time wears off, the works of judgment are like the diamond, the more they are polished the more lustre they receive. Such is the difference between Virgil's *Aeneid* and Marino's *Adone*.

It was one of Dryden's most penetrating remarks, and was an anticipation of the later 19th-Century pronouncement that every new poet has to create the taste by which his work is to be appreciated.

In addition, of interest is his further contention that true judgment in poetry, as also in painting, 'takes a view of the whole together, whether it be good or not'.[4] So that petty fault-finding was to be avoided, since ''tis a sign that malice is hard driven when it is forced to lay hold on a word or syllable'. Finally he suggests that in estimating literary values the influence of preceding writers might be taken into account. Thus 'Milton', he notes,[5] 'was the poetical son of Spenser and Mr. Waller of Fairfax; for we have our lineal descents and clans as well as other families'. Here Dryden sees more clearly than Langbaine the significance of earlier literary influences and borrowings. To Langbaine they had been but 'petty larcenies',

---

[1] W. P. Ker, *op. cit.* ii. 115.   [2] *ibid.* i. 183.
[3] *ibid.* ii. 225.   [4] *ibid.* i. 264.   [5] *ibid.* ii. 247.

on the part of the later writers; to Dryden they were of an active
and more subtle character. Great writers, he explained, 'whet
and cultivate one another'; and again, 'Spenser more than once
insinuates that the soul of Chaucer was transfused into his
body; . . . Milton has acknowledged to me that Spenser was his
original'.

But while a wider and more generous conception of the
judicial side of criticism emerges from these varied pronouncements of Dryden, not less significant are his actual appreciations
of literature in the concrete, of earlier native, as well as ancient,
literature; and among the former he includes three of the greatest
of English poets, Shakespeare, Milton and Chaucer. With Shakespeare, to begin with, he had dealt during his earlier period in
general terms, praising in glowing language his unrivalled genius,
his unlaboured art, his power of characterization, while lamenting his bombast and obscurities, his Janus-like character, his
low expressions, and the unevenness of his style; though he also
hints at his unique quality, stating that

> Shakespeare's magic could not copied be,
> Within that circle none durst walk but he.[1]

In this later period, however, his treatment is of a more detailed
and inward kind and is mainly concerned with characterization.
He still finds difficulties in Shakespeare's expression, though he
now ascribes its defects to the fury of the poet's fancy, and
besides shrewdly suggesting that the Player's speech in *Hamlet*
was no work of Shakespeare's originally[2] he concedes that in his
later plays he had 'worn off somewhat of the rust'.[3] Moreover,
his admiration for Shakespeare is still unbounded; and to
that admiration he gives expression by a comparison with the
popular Fletcher, in which Shakespeare's prolific and well-
drawn characters are once more extolled, whereas Fletcher is
described as 'a limb of Shakespeare', his characters as 'pictures
shown you in the twilight'.[4]

It is in his more detailed appreciation of Shakespeare's art
that an advance in critical insight and method now becomes
perceptible, as when for instance he submits to the test of
emotional values the quarrel scene in *Julius Caesar* and the
description of the king's entry into London in *Richard II*.[5] The
former he commends on account of its natural emotions naturally expressed; the latter as a moving scene, almost unparalleled

---

[1] Prol. to *The Tempest* (1670).   [2] W. P. Ker, *op. cit.* i. 225.
[3] *ibid*. i. 203.   [4] *ibid*. i. 217, 228.   [5] *ibid*. i. 226.

in its poignancy. And while this increased inwardness had previously been displayed in his appreciation of the complex and
rounded character of Falstaff, it is still more markedly illustrated in the light he now sheds on the character of Caliban.[1]
He had already claimed for poetry, in accordance with Aristotle's teaching, the liberty of describing things outside the
realm of Nature, provided they were founded on popular belief;
and Caliban, he now states, is represented as an unnatural and
impossible monster, 'a species in himself, begotten by an incubus
on a witch'. Yet this, he points out, 'is not wholly beyond the
bounds of credibility, at least the vulgar believe it'; and that
being so, the fiction is of a defensible kind. Moreover, this impossible monster, he adds, has been rendered probable by
Shakespeare's artistic treatment. To the monster, it is explained,
have been given a form, a language and a character, all in keeping with his supposed origin. Thus his ugly form is the product
of unnatural lust; his language is as 'hobgoblin' as his form; and
as for his character, it is a complex made up of the discontents,
the malice and wickedness associated with witch and devil,
together with 'the dejectedness of a slave and the ignorance
of one bred up on a desert island'. In other words, he is represented as an intelligible personality, the product of circumstances, distinct from all other beings; and in presenting him
in this coherent and convincing fashion Shakespeare is said to
have created an illusion of truth to Nature in accordance with
the art of 'telling lies skilfully'.[2] Such then is Dryden's masterly
interpretation of Caliban's character; and here he is applying yet another of Aristotle's principles, namely, that an im-
possibility made plausible is preferable in art to a possibility
presented in unconvincing fashion.[3]

Then, too, Dryden has something to say on Milton's great
epic; and already in 1677 he categorically declares *Paradise Lost*
to be 'one of the greatest, most noble and most sublime' of
modern poems.[4] And this admiration for its lofty thought, its
grandeur of expression, and its happy assimilation of the manner
of Homer and the elegancies of Virgil, remained with him until
late in his career. At the same time there is some inconsistency
in his actual judgments, occasioned probably by Rymer's threat
in 1678 to undertake some reflexions on that work and 'to
assert rhyme against the poet's slender sophistry'.[5] At any rate,

[1] W. P. Ker, *op. cit.* i. 219–20.   [2] Aristotle, *Poetics*, 1460 a, 19.
[3] *ibid.* 1460 a, 26–7.   [4] W. P. Ker, *op. cit.* i. 179.
[5] Spingarn, *op. cit.* ii. 208.

some fifteen years later, when Rymer was still 'promising the
world a critique' on Milton, Dryden deferentially hopes that
although that trenchant critic might find it necessary to condemn *Paradise Lost* as a heroic poem, he would at least take
cognizance of the merits already mentioned; and it is noteworthy that Dryden now finds it politic to temper his admiration for the poem. 'It is as much commendation as a man can
bear', he writes, 'to own him excellent; all beyond is idolatry.'
And he detects now in Milton's treatment certain defects that
called for notice. Thus Milton's theme, he suggests, is unsuitable, in that, treating of 'the losing of our happiness', its ending
is 'not prosperous like that of all other epics'.[1] Or again, the epic
hero is the Devil, not Adam. The knight has been foiled by the
giant and has been 'driven out of his stronghold to wander
through the world with his lady errant'.[2] Moreover, human
interest is said to be lacking, in view of the many supernatural
beings presented as opposed to the two single mortals. Nor is
this all, for in Milton's verses Dryden now discovers many
uninspired 'flats of thought among his elevations', when the
poet 'creeps along sometimes for a hundred lines at a time';
though this defect he attributes later to the poet's attempt to
follow faithfully his Scriptural text. In addition, he maintains,
something is lost owing to the absence of elegant turns on words
or thoughts;[3] archaisms, too, are overdone, though these, he
grants, may on occasion be effectively revived; and finally, he
cannot approve of his use of blank verse,[4] though he recalls
that Hannibal Caro (1507–66) and other Italians had used it.
Milton, he suggests, had discarded rhyme because 'it was not his
talent',—a fact which, Dryden strangely enough asserted, had
been proved by his early poems, in which the rhymes had
always been 'constrained and forced'. In all these comments
there is much that suggests a craven concession made for the
time being to Rymer's standards and methods. A few years later
he reverses his judgment concerning blank verse;[5] and despite
his various strictures and in view of his earlier pronouncement
on the grandeur of epic (and Milton's) style, it is not fanciful to
suppose that his first impressions of *Paradise Lost* were those
that remained with him to the end.

His finest piece of judicial criticism, however, is to be found
in his appreciation of Chaucer, an effort remarkable at this date
for its keen insight into the merits of a medieval poet. His

---

[1] W. P. Ker, *op cit.* ii. 29.   [2] *ibid.* ii. 165.
[3] *ibid.* ii. 109.   [4] *ibid.* ii. 29–30.   [5] *ibid.* ii. 220–1.

immediate aim was to introduce to his readers the authors of his *Fables*. But fired with enthusiasm for Chaucer's performance he daringly claims for him the right to rank with well-established classics, such as Ovid and Boccaccio; and his *Preface* with all its ramblings becomes little more than a masterly analysis of Chaucer's achievement. Of interest, in the first place, are the comparisons he institutes between Chaucer and those earlier masters, by way of establishing his claim. It was significant, he notes to begin with, that Ovid had written at the close of a golden age, Chaucer in the dawn of English letters; but while both had written easily and clearly, looking, one to the Greeks, the other to Italians, for their subject-matter, Chaucer alone had improved on his borrowed material, and had besides on occasion created something of his own.[1] Apart from this, Chaucer's characterization was more life-like and 'set in a better light' than that of Ovid; and if Ovid's diction was inevitably more refined than that of Chaucer, yet his style in general was disfigured by unnatural conceits and word-jingles, by glittering trifles and untimely wit, from which Chaucer was free. As for Boccaccio,[2] here Dryden points out that he like Chaucer had related amusing stories in a pleasing familiar style; but in more serious poetry Chaucer had clearly excelled. Moreover, by his treatment, Chaucer had improved on material borrowed from Boccaccio, despite his handicap of writing in verse, for Boccaccio's use of prose normally allowed greater freedom of thought. So that here again, argued Dryden, 'our countryman carries weight and yet wins the race at disadvantage'. He even suggests in his enthusiasm, that *The Knight's Tale*, a story of the epic kind, was 'not much inferior to the *Iliad* or the *Aeneid*'.

Having thus submitted a *prima facie* case on behalf of Chaucer, Dryden proceeds to substantiate his claim by a detailed examination of the poet's actual work; and in so doing he reveals his own critical genius, despite some blind spots which later scholarship was to remove. His inaccuracies, for instance, with regard to the sources of *Troilus and Criseyde* and *The Knight's Tale*[3] are not surprising at this date; and they do not invalidate his main argument. Rather more serious was his failure to recognize the full flavour and beauty of Chaucer's old-fashioned language, which was calculated to appeal to others than 'old Saxon friends' and with something more than 'a reasonable veneration for antiquity'. To him Chaucer was con-

---

[1] W. P. Ker, *op. cit.* ii. 254 ff.   [2] *ibid.* ii. 268 ff.
[3] cf. his reference to the 'tragedy of *Queen Gorboduc*' (i. 5).

fessedly 'a rough diamond'[1] who 'must first be polished ere he shines'. Hence his refining process by means of translation and the efforts of those others who at this date were submitting Latin versions of the old poet. 'Words', so Dryden suggests,[2] 'are not like landmarks, so sacred as never to be removed.' Yet from Chaucer so treated, whether in ancient or modern dress, something vital had necessarily vanished. And similarly defective is his appreciation of Chaucer's verse,[3] which, he confessed, lacked harmony to his ear, though doubtless musical enough to earlier generations. That it was an improvement on Gower and Lydgate, and that there was in it 'the rude sweetness of a Scotch tune', this much he is prepared to allow. But that it was 'correct', with ten syllables in each line, this he cannot concede, since some verses were palpably 'lame for want of half a foot'. This he maintains, in spite of Speght's explanation of 1597,[4] rashly adding that no changes of pronunciation could possibly account for this irregularity; and here he shares in the contemporary view illustrated by Waller's lines:[5]

> Chaucer his sense can only boast;
> The glory of his numbers lost.
> Years have defac'd his matchless strain,
> And yet he did not sing in vain.

It was left for Gray and Tyrwhitt later to clear up the mistake; and meanwhile Dryden is content to recall that Chaucer after all had 'lived in the infancy of our poetry'.

It is when he deals with other aspects of Chaucer's work that Dryden's keen sense of aesthetic qualities becomes really apparent, in his realization, not only of sundry artistic effects, but above all in the outstanding merits of Chaucer's character-drawing. What he sets out to do is to convince his contemporaries that Chaucer, so far from being merely 'our English Ennius' or a 'dry old-fashioned wit not worth reviving', was in reality a great artist, as well as 'a perpetual fountain of good sense'. To begin with, he notes the unaffected naturalness of all Chaucer's work. He is said 'to follow Nature everywhere', free from all affectation, and Dryden happily recalls in this connexion Martial's distinction between *poeta* and *nimis poeta*.[6]

---

[1] W. P. Ker, *op. cit.*, ii. 265.
[2] *ibid*. ii. 267.   [3] *ibid*. ii. 258–9.
[4] See Atkins, *Eng. Lit. Crit.: the Renascence*, p. 291.
[5] *Of English Verse*.
[6] W. P. Ker. *op. cit.* ii. 258: cf. Martial, *Epig.* iii. 44.

Moreover as a specific example of this natural treatment he selects Chaucer's dignified and pathetic handling of Arcite on his death-bed, and contrasts it with Ovid's elaborate 'wit' in his account of the death-agony of Narcissus. Then, too, he rightly detects in Chaucer's narrative methods a general observance of the fundamental law that it is the business of the artist to select. 'As he knew what to say', observes Dryden, 'so he knows when to leave off',—a quality illustrated for instance by his frequent use of such phrases as 'shortly for to tellen' and the like. It was an artistic quality, adds Dryden, attained by few contemporary writers, though in point of fact emphasized by many critics.[1] And he stresses once again its importance as a basic literary principle in stating that 'an author is not to write all he can but only all he ought'.[2]

Such instances of critical insight are, however, overshadowed by Dryden's acute and illuminating appreciation of Chaucer's character-drawing, which represents something rare and of permanent value in English criticism. In the first place he points out the vivid and life-like effects of the characters depicted in the *Canterbury Tales*.

I see ... all the pilgrims ... [he writes],[3] their humours, their features, and the very dress as distinctly as if I had supped with them at the *Tabard* in Southwark.

And the characters thus drawn are further described as of a comprehensive kind, embracing the manners and distinctive qualities of the whole English nation in his day; 'not one', adds Dryden, 'has escaped him'. Moreover each character is said to represent a single individuality, easily distinguished from all others in disposition and outward appearance; and at the same time fine shades of character are also clearly discriminated. Serious characters, such as the Knight and Parson, are serious in different ways; low characters like the Miller and Reeve stand for different brands of ribaldry; while 'the mincing Prioress' and the 'broad-speaking, gap-toothed Wife of Bath' are poles asunder. Then too, by way of increasing the illusion of truth, to all are given qualities appropriate to their respective callings, their breeding and social conditions; and, as Dryden shrewdly remarks, the tales they tell are all in keeping with their different

---

[1] cf. Rapin, *Réflex. sur la Poétique*, I. ch. xvi: 'c'est un grand talent que de ne pas dire tout ce qu'on pense et de laisser penser aux autres ce qu'il faut.'

[2] W. P. Ker, *op. cit.* ii. 265. [3] *ibid.* ii. 255 ff.

personalities. In this way realistic and convincing portraits of
14th-Century individuals had been supplied; so that we have
'our forefathers . . . all before us as they were in Chaucer's
day'.

Yet in recalling to life his picturesque medieval community,
Chaucer, as Dryden pointed out, accomplished something more
than even this; and this he did in giving to his portraits a
general and universal significance. The essential qualities of the
pilgrims were said to be confined to no one age; they were to be
found in 17th-Century England, though attached to other
beings than monks and friars, Lady Abbesses and nuns. The
truth was, as Dryden stated, that 'mankind is ever the same,
and nothing is lost out of Nature though everything is altered';
so that to depict truly is to depict for all time. It was this
blending of the particular with the universal, the evanescent
with the permanent, that had gone to the successful creation of
the characters in *Absalom and Achitophel*; and Dryden now
detects the same method in Chaucer's practice. To Dryden's
generation this masterly analysis of Chaucer's character-drawing must have come as a revelation of some of the mysteries of
art; and to it later ages have added little or nothing that is
essential.

Less significant perhaps, yet still of interest, are Dryden's
scattered judgments on other literary works, notably those of
Spenser, Donne and Cowley. Concerned at this later date with
the development of the epic, he considers Spenser in the first
place as a possible model, but finds him defective, while acknowledging his great genius and the unrivalled quality of his musical
verse.[1] Thus the *Faërie Queene*, he points out, lacked unity of
action, as well as a true epic hero; though Prince Arthur, he
recognizes, 'who succours the rest when they are in distress',
might possibly make up for that defect. Other difficulties, however, were its obsolete diction and ill-chosen stanza; and when
he adds that 'Spenser only wanted to have read the rules of
Bossu',[2] it is evident that the tests he has in mind are those
of the neo-classical kind. On Donne, however, his remarks are
of interest as throwing light on the current estimate of that poet
during the latter half of the 17th Century; and in them some
amount of perplexity is apparent. He is said to possess 'a talent
for satire', skill, too, in the expression of 'deep thoughts in
common language'.[3] On the other hand his poetry is described
as lacking in charm, his versification as faulty with rough

[1] W. P. Ker. *op. cit.* ii. 28.   [2] *ibid.* ii. 220.   [3] *ibid.* i. 52; ii. 102.

cadences; and Dryden's conclusion is that 'if nowadays we are not so great wits (i.e. scholars) as Donne, yet certainly we are better poets'. The main cause ascribed by Dryden for these defects is, however, of considerable interest. 'Donne', he disparagingly states, 'affects the metaphysics',[1] not only in his satires but also in his love-poems, where 'nice speculations of philosophy' were out of place and where charm alone was needed. This explanation, suggested by Donne's psychological treatment and his use of medieval Scholasticism, was subsequently adopted by Dr. Johnson, who incidentally gave currency to a new term in the critical vocabulary. As yet, however, apart from an acknowledgment of his intricate thought, his masculine and colloquial expression, the true merits of Donne's work were far from being understood; and greater insight had previously been shown by Thomas Carew in his appreciation of that poet in his *Elegy* of 1640. In addition, Dryden's casual comment on Cowley is also worthy of note, as marking the decline of his popularity. Writing in his last years Dryden explains that the decline was due to Cowley's excessive indulgence in far-fetched fancies, especially in his *Mistress*, into which he had 'swept like a drag-net conceits great and small'.[2] It was a lack of judgment on the part of one who was otherwise a great poet; and his works, added Dryden, were no longer in great demand.

No account of Dryden as a critic, however, would be adequate without some mention of his judgments on ancient literature, on Virgil and the Roman satirists in particular, though here he owed not a little to the guidance of Segrais and Dacier. At the same time he rightly claims to have added 'something of his own'; and his remarks are of value as further illustrating his wide outlook, his literary doctrines and critical acumen. The causes which led to his concern with ancient literature have already been mentioned, as being primarily due to the vicious attacks of the moderns in France; and it is in reply to Perrault and others that he undertakes, first, a defence of Virgil as an epic poet. The main charges brought against Virgil were five in number: a worthless moral, a defective hero, errors in the narrative, obvious borrowings, and a lavish use of similes; and with these Dryden deals, contemptuously ignoring other pedantic 'cavils of grammarians'.

With regard to Virgil's moral,[3] in the first place, he concedes that in urging the necessity for unity in a state Homer had

---

[1] W. P. Ker, *op. cit.* ii. 19.   [2] *ibid.* ii. 258.   [3] *ibid.* ii. 166 ff.

supplied the nobler teaching; yet Virgil, he held, in inculcating loyalty to the reigning Augustus as the urgent need of his time had also provided wise counsel. Then, again, Aeneas was decried as a hero in whom piety and the softer virtues were more conspicuous than his valour, as a sort of 'St. Swithin hero, always raining';[1] and one, besides, who was false in love. To these charges Dryden replies that there was no evidence of cowardice on the part of Aeneas, that 'more could not be expected from an Amadis or a Sir Lancelot'; and as for the charge of faithlessness in love, his treatment of Dido had been dictated by Jupiter himself. Rather more weighty was the complaint that in representing the Trojan Aeneas and Dido as contemporaries Virgil had perpetrated a glaring anachronism; and this calls forth from Dryden a striking pronouncement. He first recalls that the point had been humorously treated by an imitator of Boccalini's *Ragguagli di Parnasso* (1612), when Virgil was graciously pardoned by Apollo for his error, on the understanding that no future poet 'should presume to make a lady die for love two hundred years before her birth'.[2] And then Dryden submits Segrais's argument in defence, assigning to Virgil as the original law-giver a dispensing power which freed him from a slavish observance of orthodox law. 'Chronology at best', states Dryden, 'is but a cob-web law, and Virgil broke through it with his weight.' Moreover, that poet, he explains, had chosen a remote and obscure period for imaginative treatment, and in violating historical truth he was merely superseding a 'mechanic rule of poetry', a rule not really fundamental. And then in support he recalls Aristotle's teaching that 'nothing is to be called a fault in poetry but what is against the art' (i.e. an artistic error);[3] so that a man might be a good poet without being 'an exact chronologer'. Well-known facts of history should not be contradicted; Hannibal, for instance, should not be made a contemporary of Alexander. But for the rest, provided the poet's fiction was pleasing and all of a piece, such departures from historical truth were fully justified; and such, added Dryden, is Virgil's episode of Dido and Aeneas, one of the beauties of the poem.

Furthermore there was the charge that Virgil had shown a lack of originality, having borrowed extensively from Homer, Apollonius and others. To this Dryden replies that such borrowed material—fables, descriptions, and the rest—were none

---

[1] W. P. Ker, *op. cit.* ii. 179 ff.   [2] *ibid.* ii. 193.
[3] *ibid.* ii. 194: cf. *Poetics*, 1460 b, 3.

other than the commonplaces of poetry, 'furnished from the magazine of Nature', and therefore material to which 'every poet hath as much right . . . as every man hath to air and water'.[1] The important point, he explained, was that Virgil's 'economy' (i.e. treatment) of such material was new and original; and 'it was one thing to copy and another thing to imitate from Nature'. Moreover, 'the poet who borrows nothing from others', he added, 'is yet to be born'. And, lastly, there was Virgil's use of long-tailed similes, which were said to distract attention from the main theme, 'pouring cold water into the cauldron when the business is to make it hot'.[2] Such usage, however, Dryden defends as contributing to that heightening of epic style to which he had previously called attention.[3] In the excitement of tragedy he allows that similes of any kind are out of place. But in the epic, which aimed primarily at arousing admiration or wonder, it was different; though even there, he granted, they could be overdone and abused. Yet Virgil, he maintained, had made a judicious use of his similes, introducing them 'not in the heat of action but generally when excitement is declining'. And explaining further the function of such similes he adds that when Virgil 'has warmed us in his descriptions, . . . then lest that warmth should languish, he renews it by some apt similitude which illustrates his object and yet palls not his audience'.

Apart from this defence of Virgil, however, Dryden has further remarks on Virgil and other ancient writers which are of interest as illustrating his critical standards and methods. In the first place the soundness of his critical taste is revealed by his appreciation of Virgil elsewhere, whom he commends, not for the observance of rules, but for his aesthetic effects which are discussed in some detail. He points for instance to Virgil's inimitable power of expression, his graceful diction, his admirable choice and placing of words. 'They must be read', he explains,[4] 'in order as they lie; the least breath discomposes them; and somewhat of their divinity is lost.' Then, too, there was the glory of his style, 'succinct and majestic', with its ever-varying rhythm, 'sounding the very thing . . . whose sense it bears',[5] a vivid contrast to that of Ovid who lacked variety and was 'always at the hand-gallop'. Moreover, his verse, Dryden points out, was free from conceits and crude hyperboles, so that 'he shines but glares not',—a highly significant tribute in Dryden's

---

[1] W. P. Ker, *op. cit.* ii. 197 ff. [2] *ibid.* ii. 202 ff.
[3] See p. 120 *supra*. [4] W. P. Ker, *op. cit.* ii. 215. [5] *ibid.* i. 255.

own day. And with his economy of words, it is added, he has the
virtue of 'leaving much to be imagined by the reader'.[1] With
regard to structural qualities Dryden has not much to say,
though he notes the particular effects of Virgil's use of epic
machinery. In this device he is said to have imitated Homer, but
with a difference. In general, so Dryden explains, his divinities
were not necessarily employed in performing supernatural functions, but in 'performing those things which might possibly
have been done without them'.[2] At the same time they were
also used to give plausibility to deeds otherwise incredible, and
'to soothe the vanity of the Romans' at finding the power of
their gods so visibly demonstrated.

In his appreciation of the Roman satirists the same aesthetic
treatment is visible, though here he makes use of other critical
methods. Among other aesthetic qualities, for instance, he notes
the crabbed, obscure style of Persius, the elegance and 'secret
happiness' (*curiosa felicitas*) of Horace, and the more vigorous
and masculine wit of Juvenal. Equally notable is the use he
makes of the comparative method as a means of revealing
characteristic qualities. It was a method that he had found
useful from the first; and its use was doubtless encouraged by
the appearance of Rapin's *Comparaisons* and other French
Parallèles. It was amply illustrated not only in the early *Essay
of Dramatic Poesy* but also in the later comparisons drawn
between French and English geniuses,[3] between Homer and
Virgil,[4] and Chaucer and Ovid. And now he clearly distinguishes
between the Stoic gravity and sincerity of Persius as a satirist,
the good-humoured treatment of folly in general at the hands
of Horace, and the savage handling of particular vices characteristic of Juvenal. More than this, however, he here makes
use of what he claims to be a new method of arriving at literary
judgment,[5] namely, by taking into account historical factors
and the conditions of the age. Thus Persius, he explains, living
under Nero, directed his attack against the lewdness of Nero's
court; and in like manner the satires of Horace and Juvenal
were conditioned by the ages in which they lived. Approached
from this angle, so Dryden maintained, Horace is seen to have
laboured under certain disadvantages. As a courtier in the
peaceful days of Augustus he had less scope for vigorous satire
and had to be content with ridiculing common follies and the
false opinions of philosophers; whereas Juvenal, on the other

[1] See Rapin's note, p. 137 *supra*. [2] W. P. Ker. *op. cit.* ii. 208.
[3] *ibid*. ii. 219. [4] *ibid*. ii. 251. [5] *ibid*. ii. 91.

hand, lived under Domitian and so had a larger field for satire, since gross vices then abounded and Roman liberty was at stake. Such comments were a welcome sign of the extension of critical methods and of a widening conception of the critical business.

These then were Dryden's main pronouncements on literary theory and his judgments on literature; and it now remains to attempt some estimate of his many-sided critical achievement. That his critical powers, considerable from the first, matured in due course, along with a widening of outlook, would seem evident from what has been said. Evident also are the facts that in output he had excelled all that had gone before; and that, despite his lack of system, his inconsistencies and digressions, he has something substantial to offer his own and later ages. It is not without its significance, for instance, that in his literary theorizing he recalled not a few of the seminal and lasting principles generated in antiquity; that poetry, for example, was not confined to factual truth, that there was an 'imitation' that looked to the great masters for inspiration rather than for rules, that too much 'filing' killed the spirit, or again, that grandeur of style was the glory of the epic, and that there existed yet another 'harmony of prose'. To these he added advice gleaned from his own experience. He decried bombast in the drama, for instance, conceits and 'false wit' in poetry, irrelevance and superfluity in prose; he called attention to the importance of dramatic characterization, whereas the ancient Chorus and the Unity of time he regarded as unnecessary features of English drama; and besides commending a subtler form of satire, he noted also the emotional values of literature in general, and the relations existing between poetry and one of the sister arts. Furthermore, and not least, he drew attention to the higher function of criticism, that is, the appreciation of positive literary excellences, and to the fact that time was the final test of literary values. He also illustrated his doctrine by revealing fresh 'beauties' in three of our greatest poets, and by making an effective use of the psychological, comparative and historical methods in forming literary judgments. It all marked an advance in critical activities, and opened up new possibilities in theorizing and judgment alike.

The advance thus made was due in some measure to contemporary French influences, to that of Corneille in his earlier period, to Rapin, Boileau's *Longinus* and Saint-Evremond in his later years; though equally apparent, if less fruitful, was the use he made of the works of Segrais, Le Bossu, Dacier and others. Nowhere, however, does Dryden's critical acumen stand out more clearly than in the discriminating use he makes of the several influences, and in the certainty with which he adopts what was most vital in their theories, at the same time 'adding something of his own'. He makes, for instance, no formal attempt to expound the details of their doctrines; and was less subservient than is sometimes supposed to the reigning neo-classical school. What on the other hand he assimilated were those influences which found a response in his own nature and temperament: the free critical spirit fostered by Corneille, 'Longinus' and Saint-Evremond, for instance, Aristotle's sane doctrine presented anew by Rapin and Dacier, but, above all, the inspiring outlook of 'Longinus' revived by Boileau.

Yet the secret of Dryden's greatness as a critic lay after all in himself, in that native sensibility which made him keenly alive to artistic values, capable also of a dispassionate psychological analysis of those values. What he found to admire in Shakespeare or Chaucer was based on no formal rules, but on his own instinctive reactions submitted to the test of Nature or reason, a test, it should be added, which to him represented something more than mere common sense or the prose understanding. The truth was that his judgment, at its best, both in theorizing and appreciating, was of a supra-rational kind. It sprang from an imaginative sympathy which soared beyond anything that the pure unaided intellect could discern. Firmly based on his own impressions, his appreciations were something more than the result of acute analysis and sound reasoning, though these too played their part in confirming the faith that was in him. They were rather the result of a synthetic process which viewed the effects observed with a critical insight akin to the creative vision, that detected in the multiplicity of those effects meaning and coherence, thus penetrating to the heart of things. In short, it is not too much to say that with Dryden in his psychological judgments the creative imagination was unconsciously at work, a century or more before the process itself had been realized and defined.

Nor was it merely this balance of feeling and reason that made Dryden so successful a critic. Much was also due to his manner of presentment, to the charm, the urbanity and liveliness with which he communicated his judgments, to the absence of pedantry, and to that clear and picturesque style which has given a host of arresting phrases and an unfading freshness to all he wrote. Then, too, there were his unfailing good sense, his skill in argument, his independent judgment and his quiet dignity in replying to hostile and malevolent critics. All these commend him to modern readers; as do also occasional suggestive thoughts such as, ' 'tis difficult to write justly on anything, but almost impossible in praise',[1] or again, 'anything . . . which a man speaks of himself . . . is still too much'.[2] Yet what gives to his work its distinguishing flavour is the personal note that is heard throughout. A man's character, it has been said, may often be judged from his asides; and the *obiter dicta* of a critic may give a clue to his profounder thought. Besides, an endearing human touch is supplied by Dryden's references to his own distressful circumstances, as towards the end the clouds gathered ominously around him. But when all is said what gives to his criticism its supreme value is that personal, irresistible quality which Gibbon later on ascribed to 'Longinus'. 'Longinus', he states, 'not only lays bare his own spiritual experiences, . . . but he does so in such a way and with such enthusiasm that he succeeds in communicating his feelings to others'; and this compelling treatment, this infectious praise of great literature, is characteristic of Dryden as well. Of this quality he himself was not unaware in the abstract; as when he saw in the best critics 'a certain magnetism in their judgments which attracted others to their sense'. His reputation as a critic therefore rests on sure and lasting foundations. In an age of transition and much confusion he set criticism on new and fruitful lines, pointing to other standards and methods than those commended by the French neo-classical school. And his work remains to-day as readable and suggestive as ever, the legacy of one of the greatest of English critics.

[1] W. P. Ker. *op. cit.* i. 249.   [2] *ibid.* ii. 80.

CHAPTER V

NEO-CLASSICISM CHALLENGED: DENNIS, ADDISON, POPE, SWIFT, WELSTED AND BLACKWELL

WITH the passing of the age of Dryden English criticism entered on a new phase, marked by a definite increase in both volume and scope; so that already in the opening decades of the 18th Century the main lines emerge along which criticism was to develop for the best part of that century. Hitherto French influence had been tentative, intermittent and partial; whereas after 1700 the teaching of Boileau, Rapin and Le Bossu, now viewed in clearer perspective, became yet more influential. In place of Dryden's occasional references to neo-classical rules and principles, and the more systematic but limited efforts of Mulgrave, Roscommon and others to expound certain aspects of the neo-classical creed, a maturer acquaintance with the works of French critics now brought about a general acceptance of their teaching, and neo-classicism was ostensibly recognized as the orthodox creed. At the same time it is important to note that from the first there were signs that such doctrines were not being passively or wholly adopted. With rare exceptions little more than perfunctory approval was given to the more rigid doctrines of that body of theory; while owing to the native dislike of abstract reasoning and systems as such, the neo-classical code was never fully deployed in England by representative critics. From the first Dryden's selective treatment, with a difference, persisted. Increasing value was attached to the more liberal theories submitted not only by 'Longinus', but also by Saint-Evremond, Bouhours, La Bruyère and the like; and their doctrines were now applied to practical uses and were accompanied by some independent thinking as well. In short, critical efforts were now devoted, not so much to the formulation of an adopted creed, or the discussion of specific questions, as to inquiring into the aims and methods of criticism in general, in furthering an appreciation of literature in the concrete, while signs of a distinct challenge to the whole basis of neo-classicism were now forthcoming.

For the renewed vitality of critical activities during these opening decades of the 18th Century there were many causes, both social and intellectual. Not least significant, for instance, was the new dignity accorded to men of letters for party services, a recognition that gave them greater assurance and freedom of thought, releasing them from subservience to the whims of patrons, and making of literature a lucrative career. And as a result, criticism now assumed a more varied and independent form, being no longer confined to explanatory Prefaces and the like. Then, too, for the expression of critical views fresh mediums had become available in the periodical literature inaugurated by *The Athenian Mercury* (1690–7), with its later developments; and with Jacob Tonson had appeared the first of the race of modern publishers. The clubs and coffee-houses, again, that now became fashionable, offered increased facilities for lively interchanges of views among wider circles; and whereas an addition to the reading public came with the rise of a prosperous and serious-minded middle class bent on culture, a marked increase in the volume and variety of the literary output offered wider scope for critical treatment.

Nor were there wanting influences of an intellectual kind. Apart from the reaction against the immorality of the Restoration period, a critical temper, for one thing, had been fostered by the current of rational thought generated by the works of Hobbes and Newton (1642–1727); while Locke (1633–1704) in the meantime had aroused fresh interest in psychological inquiries. Moreover, politics, theology and morality were all being subjected to rational scrutiny at the time; and literature could not well escape similar critical treatment. On more than one point, indeed, most contemporaries were agreed. It was felt, for instance, that the craze for Italian opera had a devastating effect on literary taste; that in the native literature there were glaring defects to be remedied, hidden beauties to be revealed; and, in addition, there was the conviction that criticism generally was in a bad way. For guidance in these matters there were available those French theorists who were generally acknowledged as arbiters of taste. But they were found to be at variance with the suggestive new theories and judgments of Dryden, as well as with the doctrines of 'Longinus', whose influence now for the first time became really operative in England. Under these conditions not only was fresh impetus given to critical inquiries but a new spirit and a new direction were imparted to literary studies. The all-absorbing object from now on became the solution of this discord; and in the varied attempts made at establishing sound critical principles and methods, a challenge to neo-classicism became inevitable and persisted for the best part of the century.

Of the critical works belonging to this opening period those of Gildon and Dennis first call for notice, as marking the transition from the 17th to the 18th Century. Admirers of Dryden in the preceding generation, they and their earlier works bear ample traces of his influence; whereas their later writings, being out of touch with the spirit of the new age, were subsequently denounced by Queen Anne's men in no uncertain terms. It cannot be said that the contributions of Charles Gildon (1665–1724), to begin with, are of any great intrinsic value. Little more than a literary hack, he writes on various subjects; but while his *Miscellaneous Letters and Essays* (1694) and his *Complete Art of Poetry* (1718) have some historical interest, his discussions in the years between on stage matters and *Robinson Crusoe*, and his revision of Langbaine's *English Dramatic Poets*, have but little to recommend them.

What is of interest in his *Miscellaneous Letters*, in the first place, are the liberal views he expounds in his defence of Dryden against Rymer and others. He maintains, for instance, as against Rymer, that the rules of Aristotle are not binding on modern poets;[1] he defends the use of love-themes in tragedy and in the verses of Cowley and Waller; and above all, he demands the observance of relative standards in literature. 'As in physic, so in poetry', he writes,[2] 'there must be a regard had to the clime, nature and customs of the people'; so that, so far, he is a clear opponent of the neo-classical school. A different story is, however, revealed in his *Complete Art of Poetry*; for there he has discarded his earlier views, and the work represents the most detailed statement of that creed made during this period.[3] Written in dialogue form, it was compiled to supplement the partial treatment of Edward Bysshe's *Art of English Poetry* (1702), which had dealt merely with prosody, and that in mechanical fashion; and Gildon now reproduces the strict teaching of neo-classical theorists, with their concern for the rules and the greater and lesser 'kinds' of poetry.

In his treatment nothing is more characteristic than his insistence on the need for rules as conducing to order and harmony. For one thing, he attempts to meet all the current objections to that doctrine. Homer's work, he contends, though ostensibly based on no rules, was nevertheless the result of

[1] Durham, *Critical Essays of the 18th Century*, p. 17.
[2] *ibid*. p. 4.   [3] *ibid*. pp. 18 ff.

rules of his own devising. Besides, what pleased in Athens might well seem dull to London audiences; yet the taste of the town, he observes, was not necessarily final. Or again, there was Temple's condemnation of rules for poetry. Yet here, Gildon maintained, that critic was only contradicting himself; for elsewhere he too demanded some knowledge of art. Apart from this, Gildon, in defence of the rules, sees fit to decry Shakespeare's achievement. That dramatist, he pontifically explains, is great in nothing but what is according to the rules. Otherwise men of judgment, he adds, see nothing in his works either great or judicious, nothing but absurdities; and as for Shakespeare's popularity, that he ascribes to the ignorance of his audiences. The truth was that, according to Gildon, the one hope for poetry lay along neo-classical lines; and innovations like those of Lope de Vega and Corneille were absurd and futile. Built up by French critics on the findings of Aristotle, the greatest of philosophers, and consisting of rules drawn from the great literature of Greece, that system, he held, was firmly based on Nature, reason and the practice of the ancients, while its effects were seen in the best works of ancients and moderns alike. This then was the main gist of Gildon's manifesto; and with its crude, dogmatic pronouncements it stands practically alone in the theorizing of the time.

Rather more, however, must be said for the critical works of John Dennis (1657–1734), that formidable, heavy-handed critic who, respected, then feared and derided during his lifetime, has since received less than justice from later historians. In his early years as one of the 'young fry' who paid court to Dryden at Will's, his first efforts, like those of Gildon, were devoted to championing the views of the master against divers assailants; and in quick succession there appeared his readable *Impartial Critic* (1693), consisting of five dialogues replying to various points raised in Rymer's *Short View of Tragedy*; also his *Remarks on Blackmore's Prince Arthur* (1696), censuring Blackmore for his inadequate observance of Bossu's rules; and, again, his pamphlet *On the Usefulness of the Stage* (1698), a reply to Collier's savagery, in which he conceded Collier's right to attack abuses but not the stage itself. In the next ten years or so his more original thinking was done; and in his *Advancement and Reformation of Modern Poetry* (1701), his *Large Account of Taste in Poetry* (1702), and his *Grounds of Criticism in Poetry* (1704) he submits his real message to his age, namely, the need for an impassioned poetry, fired by religious 'enthusiasm'. The one other critical work belonging to this his most fruitful period was his *Essay on the Genius and Writings of Shakespeare*[1] (1711): after which troubles began to accumulate for one who had previously been hailed as 'the critic'. Subsequently until his death in 1734 he became embroiled in unseemly quarrels with Pope, Addison and others. Devoid of all sympathy with the new generation of writers and embittered by lack of recognition from any quarter, he developed the character of a pugnacious and virulent Zoilus, which has since diminished his stature in the eyes of posterity. Not that these latter years were wholly without useful work; for amidst all the captious fault-finding in his judgments on Pope's *Essay on Criticism*, Addison's *Cato* and the like, there are good things, as there are also in his original *Letters* published in 1721.

That the respect paid to Dennis in his earlier years was not altogether unwarranted is shown by his sensible outlook on current questions in his *Impartial Critic*, whereas of lesser importance are his treatment of Blackmore and his reply to Collier. In the spirited dialogues of the *Impartial Critic*, however, he effectively challenges the redoubtable Rymer, calling him to account on more than one score, and censuring his crude 'pleasantries' as being neither fitting nor convincing. In the first place he disputes Rymer's demand for the restoration of the Greek Chorus to revive the English stage. The Greek Chorus, he asserts,[2] was not adapted to a modern age, in which 'religion, climate and customs' were all different; and its success at Athens was no argument for its adoption on the English stage. It would be as absurd, he added (here alluding to another vexed question of the time), to suggest that love-themes should be banished from English plays because they were rare in Greek drama.[3] Then, too, the same independent attitude is revealed when he counters Rymer's sneer at Dryden's *Oedipus* (1679) because the tragic hero was not strictly in accordance with Aristotelian rules.[4] He concedes the departure from Aristotle's principles: yet Dryden, he maintains, by his 'extraordinary address' had nevertheless produced the necessary tragic effects. The rules of Aristotle, he recalled, were nothing but 'Nature and good sense reduced to a method';[5] and a judicious use of the rules is all that he recommends. In addition he denounces Rymer's inability to see in Shakespeare anything but faults;

[1] See pp. 244–5 *infra*.   [2] Spingarn, *op. cit.* iii. 148.
[3] *ibid*. iii. 151, 180.   [4] *ibid*. iii. 161.
[5] *ibid*. iii. 194.

and in order to illustrate that critic's imperfect judgment he queries by the way the soundness of his estimate of Waller. That Waller's verse with its wit, good sense and delicate turns of thought was worthy of praise, and that he had first accustomed English ears to the music of a just cadence, this he does not dispute. Yet elsewhere in Waller, he asserted, were improprieties of expression, much prose, and an abuse of epithets; and 'every epithet', he sagely remarks,[1] 'which does not add to the thought is to be looked upon as a botch'. These and other defects, he states, had passed unnoticed by Rymer, and his judgment was therefore of a one-sided kind. Blind to the faults of Waller, he was equally blind to the merits of Shakespeare. And on the necessity for balanced judgment, Dennis, it might be noted, lays some stress at this date. Pointing out that it was easier to find faults than to discern beauties, he explains that 'to do the first requires but common sense, but to do the last a man must have genius'; and again 'to expose a great man's faults without owning his excellences is altogether unjust'.[2]

Of an original kind, however, were the doctrines submitted in the three noteworthy publications that followed, in which he put forward new views concerning poetry in general, and English poetry in particular. He had previously given some indication of the lines along which his mind was working. 'The poet', he had stated,[3] 'is obliged to speak always to the heart', and therefore 'point and conceit and all they call wit is to be banished from true poetry.' And here he revealed the influence not only of 'Longinus', but also of French critics who had emphasized the emotional side of poetry. It was thus upon this emotional element that he now based his conception of poetry. That art he defined as 'an imitation of Nature by a pathetic (i.e. emotional) and numerous (i.e. rhythmical) speech';[4] and this idea he elsewhere elaborated when he explained that poetry excites emotion in order to delight and reform the mind, and that it performs that task more effectively than philosophy, since it stirs men's minds more powerfully. Moreover he analyses the nature of the emotional element.[5] There are 'vulgar' or ordinary emotions, he states, that are inspired by objects in actual life; there are also 'enthusiastic' or heightened emotions inspired by 'ideas in contemplation'; as

[1] Spingarn, *op. cit.* iii. 175.   [2] *ibid.* iii. 176.
[3] *Remarks on Blackmore's Prince Arthur*, p. 186.
[4] *Adv. and Reform. of Mod. Poetry*, p. 23.
[5] *Grounds of Criticism*, ch. iv.

when the sun is regarded, not merely as a shining orb, but as an 'image of divinity'. And it is this 'enthusiastic', this heightened and subtler, emotion that he assigns to poetry, a conception that forestalls, if it did not inspire, Wordsworth's idea of poetry as 'emotion recollected in tranquillity'.

With this as the basis of his theory he therefore contends that for the advancement of modern poetry it was necessary to endow it with greater emotional quality. And this, he suggests, would be best achieved by infusing religious 'enthusiasm' as the ancients had done.[1] For such a task, he argued, the Christian religion was specially suitable, since it reconciled the old conflict between reason and passion which dated from the fall of man; and this it did by seeking not to suppress the passions but to exalt them. Moreover religious poetry necessarily dealt with the loftiest conceptions of which man was capable and was therefore calculated to inspire the most sublime emotions. Thus does he appeal to reason in support of his theory; and if his references to the authority of Aristotle, Hermogenes and 'Longinus' are less convincing, his illustrations drawn from Milton are not without their effect, for it was his admiration for that poet that had largely inspired his theory. Least important in that theory is his advocacy of religious themes, the use of which had previously been attempted in France in connexion with the epic, but without success. What, however, is of value is the stress he lays on 'fine frenzy' as the indispensable emotional element in poetry, thereby running counter to the rationalistic tendencies of his age; and for this he was dubbed 'Sir Longinus' by angry opponents in his later entanglements.

Nor is it in this respect alone that Dennis gives evidence of independent thinking, though his theorizing, for the rest, is along neo-classical lines. Thus he recognizes the necessity for rules in poetry, as well as the existence of the 'kinds'; but his adherence to orthodox principles is by no means absolute. Rules are necessary, he states,[2] to ensure that rational order and harmony which ultimately govern the whole universe. But he notes also some irregularities in Nature which likewise contribute to the harmony of the whole; and the same, he maintains, holds good in poetry.[3] And this he illustrates from *Paradise Lost* with its 'new thought, new images, and an original spirit, all new and different from those of Homer and Virgil'. Then, too, his conceptions of the 'kinds' are in the main

---

[1] *Adv. and Reform. of Mod. Poetry, passim.*
[2] *ibid.* Part II.   [3] *ibid.* Epist. Dedic.

neo-classical, though here again he has certain views of his own. With regard to tragedy, for instance, he notes that an observ- ance of the Unities might strengthen the reasonableness of the action, and add clearness and grace;[1] but then, together with Dryden, he considers it to be a 'mechanic rule', not neces- sarily binding, but one to be set aside in order to obtain some greater artistic beauty.

Less convincing, however, are his arguments for the need of the observance of 'poetic justice' in both tragedy and the epic, a doctrine previously advanced by Rymer, and later condemned by Addison as 'a ridiculous doctrine of modern criticism, without foundation in Nature, reason, or the practice of the ancients'.[2] Dennis, however, asserts that if tragedy and the epic are to instruct with their fables and morals (as Bossu required) then 'poetic justice' was essential, for without it neither pity and terror in tragedy nor admiration in the epic could possibly be evoked.[3] It was a doctrine which led to many unfortunate tamperings with Shakespeare's plays at this date. On the remaining 'kinds' he has less to say, though not without its interest is his declaration in favour of the comedy of humours with its characters of low life as against the comedy of wit with its characters of a more artificial type;[4] or again, there is his preference for the earlier burlesque, as seen in *Hudibras*, as against the mock-heroic recently introduced by Boileau. This latter pronouncement may, however, have been inspired by his hatred of Pope, just as his disapproval of ancient ballads[5] was definitely his retort to Addison's praise of that literary form in the *Spectator* (40).

But it is owing to his judgments in the last phase of his career that he has since incurred the wrath of later historians. And in his various *Remarks* of that period there is much that is de- plorable, much scurrility, captious fault-finding and indulgence in personalities, inspired by hostility to the new school of *lit- térateurs*; so that he has come down as little more than 'a grumbling pedant' or 'a worthless Zoilus'. Thus Pope, for in- stance, is condemned as an enemy of religion who read into Homer Popish beliefs, while his verses are described as 'an eternal monotony' and 'his Pegasus, a battered Kentish jade'. Then, too, some of his judgments are lacking in insight and are of a misguided kind, as when he decries the delicate spirits in

---

[1] *Remarks on Cato.* [2] *Spectator*, 40.
[3] *Original Letters*, pp. 1, 10, 376.
[4] Durham, *op. cit.* p. 118. [5] *Original Letters*, p. 166.

The Rape of the Lock on the ground that they are pagan, devoid of allegorical significance, and not justly proportioned to the main theme. On the other hand he is not without his better moments when he gives evidence of sound views and submits some penetrating judgments. Like most of his contemporaries he complains of the degeneration of literary taste, which he attributes to the growing concern of his generation with politics and business affairs; and he has some interesting suggestions to offer concerning the improvement of critical methods and standards. He had previously pointed out the need for balanced judgments; and he further explains that literature appealed not only to the intellect but to the emotions as well. It inspired 'longings which by their pleasant agitation disturb and delight the mind'.[1] And, for actual appreciation, he adds, such things as 'a lively imagination, a piercing judgment, and an ability to enter into the various emotions', all are necessary; since 'for the judging of any sort of writing', he acutely adds, 'those talents are in some measure requisite which were necessary to produce them'.[2]

Nor are his further judgments wholly of a destructive kind, though he has a shrewd eye for defects of various sorts. Pope's power of expression, for instance, he declares, surpassed his power of thought; and he calls attention to the equivocal manner in which that poet employed the terms 'Nature' and 'wit'. In Addison's *Cato*, again, he points out the absurdities that resulted from the strict observance of the Unities; and how lovemaking, conspiracies, debates and fighting all take place perforce in 'the large hall of the Governor's palace at Utica'. At the same time he is also capable of appreciating good things, as was shown by his rapturous and well-founded praise of Milton. That poet had not lacked earlier admirers; but Dennis was the first, after Dryden, to perceive what are perhaps his distinguishing qualities, namely, 'his sublimity and matchless harmony'. It was in virtue of its sublimity that *Paradise Lost* made its appeal to the emotions; and to Dennis it was 'the most lofty and most irregular poem ever produced by the mind of man'. Nor should it escape notice that under the same influence Dennis becomes an early champion of blank verse. That verse-form had previously won but little attention from critics; whereas Dennis now commends it for 'the diversity that distinguishes it from the heroic couplet, bringing it nearer to common use', and making it 'more proper to gain attention and also more fit for action and

[1] *Remarks on Cato*, p. 16.   [2] Durham, *op. cit.* p. 133.

dialogue'.[1] It might also be added that he notes that 'neither painting nor sculpture can show local motion',[2]—a passing glance at the sister arts not without its significance.

Such then in the main was the critical achievement of Dennis; and he is obviously something more than 'a hectoring bully' or a tame purveyor of neo-classical doctrine. From the first he gave signs of independent and even acute thinking, which opened up liberal views concerning literature and criticism as well. And it was in declining to recognize neo-classical rules as absolute and final, in calling attention to the emotional values of poetry in a rationalistic age, and in requiring from the critic poetic insight and sympathy that his best work was done. Of defects of temperament he had his share, defects that increased as time went on and transformed him into an assertive, truculent, fault-finding pedant, thus exciting the hostility and ridicule of Pope, Gay, Parnell and others. Yet to accept their estimate of his critical value is to neglect what had gone before their fierce feuds; for he had carried over into the 18th Century something of the beneficent influences of Dryden, 'Longinus', and certain French critics, and had helped his generation to realize anew the greatness of Milton. This in itself was a valuable performance. And not without its significance is the fact that later on Dr. Johnson, that most sensible of mortals, took him seriously, noting more particularly his faculty of hitting on weak points; though such testimony failed to dissipate the mists of prejudice generated by Pope and others. The truth is that Dennis, if not a great critic, is by no means negligible; for among his prolific writings are to be found many good things that marked an advance in the critical development.

The main direction of critical activities during this period, however, emerges, not in the works of Gildon and Dennis, but in those of the new school of writers, including Addison, Pope, and Swift. With them criticism concerns itself, not, as before, with specific questions occasioned by the publication of this or that work, or with isolated problems presented by contemporary conditions, but rather with a general inquiry into the methods and standards of criticism itself, with the practical business of correcting prevailing literary faults and of fostering a sounder appreciation of literature in general.

Already in the works of Joseph Addison (1672–1719) the new critical trend clearly appears, and is amply illustrated in his *Spectator* papers (1711–14). He had previously written *An*

[1] *Orig. Letters*, p. 373.   [2] *Remarks on Pope's Homer*, p. 56.

Account of the Greatest English Poets (1693), a youthful and
immature production, which, however, is not to be taken too
seriously. In that work he recognized only Chaucer and Spenser
before Cowley's time as worth the notice of 'an understanding
age'; even Shakespeare is not mentioned. Chaucer is nothing
more than 'a merry bard' long since antiquated, Spenser one
who amused 'a barbarous age' with fanciful tales, tiresome
allegories and dull morals; and whereas Cowley is hailed as 'a
mighty genius', and Milton as a notable and gifted poet, the
Muse of Dryden is said 'to wear all dresses' and 'to charm in all'.
The work is obviously as superficial as it is ill-informed; and,
it is worth noting, it was never published by the author himself.

In the *Spectator* papers, however, Addison approaches literary
questions with a widened outlook and in altogether a different
spirit; and although his main object in those essays was to
inculcate a new sense of values in life as a whole, to literature
as a means of culture he devotes considerable attention. In the
first place, nothing is more illuminating than his remarks on
the critical standards and methods of those who posed as guides
in literary matters; for what he has to say constitutes a direct
attack on the orthodox creed of the time. Steele had already
defined your contemporary critic as 'a sort of Puritan in the
polite world who quotes his authorities as the enthusiast quotes
Scripture';[1] and later on he charged critics with applying rules
ill-understood, with a servile deference to authority, and with
a persistent demand for tame regularity, regardless of the fact
that bold and impassioned expression is sometimes demanded.[2]
And this is likewise the burden of Addison's complaint. Already
in 1710 he declares that

A critic nowadays is one that without entering into the sense and
soul of an author has a few general rules which, like mechanical
instruments, he applies to the works of every writer. . . . He is master
of a certain set of words, such as unity, natural, turn, sentiment and
the like; . . . he hath formed his judgment from the works of . . .
Rapin and Bossu; and he never dares praise anything in which he has
not a French author for his voucher.[3]

At a later date he enlarges further on this same theme, when he
derides critics who judge merely by the rules as being ignorant
of the fact that 'there is sometimes greater judgment shown in
deviating from the rules of art than in adhering to them'.[4]

Our inimitable Shakespeare [he adds] is a stumbling-block to the

---

[1] *Tatler*, 29.   [2] *Guardian*, xii.   [3] *Tatler*, 165.   [4] *Spectator*, 592.

whole tribe of these rigid critics. Who would not rather read one of his plays where there is not a single rule of the stage observed than any production of a modern critic where there is not one of them violated?

Here Addison's attitude to the neo-classical school is unmistakably plain; and a clue is also given to his conception of the true method of forming literary judgments. Neither rules nor other 'mechanical instruments', but that 'good taste' which La Bruyère had defined as merely 'good sense' in its critical function, this was to be his test of literary excellence; and the results are seen in his subsequent judgments.

It is with pillorying what he regards as the more glaring defects in contemporary productions that he is first of all concerned. And he falls at once on the mixture of absurdities bound up with the then popular Italian opera,[1] with its florid and forced expressions, and with 'generals singing in recitative their words of command'. To him it was an outrage on common sense, degrading to the taste; and 'taste', he maintains, 'was not to conform to the art but the art to the taste'. Then, too, he is equally severe (and with greater justice) on the stock devices which disfigured contemporary drama,[2] in which kings were necessarily accompanied by halberds and battle-axes, princesses indicated by their long trains, and battles announced with drums and trumpets. 'Brutus', he curtly remarks, 'in a few lines of Shakespeare acquires more pomp and majesty than by all these devices.' Or again, there were the melodramatic artifices for increasing pity and terror; the sight of a 'disconsolate mother with a child in her hand', the use of ghosts, the tolling of bells, and the awesome effects of thunder and lightning. All these in general he ridicules as inartistic thrills and crude appeals to the emotions; though, discreetly handled, he allows, they had dramatic possibilities, as was seen in the weird effect of the ghost in *Hamlet*, or the eerie chiming of the clock in *Venice Preserved*. Nor again has he any use for those antiquated tricks in verse-writing, of which figure-poems, acrostics and anagrams and other ingenious trifles were the chief product.[3] He condemns them all as a species of 'false wit'; and noting that figure-poems, shaped like an egg, an altar, a pair of wings and the like, were of venerable antiquity, that they had been revived by Herbert and derided by Dryden,[4] he forthwith dismisses them as the work

---

[1] *Spectator*, 5. 13, 18, 29.   [2] *ibid*. 42, 44.   [3] *ibid*. 59–61.
[4] cf. *MacFlecknoe*, 196 ff.; also Butler's *Character of a Small Poet* (*Remains*, ii. pp. 118–20).

of writers who, more intent on form than on sense, would submit poetry to the Procrustean bed.

Less trenchant are his further comments on contemporary literature; though on the drama, in particular, he has some interesting remarks to make. Tragedy, in the first place, he regards as 'the noblest product of mankind', by reason of its uplifting influence in softening insolence and soothing the afflicted.[1] His conception of the tragic hero (embodied in *Cato*), moreover, is that of 'a virtuous man struggling with misfortune'; and in general he suggests that modern tragedy excels that of the ancients but is inferior in its moral teaching. What he finds defective in modern tragedy, apart from the rant that inflamed passions with curses, blasphemies and the like, were the attempts to employ rhyming verse, which was tantamount to transforming Greek tragedies into hexameters. Aristotle, he recalls, had approved of iambic verse for tragic purposes as being more elevated than prose, yet nearest to the speech of ordinary discourse; and for similar reasons he held that blank verse was more suitable than rhyme for English tragedy, though he allowed that rhyme was effective at the end of every act as affording a graceful exit.

Then, too, in commenting on Dennis's theory of 'poetic justice' he argues[2] that to make virtue triumphant in every tragedy would remove suspense, thus defeating the tragic purpose, that of exciting pity and terror; whereas ancient tragedies, with their unhappy endings, were more effective, besides being more true to life. On the other hand tragedies like *The Mourning Bride*, with happy endings, were not to be ruled out, though such plays, he contended, gave a wrong bias to English tragedy. The recent revision of *Lear*, he pointed out, in the light of 'poetic justice' had sacrificed half the beauty and force of Shakespeare's play. Moreover, he has a word or two to say on other questions of the day. Tragicomedy, for instance, is to him 'a monstrous invention, a motley piece of mirth and sorrow', as absurd as a mixture compounded of the stories of Aeneas and Hudibras. Elsewhere he objects in general to the use of double plots in tragedy as distracting attention from the main action; though he would admit that an underplot related to the main plot might well be effective. Nor should his occasional references to other contemporary defects pass unnoticed; as when he con-

---

[1] *Spectator*, 39–40: cf. Rapin's *Réflexions sur la Poétique*, II, chs. xvii and xviii.

[2] *ibid.* 40.

demns, for instance, untimely imitations of Milton's archaisms,[1] which in him had been 'a pardonable vice', or again, those imitations of Cowley's 'points and turns' which earlier had been so much admired. Such imitators, he briefly remarks, 'go fine but not well dressed'.

It is not, however, in these various strictures on the literature of his day that Addison's most illuminating critical work was done. For that we must turn to those eighteen *Spectator* papers on *Paradise Lost*,[2] which represented the first detailed study of a great masterpiece and contain much that is of interest. Of earlier occasional appreciations of Milton there had been no lack, despite Rymer's insensate judgment. His greatness, as we have seen, had already been recognized by Phillips, Roscommon, Dryden and Dennis; and illustrative also of the growing appreciation was that anonymous *Letter*[3] (1694) in which were noted the 'sublime grandeur of Milton's theme and expression', the 'venerable antiquity' conferred by his archaisms, while as if conscious of his inability to do justice to his subject, the writer finally declares that *praestat de Carthagine tacere quam pauca dicere*. To Dryden of all these critics Addison owed most; but into his treatment he also infused something of his own, and much of his praise is of permanent value. Besides, his works being widely read for a century or more, their influence was probably decisive in establishing Milton's supremacy among English poets.

Hitherto there has been a tendency to dismiss Addison's appreciation of Milton as little more than a judgment based on neo-classical rules, the tests ostensibly applied being those of Aristotle, Bossu, and the practice of the ancients. It is true that references are made to those authorities, while the subject is treated under Bossu's four heads, namely, fable, character, thought and expression. And in thus making use of earlier authorities Addison proceeds in accordance with the conventions of his time; but he has also in mind tests that to him were more vital and fundamental. What those tests were he explains in the course of his treatment. 'A few general rules', he states,[4] 'extracted out of French authors, with a certain cant of words', is not enough for forming judgments. It was rather 'by entering into the very spirit and soul of fine writing, and by shewing the several sources of that pleasure that rises in the mind of the reader'[5] that a just appreciation was attained; and this is the

[1] *Spectator*, 140.   [2] *ibid.* 267 ff.
[3] Spingarn, *op. cit.* iii. 198 ff.   [4] *Spectator*, 291.   [5] *ibid.* 409.

method here adopted by Addison. He makes use of Aristotle, 'Longinus', French critics and Dryden, in so far as they were in accord with his own impressions; but his aim throughout is to introduce his readers to the artistic qualities of the poem by making articulate his own impressions, and attempting psychological explanations of the same. It was, in short, that judgment by 'taste', which had been successfully employed by Dryden in expressing his instinctive reactions to Chaucer and others.

Nothing is more admirable in Addison's treatment of *Paradise Lost* than the clarity with which he indicates, first, its general excellences, then what he conceives to be its main defects, while affording, besides, scattered glimpses of its more subtle artistic effects. The plot, in the first place, he shows to be in accord with Aristotle's principles.[1] The action is single, that of the fall of man; it is complete, being 'contrived in hell, executed upon earth and punished by heaven'; it is also great, comprising 'not the fate of a single person or nation, but all mankind'. Moreover, he points out how skilfully the poet had hastened *in medias res*, beginning first with the scene of the fallen angels and the fateful conspiracy formed in the infernal Council, then utilizing as significant episodes preceding events such as the battle of the angels and the creation of the world, all bearing intimately on the main theme. The characterization,[2] he next claims, has all the variety that was possible; and the characters are for the most part clearly distinguished. Satan's complex nature, for instance, he states, is amply revealed in both speech and action; the characters of the fallen angels emerge in debate; while Adam and Eve in their state of innocence are also naturally and consistently drawn. Moreover, the style of the poem is said to be in keeping with the sublimity of the theme.[3] Milton, states Addison, 'has carried language to a greater height than any English poet', though his expression in places is 'stiffened and obscured' by Latinisms and archaisms. On the other hand it is said to be free from false refinements, from epigrammatic turns, fustian and the like; attention is specially called to the exquisite nature of his similes,[4] which not only added beauty to the narrative but also gave relaxation to the mind of the reader; and in Milton's blank verse he detects that grandeur and energy of expression necessary for the treatment of his great theme.

Less valuable are his remarks on what he conceives to be the technical defects of the poem,[5] among which he includes such

[1] *Spectator*, 267.   [2] *ibid*. 273, 279, 303.
[3] *ibid*. 279, 303.   [4] *ibid*. 285.   [5] *ibid*. 297.

minor points as trifling word-jingles, e.g. 'beseeching or besieg-
ing', and the use of obscure technical terms, e.g. 'pilaster,
eclipse, architrave'; for the poet, he suggests, should make hard
things intelligible. There are also the objections to Milton's
personal reflexions as intrusions into the narrative, as well as
his display of vast learning, though to later ages these digressions of the poet present no difficulty; while his use of universal
history has the merit of adding greatness to the tenuous details of the simple Bible story. Or again, the representation of
Sin and Death in action is said to be out of keeping with epic
principles, for in Homer and Virgil such allegorical figures are
referred to only in short allusions. His main objections however
are based on other departures from epic rules, inasmuch as the
nominal hero, Adam, is unsuccessful, the Devil being the real
hero; while the poem has an unhappy ending more suitable for
tragedy than for the epic. Both of these matters had been raised
by Dryden; but Addison now tries to extenuate the apparent
irregularities.[1] The unhappy ending, for instance, he suggests,
was inevitable; otherwise the 'fall' would have been incomplete
and the main action imperfect. Moreover, Adam and Eve, he
points out, cheered with the promise of ultimate salvation, were
in reality triumphant, whereas Satan was defeated. He fails
however to realize the effectiveness of the last two lines of the
poem, and suggests that the more cheerful note of the lines
preceding would have provided a better ending.

Apart from the more formal criticism of beauties and defects,
Addison has greatly increased the value of his appreciation by
calling attention to some of the more subtle effects of the poem,
and to the sources of aesthetic pleasure thus provided. He
notes, for instance, the varying shades of expression called
forth by the changing situations; how, where the Almighty
appears, Milton, fearing to give free rein to his imagination, has
confined himself to the bare exposition of orthodox doctrine,
whereas in his descriptions of Eden and Paradise he indulges in
the ornate diction lavished elsewhere on the static parts of the
narrative.[2] Elsewhere reminiscences of Biblical and classical
literature are recalled; or again, the poet's skill in preparing the
reader for later happenings is revealed, notably by his hints of
Satan's machinations against Eve as she lay asleep.[3] Then, too,
the grandeur and terror inspired by the battle of the angels are
duly noted, with comments on Milton's masterly handling and
his power of imagination. The poet, in that scene, it is stated,

[1] *Spectator*, 363, 369.   [2] *ibid.* 315, 321.   [3] *ibid.* 333.

'knew all the arts to affect the mind';[1] and praise is given to his avoidance of all trivialities, and to his provision, there and else-where, 'of resting-places to ease the attention', by means of reflexions, similes and the like. Above all, in the story of the Creation and the description of Chaos attention is called to the sublimity of the poet's utterance, in which, it is suggested, he had successfully recaptured the spirit of the opening chapter of *Genesis*.[2] The simple majesty of one famous passage had been extolled by 'Longinus'; and Addison claims that Milton has here illustrated the Longinian conception of 'imitation', in 'catching the flame from a great poet and writing in his spirit without slavishly following him'. It is such comments as these that give illumination to Addison's exposition; and his treatment marks a distinct advance in the business of literary appreciation.

This freedom of judgment, it must however be added, was not everywhere characteristic of Addison's criticism; for in his comments on the old ballads[3] he does not trust his own impres-sions, but falls back mainly on neo-classical standards instead. His instinctive feelings for this old popular poetry had been confirmed by Sidney's admiration for *Chevy Chase*; and in its artless simplicity he detected a much-needed antidote to the 'Gothic manner of writing' that had been fostered by the artificial taste of a later age; while Percy's lament over his enemy he describes as 'generous, beautiful and passionate'.[4] Yet he bases his judgment wholly on its conformity with the rules of epic poetry, according to Bossu's scheme. He praises, for instance, its moral teaching, its stories of great and stirring deeds, its simple and natural sentiments, and its manly and unstudied expression, all of which are said to have their counter-parts in Virgil's *Aeneid*; and it is on these grounds that he commends this old poetry to his generation.

So far Addison had sporadically submitted, both in theory and practice, a more enlightened conception of the critical function; and it remains to notice his no less important efforts to define those critical terms—taste, wit, and imagination—which were still being loosely and vaguely employed. 'Taste', for instance, he describes as a new word that needed definition;[5] and referring to the Spanish Jesuit, Gracián (1600–58), who was said to have originated the term, he defines it as 'a faculty of the soul' which distinguishes the merits and defects of literary works. He does not further specify its exact relations to the

---

[1] *Spectator*, 339.　　[2] *ibid*. 345.　　[3] *ibid*. 74.
[4] *ibid*. 70.　　[5] *ibid*. 409.

intellect on the one hand, and to feeling on the other, as certain French critics had done; but from his own critical practice it is clear that to him it stood for an instinctive reaction guided by good sense. And, inspired by Bouhours, whom in one place he describes as 'the most penetrating of all French critics',[1] he doubtless agreed with La Bruyère's sage counsel that 'when the reading of a book elevates the mind and inspires brave and noble sentiments, seek no other rule by which to judge it'. In other words, his main guide in judging by 'taste' was the appeal made, not to the mere intellect, but to the whole man, a test which took cognizance of 'graces beyond the reach of art', and those fine shades expressed by the French *je ne sais quoi*.

Then, too, concerning the much-abused term 'wit', he has also something to say. With much respect he dismisses Dryden's earlier definition of the term, i.e. 'a propriety of words and thoughts adapted to the subject'. That, he states, was 'a definition, not of wit, but of good writing in general'; for, if it were true, 'Euclid would be the greatest wit and Virgil more facetious than Martial'.[2] A more satisfactory attempt, he added, had been made by Cowley, when in his *Ode on Wit* he suggested that it was best described by what it was not. On the other hand Addison accepted Locke's conception of 'wit', i.e. 'the resemblance and congruity of ideas giving . . . pleasure to the fancy'; but to this he would add that the pleasure thus given should involve ingenuity and surprise, and that therefore the ideas should not be closely similar. And here he was approaching our modern conception of the term, into which delight, facetiousness and the unexpected all enter. But while this he regards as 'true wit', he condemns as 'false wit' those surprising but distorted resemblances employed by Cowley, as when, for instance, that poet had compared 'the cold regard of his mistress's eyes' to that of 'burning glasses made of ice'.[3] Such irregular flights of fancy, Addison maintained, 'had no foundation in the nature of things'. It was an unnatural way of writing, entirely lacking in the 'majestic simplicity' of the ancients; and such poets, of whom there had been many in England, he described as 'the Goths in poetry', and their manner as 'the Gothic way of writing'.

His most ambitious effort of this kind, however, is his attempt to explain the pleasures of the imagination as the secret of the poetic appeal;[4] and already from his opening statement that sight is the one sense that fires the imagination it becomes

[1] *Spectator*, 62.   [2] *ibid*.   [3] *ibid*.   [4] *ibid*. 411-21.

apparent that his idea of imagination is of a limited kind. Those pleasures he describes as either primary or secondary; primary, when they result from objects before our eyes, secondary, when the ideas of those objects are recalled to memory by means of paintings, descriptions and the like. And all such pleasures, he adds, are less gross than those of sense; they are innocent and healthy and add in general to the pleasures of life. As for the sources of the pleasures thus afforded, they are said to be supplied by what is great, strange, or beautiful.[1] Thus primary pleasures are aroused by the sight of stupendous mountains, by surprising imperfections of external Nature, or again, by its refreshing comeliness. And in this process 'the bold, rough, careless strokes of Nature' are said to be more effective than 'the nice touches and embellishments of art'; foreign gardens with their artificial rudeness than English gardens with their stiff and formal arrangements. With regard to secondary pleasures, those compounded by the memory, he has rather more to say; for these, he holds, are inspired, not only by what is great, strange and beautiful, but also by what is ugly and disagreeable, provided such things were aptly and convincingly treated. Moreover, 'a secret ferment of the mind' might be raised by the supernatural, as, for instance, in 'the fairy way of writing', which dealt with fairies, witches and magicians.[2] It was a vein, he held, in which Englishmen had excelled by reason of their gloomy and melancholy turn of mind, and in which Shakespeare had been supreme. And although men of cold fancies and philosophical temperaments might object to poetry of this kind, Addison's advice was to surrender to so agreeable an imposture.

To this disquisition on the 'imagination' considerable importance has sometimes been attached as the earliest recognition of the workings of that faculty in its more modern sense. The truth however is that to Addison, as to his contemporaries in general, 'imagination' and 'fancy' were synonymous terms;[3] and this he makes plain from the first in stating that he uses both in 'promiscuous' fashion. Hence what he treats of is really 'fancy', the image-forming faculty, limited to fact and ideas of sensation; whereas no suggestion is made of the transcendental quality of 'imagination', that creative faculty which transmutes facts and penetrates to the heart of things. At the same time not without its value is his attempt to treat of one of the vaguest critical

---

[1] *Spectator*, 412–14.   [2] *ibid.* 419.
[3] cf. 'Imagination, that forward, delusive faculty ever obtruding beyond its sphere' (J. Butler, *Analogy of Religion*, ad init.).

terms of his day. His psychology is obviously based on Locke; and Dennis, with his 'vulgar' and 'enthusiastic' emotions, may have suggested Addison's 'primary' and 'secondary' pleasures. Notable also is his appreciation of the delight to be derived from the element of strangeness in literature, the appeal of great mountains and of wild, disordered Nature. Yet the real value of Addison's exposition lay after all in the new direction he gave to critical inquiries, in his effort to render intelligible the current critical terminology, and to foster on sound lines aesthetic taste and appreciation.

And in estimating Addison's critical value the final verdict must be that he did much to encourage among ordinary readers a genuine taste for good literature; and that after all is no mean achievement for any critic. It may be argued that he was not profound, that he did little to enlarge the field of critical theory, that he fell back at times on neo-classical guidance, and that his knowledge of psychology was somewhat limited. What he did however was to bring within the reach of the plain man the best critical ideas of his day, besides urging his readers to look for artistic qualities, not by applying rules, but by 'entering into the very spirit and soul of fine writing', and by making articulate their own impressions. For the subtler beauties perhaps he had no adequate touchstone, his main test being that of cultured good sense; but within those limits he succeeded in revealing not a few literary excellences. Moreover, his teaching commended itself by his skill in communicating it. For his easy, well-bred, conversational style, his adoption of the short essay as his chosen vehicle, and his use of illustrative passages in his examination of literature in the concrete, all were welcome at tea-tables and clubs alike, and did much to modify the unformed taste of his contemporaries.

Nor was his influence confined to his own generation; for the continued popularity of his *Spectator* papers led to the widespread acceptance of his critical doctrines and methods. In challenging the neo-classical system, it is true, he was not alone at this date. But he anticipated, as did no other, the main lines along which that challenge was subsequently to develop; and this he did by his description of Shakespeare as 'the stumbling-block to the whole tribe of rigid critics', his timely (if equivocal) comment on the merits of the old ballads, and his praise of Milton, the *Psalms* and other non-classical poetry. Apart from this his essays are full of good things; and of interest, in the light of Boswell's later achievement, was his suggestion that

12

'men were better known by a perusal of their private letters than in any other way'.[1] So that Addison's position in critical history is one of considerable importance. It was not only that he tried to correct some of the more glaring literary abuses of the time and to define more clearly the current critical terminology, but in inculcating among wider circles of readers a taste for literature he gave fresh impetus to literary appreciation and carried on in his own way the tradition of Dryden.

Hardly less important, however, is the critical contribution of Alexander Pope (1688–1744), whose efforts, like those of Addison, were mainly directed towards improving the methods and standards of criticism in general, though he is perhaps more interested in denouncing literary abuses than in fostering a positive appreciation of literary excellences. His views on the critical business, for instance, are presented in his *Essay on Criticism* (1711), his judgments in his *Preface to Shakespeare* (1725), his *Art of Sinking* (1727–8), and his *Epistle to Augustus* (1733); while further critical matter is to be found in his *Preface to the Translation of the Iliad* (1715), and here and there in his *Letters*. And of these the most notable were the youthful but elegant *Essay on Criticism*, written possibly first in prose,[2] together with the lively *Art of Sinking*, which, with its pungent attack on current abuses, formed the prelude to the *Dunciad*.

In formulating his views on criticism, in the first place, Pope resorts to different methods from those adopted by Addison. Whereas Addison had endeavoured to inculcate a sound taste and the necessity for making articulate one's own impressions, Pope is content to collect together what he regarded as the best that had been said on the subject by earlier authorities. His early Preface to his *Pastorals* (1709) had been compiled from the works of Heinsius, Rapin, and Fontenelle; and in his *Essay* he likewise draws freely on ancient and modern sources, on Horace and Quintilian, Vida, Rapin, Boileau and others. In form the *Essay* follows the Horatian tradition in its desultory character; but while lacking in system it is not wholly without a plan. In it comes first a consideration of the art of criticism in general (1–201), then a treatment of the chief causes of faulty judgment (202–560), and finally a sketch of the ideal critic (561–640), followed by a brief account of the history of criticism (641–end). The result is a miscellany in which principles, originated at different dates and of varying value, are submitted and

---

[1] *Spectator*, 27.
[2] See J. Warton, *Essay on Pope*, i. 106.

discussed, for the most part without prejudice. There are repetitions and inconsistencies, some conventional pronouncements along with injunctions of lasting value; but nowhere (and this should be emphasized) are the principles organized into a coherent whole, and no cut-and-dried theory therefore emerges. Nevertheless the *Essay* is often regarded as a considered statement of Pope's guiding principles, though written at the age of twenty-three, and as a definite pronouncement on behalf of the neo-classical system. And this assumption derives support from his opening remarks on what he submits as the true basis for forming judgment. Thus he laments the corrupt taste of his day, blinded as it had been by ignorance and pedantry; but on 'taste' as a touchstone he does not enlarge, beyond stating that 'true taste' was rare, though elsewhere he defines it as none other than 'common sense, a gift from heaven'.[1] For sound judgment, however, he maintains, the surest test was conformity to Nature, 'the source, and end and test of art';[2] and here he recalls the Renascence doctrine voiced by Vida and by most other contemporary critics. But this test, he added, was best arrived at by a study of the rules, which after all were none other than 'Nature methodiz'd';[3] and here he makes use of Rapin's dictum. Moreover, the rules, he explained, were no arbitrary precepts, but laws deduced from the great works of antiquity, and on them judgment could safely be based, since 'to copy Nature was to copy them'.[4] All this of course is conventional neo-classical doctrine, and it is further noteworthy that in treating of the merits of the *Iliad*[5] about this date (1715), he is palpably influenced by Bossu's 'admirable treatise'.

Yet it does not follow that Pope is therefore a representative, pure and simple, of the neo-classical school. In Homer, for one thing, what he admires is not the poet's 'correctness', his observance of the rules, but his 'poetic magic', his wealth of fancy. And yet more significant is his considered estimate of that system when, later on in 1728, he ridicules Bossu by a lively burlesque of his critical scheme;[6] though from the first he is conscious of the abuses connected with that system, and how some critics compiled 'dull receipts how poems may be made'.[7] Apart from this, already in the *Essay* he states definitely that the rules alone with their fixed standards would not suffice, and

---

[1] *Moral Essays*, iv. 43.   [2] *Essay on Crit.* 73.
[3] l. 89.   [4] l. 140.   [5] See *Pref. to Trans. of Iliad.*
[6] See p. 171 *infra.*   [7] l. 115.

that in forming judgment a poet's aim and his environment had to be taken into account.[1] Elsewhere he states that each work should be judged 'with the same spirit as the author writ';[2] and there again the suggestion is that something more than a mere application of the rules was needed. In addition, there were said to be 'nameless graces which no methods teach';[3] so that departures from the rules were justified provided they resulted in an appeal to the heart of the reader. These were fruitful ideas developed at a later date; and if any judgment can be formed from the *Essay* of Pope's attitude to neo-classicism it is that he accepted the system with some reserve, that he cannot be included among the rigid theorists of that school, and that the *Essay* is essentially a collection of approved critical precepts industriously gathered, as was his wont, from many sources.

Viewed in this light the *Essay* has further sensible advice to give concerning the critic's craft; though in one place Pope adopts Pliny's debatable opinion that the artist alone was capable of judging art.[4] For the rest, he warns, for instance, against judging by parts while neglecting the effect of a work as a whole,[5] against attaching undue value to the false brilliance of flashy conceits,[6] or again, to mere diction, style, or verse apart from the sense.[7] Furthermore he condemns judgments based solely on popular opinion, or animated by prejudices in favour of either the old or the new.[8] Nor, he held, should political or ·sectarian interests, any more than personal feelings, be allowed to influence the critic; while equally harmful was judgment too meticulous,[9] or that extreme fastidiousness 'where all looks yellow to the jaundic'd eye'.[10] On the other hand your true critic, he urges, ·was one who, endowed with knowledge and discrimination, uttered disinterested judgments with modesty, courtesy and good breeding, and who, refraining from magnifying trifling faults, 'loved to praise with reason on his side'.[11] Such qualities, he added, had distinguished the long line of critics from Aristotle to Boileau. But in his attempt at sketching earlier critical history he betrays signs of superficiality and a want of acquaintance with the facts. In ranking Petronius, for instance, with 'Longinus' and Quintilian he shows a lack

---

[1] ll. 120, 255.   [2] l. 233.
[3] l. 144: cf. Quintilian, *Inst. Or.* ii. 13, and Rapin, *Réflex. sur la Poétique*, i. xxxv.
[4] l. 15: cf. p. 69 *supra*.   [5] ll. 235 ff.   [6] ll. 299 ff.
[7] ll. 305 ff.   [8] ll. 408 ff.   [9] ll. 262 ff.
[10] ll. 559 ff.   [11] l. 640.

of perspective, with which Dr. Johnson dealt later in drastic
fashion.

Pope [suggested Johnson] [1] had never read Petronius, and mentioned him on the credit of two or three sentences which he had often
seen quoted, imagining that where there was so much, there must
necessarily be more. Young men [adds the Doctor] in haste to be
renowned, too frequently talk of books which they have scarcely
seen.

Moreover, Pope's tributes to Mulgrave and Roscommon as
representative English critics (with Dryden excluded) are hardly
less strange than the extravagant praise accorded to William
Walsh (1663–1708), whose sole claim to recognition apparently
lay in advice given to the youthful Pope that 'correctness' in
poetry should be his aim.

Such then were Pope's chief pronouncements concerning the
art of criticism; though elsewhere, it might be noted, he also
ridicules Scaliger's (and Rymer's) method of assessing the comparative value of poets by examining parallel passages in their
works.[2] His remarks on critical theory, however, do not exhaust
the interest of the *Essay*. On points of literature he has also
something to say; as when he recalls that beauty depends on
context or setting,[3] that in verse 'the sound must seem an echo
of the sense',[4] or that in the choice of diction, 'the oldest of the
new and the newest of the old'[5] were to be commended. Among
the most familiar of such pronouncements is his definition of
'true wit' (possibly suggested by Boileau) as 'what oft was
thought but ne'er so well expressed';[6] even though elsewhere he
uses that term and also the term Nature, in vague and confusing fashion. In addition there are many wise maxims that have
since passed into familiar use, all alike enshrined in terse, un-
forgettable phrase, and consisting of old truths presented in a
new guise. It may be argued that the work lacks originality, that
it is little more than a collection of trite commonplaces, the
virtue of which has long since vanished. Yet the value of its
teaching on the art of criticism can easily be underrated; for
among its many precepts are not a few of lasting validity. The
work is, in short, a mosaic not without its precious stones, and
is the result of wide and judicious selection among 'the mazes
of the schools'. Much of its contents was doubtless new to Pope's

---

[1] *Literary Magazine* (1756), i. 35–8.   [2] *Pref. to the Iliad.*
[3] *Essay*, ll. 171–4; cf. Hor. *A.P.* 361–3.   [4] ll. 365 ff.
[5] ll. 334 ff.; cf. Quin. *Inst. Or.* i. 6, 41.   [6] ll. 297–8.

own generation; and to modern readers it remains of more than historical interest, for it comes as a reminder of some important truths not included in neo-classical teaching.

Critical work of a different and more judicial kind is represented in his *ΠΕΡΙ ΒΑΘΟΥΣ* or *The Art of Sinking in Poetry*[1] (1727), a lively prose treatise included in the third volume of the *Miscellanies* (1728) produced by the Scriblerus Club. In it he ruthlessly attacks what was the most glaring defect of the poetasters of his day, namely, their futile attempts at attaining the 'sublime', attempts fostered by a woeful misunderstanding of 'Longinus's' teaching and Milton's practice. Traces of the same fault had been present in Pope's own *Messiah* (1712); but in the *Guardian*[2] (1713), one year later, he had taxed Ambrose Philips with similar defects, and in his *Art of Sinking* he now arraigns a whole group of writers, including Blackmore, 'the father of bathos', Dennis, Theobald, Eusden and others. The matter, it might be noted, had previously been raised by Lord Lansdowne in his short essay, *Upon Unnatural Flights in Poetry*[3] (1701), a work which, largely based on Bouhours's *La Manière de bien penser*, had urged that the poet in his flights should avoid all excesses and bring all things to the touchstone of truth. And Pope, in his *Art of Sinking*, now enlarges on this theme by an ingenious parody of 'Longinus's' *On the Sublime* (*ΠΕΡΙ ΥΨΟΥΣ*), in which, by misinterpreting the Longinian term *Βάθος*[4] (i.e. profundity) as meaning 'a ludicrous descent from the elevated to the commonplace', he incidentally introduced into English a new word, 'bathos', with a meaning which it has since retained.

In this work Pope describes 'bathos' in grave and ironical fashion as a quality natural to man and conducive to sleep and tranquillity of mind; yet for its full development, he adds, some knowledge of art was really required. The first essential rule, he states,[5] was the avoidance of both common sense and the imitation of Nature. And this, he points out, had been finely achieved by Blackmore when in his *Prince Arthur*, for instance, the acclamation at the Creation when 'the morning stars sang together' reminded the poet of 'the rejoicing of the Lord Mayor's day'. Secondly, 'triticalness' or mediocrity of thought[6] was said to be necessary for perfect bathos; and what could be finer,

---

[1] See Elwin and Courthope, *Pope's Works*, x. 394 ff.
[2] No. 40, cf. *Essay on Crit.* 350 ff.
[3] Spingarn, *op. cit.* iii. 292 ff.
[4] ch. 2. 1.   [5] ch. v.   [6] ch. vii.

he asks, than the poet's picture of the hard-pressed stag in terror lest his hind-feet should overtake his fore-feet? Then, too, amplification or making the most of a thought was said to be useful;[1] and here Blackmore's masterly enlargement with grandiose periphrases of such simple Biblical phrases as 'He touches the hills and they smoke' is highly commended, as successfully diminishing their energy and simplicity. Or again, much valuable help might be obtained from earlier models, especially from their defects;[2] and reference is made to Philips's *Cyder* with its grotesque imitation of Milton's antiquated words.

The most glorious effects, however, were to be won from the use of figures which enabled men 'to say nothing in the usual way, but (if possible) in the direct contrary';[3] and the opportunities for bathos afforded by unsuitable metaphors, mixed figures, obscure and impossible hyperboles, as well as by the infantine simplicity of Philips's *Pastorals*, are all faithfully represented. Nor were considerations of style to be neglected.[4] In general, it was said, expression should not always be grammatical, lest it should seem pedantic; nor was it to be too clear for fear of becoming vulgar, since obscurity gave a touch of the wonderful and an oracular dignity to a passage that had no sort of meaning whatever. Besides, there were certain styles that in themselves conduced to bathos; though sometimes a single word could produce the desired effect, as, for instance, in Blackmore's picturesque line, 'He from the clouds does the sweet liquor squeeze.' Of the specific styles proper to bathos there were, among others, the florid style with its 'trembling palms' and its 'sighing alders'; or the buskin or stately style, in which a mere 'open the letter' was transformed into 'Wax! render up thy trust', or again, 'shut the door' into 'the wooden guardian of our privacy quick on its axle turn'. These were among the basic principles laid down, with abundant illustrations from masters of bathos; and Pope concludes with an elaborate skit on Bossu,[5] consisting of a recipe for making an epic poem, in which the whole mechanical teaching of that critic is turned to ridicule.

This then is Pope's *Art of Sinking*, the most delightful of satires, which had the additional merit of denouncing in ironical fashion some of the most glaring literary abuses of his time. As a prelude to the *Dunciad* it was doubtless actuated in part by

---

[1] ch. viii.   [2] ch. ix.   [3] chs. x–xi.   [4] ch. xii.
[5] ch. xv; this chapter had previously appeared in the *Guardian*, No. 78 (1713).

personal animosities against the poetasters in question. At the
same time Pope does not hesitate to include as illustrations
earlier lapses of his own; and beneath his irony there lurks a
substantial element of critical judgment based on the test of
common sense. As Thomas Warton remarked, 'there is scarcely
a species of bad writing but what is exposed in . . . this little
treatise, in which the justest rules are delivered under the mask
of ridicule, *fortius et melius* than in professed and serious
critical discourses'; while Joseph Warton, for his part, notes
how strange it was that 'some of the most useful criticism
in our language should be delivered in two ludicrous pieces,
Rehearsal and *Bathos*'.[1] Nor should the method adopted pass
unnoticed, for it was that of Swift in his *Gulliver's Travels*
(1726); and in one place Pope actually refers to the distortions
resulting from the 'anti-natural way of thinking' as being
obtained by applying one's eye to the wrong end of a telescope'.[2]
Altogether, this *jeu d'esprit* is therefore of some importance in
the critical development. It was not left for later generations to
decry the jargon, the windy periphrases, and the false elevations,
which were the peccant humours of this period; and the work
is worthy of more attention than it has hitherto received.

Of less positive value is the remaining critical work of Pope,
that is, his more familiar *Epistle to Augustus*, which represents
an imitation or adaptation of Horace's *Epistle* of the same name.
Its general lines follow closely those of its original; and Pope's
main theme of undue reverence paid to earlier English poets,
his reference to 'the mob of gentlemen' who wrote in Charles
the Second's days, and to the influence of 'conquered France',
all have their counterparts in Horace's poem. Yet the results
are something less than fair or free judgments of the English
poets concerned. Pope's complaint, for example, of the un-
deserved popularity of Chaucer, Skelton and the old ballads
at this date was not well-founded; and of the later poets he
emphasizes the defects in accordance with his main theme
already mentioned. Thus despite references to 'immortal Shakespeare' and his skill in tragedy, it is to Shakespeare's mercenary
aims and his unchecked fluency that he calls attention. Milton's
sublimity, again, is cursorily recognized, but the presence of
pedestrian passages and quibbling angels is also noted, while
the Deity is said to be represented as a 'school divine'. Then,
too, Cowley is commended for his moral teaching, whereas his
'pointed wit' and his Pindarics are described as out of date; and

[1] *Essay on Pope*, ii. 399.   [2] ch. v.

all that is said for Dryden is that although a master of verse he 'wanted or forgot . . . the art to blot'. Such judgments are obviously inadequate; and equally inadequate are his comments on the poverty of the 'wits' of Charles's days, or on the influence of 'conquered France', which is limited to that of 'correctness'. The truth is that Pope was here writing to a brief drawn up by Horace, who in pleading for a new school of poetry had decried Ennius and other early Roman poets; and Pope's judgments, following suit, are directed without discrimination to the same end in connexion with English poets. As a contribution to literary judgment the work therefore embodies estimates of a biased and unbalanced kind; it is a work of imitation rather than of genuine criticism. At the same time its poverty of judgment is successfully veiled under much happy phrasing and charm of verse; and it is these qualities, not its critical element, that commend the poem to modern readers.

Somewhat disappointing and altogether different from the critical writings of both Addison and Pope is the contribution of that great genius, Jonathan Swift (1667-1745). His criticism, scattered throughout works of various kinds, has little to offer in the way of constructive theories or appreciations, is in fact confined almost entirely to correcting current literary abuses; and though, like Addison and Pope, he too discusses criticism in general, unlike them he concerns himself mainly with matters of prose style. Moreover, no one of his greater works is devoted to literary criticism as such. His brilliant travesty *The Battle of the Books* (1704) is a perverse but delightful contribution to the Ancient and Modern Quarrel, with Temple represented as the advocate of the ancients, and Bentley and Wotton as advocates of the moderns, though it also contains more than one place of critical interest. His *Tale of a Tub* (1704), again, treats mainly of religious matters in his allegory of the three coats, whereas literary matters are incidentally discussed in some lengthy digressions. It is in his occasional letters and pamphlets that he treats of literary questions in more or less direct fashion; and from a *Tatler* paper[1] (1710), from his *Proposals for correcting the English Tongue* (1711), and his *Letter to a young Clergyman* (1720), his views on certain literary matters rather more clearly emerge.

Concerning his views on contemporary criticism, in the first place, there can be no doubt. They are amply displayed for instance in *The Battle of the Books*, in his vivid and scathing

[1] No. 230.

description of 'the malignant deity called Criticism', who dwelt with blind Ignorance, her father, with Pride, her mother, and with giddy Opinion, her restless sister, while around her were gathered her ugly brood, Noise and Impudence, Dulness and Vanity, Positiveness, Pedantry and Ill-manners. As for the goddess herself, she is said to have claws like a cat, the ears and voice of an ass, eyes that turned inward, while she fed daily on her own gall. Nor less devastating is the description of her function, which is said to be that of giving wisdom to babes and idiots, of making schoolboys judges of philosophy, and enabling coffee-house wits to pronounce on literature without understanding either matter or style. And the same unflattering estimate of contemporary criticism is revealed in his *Tale of a Tub* where savagery of description is exchanged for a characteristic use of irony. Two types of critics, he explained,[1] were then extinct, namely, textual critics who restored texts from 'worms and the dust of Mss.', and again, those who drew up rules for forming judgments and who (erroneously) held that, their business being both praise and censure, they who censured only were no better than hanging judges. At the same time, he added ironically, the place of such critics had happily been taken by others of a better sort, keen fault-finders, who traced heroic descent from Momus, Hybris, Zoilus, Bentley, Rymer, Perrault and Dennis, and who battened on the greatest writers with an eye to garbage alone. Nor, he explains further,[2] were your true critics concerned with such matters as relative standards, or the necessity for considering the conditions under which a work was written. Such doctrines he briefly dismissed by recalling that much of *The Tale of a Tub* had been composed in bed, in a garret and in a state of hunger; circumstances, he claimed, that threw but little light on its literary value.

Methods of a more direct kind characterize his remarks on linguistic and stylistic defects of his day, matters which apparently caused him some amount of genuine concern. He attributes, for instance, to the depravity of English taste the recent corruption of language and style; and while conceding that both had improved between 1558 and 1642, after 1642, he held, there had been a marked decline, owing to the infusion of 'enthusiastic jargon', and to false refinements introduced during the lawless Restoration period. With regard to language[3] he complains of the 'maiming of words' and the loose use of such forms as

---

[1] Section iii.   [2] Preface.
[3] *Tatler* (230), and *Proposals for correcting the English Tongue.*

'mobb', 'phizz' and 'incog'; of the use of polysyllabic words introduced during the recent wars, such as 'battalions', 'ambassadors' and 'preliminaries', forms, he ventured to think, that would not survive; or again, of the use of society slang invented by 'pretty fellows' of the day, such as 'banter', 'bamboozle' and 'kidney', besides affected phrases in plays which were really unintelligible. Moreover, orthography, he added, had become chaotic. There was a wide-spread idea that 'we ought to spell exactly as we speak'; to which Swift replied that pronunciation varied in different localities, was besides constantly changing; and he therefore advocates the formation of an Academy to fix the language.

Equally specific are his comments on stylistic abuses. He decries in strong terms, for instance, the slipshod formless prose of 'the gentlemen who wrote with ease', with their short, abrupt sentences, marred with abbreviations and elisions—a 'Gothic strain', as he termed it, 'lapsing into barbarity'. Then too he condemns all fine writing, with its conceits, 'its flat, unnecessary epithets', as well as the crude colloquial style, with its smart phrases, its abundant clichés, devised in defiance of old unfashionable standards in order to display a knowledge of men and manners. His views on style are therefore tolerably clear. Scorning all affectation, whether of the Court or of the town, as well as all factitious ornaments and emotional appeals, he stands for plain good sense, for the use of 'proper words in proper places'[1] as 'the true definition of a style', and for simplicity of utterance, that simplicity which he describes as 'the best and truest ornament of most things in human life'.[2] And in this connexion he notes, significantly enough, that he had been better informed by a few pages in the *Pilgrim's Progress* than by a long discussion on the will, the intellect and the rest;[3] while elsewhere he does not fail to call attention to the glorious style of the English Bible and the sublime eloquence of the English Prayer Book.

Concerning poetry, on the other hand, he has less to say. It was as if he lacked interest in that branch of literature, for he cryptically remarks that Sidney in his *Defence of Poesie* had argued 'as if he really believed himself'; and what he in turn writes is in the vein of irony, directed against what he regarded as the prevailing tendencies of his day. Thus he ironically suggests that it was unnecessary for a poet to believe in God,[4]

[1] *Letter to a young Clergyman.*
[2] *Tatler* (230).
[3] *Letter to a young Clergyman.*
[4] *Letter to a young Poet.*

since a taint of religion might ruin the noblest work; though the Scriptures, he allowed, might be useful in supplying similes, allusions and the like. Moreover he notes that Petronius's demand for a *liber spiritus* on the part of the poet was commonly taken to mean 'not a sprightly imagination', but a mind free from all prejudices concerning the divine nature. Nor could learning be regarded as really necessary for the poet; yet the ancient classics, even 'the most worm-eaten', might on occasion serve some purpose or other. On the other hand the poet, in spite of Milton, should study rhyming carefully; and happily an ingenious youth was then engaged in turning *Paradise Lost* into rhyming verse, thus making it more 'heroic and sonorous'. Apart from this, it would be well, he adds, to master the tricks of figure-poems, to head all poems with quaint mottoes, to be diligent in invoking the Muses, to avoid all natural and concise expression, and to be unsparing in 'epithets which cost nothing'. In addition the wise poet would begin with lampoons and satires, thus using 'the point of his pen and not the feather'; for this would enable him to display his wit and to add to his reputation, thus qualifying for inclusion among the *genus irritabile vatum*.

These then are among the chief places where Swift comments on literature; and they are mostly of a destructive kind, part of his campaign against dullness and stupidity. To these, however, might be added his parody on the trite commonplaces of moralists in his *Tritical Essay* (1707), his satire on current Dedications with their fulsome praise of patrons,[1] and his tirade against irrelevant digressions, devised to add to the bulk of a volume[2]—all attacks on actual practices of the time. In one place, it is true, he recognizes posterity as 'the sole arbiter of the productions of human wit';[3] but on occasion he rails indiscriminately against Dryden, Nahum Tate, Rymer and Dennis. And, for the rest, his comments are limited in range and mostly ironical in character. His one serious contribution, appropriately enough, was in connexion with prose style; and here a great master was revealing the secret of his own art, which extended the earlier tradition of Sprat and Glanvill.

So far our inquiry into the critical pronouncements of this period has revealed no overwhelming concern with neo-classical doctrine, though regard was undoubtedly paid to the orthodox doctrines of Boileau, Rapin and Le Bossu. On the other hand

---

[1] *Tale of a Tub*, Ded. [2] *ibid*. Section vii.
[3] *ibid*. Ep. Dedicatory.

it is evident that in the general attempt to arrive at a clear conception of the business of criticism, influences derived from 'Longinus' and from the less rigid teaching of Bouhours, La Bruyère and others had been fostering a more independent attitude to literary questions, and had tended to set up judgment by taste in place of judgment by the rules. And this independence, it should be noted, was not confined to Addison, Pope and Swift alone. It was shared just as clearly by less distinguished writers of the period, notably by Farquhar, Welsted, John Hughes and others; and their evidence is also important in tracing the development of critical thought at the time. So that hasty generalizations concerning the unchallenged position of neo-classicism are in need of some revision.

There is first the protest of the successful playwright, George Farquhar (1678–1707), in his somewhat rambling *Discourse on Comedy*[1] (1702), a work directed against the convention requiring all plays to submit to the rules of 'Aristotle, Scaliger, Vossius and the French critics'. Observing, to begin with, that dramatists who had adhered to the rules had met with indifferent success, he urges his reader 'to lay aside his superstitious reverence for antiquity'; and then he proceeds to confute the claims of Aristotle to be regarded as dictator and law-giver. For one thing, he urged, Aristotle was no poet, and therefore without the practical experience needed for teaching the art. Moreover, his *Poetics*, an admirable work, was nevertheless based on limited observations, confined mainly to the works of Homer and Euripides; so that no guarantee was given that the principles deduced were either essential or exhaustive. Then turning to his actual subject, he submits his views on the proper form of English comedy by inquiring first into the aim of comedy in general, and then into the best means of achieving that end.

The aim of comedy, he briefly states, is that of 'schooling mankind into better manners' by counsel and reproof; and here he is obviously following the Jonsonian tradition. Concerning the appropriate means however he has rather more to say. First he insists that the dramatist's appeal was to be made, not to French or Spanish, but to English, audiences—audiences distinguished for their 'most unaccountable medley of humours'; and this fact involved not only many foibles calling for remedy, but also a variety of tastes demanding satisfaction. But to make moral instruction effective, he added, comedy must amuse, and amuse as well many different tastes. And this was done, not

[1] Durham, *Critical Essays*, pp. 257 ff.

by 'tumbling over volumes of the ancients', but by studying
modern character and the methods adopted by successful English dramatists, such as Shakespeare, Fletcher and Jonson.
These methods, he noted, had dispensed with most of the conventional rules, had ignored for instance the Unities of time and
place, and had followed no strict lines in the structure of plots.
For the truth was, he significantly added, that the rules of
comedy did not 'lie in the compass of Aristotle and his followers, but in the pit, box, and galleries', that is, in the delight
given to English playgoers. Nor did the freedom thus implied
mean simple lawlessness; for your ordinary playgoer would
find no delight in incoherent plots or unnatural, unconvincing
characters. And as for breaches of the Unities, 'why', he asks,
'should a poet fetter and starve his action for considerations of
time and place', since with the aid of fancy the thoughts of man
could compass a thousand years and all space in a moment of
time; and an exercise of fancy was all that was required to make
up for such imperfections. Hence his declaration for the earlier
native tradition in comedy, free from the niceties of Aristotle's
rules, which he maintained were fruitful only in exciting futile
controversies.

In this way does Farquhar reject the rules in defending his
own practice; and what is of special interest is that, either
consciously or unconsciously, he is here recalling the principles
suggested from time to time by Elizabethan dramatists in
defence of their 'new art'. Lyly, for instance, followed by others,
had declared that the function of comedy was primarily to give
pleasure and to amuse. The necessity for appealing to the taste of
playgoers, apart from all rules, had been urged by more than one
dramatist; even Jonson had stated that his aim had been to please
'not the cook's taste but the guests' '. And Shakespeare, again,
was not alone, in view of the liberties taken with time and place,
in calling upon his audience for an exercise of fancy, so as 'to
piece out all imperfections' with their thoughts. An application
of these principles devised by gifted dramatists had resulted in
the glories of Elizabethan drama, with its appeal, not to coteries,
but to the public at large; and it is a significant fact that they
now suggest themselves to one who was also an experienced
dramatist and a successful one at that.

Illustrative of the same emancipatory tendency was the *Dissertation concerning the Perfection of the English Tongue, and the
State of Poetry*[1] (1724) of Leonard Welsted (1688–1747), a

---

[1] Durham, *op. cit.* pp. 362 ff.

minor poet, who in his *Translation of Longinus* (1712) had given evidence of critical ability in occasional remarks on Spenser and Shakespeare. The *Dissertation*, despite its unattractive title, is largely an attack on neo-classical rules, though it contains much else besides, including notes on poetry in general, on the language and prose style. And if it lacks the distinction of style characteristic of its greater contemporaries, it nevertheless forms a valuable side-light on the critical unrest of the time. That its author was no fanatic opponent of the neo-classical school is shown by his tribute to French critics, allowing that they 'had taken criticism out of pedantry' and had made it 'delightful by elegant treatment'. What he attacks, however, is the body of rules bound up with their system and handed down with authority and a show of learning; and as an example of what he has in mind he quotes from the otherwise much-admired *Essay on Poetry* by Mulgrave.

He begins his discussion with some complacent remarks, characteristic of the period, concerning the happy cultural conditions of his day. Everything, he notes, was then conducive to the advancement of poetry, notably, trade developments, the peace prevailing, the sense of liberty and the national character. Moreover, poetry and the polite arts, he claimed, 'had begun to spring up at the Restoration', so that now 'we have far advanced towards a classical age'[1] marked by a standard of perfection. And this claim he endeavours to substantiate by recalling the recent improvements in language and literature generally. Thus the language of his day, he held, was not capable of much further development. It had been enriched with foreign borrowings which had become naturalized, unlike 'the uncouth unnatural jargon' of that 'immortal poet, Milton', whose diction was none other than 'a second Babel or confusion of all languages'.[2] For the rest, he added, the native 'Teutonic rust was quite worn away'; and English at last was capable of choice expression, variety and beauty of sound, as well as of many of the ancient graces of form and rhythm. And as for prose style, it was described as 'little inferior to the French in neatness and perspicuity'; though Addison, who was said to have developed essay-writing and to have furnished models of terse and chaste diction, was at the same time condemned for his lack of masculine vigour and freedom. His main defect, according to Welsted, was his use of short sentences in which the chain of thought was wanting; and the popularity of this style, ascribed to the

[1] Durham, *op. cit.* p. 362. [2] *ibid.* pp. 385–6.

influence of Fontenelle, was stated to have been already spent and exhausted.

Along with these unpromising and misguided comments, however, Welsted had something better to offer. He is conscious, for instance, of certain causes that were hindering the progress of poetry; and among them he reckons the rules laid down for the creation and judgment of that art, rules, he contended, that had never made a good poet or mended a bad one.[1] Originally, he points out, those rules had been merely comments on works composed without their assistance; and modern treatises had but hackneyed the same precepts, making them still more trite and commonplace. Moreover, such rules touched only on externals without entering into the spirit of poetry; and the secret of good writing, too subtle for pedants, was not to be arrived at by such mechanic laws. On the other hand, the beauties of poetry, it was added, are to be felt rather than described, though many of its graces might be discussed in intelligible language by those gifted with 'taste'. And to have 'taste' was to have 'a new sense or faculty superadded to the ordinary ones of the soul'; though, as he adds later, we cannot physically account for it any more than for the soul. Even so, however, there were poetic graces that would not yield to the torture of explanation, and many beauties resulted merely from a 'happy felicity'. 'We are captivated by them', writes Welsted, 'without being able to say precisely wherein lies the enchantment.' In short, 'poetry . . . may be said to flow from a source, which, like the Nile, it conceals', and here at least rules were useless.

Nevertheless, poetry, he continues, is 'no lawless mystery'. Everything, he explains, depends on reason; but reason operates differently at different times, and 'poetical reason is not the same as mathematical reason'. There is, for instance, truth in poetry; but that truth is not revealed by mathematical reason, for poetry depends largely on 'imagination' (i.e. fancy), that 'bright emanation of reason, painting or throwing light upon ideas'. And in judging things it is important to try them by tests appropriate to themselves. His conclusion, therefore, is that rules of poetry as ordinarily expounded were useless for practical purposes, seeing that poetry could not be reduced to a formal science or taught by set precepts. With certain general principles, such as the need for thinking clearly, for fine 'imagining', and for choosing themes to suit a particular genius, he

---

[1] Durham, *op. cit.* pp. 364 ff.

would agree. Apart from this, he urges, your poet should be guided by his own genius, scorning mere imitation which in reality was the bane of writing. 'Works of imitation', he adds, 'differ from originals as fruits brought to maturity by artificial fires differ from those ripened by the natural heat of the sun'; and 'what pleases truly and lastingly . . . is always the result of a man's own force'.

Such then is the main gist of Welsted's *Dissertation*; and with these illuminating remarks he was not only challenging the neo-classical regime, but was also suggesting a new approach to the proper appreciation of poetry. At the same time, concerning the value of poetry in general he has also something more to say, when he compares the social value of poetry with that of the sciences, the sister arts and history, and asserts that whereas poetry discharges the functions of all combined, in it besides there is something 'imperishable and free from decay'.[1] Moreover, he is among the first to call attention to the need for 'originality' and the free exercise of 'genius', a term which Swift had previously defined as 'one who is able to open new scenes and to discover a vein of true and noble thinking'.[2] And, influenced possibly by Addison, he adopts the more modern conception of that much-abused term 'wit', when he describes it as 'an uncommon thought couched in images that create a sudden pleasing surprise and illumination'.[3]

On the other hand it is true that he is sometimes short-sighted in his particular judgments. His disparaging remarks on Milton's diction and Addison's style have already been noted; and there is also his slighting but interesting comment on Dryden as a critic, whom he described as one 'whose way was to say everything that came into his head, whose critical discourses were an amusing mixture of wit and ribaldry, good sense and impropriety', being endowed with 'a liveliness that never tires one, but wanting in solidity and justness'.[4] Yet such lapses of Welsted are of minor importance compared with the positive illumination supplied in connexion with poetry. In his remarks on 'original genius' he prepared the way for Young's later *Conjectures on Original Composition*; and with a lively sense of the mystery of poetry he pointed out that it embodied much that no analysis could explain, and that an exercise of pure intelligence would not suffice. Concerning the nature of what he calls

---

[1] Durham, *op. cit.* pp. 380 ff.
[2] *Proposals for correcting the English Tongue.*
[3] Durham, *op. cit.* p. 392.   [4] *ibid.* p. 379.

13

the 'poetic reason' he is rather more vague, but suggestive as well; for he is conscious of the problem that was to be solved only in Coleridge's day. To have realized the problem was a definite advance; and his work is in its way among the more illuminating in the age of Addison and Pope.

There still remain a few minor works of this period that call for brief notice, as witnessing to an awakening interest in Spenser's poetry and to an attempt at developing the historical approach to literature, both tendencies being destined to militate later against the neo-classical regime. Of some importance, for instance, was the critical contribution of John Hughes (1677–1720), another of Pope's 'mediocrities', among whose miscellaneous works were an essay, *On Style*[1] (1698), together with the first attempt at a critical edition of Spenser's poetry (1715). That he was no blind adherent of the rules is already apparent in his remarks on style; for there, along with much that was conventional, he has some interesting comments to make. Thus elegance in writing, he asserts,[2] cannot be taught by rules; indeed, too close an observance of rules, he adds, is apt to cramp one's style. He likewise calls attention to the need for varied rhythmical effects in prose, which he describes as 'a considerable part of eloquence'; and while decrying in general the use of archaisms, he states that in poetry they might add force and majesty to expression. And to these remarks he adds short appreciations of writers of his day, noting the varied graces of Temple, the manly style of Sprat, and the lucid simplicity of Tillotson, apparently so easy yet so hard to attain.

Yet more important at this date was his edition of Spenser's works, to which was prefixed an essay, *On Allegorical Poetry*,[3] together with *Some Remarks on the Faërie Queene*.[4] In the former, it is true, he prescribes rules for allegorical poetry, since the subject, he claims, had been neglected by earlier critics; but in treating of the *Faërie Queene* he is conscious that something more than neo-classical doctrine was needed for its proper appreciation, and he discards throughout the conventional teaching of Bossu and others. What he admires in the poem is not its observance of rules, but its original treatment of old-world fable, its 'poetical magic', its rich variety of description, and its imagery abundant even to excess. He is not blind to certain defects; he notes, among other things, its lack of unity, its imperfect characterization, whereby fairies, in contrast with

---

[1] Durham, *op. cit.* pp. 79–85.   [2] *ibid.* p. 82.
[3] *ibid.* pp. 86 ff.   [4] *ibid.* pp. 105 ff.

Shakespeare's practice, were indistinguishable from human beings; or again, there was the unconvincing part played by Prince Arthur, and the monotonous, if harmonious, stanza of the poem. But this lack of unity he defends, though aware that the multiplicity of stories had a distracting effect, and that the poem appeared 'monstrous' if judged by epic rules.

Yet Spenser, he maintains, had not aimed at conforming to those rules. To compare his work with that of the ancients was like comparing Roman architecture with the Gothic kind; and for the poem, as for Gothic architecture, he claims some positive merits. The ancient epic, he allows, might be more majestic with its natural grandeur and simplicity; but Spenser's poem, with its mixture of beauty and 'barbarism', offered many delights of a surprising kind. And he further explains Spenser's neglect of the traditional rules. In the first place, he asserts, the English poet was inevitably influenced by Italian poets then in vogue, and notably by Ariosto, whose 'air of romance' and wide-ranging fancy made a special appeal to Spenser's particular genius. Moreover, something was also due to the spirit of the age, with its love for 'old Gothic chivalry'. Knights errant, he held, were not as antiquated to the Elizabethans as they were to later generations; and Spenser was therefore amply justified in his choice of material. Hence for Hughes it may be claimed that he here points the way to sounder methods of understanding earlier poetry. His comments on Spenser have their limitations; but in recognizing the part played in poetic creation by individual genius and environment, and in redeeming the term 'Gothic' from being merely one of reproach, he marks an advance on earlier methods of forming judgment, and joins hands with Farquhar, Welsted and others in challenging the neo-classical rules.

A further recognition of the importance of the historical approach to literature came, however, from Thomas Blackwell in his *Inquiry into the Life and Writings of Homer* (1735), a work representing the first real application of the method to a single writer. His object was to discover those conditions which made Homer the greatest of poets; and he finds that 'a concourse of natural causes' had conspired to produce that mighty genius. Native gifts of course he had, and in great abundance; but those gifts, Blackwell maintained, were enhanced by a happy combination of circumstances, by gracious climatic conditions as well as by the nature of the heroic age in which he lived. It was an age, Blackwell points out, of great simplicity, an age in which men, free from rigid conventions, were enabled to develop marked individuality of character, and to give voice to elemental passions without fear or restraint. Language, too, was at that elementary stage of its development best calculated to give natural and forceful expression to men's thoughts and emotions; for, it was added, 'a polished language is not fit for a great poet'.[1] Apart from this it was noted that Homer's poems were made to be recited to popular audiences, and had in consequence an appeal of a universal kind.[2] And this appeal was heightened since poets at that time were held in reverence as the inspired religious teachers. Altogether, then, Blackwell's finding is that Homeric conditions had contributed largely to the excellence of his work; and he concludes with an assertion of the need for adopting the historical approach in literary criticism. True appreciation of Homer, he states, can only come when we put ourselves in the place of his audience;[3] and this truth in general was more fully recognized as time went on by Thomas Warton, Hurd and others.

While these were then the more important additions to criticism during the opening decades of the 18th Century no account of the critical activities of that period can, however, omit some mention of the work of the famous and redoubtable Richard Bentley (1663–1742), with whom are associated what Porson later called his immortal *Dissertation on the Letters of Phalaris* (1692) and an ill-advised edition of *Paradise Lost* (1732). In the former Bentley deals with an unfortunate reference of Temple's to Phalaris's *Epistles* as the 'oldest' and the 'best' in the world; and by means of unrivalled erudition and acute critical and historical sense he proves conclusively, applying chronological, linguistic, and stylistic tests, that the *Letters*, so far from dating from the 6th Century B.C., were none other than forgeries of a later date. It was a masterly performance, revealing the possibilities of historical criticism; and it is not too much to say that it heralded a new era in critical method. On the other hand his work on *Paradise Lost* was of an inept and wholly misguided kind. Assuming without foundation that Milton's text had been vitiated by errors due to an amanuensis and an imaginary editor, he recklessly introduced capricious and ill-founded emendations, interpolations and the like, which made in his opinion for greater 'correctness'. Following Addison, for instance, he deplores the Miltonic ending of the poem, and suggests as a better reading:

[1] *Inquiry*, p. 71.   [2] *ibid*. p. 103.   [3] *ibid*. p. 118.

Then hand in hand with social steps their way
Through Eden took, with heav'nly comfort cheer'd.

It was altogether a lamentable business which was subsequently condemned by Johnson and others.

The general advances thus made at this stage are, therefore, of some importance. One thing is clear, and that is that, despite Johnson's later declaration that neo-classical standards were still recognized by some in his day, yet at this earlier date they received no absolute endorsement, and neo-classicism was nowhere passively accepted as the orthodox creed. Amid conflicting cross-currents there was already an awakening to the need for something more than the rules, a realization that the poetic appeal was not to the intellect alone, but to the emotions as well; and methods of appreciation, as distinct from methods of composition, became now the main consideration. Certain general principles, for instance, were either emphasized anew or tentatively set forth for the first time. Fixed rules, it was asserted, were inconsistent with a changing environment; a distinction was drawn between the 'mathematical reason' and the 'poetical reason'; 'good taste' was advocated as the test of literary excellence; and attempts were made to clear up obscurities in the critical terminology. As yet these more enlightened conceptions of art were but imperfectly expounded; but the discussion prepared the way for what was to follow. It indicated the lines along which criticism was to advance; as when, for instance, it was significantly noted that Shakespeare and Spenser had successfully violated many of the established rules.

CHAPTER VI

THE WIDENING OUTLOOK: LOWTH, YOUNG, GRAY, THE
WARTONS, HURD

I N order to understand the course of the critical development
after the Age of Pope it is necessary to recall some of the changes
which took place in the intellectual atmosphere in the years
that followed, changes which led to a widening of the critical
outlook, and in particular to the crowded and more searching
inquiries of the middle of the century. As before, lip-service was
still paid to the neo-classical tradition of Boileau, Le Bossu,
and the rest, as the orthodox creed; and as such, things remained more or less, till the close of the century. After 1740,
however, the tentative challenge of the preceding years gathered
strength and assurance; and critics, extending their view over
wider fields of literature, influenced also by suggestions from
various quarters, now prepared the way for the ultimate rejection of that body of theory. Of marked effect, for one thing,
was the growing interest taken in the work of 'Longinus', which,
already translated by more than one English writer, was now
said to be 'in everyone's hands'; and this was accompanied, as
time went on, by a closer acquaintance with Greek scholarship
and art. Equally important was the increasing readiness, fostered by a growth of the antiquarian spirit, to find merit in a
variety of non-classical literatures, in old-world ballads, for
instance, in Hebrew poetry, in Old Norse and Welsh poems, as
well as in the works of Chaucer, Shakespeare and Milton.
Moreover, new influences were at work abroad. In France
Fontenelle, Brumoy, Du Bos and Montesquieu had written, in
Italy Vico, Gravina and Crescimbeni, while in Germany
Baumgarten was preparing the way for Lessing. Altogether
fresh impetus was thus being given to wider and more liberal
studies, to the application of historical and psychological
methods to critical problems, to attempts at historical surveys
of poets and poetry, and to aesthetic inquiries into poetry and
the sister arts. And in the meantime increased facilities for
critical pronouncements were provided by the numerous
periodicals which from now on became a characteristic feature
of the literary output; while the founding of the Oxford Chair
of Poetry (1708) gave occasion for the contributions of two

important critics, namely, Lowth and Thomas Warton the younger. The results are seen in the new direction taken by critical activities. Between 1750 and 1765 there appeared a remarkable body of criticism—the works of Lowth and Young, of Gray, the Wartons and Hurd—works which, by their methods and findings alike, suggested a fresh approach to the whole critical business. From now on, criticism was to be concerned with the art of interpreting literature; and by the development and refining of contemporary taste the established neo-classical position was gradually shaken and undermined.

In this advance towards sounder critical standards and methods the influence of 'Longinus' must first be taken into account; for, it has been well said, 'he taught criticism a new language and breathed into it a new soul'. The translations of Pulteney and an anonymous scholar of the preceding century had been followed by several later versions, including those of Welsted (1724) and William Smith (1739); and as Dryden, Dennis, Addison and Pope had all written with his work in mind the influence of 'Longinus' at this date admits of no doubt, and is to be seen in the works of Lowth, Burke and Young as well as in admiring tributes of Hurd, Reynolds, Gibbon and others. The most popular of the translations would seem to have been that of William Smith, whose version ran through several editions; and since his work is of special interest as illustrating by its comments the way in which contemporary taste was being affected by 'Longinus's' teaching, it calls, to begin with, for brief notice at this stage. His translation had the merit of presenting to English readers a more complete version than Boileau had furnished. But what is more important, at least for our present purpose, is the light he incidentally throws, by applying Longinian doctrine to literature in the concrete, on subtle literary excellences beyond the range of neo-classical teaching, excellences which he detected in the Bible and in the works of Shakespeare and Milton.

It is therefore of some significance that in the notes appended to his translation he calls attention to 'sublime' effects in English works similar to those attained by the tremendous utterance of the Creator at the beginning of things in the command, 'Let there be light', previously noted by 'Longinus'. To the grandeur of the conception, together with the simplicity of expression, were due, so Smith explains,[1] the emotional effects of that particular passage. And this 'sublimity', he adds, is

[1] *Trans. of Longinus*, pp. 40–2.

ever-present in the Psalmist's overpowering descriptions of
God,[1] or again, in Milton's account of the fight of the angels,
with its suggestion of a cosmic upheaval;[2] though similar effects,
he states, were obtained by the selection of significant details
(as taught by 'Longinus') in the stirring description of the
storm in *Psalm* 107, or again of the tempest in *King Lear*.[3] At
the same time special stress is laid on simplicity of utterance.
'Great emotions', Smith asserts, 'can be expressed as strongly
by silence or a bare word'[4] as by a long speech; and this he illustrates by Brutus's laconic exclamation, 'Portia is dead', and by
the Biblical command, 'Peace be still'. He even commends the
occasional use of ordinary familiar phrase as being sometimes
more effective than elegant language, adding that 'a true genius
. . . with bold rashness on particular occasions . . . will almost
touch upon rocks yet never receive any damage'.[5] And in
addition he notes various devices for obtaining the same ends.
There is, for instance, the use of reiterated rhetorical questions
as in *Job* (ch. xxxviii), where 'every question gives lofty ideas of
the Deity and awes us into silence';[6] or again, the resort to
broken utterances and abrupt transitions as in Hamlet's speech
beginning 'But two months dead';[7] and sometimes, he adds, peri-
phrasis could achieve the desired effect, as in John of Gaunt's
famous speech in *Richard II*.[8] Thus with the help of 'Longinus'
Smith calls attention to literary effects unnoticed so far and for
which no reasoned explanation had hitherto been attempted.
And while his comments point to a growing insight and refinement of taste, which were to lead to a more intelligent appreciation of Shakespeare and others, they also supply evidence that
critical minds were already definitely working on lines other
than neo-classical.

Of far greater importance, however, was the contribution of
Robert Lowth (1710–87), Bishop of London, who, as Praelector
of Poetry at Oxford (1741–51), delivered a course of lectures,
subsequently published as *De Sacra Poesi Hebraeorum* (1753), a
volume which immediately won European fame, was frequently
revised and reprinted, and which was translated into English
by G. Gregory in 1787 under the title of *Lectures on the Sacred
Poetry of the Hebrews*. In it the influence of 'Longinus' is
abundantly seen; and already in 1756 it was being hailed by
Joseph Warton as something 'entirely new, . . . the richest

---

[1] *Trans. of Longinus*, pp. 38–9.   [2] *ibid*. p. 35.
[3] *ibid*. pp. 55–7.   [4] *ibid*. p. 28.   [5] *ibid*. p. 127.
[6] *ibid*. p. 93.   [7] *ibid*. p. 102.   [8] *ibid*. p. 122.

augmentation literature has lately received'. Treating of a literature which owed nothing to Graeco-Roman traditions, it not only
interpreted with keener insight the poetry of the Bible, but,
opening up new vistas of aesthetic possibilities, it enlarged
literary taste and suggested critical principles of a new and
illuminating kind.

In the first place Lowth is so far influenced by the current
orthodox theory as to attempt a classification of Hebrew poetry
on the basis of the 'kinds', in accordance, however, not with
any traditional scheme but with the passions treated. He finds
therein, for example, elements of elegiac poetry in *Jeremiah* and
Ezekiel, of didactic poetry in *Proverbs* and *Ecclesiastes*, of lyrical
poetry in the *Psalms* and the *Song of Deborah*, of dramatic
poetry in *Job* and the *Song of Solomon*; and to these he adds
what he calls prophetic poetry as the most effective and characteristic of the 'kinds'. All these, however, he regards as 'nice
and artificial distinctions', to which he attaches but little
importance. The lyric, he explains, admits of every passion,
didactic poetry of none. Moreover, he holds that the ancient
classification of poetry as narrative, dramatic and mixed was
'not of much use', since, as he shrewdly adds,[1] 'there is scarcely
any species of poem . . . which does not occasionally unite these
different modes of expression'. The dramatic *Song of Solomon*,
he notes, was of the nature of an epithalamium, whereas *Job*
was no perfect drama though of great dramatic quality; and the
suggestion is that here was a body of literature to which the
constricting rules of the neo-classical system did not apply.

It is in his positive appreciation of Biblical poetry, however,
that the greatness of his work consists; and this appreciation he
achieves with a mind set aflame by 'Longinus's' doctrine, and
by applying reasoned methods of a psychological and historical
kind. His claim in general is bold enough. Than Hebrew poetry
'he can conceive nothing more elevated and beautiful'. 'The in-
effable sublimity of the subject', he states,[2] 'is fully equalled
by the energy of the language and the dignity of the style, . . .
and in sublimity it is superior to the most finished productions
of the Greeks.' Nor are the critical principles by which he is
animated any less notable. In approaching ancient literature,
he asserts,[3] 'it is the first business of a critic to remark . . . the
situation and habits of the author, the natural history of his
country and the scene of the poem'. Then, again, 'we must

---

[1] *Sacred Poetry of the Hebrews*, p. 330.
[2] *ibid.* p. 30.   [3] *ibid.* p. 77.

endeavour', he states,[1] 'to read Hebrew poetry as the Hebrews would have read it'; and he further maintains that 'each language possesses a peculiar genius and character, on which depend the principles of its versification and in a great measure the style and colour of the poetic diction'.[2] There had been nothing quite like it since Colet and Erasmus had thrown a vivid light on Biblical writings.

Not content, however, with mere generalities, he endeavours to bring out, with explanations where possible, those unique qualities which distinguish Biblical poetry; and in the first place he has something to say on Hebrew verse. Thus he notes in passing that in some poems the initial letter of each line or stanza followed the order of the alphabet.[3] But this was merely an occasional device, obscured in the English version; and he proceeds to reveal, and that for the first time, the secret which had hitherto eluded earlier critics.[4] Hebrew poetry, he states, was really metrical in form; but not in Jerome's sense, when, attempting to trace a similarity with Greek metres, that authority affected to detect in Hebrew verse the presence of hexameter and other measures.[5] Its metrical form, so Lowth explains,[6] was of a different order, and was due to the early use of Hebrew poetry in public worship, when sacred verses were sung alternately by opposing choirs, one choir chanting a verse the sense of which was repeated, completed, or opposed by another choir. Hence the now familiar system of parallel clauses, which, broadly speaking, might be synonymous, synthetic, or antithetic in kind. It was a revelation of something new in metrical matters and of effects nearer to the Old English, than to classical, tradition.

But this free, unshackled verse, he goes on to show, was admirably fitted to express the profound thought enshrined in Biblical poetry. To begin with, there was the predominant style of that verse which he describes as 'sententious', that is, marked by the utmost brevity and simplicity.[7] It was a style unadorned with epithets, but one in which the poet repeated, varied, and amplified his thought; and this repetition, superfluous and tedious in other languages, in Hebrew poetry was really the source of its splendour and strength, of that forceful and animated

---

[1] *Sacred Poetry*, p. 65. [2] *ibid.* p. 59.
[3] *ibid.* p. 40: cf. *Psalms* 25, 34, 37, &c.
[4] For earlier comments on Hebrew verse, see Atkins, *Eng. Lit. Crit.: the Renascence*, pp. 108, 191.
[5] See Atkins, *Eng. Lit. Crit.: Medieval*, pp. 19–20.
[6] *Sacred Poetry*, pp. 206 ff. [7] *ibid.* p. 59.

phrasing specially characteristic of the Hebrew genius. At the same time, he added,[1] it was a style that might be richly coloured, after the Oriental manner, by figurative expressions which displayed objects in striking and arresting fashion. And ignoring as irrelevant the complications due to Greek and later rhetoricians, he confines his treatment to the more common of the figures. Thus frequent use, for instance, he states, is made of daring and magnificent metaphors and similes, which, often vague and indefinite, are yet seldom obscure; and this was due to the concrete character of such imagery, which, drawn mainly from external Nature or from familiar Palestinian life, was invariably invested with dignity and grace.

What, according to Lowth, constituted the supreme glory of Hebrew poetry was, however, its ultimate sublimity, a quality which he defines as 'that force . . . which strikes and overpowers the mind, . . . excites the passions, and . . . expresses ideas with perspicuity and elevation, . . . whether the language be plain or ornamented, refined or familiar'; and in his use of the term he freely acknowledges his debt to 'Longinus'.[2] Such sublimity, he explains, may be due to the quality of either the thought or the expression. And, dealing first with the grandeur of the subject-matter, he notes that Hebrew poetry treats above all of the infinite power and wisdom of God, and in a fashion unrivalled in any other literature. Thus recalling 'Longinus's' famous reference to the opening pronouncement of *Genesis*, he explains that 'the more words you would accumulate upon this thought the more you would detract from the sublimity of it'.[3] Moreover, the understanding, he adds, quickly comprehends the divine power from the effect thus obtained, and perhaps most vividly and completely when no explanation is attempted. Elsewhere the same theme, he points out, is treated more elaborately by the Psalmist and the prophets, and then with imagery, interrogations and negations; but everywhere the same sublime effects are attained. 'The mind', he states, 'is insensibly led on towards infinity, and is struck with inexpressible admiration and a pleasing awe.'[4] Then, too, the expression itself was also a contributory factor. And reminding his readers that every language has its own particular form of poetic expression, different from that of ordinary life,[5] he states that Hebrew excelled all in its emotional quality. In it, he explains, the free spirit is hurried along, impulsive and unconstrained, expressing itself

[1] *Sacred Poetry*, pp. 71 ff.   [2] *ibid*. p. 155.   [3] *ibid*. p. 176.
[4] *ibid*. p. 178.   [5] *ibid*. pp. 157 ff.: cf. Gray, pp. 197–8 *infra*.

with matchless force, in broken and irregular sentences, in abrupt transitions, in statements often redundant, and in bold magnificent imagery, all of which was calculated to excite the strongest emotions. 'There is no sublimity', added Lowth, 'where no passion is excited'; and the fervent emotions of the poet, communicated with compelling force to the reader, result in the 'transport' described by 'Longinus'.

Such then is the work of Lowth, one of the most illuminating and suggestive of 18th-Century critical writings; though its influence was probably limited by its original appearance in Latin dress. A work of sound scholarship, written with enthusiasm, clear insight and sane judgment, it marks an advance in literary appreciation by its application of historical and psychological methods, and by an abundant and skilful use of illustrative quotations. Like the treatise of 'Longinus' himself, in treating of a specific theme it contrives to inculcate certain critical principles of lasting value; and not least is that which suggests the necessary limitations of the orthodox neo-classical creed. The nature and principles of Hebrew poetry, he categorically affirms,[1] cannot be comprehended in minute and artificial precepts nor reduced to rule or method; for its true appreciation an acuteness of judgment and delicacy of taste are required. And in thus opening men's minds to a wider conception of poetry he also pointed the way to a truer appreciation of what after all is one of the world's greatest books.

Yet another factor in this widening of the critical outlook, which likewise revealed in some measure Longinian influence, was the *Conjectures on Original Composition*[2] (1759) of Edward Young (1683–1765). It was in some sense a surprising piece of work written at the close of a long life by one whose earlier odes, plays and satires had betrayed no great originality, and whose famous but tedious *Night Thoughts* (1742) was destitute of initiative and inspiration alike. Disappointed in failing to obtain the patronage which he notoriously sought throughout his lengthy career, it may have been, as is sometimes suggested, that he petulantly revolted in his latter years from the ideals and methods that had brought recognition to more favoured contemporaries; and in this connexion his glancing hits at Pope, Addison and Swift are of significance. On the other hand it is significant also that he does more than revolt; he has something positive to offer that might well have been suggested by the

---

[1] *Sacred Poetry*, p. 173.
[2] *English Crit. Essays*, ed. E. D. Jones (World's Classics), pp. 315–64.

teaching of 'Longinus', as well as by scattered hints derived from earlier writers. But whatever the actual cause of writing, the essay must be described as a work of considerable critical interest, embodying not only an attack on neo-classicism, but also a declaration of literary independence which heralded some of the fundamental doctrines of a later generation.

The main theme of the *Conjectures* is that in all artistic creation free play should be given to native genius, as against the constricting method of imitation bound up with the generally accepted creed. Apart from Temple's striking observation it had been tentatively suggested by various earlier critics. Swift, as we have seen, had in a sense prepared the way by defining what was meant by an 'original genius';[1] and Welsted in the meantime had pointed out the artificiality of works of imitation as compared with the achievements of native genius. Joseph Warton (1753), moreover, had noted with regret the absence of original writers;[2] and Gray, about the same date (1754), was planning an ode on *The Liberty of Genius*, which, though never completed, was intended to maintain that 'all that men . . . can do for men of genius is to leave them at their liberty'. And Young now enlarges on the matter in discursive, but not uninteresting, fashion.

In the first place he considers the principle of 'imitation' and the rules prescribed by the neo-classical school. At best, he asserts, all that formal imitation could provide was 'a sort of duplicates'[3] of earlier masterpieces laboriously wrought out of borrowed material; whereas the rules were said to militate against natural unstudied graces, to impose fetters on the liberty of the poet, and even on occasion to mislead with pedantic prejudices. In short, 'rules, like crutches', he added,[4] 'are a needful aid to the lame though an impediment to the strong' for 'there is something in poetry beyond prose reason, there are mysteries not to be explained'. Moreover the establishment and recognition of the rules he ascribes, not to a conviction that *tout est dit*, still less to a decline in modern intellectual powers, but rather to a superstitious reverence for the ancients. And it was for modern writers to choose between poetic liberty and 'the soft fetters of easy imitation'.

Not that he undervalued the inspiration to be derived from the ancients. 'Their beauties', he regarded as 'stars to guide, their defects as rocks to be shunned, and the judgment of

---

[1] See p. 181 *supra*.   [2] See p. 205 *infra*.
[3] Jones, *English Crit. Essays*, pp. 319 ff.   [4] *ibid.* p. 326.

ages . . . as a chart to conduct . . . to greater perfection than theirs'. Nevertheless it was as allies that these ancients were to be considered; they were not 'to enslave or over-awe' modern efforts. And then in a notable passage he recalls the Longinian idea of imitation as the best means of deriving inspiration from ancient masterpieces. Thus he enjoins,[1] to begin with, 'let us be as far from neglecting, as from copying, their admirable compositions. Let our understanding feed on them, . . . but let them nourish not annihilate our own; and when we read let our imagination kindle at their charms'. Beyond this, however, he urges, modern poets were to write 'with the spirit, and in the taste, of the ancients, but not with their materials'. They were to imitate, not Homer's formal details, but his methods; for, as was shrewdly added, 'the less we copy the renowned ancients we shall resemble them the more'. All this was none other than Longinian teaching on the process of imitation, with its injunctions to submit to the spell of the great masters and to aim at recapturing, not formal details, but the vital force, the imaginative stimulus, that had animated their work; and in thus advocating an imitation that was in essence a spiritual process Young had broken new ground in critical history.

Having thus claimed for poetry freedom from formal rules, Young takes up his main theme, and, encouraged by what had been implied in 'Longinus's' conception of the poetic process, he attaches supreme value to the original efforts of native genius and to spontaneous flights of poets inspired. By such means, he maintained, were accomplished great things without the means generally conceived to be necessary; unprescribed beauties and unprecedented effects, as well as countless excellences unattainable by recognized rules. Besides, free to range in the wide fields of Nature or in the fairyland of fancy, original genius, he urged, might wander at will, exploring untrodden paths, or giving life to supra-natural worlds with their shadowy beings. In this way, he argued, would the republic of letters be extended; and although originality had not always been regarded as a merit, it was along these lines that true progress lay.

Nor was the cultivation of originality in art an idle dream. All ages had given evidence of its workings; and modern powers, he reiterated, were undiminished, while modern advances in arts and sciences all provided fresh fields for the exercise of original genius. Apart from this, in Englishmen, more particularly, he detected a strong vein of originality,[2] seen for instance

[1] Jones, *op. cit.* p. 323.   [2] *ibid.* p. 347.

in Shakespeare and Bacon, Milton and Newton; and he calls
Bacon to witness that men ought not to be content with what
had previously been known and done. Some conditions, rather
than others, he added, were conducive to the emergence of
original genius, as was seen in the great ages of Greece and
Rome when political and social liberties flourished. Nevertheless
it was true to say that all men were born 'originals', with
'imitation' the 'great leveller'; that in literature 'all eminence
and distinction lay outside the beaten road'. And in this connexion he ventures to state that original creations 'often then
deserve to be most praised when they are most sure to be
condemned', owing to their unfamiliar excellences.

It was along these lines that Young urged the need for a
break-away from the tradition of poetic imitation, and for free
scope to be given to native genius; and this constitutes his
contribution to literary theory. Looking back to earlier writers
however he is less successful. He finds in Shakespeare, it is true,
his ideal of a great 'original'; though Ben Jonson he unfairly
dismisses as a mere imitator, 'very learned, as Samson was very
strong, to his own hurt'.[1] Nor does he refrain from censuring his
own admired contemporaries. Dryden's genius, for instance, is
said to have lacked concentration and his plays emotional
appeal; Pope, with all his merits, was 'an avowed imitator,
choosing rather to triumph in the old world than to look out
for a new'; while Swift was an example of great genius gone
wrong, with judgment wanting and imagination soiled. Apart
from this, not without its interest is his plea at this date for a
revival of blank verse. The use of blank verse, he suggests,[2]
had been prejudiced by its unhappy description; whereas in
reality it was 'verse reclaimed and re-enthroned in the language
of the gods'. Rhyme, it was true, was necessary and effective in
the lesser forms of poetry; but for the epic and tragedy alike it
was unsuitable. Its use by Dryden in his tragedies, he maintained, had been disastrous; and hardly less culpable was Pope's
'tinkling verse' in his *Iliad*, which degraded a great theme and
'put Achilles into petticoats', whereas what was wanted were
the glorious harmonies of Miltonic blank verse.

In all this there was much that was salutary at the time; and
it is worth noting that Young does not recommend complete
abandonment for the poet, but is conscious of the inspiration to
be derived from earlier masterpieces. In one place, in fact, he
warns against 'too great indulgence of genius'.[3] Some of his

---

[1] Jones, *op. cit.* pp. 349 ff.   [2] *ibid.* p. 340.   [3] *ibid.* p. 331.

claims, it is true, read apart from their context, may seem somewhat excessive; but over-emphasis is often the outcome of reforming zeal, and the epistolary form adopted, that of a letter
addressed to Richardson, doubtless accounts for some extravagant statements on the part of one thinking aloud. On the other
hand he lets fall by the way some suggestive thoughts, as when
he notes that 'what comes from the writer's heart reaches ours',[1]
or again that 'in the theatre, as in life, delusion is the charm';[2]
and while of interest is his remark concerning the mixed pleasure
of tragedy, namely, that 'the movement of our melancholy passions is pleasant when we ourselves are safe',[3] most illuminating of all is that comment of his already quoted, that 'in poetry
there is something beyond prose reason, there are mysteries in
it not to be explained'. Altogether this belated and rhetorical
essay of the poet of *Night Thoughts* is of considerable significance as voicing the thoughts of more than one of his contemporaries. Its effect on English readers may have been slight; but
in Germany its influence was undoubted; and it anticipated
the spirit that was to animate much of the later critical thought.

Meanwhile along with the pervasive influence of 'Longinus's'
teaching—and Burke's *Essay on the Sublime and Beautiful*[4]
supplies yet further evidence—there were other factors which
contributed to the widening of critical activities at this date;
and with the awakened interest in antiquarianism and in earlier
literature, and the more intensive studies that followed, a further advance was made in literary appreciation which led to a
more generous conception of literature in general. Attempts had
previously been made to bring to light many of the old ballads;
interest had been revived in the works of Chaucer; and the
earlier studies of Old English and Old Norse, represented by
Somner, Hearne, Hickes, Wanley, Wormius and others, had
opened up new fields of literary value. Moreover, fresh light had
in the meantime been thrown on literary history by the Italian,
Crescimbeni, and on Dante by Gravina, while the appearance
at this stage of the Ossian poems, the works of Chatterton and
Specimens of Old Welsh poetry likewise fostered the growing
interest in earlier and non-classical literature. And among the
main contributors to the critical activities that resulted were
Gray, the Wartons, and Hurd.

Not the least important of these critics was the poet
Thomas Gray (1716–71), even though his contribution was com-

---

[1] Jones, *op. cit.* p. 351.   [2] *ibid.* p. 355.
[3] *ibid.* p. 356.   [4] See pp. 333 ff. *infra.*

paratively slight, consisting as it did mainly of casual remarks
in *Letters* (1742–71) to his friends, Richard West, Horace Wal-
pole and Wharton, together with a few essays, *On English
Metre, On Rhyme* and *On the Poems of John Lydgate*,[1] written
after 1759, during a short period of study at the British Museum,
as well as fragments of a projected *History of English Poetry*
which was never completed. In his *Letters* he touches lightly on
questions of the moment and submits lively judgments on contemporaries both at home and abroad; whereas in the essays he
prepares the way for a sounder understanding of earlier native
literature by a scholarly and detailed examination of medieval
manuscripts. For such critical work he was by nature amply
equipped. From the first, evidence was forthcoming of a
heightened sensibility in his reactions to both Nature and art.
To him in his early years, for instance, the venerable Burnham
beeches stood ever 'dreaming out their old stories to the winds';[2]
the rugged precipices and wild torrents of the Alps were 'pregnant with religion and poetry';[3] and, besides, he was among the
first to realize the beauty and mystery of Gothic architecture
with 'its rude kind of majesty' resulting from its lofty naves, its
gloomy aisles and massy pillars, which seemed 'calculated for a
long duration'.[4] This imaginative sensibility was a development
of aesthetic taste that, along with broad sympathies, wide
learning [5] and a penetrating judgment, coloured his criticism
throughout, and endowed him with the qualities of a potentially
great critic.

The results are seen, to begin with, in occasional remarks
scattered throughout his *Letters*, in his pronouncements on
literary theory as well as in judgments on his contemporaries
and others. Thus, first, in the matter of literary theory, West's
objection to the style of Gray's unfinished tragedy, *Agrippina*,
as being 'too antiquated', evokes from the poet a pronouncement of lasting value, insisting on the necessity for a judicious
heightening of poetic style and diction.

The language of the age [he states] [6] is never the language of
poetry; except among the French whose verse . . . differs in nothing

---

[1] Gray, *Poems and Letters*, ed. J. Drinkwater (Everyman's Library).
[2] *Letters*, Sept. 1737.   [3] *ibid*. Oct. 1739.
[4] *Essay on Norman Architecture*.
[5] 'Perhaps the most learned man in Europe'—an estimate due to
Rev. Mr. Temple, a Cornish rector (ancestor of Archbishop Wm.Temple),
and adopted by Johnson (see *Lives*, iii. 429).
[6] *Letters*, April 1742.

14

from prose. Our poetry, on the contrary, has a language peculiar to itself; to which almost everyone that has written has added something by enriching it with foreign idioms and derivatives; nay, sometimes words of their own composition or invention.

Such, he explains, had been the practice of Shakespeare and Milton, Dryden and Pope, adding further that 'our language not being a settled thing, . . . has an undoubted right to words of an hundred years old, provided antiquity have not rendered them unintelligible'. Moreover, contrary to earlier opinion, 'Shakespeare's language', he declares, 'is one of his principal beauties. . . . Every word in him is a picture.' And the fact that many of his passages could not be modernized suggested that English since his day had 'greatly degenerated', having become 'too diffuse and enervate',—an astounding pronouncement to complacent 18th-Century readers. Here Gray is pronouncing on a much-vexed question which dated from Renascence times; and his solution, which was to be challenged later, is rightly based on the practice of great English masters.

Then, too, his remarks on yet another much-debated question are also illuminating, when in commenting on Mason's tragedy *Elfrida*,[1] he decries his friend's use of the Greek Chorus on grounds similar to those suggested by Brumoy in his *Théâtre des Grecs* (1730). The ancients, Gray maintained, had really been hampered by that convention; and it was 'not caprice but good sense' that had led to its dismissal from the modern stage. For one thing, a wider liberty in plotting was thus made possible; and it was unreasonable to condemn the greater complications of Spanish plots with their abuses and love-stories, because of French scenes of 'mere insipid gallantry'. Apart from this, the very presence of a 'singing, moralising and uninteresting chorus on the stage during an affecting scene of love or passion was nothing short of an intrusion'. Under such conditions, he asked, 'how could Macbeth and his wife have laid the design for Duncan's murder?' Moreover, the employment of the Chorus was unnecessary to ensure verisimilitude, seeing that Shakespeare had obtained convincing results without it, not only in *The Tempest* but also in his treatment of witches and fairies. Nor again was it needed in order that passages of pure poetry and moral reflexions might be conveniently introduced into tragedy. Many of Shakespeare's most impassioned scenes, he points out,

---

[1] *Letters*, 1751 (to Mason).

were none other than pure poetry; and, besides, there were minor scenes which permitted 'a variety of *nuances*' of poetry. And in these 'cooler' scenes moral reflexions might well be introduced. Such reflexions, he stated, were 'great ornaments' provided they were in keeping with character. Otherwise, he added, 'they are better omitted than put into the mouth of professed moralists' (i.e. the Chorus).

Equally interesting, however, are his comments on poetry, and more particularly on lyric poetry, a subject all too rarely handled by earlier critics. Drawing on his own experience he declares that 'extreme conciseness of expression, yet pure, perspicuous and musical, is one of the grand beauties of lyric poetry';[1] or again, that 'the true lyric style, with its flights of fancy, its ornaments, its heightening of expression and harmony of sound, was in its nature superior to every other style'.[2] Moreover, he explained, it was owing to its very intensity that lyric style could not be maintained in a work of great length, that the epic perforce assumed more sombre colours, with but occasional ornaments drawn from lyric poetry. And he wishes that some of the allegorical figures favoured by his contemporaries were stripped of their allegorical garb and a simpler expression introduced here and there.

Apart from this he insists that the essence of poetry consists not in its subject-matter but in its treatment; that 'sense is nothing in poetry but according to the dress she wears and the scene she appears in'.[3] And incidentally he refers to certain prevailing defects in contemporary poetry. Disliking (according to Mason) the long chain of irregular stanzas which with Cowley had passed for Pindarics, he not only submitted a truer conception of Pindar's odes, but also urged the limitation of strophe and antistrophe to nine lines at most, since stanzas of greater length 'prevented the regular return of metres' from having its proper effect.[4] Then, too, he condemns the excessive use of description in poetry. 'Description', he states,[5] 'makes the most graceful ornament of poetry but never ought to make the subject.' Elsewhere he decries the current affectation of unnecessary old phrases, such as 'or ere' for 'before'; and in his *Observations on English Metre* he has something to say on the fixed caesura advocated by Puttenham and later on by Bysshe. He concedes, for instance, the necessity for its use in the Alexandrine line, but protests against its observance in octo-

---

[1] *Letters*, Jan. 1758.   [2] *ibid*. Nov. 1758.   [3] *ibid*.
[4] *ibid*. March 1755.   [5] *ibid*. July 1770.

syllabic and heroic measures; and his protest is based on the
practice of Milton, 'the best example of an exquisite ear'.

The more we attend to the composition of Milton's harmony [he
writes] [1] the more we shall be sensible how he loved to vary his
pauses, his measures and his feet, which gives that enchanting air of
freedom and wildness to his versification, unconfined by any rules
but those which his own feeling and the nature of his subject
demanded.

Less weighty, though fresh and unconventional, are the
running judgments on various writers in his *Letters*. Among his
judicious comments on contemporaries there was, for instance,
his generous remark on Johnson's early poem *London*, a work
written, so he states, 'with the ease and spirit of an original'; or
again, his praise of Dyer for his imaginative qualities, despite
an occasional roughness; though Akenside's *Pleasures of Imagination* is briefly dismissed as 'too much infected with the Hutch-
eson-jargon'; and all that could be said for Boswell's *Account of
Corsica* is that 'any fool may write a most valuable work by
chance, if he will only tell us what he heard and saw, with
veracity'. Less happy are his remarks on Collins, who is charged
with 'a bad ear' and defective imagery; and while he owns to
being *extasié* with the beauty of the Ossian fragments he is
nevertheless puzzled as to whether they were genuine or not.
On the other hand he recognizes great possibilities in the newly
created novel at a time when it had yet to be regarded as serious
literature. The plot of Fielding's *Joseph Andrews*, he remarks,
might be poor, but its life-like characters and its reflexion of
the age would always please; and in *Tristram Shandy* he detected a rich vein of humour. Moreover, 'many exalted minds',
he added,[2] 'might scorn such things; yet they are more useful
than your grave discourses upon the mind, the passions and
what not'.

Nor are his judgments on ancient and foreign works less interesting and original; and original is the frank comment on
Aristotle by one who was an outstanding Greek scholar. Writing
confidentially, and mischievously, to his friend Wharton in this
connexion he complains of reading matter that 'tasted for all the
world like chopped hay',[3] that the author 'often loses himself in
trifling distinctions and verbal niceties', and had 'suffered vastly
by transcribblers, as all authors of great brevity must'; adding,

---

[1] Drinkwater, *op. cit.* p. 29 ff.
[2] *Letters*, April 1742.   [3] *ibid.* Sept. 1746.

however, that 'there was in him an abundance of fine uncommon things which made him well worth the pains he gives one'. On more modern works he has also something to say, for his taste is of a catholic kind. Hall's *Satires*, for instance, are said to be as spirited as Donne's and with more poetry in them. An admirer of Jeremy Taylor, he longs for a return to that author's warm imaginative style in place of the naked expression and 'chopped logic' of contemporary divines. And, lastly, there are his lively comments on French literature. Thus in Froissart's stirring pictures of the past he finds delight, and happily describes him as 'the Herodotus of a barbarous age'. Rousseau, often dull, absurd and unpractical, is yet said to have passages of 'important truths better expressed than ever before'. And whereas in the *Letters* of Madame de Maintenon he detects marks of a noble spirit, Voltaire is characteristically referred to as 'that inexhaustible, eternal, entertaining scribbler'.

More far-reaching in their significance, though perhaps less entertaining, are his essays on earlier English literature, the results of wide reading and independent research, inspired however in places by the *Commentarii intorno alla volgar poesia storia* (1702–11) of G. M. Crescimbeni (1663–1728), while an acquaintance for the first time is shown with Dante's *De Vulgari Eloquentia*, due to Gravina's exposition of that work.[1] The essays are of a scholarly but discursive kind, conveying to English readers a mass of fresh information concerning medieval and Elizabethan literature, and bringing to light a large number of Middle English poems, including the *Poema Morale, The Owl and the Nightingale* and the work of Robert of Gloucester, besides speculations with regard to romances, Provençal origins and the like. English verse-forms, fifty-nine in all, are treated in great detail; and Dante's remarks on heroic verse, terza rima and the canzone are recalled. An original appreciation of Lydgate and a note on Samuel Daniel are also provided; and altogether, valuable material was collected for a History of English Poetry, a scheme which was subsequently abandoned on hearing that Thomas Warton was planning a similar enterprise.

Apart from the erudition here displayed Gray gives evidence also of a keenly critical mind which renders his treatment of medieval literature a remarkable performance at this particular date. He occasionally makes use of unsifted learning which later inquiries have corrected; as when, for example, he looks for Chaucer's 'riding rhyme' in *Sir Thopas*, or when he attributes

[1] See J. V. Gravina, *de Poesi*, added to his *della Ragion Poetica* (1716).

the origin of rhyme itself to the early Britons rather than to the Latin hymns of the early Church as suggested by Crescimbeni.[1] On the other hand he has some striking suggestions to make which threw altogether a new light on medieval literature. Thus he condemns the practice of recent editors of Chaucer, Urry (1721) for instance, who had arbitrarily added or omitted syllables in order to regularize the versification of the original text.[2] Irregularities, he conceded, existed in the earlier MSS.; but while some were due to the errors of copyists, many others, he explains, resulted from the linguistic conditions of the time. In the 14th Century, he states, 'our orthography was unsettled, the syntax very deficient and confused'; and he recalls Crescimbeni's evidence that similar irregularities, due to the same causes, had been present in the MSS. of Petrarch, Dante and Boccaccio.[3] Yet despite these inconsistencies of spelling and syntax he boldly suggests that the verse of early English writers was less irregular than was commonly supposed. 'I am inclined to think (whatever Mr. Dryden says)', he writes,[4] 'that their metre, at least in serious measures and in heroic stanzas, was uniform; not indeed to the eye, but to the ear, *when rightly pronounced.*' And in order to attain the right pronunciation it was necessary, he explains, to give syllabic value to final *e* and to assign to words of French origin their original French accent.[5] Here then was one of Gray's most illuminating pronouncements; it was a hint developed by Tyrwhitt at a later date.

Moreover, on medieval literature in general he has also one further noteworthy comment to make, when he accounts historically for the long-windedness of those early writers and defends such procedure. These 'long processes', as he terms them, when stories were told with unending and tedious detail, were really due to 'the simple curiosity of the age'.[6] Men loved 'a train of circumstance in a narration', he explains, for it fixed their attention, kindled their imagination and 'kept pace with the slow motion of their thoughts'. And such treatment, judiciously employed, was not without artistic effect even in a more cultured age. It was said to 'give an air of reality to facts'; since 'circumstance (i.e. detail)', he maintained, 'ever was, and ever will be, the life and essence of oratory and poetry'. And examples of its effective working, it might be added, had already been afforded by Defoe and Swift. Nor, finally, must his remarks

---

[1] Drinkwater, *op. cit.* pp. 57, 69.
[2] *ibid.* p. 21.   [3] *ibid.*   [4] *ibid.* p. 94 f.n.
[5] *ibid.* pp. 25, 94.   [6] *ibid.* p. 92.

on Lydgate and Daniel be overlooked, though his account of
Lydgate is mainly of a factual kind, concerned with details of
his life and works. And while that poet's debt to Chaucer is
recognized and he is doubtfully placed above Gower, he is
credited with grave and sententious reflexions and with occasional touches of satire directed against women and the clergy.
Concerning Daniel, Gray is less enthusiastic, and also less happy,
in maintaining that his natural talents had been blasted by a
pedantic admiration and reverence for the ancients, the effects
of which were seen in his imitation of Senecan tragedy in his
Cleopatra. He is also charged with a coldness and redundancy of
expression which marked his treatment of history; though his
Musophilus rightly wins for him praise, as the result of 'a feeling
mind strongly possessed by its subject'.

From these varied and sporadic remarks of Gray some idea
may now be gathered of the place he occupies in the critical
development. That he shared in the widening outlook is amply
shown by his broad sympathies and catholic tastes, his independent judgments, and his pioneering efforts in the more
intensive study of earlier native literature. His attitude to neo-
classical doctrine, on the other hand, is sufficiently clear from
his remark that 'rules are but chains, good for little except
when one can break through them';[1] and it is worth noting
that he adopts throughout the historical method of approach,
the tests and standards of the great English masters. Hence the
value of many of his critical utterances which are nearly always
fresh, disinterested and suggestive. Most important were his
inquiries into earlier native literature. Forming as they did a
landmark in English scholarship, they threw new light on
Chaucer and others, while they also prepared the way for a
truer understanding of texts hitherto inaccessible. Elsewhere,
again, he reveals some general principles of his own craft; and
in his scattered judgments he gives evidence of profound critical
insight. Well equipped with good sense, artistic sensibility and
sound scholarship, he contrives to scatter throughout his work
not a few seminal ideas; and despite his disclaimer of any critical
ambitions he was notwithstanding one of the most inspiring
and suggestive of 18th-Century critics.

Meanwhile closely bound up with the new critical movement
were the works of Joseph Warton (1722–1800), son of Thomas
Warton the elder (1688–1745), Oxford Professor of Poetry
(1718–28), whose translation of two passages from the *Song of*

[1] *Letters*, March 1771.

Ragnor Lodbrog in his *Runic Ode* (pub. 1748) represented perhaps his most notable performance. Already in 1744 Joseph
Warton had revolted against the vogue of Augustan poetry;
and this attitude, revealed in his blank-verse poem, *The Enthusiast or Lover of Nature*, was confirmed in the Advertisement
to his volume of *Odes* (1746), where he stated that 'the fashion
of moralizing in verse' had been carried too far, that 'invention
and imagination' were the chief faculties of a poet, and that he
was therefore endeavouring 'to bring poetry back into its right
channel'. It was an attitude that determined the character of
his later critical writings, which consisted of contributions to
The Adventurer (1753) and an *Essay on the Genius and Writings
of Pope* (vol. i. 1756, vol. ii. 1782); and in the latter he startled
his age by questioning the greatness of the leading Augustan
poet himself. As a prelude to the later 'romantic' revolt that
attack is undoubtedly of critical interest; but the *Essay* is also
something far more than this. In the first place it represents a
widening of critical activities, being one of the earliest studies
of an individual poet. But more important still is its discerning treatment of contemporary literary problems, and above
all, its aliveness to most of the emancipatory tendencies of the
day. To his task its author brought unusual stores of fresh
learning; and of his influence as Head Master of Winchester
and a member of Johnson's Literary Club there can be little
doubt.

Already in his *Adventurer* essays, written to improve contemporary taste, may be found traces of that new critical outlook which, with Lowth, Gray and others, was producing a more
profound and subtle appreciation of literature. Thus he decries,
for instance, the shallow learning upon which neo-classical doctrine was based, ridiculing in particular the second-hand knowledge of Rapin, Bouhours and others;[1] though for Le Bossu
and Brumoy he has rather more respect since their teaching
was based on a direct acquaintance with Greek doctrine and
literature. His efforts were not confined, however, to disparaging
neo-classicism, for he calls attention to the changing standards
and methods of criticism which at the time were revealing
literary beauties unprescribed by the neo-classical school. In-
dulging in the pleasant fancy that a hitherto unknown appreciation of the Bible by 'Longinus' had recently been unearthed,
he points, for instance, to sublime descriptions, moving stories
and passages of strange beauty in the Bible for which, he

[1] No. 49.

maintained, no parallel could be found even in Homer.[1] Elsewhere he is among the first to lament the absence of original
writers[2]—a matter noted by Gray and developed later by
Young. And apart from this, he reminds his readers of those
merits of Shakespeare revealed by recent critics,[3] namely, his
convincing characterization, his lively creative imagination and
his lofty themes, excellences more important than mere observance of the Unities and the like.

It was in the *Essay on Pope*, however, that his real contribution to criticism was made; and that work consists not only of
a detailed study of Pope's poetry with a view to challenging
the generally accepted status of that poet. It embodies also
some interesting views on literature and literary theory, and
thus reflects, not inadequately, those main tendencies that were
making for a new poetry at the time. Yet if the attack on Pope
is not the sole interest of the work, as is sometimes implied, it
is nevertheless a significant pronouncement. And Warton's
claim is that Pope's poetry was not of the highest order,[4] that
it was a poetry of reason, of the didactic, moral and satiric
kinds, instinct with good sense and judgment, correct and
polished, but devoid of what he regarded as the supreme poetic
qualities. Those qualities he defined as the outcome of a 'glowing
imagination, the *acer spiritus ac vis*' that inspired 'sublime and
pathetic (i.e. emotional)' utterances, and irresistibly carried
away all readers. And here he was possibly influenced by Fontenelle's judgment on Boileau denying him the rank of *grand
poète*.[5] Supreme poetic qualities Warton detected in the works
of Spenser, Shakespeare and Milton; and to Pope he therefore
assigned a lower place in the hierarchy. It was a bold judgment
that was to be hotly debated at a later date; and echoes of the
discussion continue to the present day.

Less arresting, but of considerable interest, are Warton's
sporadic comments on literary theory which suggest emancipatory tendencies at work. And in the first place his general
attitude to neo-classical conventions is clear and sensible
enough. Thus he does not condemn all rules outright. 'A petulant
rejection and an implicit veneration of the rules of ancient
critics', he maintained, 'are equally destructive of true taste.'[6]

---

[1] No. 51.   [2] No. 63.   [3] Nos. 93, 113, 116, 122.
[4] See *Ded*. and ii. 404–5.
[5] cf. 'il n'était pas grand poète, si l'on entend par ce mot, comme on
le doit, celui qui fait, qui invente, qui crée' (Fontenelle, *Œuvres*, iii. 376).
[6] *Essay*, i. 120–1.

On the other hand he explains that there are certain 'fundamental and indispensable rules prescribed by Nature and necessity', and that these should be observed; whereas rules, such as
those requiring that the epic should consist of twelve Books,
that the first Book should contain no simile, or that in tragedy
three persons only should appear at one time on the stage, these
he describes as frivolous and unimportant. And in this connexion he recalls Hume's defence of Ariosto's alleged irregularities, that 'if they were found to please they could not be
faults';[1] while elsewhere he quotes with approval 'Longinus's'
teaching that flights of great genius with trivial lapses were to
be preferred to the work of faultless poets who never soared.[2]
Then, too, he has no use for the vague term 'correctness', then
in vogue; to him it was none other than 'the nauseous cant of
French critics'.[3] If the term stood for an absence of petty faults,
that he could understand; but if it meant merely that breaches
of neo-classical rules were avoided, then it seemed to him futile.
In Le Bossu, Boileau and Brumoy the French, he allowed, had
some excellent critics; but then they were inadequate guides in
matters of literary taste. For true guides, he significantly adds,
'one must have recourse to the Greek critics'. Moreover he
remarks that the establishment of rules had nowhere resulted
in the production of any great works, not even in Greece, nor
yet in Rome or France; and in England, he states, the rules of
the drama were well enough understood, yet 'uninteresting
though faultless tragedies' were alone produced. And for this
he suggests reasons; either that natural powers were debilitated
by a rigid regard for the rules, or else that poets under such
conditions were wont to write from the head rather than from
the heart.

Apart from this he has some illuminating comments to make
on details of current doctrine, which also point to a reaction
against the conventional creed. Thus he discountenances, for
instance, the use of general terms in poetry, and suggests the
pleasing effects of 'true and minute representations of Nature',[4]
and of 'common and familiar words and objects judiciously
managed', supporting his argument by references to Quintilian
and Demetrius. 'A fastidious delicacy and false refinement', he
asserts, 'have deterred our writers from the introduction of such
words; but Dryden often hazarded it and gave by it a secret

---

[1] *Essay*, i. 238: cf. Hume, *Four Dissertations*, iv. 212.
[2] *ibid*. i. 366: cf. *On the Sublime*, ch. 33.
[3] *ibid*. i. 196.   [4] *ibid*. ii. 170.

charm and a natural air to his verses.' Moreover, 'what distinguishes Homer and Shakespeare', he adds,[1] 'is that they do not give their readers general ideas; every image is the particular property of the person who uses it'.

Then, too, at a time when the heroic couplet held the field what he has to say on rhyming verse is also worth noting.[2] Fénelon, he recalls, had held that *la rime gêne plus qu'elle n'orne les vers*; and Warton for his part would limit rhyme to short pieces such as the lyric, elegy and satire, where 'smartness of style' is expected; but for longer and more impassioned poems he regarded blank verse as essential. An epic in rhyme, he maintained, was bound to be tedious, since the true harmony of a poem resulted from a variety of pauses and feet rather than from uniformity of endings; and he notes Cowley's statement that 'there could be no music with only one note'. Or again, there is his plea for the cultivation of 'romantic' themes.[3] He recognizes that poetry had latterly become sober and rational, and poets had not ventured to treat of fairy themes. 'There are some, however,' he states, 'who think that it had suffered by deserting those fields of fancy, . . . since the mind loves to lose itself in one of these wildernesses and to forget the hurry, the noise and splendour of more polished life.' 'Gothic charms', he suggests, 'are more striking to the imagination than the classical'; and he wonders that more use had not been made of 'Druidical times and the traditions of old bards', which afforded fruitful subjects for the most genuine poetry. This truth, he added, had been amply shown by 'our irregular Shakespeare' and more recently by Thomson and Gray as well.

Not less significant, however, are his conceptions of the business of the critic, together with his sane judgments on contemporaries and others, all of which point to more enlightened critical methods. In the first place, as opposed to neo-classical standards and methods, he urges that for true judgment the emotional appeal of a poem should first be taken into account; 'one must feel strongly', he states,[4] '. . . with some sparks of that fire that animated the poet'. Moreover he is conscious of the existence of relative standards and of the value of the historical point of view, his contention being that 'we can never completely relish or adequately understand any author, especially any ancient, except we constantly keep in our eye his climate, his country and his age'.[5] And, in addition,

---

[1] *Essay*, i. 318.   [2] *ibid*. ii. 148 ff.   [3] *ibid*. i. 348 ff., 382 f.n.
[4] *ibid*. i. 136.   [5] *ibid*. i. 5.

he maintains that 'general and unexemplified criticism is always useless and absurd';[1] he derides the old doctrine that the poet was the only critic as being contradicted by experience;[2] or again, he points out that all borrowing is not necessarily plagiarism, and that a discovery of sources might help the critic by throwing light on the art with which the borrowed material was employed.[3]

In keeping with this larger outlook are his various judgments, which are notable, generally speaking, for their range and insight alike. Concerning Pope he has naturally much to say, apart from those limitations that form his main thesis; and among his comments are many of a judicious and independent kind. Thus while freely recognizing Pope's supremacy in his own kind of poetry, in his moral teaching, his use of the *mot précis* and the like, Warton calls attention to his earlier weakness in introducing into his verse-paraphrase of Isaiah's prophecy 'florid epithets and useless circumlocutions' that destroyed the energy and simplicity of the Biblical original.[4] Elsewhere, again, he notes as serious defects in Pope's much-acclaimed *Translation of Homer* an excessive use of antitheses, 'pert and puerile', as well as much 'unnecessary, improper and Ovidian ornament';[5] and while quoting Bentley's remarks that the result was 'not Homer but Spondanus', to Warton himself it recalled 'Nero's gilding of a brazen statue of Alexander the Great, cast by Lysippus'.[6] Nor should his occasional use of the comparative and historical methods pass unnoticed. In suggesting, for instance, the shortcomings of Pope's lyrics he describes them as inferior to Dryden's *Alexander's Feast* in harmony and passion, inferior also to Collins's *Odes* with their fresh imagery and tuneful numbers;[7] and in his appreciations he often provides a historical setting, as when in his comment on *The Rape of the Lock* he traces the development of the mock-heroic in Tassoni and Boileau.

Even yet more illuminating are his further judgments on a wide range of literary works and their writers. Sometimes he deals with contemporary developments, as, for instance, the new Nature-poetry of Denham's *Cooper's Hill* and Thomson's *Seasons*, compositions described by Pope as 'absurd as a feast made up of sauces'. It is true that to Warton one of the virtues of this descriptive poetry was the neat introduction of moral 'sentences';[8] but he also notes its real merit, that of affording

---

[1] *Essay*, ii. 12.   [2] *ibid*. i. 109.   [3] *ibid*. i. 90.   [4] *ibid*. i. 11.
[5] *ibid*. ii. 146.   [6] *ibid*. ii. 228.   [7] *ibid*. i. 64.   [8] *ibid*. i. 29 ff.

faithful pictures of external Nature itself. And in Thomson he commends not only his depiction of scenes as 'wild and romantic as those of Salvator Rosa',[1] but also his original and realistic treatment of details mostly unobserved by poets before, such as, the fallen leaves in autumn, the white down floating in summer, the silence that precedes an April shower, or the murmurs of insects swarming at noon on a summer's day. Elsewhere he has a word to say on the fashionable *Imitations* of Spenser,[2] which for the most part he condemns as misleading and futile, being merely coloured by a few of the poet's archaisms but otherwise lacking in Spenserian high seriousness and grace. Of such poems Pope's *Imitation* of Spenser—a realistic description of an alley of fishwomen—is referred to as an example, though Shenstone in his *Schoolmistress* and Thomson in his *Castle of Indolence*, he allows, had been more successful.

Occasionally, in addition, he presents a considered judgment on the works of a particular writer, as when he indicates, among other things, the faults of Addison's *Cato*,[3] its defective action and characterization, its sententious and declamatory qualities; at the same time pointing out many strokes of genius in his essays, their unexcelled humour, and above all their chaste and simple style, which formed a vivid contrast to the pompous rotundity of phrase common at the time. Apart from this, many of Warton's judgments are of the nature of corrected impressions. Thus a common mistake concerning Chaucer was to regard him as merely a humorous old poet, whereas *The Knight's Tale*, Warton points out, was both dignified and moving, and his comic vein, like that of Shakespeare, 'one of mercury mingled with gold'.[4] Or again, he refuses to accept the current opinion that the Restoration period was the Augustan age in England. 'True taste', he argues,[5] 'had not then been formed'; what was called 'sheer wit' alone was applauded; and Cowley was esteemed the best of poets. Nor does he agree, as was sometimes urged, that Dryden's *Prefaces* were vitiated by their contradictory passages; and he calls attention to his admirable style, rhythmical, lively and pleasing.[6] Milton, too, he defends against earlier censures. The 'flat' passages condemned by Dryden, he held, were artistically effective, providing (as in music) the necessary shades to make the light more striking;[7] and for Milton he also claims what Pope had assigned to Dryden,

[1] *Essay*, i. 40 ff. [2] *ibid.* ii. 29, 35. [3] *ibid.* i. 253 ff.
[4] *ibid.* ii. 8. [5] *ibid.* i. 153.
[6] *ibid.* i. 111. [7] *ibid.* i. 133.

namely, the true origin of 'the varying verse, the full resounding line'.[1]

These then are some of the critical pronouncements of Joseph Warton; and his place in the critical development is one of considerable importance. In his theorizing and judgments alike he brought to bear not only broad sympathies, good sense and keen insight, but also unusually wide learning which embraced much of what was best in ancient and modern literatures and theories. That his main sympathies lay in the direction of a new poetry is manifest; and already in 1756 his suggestions are of a comprehensive kind. Insisting on the value of Greek literature and doctrine as opposed to those of the neo-classical school, he commends the new Nature-poetry of Thomson, anticipates later censures on the false poetic diction of his contemporaries, corrects certain wrong notions and points to the 'romantic' possibilities of fairy themes and the like. Nor is it without its significance that he revives interest in the forgotten works of Dante, when he describes his *Inferno* as 'perhaps the nearest composition to the *Iliad* in originality and profundity'.[2] It is true that his judgment is sometimes at fault, as when he states that Pope's fame would rest in part on his *Windsor Forest*; or when he fails to see in Donne's *Satires* little more than 'a vast fund of sterling wit and strong sense degraded and deformed by the most harsh and uncouth diction'.[3] For the rest, however, his work is full of good things. Less original than his brother, Thomas Warton, to whom he may have owed some suggestions, less interested also in medieval developments, he has nevertheless valuable qualities of his own. His professed design in dealing with Pope was to discourse freely on literary matters in general; and his *Essay*, with its wide culture and discursive treatment, provides a valuable introduction to literary studies which calls for more recognition than it has hitherto received.

To the achievement of his more famous brother, Thomas Warton (1728–90), Oxford Professor of Poetry (1757–67), more credit has perhaps deservedly been given. He has long been recognized as one of the path-finders in English criticism, whose untiring labours opened up fresh tracts of English literature and directed criticism into new and fruitful fields. His critical con- tributions consist of *Observations on the Faërie Queene of Spenser* (1754) and his *History of English Poetry* (3 vols. 1774, 1778, 1781). Both are works of vast erudition acquired by patient research among MSS. hitherto unprinted, and though lacking

[1] *Essay*, ii. 347.   [2] *ibid.* i. 252.   [3] *ibid.* ii. 348.

in accuracy occasionally, as was inevitable, lacking too in graces
of presentment, in coherence and appreciation of an aesthetic
kind, they nevertheless revealed for the first time Spenser in his
true light as well as the complicated progress of English poetry
from medieval to Elizabethan times. Ritson and later editors
were to point to factual errors here and there in his pages but
without seriously detracting from the merits of his performance.
He not only extended critical activities by filling a gap in historical knowledge; he also indicated a new approach to literary
studies, initiated new critical methods and gave fresh impetus
to the new 'romantic' poetry; and upon his labours later critics
have successfully built.

In his *Observations on Spenser*, in the first place, we have
undoubtedly one of the outstanding critical achievements of the
time; and in that work his critical genius is clearly displayed as
he places the *Faërie Queene* in a new light, helping readers to
understand something of its real merits, and thus dispelling
the gross misconceptions of Spenser revealed in contemporary
Imitations of his poetry. He begins by allowing that, judged by
the rules, the *Faërie Queene* is seriously defective. He recognizes, for instance, that the epic hero, Prince Arthur, is no
principal agent but merely a subordinate character; and, again,
that the poem is lacking in unity of action, since the adventures
of the several knights are all independent incidents. Having
deferred so far to the conventional tests of his day, Warton
however questions the validity of those neo-classical standards.
Spenser, he argues, did not live in 'an age of planning', with
rigid laws laid down and accepted by poets. The dictates he
followed (and Ariosto before him) were inspired by a desire to
engage the fancy and to delight readers with tales of beauty
and romance strange and marvellous, themes which required
great liberty in their treatment; and 'it was absurd', he states,[1]
'to judge Ariosto or Spenser by rules which they did not attend
to'. If therefore, he added, Spenser's poem lacked certain formal
qualities which epic severity required, yet their loss was amply
redeemed by other qualities which appealed to the heart rather
than the head, so that 'if the critic is not satisfied, yet the
reader is transported'.

This then was Warton's main thesis. It was a plea for recognizing the historical factor and relative standards in forming judgments, in place of a criticism based on a mechanical application
of the rules. As he explained,[2] 'in reading the work of a poet who

[1] *Observations*, i. 15.   [2] *ibid*. ii. 87.

lived in a remote age, . . . we should endeavour to place ourselves
in the writer's situation, . . . to discover how . . . his manner of
composing was influenced' by contemporary conditions and
taste. The doctrine was one that had been enunciated before;
but Warton, not content with the general statement, proceeds
to illustrate its workings by showing how Spenser's treatment
in particular was conditioned by contemporary influences, by
prevailing customs and the literature current at the time. Thus
Spenser, he maintains, was affected by the Elizabethan love of
pageantry, in itself an aftermath of medieval chivalry; still more
by his reading of old-world romances and the works of Ariosto
and Chaucer. And with abundant details (the most considerable
and the most original part of his work) Warton makes these
matters clear, quoting freely besides from such old works as
*Morte Arthur, Sir Bevis, The Squire of Low Degree, Huon of
Bordeaux*, and the like. It was by thus realizing the sources
upon which Spenser drew, he maintained,[1] that 'we are enabled
to regulate our ideas of his merits, . . . by showing what degree of
genuine invention (i.e. creation) he possesses, and how far he
has improved the material of another by his own art'. And by
this new method was doubtless obtained a clearer insight into
Spenser's poetic processes as well as a truer understanding of
the significance of his poetry.

On the artistic merits of the *Faërie Queene* he has less that
is vital to say. He scorns the criticism which consisted of mere
irrational praise, and distrusts those critics whose judgments
were the outcome of mere fancy and 'enthusiasm' rather than
of reason.[2] At the same time, having called attention to the free
treatment of Spenser's tales of romance, their emotional quality
and their appeal to an Elizabethan public, he attempts to remove the chief stumbling-block to their appreciation by 18th-
Century readers, which lay in their disdain for things medieval,
and, in particular, for outmoded chivalry and romances. This
old-world atmosphere revived by Spenser, he suggests, was not
undeserving of the serious attention of a more cultured age.
Chivalry, for instance, was no barbarous sport of primitive
days;[3] it was a school of fortitude and honour, it taught gallantry and civility and refined the manners of men. And as for
the old romances, 'the appendages of this ancient chivalry',
they faithfully reflected days that were past, while with their
'fictions and fabling they invigorated the imagination and stored
the fancy with those sublime images which true poetry delights

---

[1] *Observations*, ii. 36.   [2] *ibid*. ii. 263.   [3] *ibid*. ii. 267.

to display'.[1] It was a timely correction of 18th-Century prejudices concerning the earlier native literature, which claimed,
not only for Spenser but for medieval writers as well, a wealth
of literary values hitherto ignored.

Apart from this, he also remarks, less convincingly perhaps,
on certain other aspects of Spenser's work, his verse, his diction
and the like. The Spenserian stanza, for instance, he regards as
an unwise choice since it led to circumlocutions and repetitions
owing to rhyming exigencies;[2] though he concedes that it also
lent itself admirably to purposes of description. Of Spenser's
use of archaisms and foreign borrowings he approved in general;
and Ben Jonson's well-known censure he held was unreasonable
and unfounded, seeing that the poet's style, which was always
clear, being based on the language of the age, was by those
means definitely strengthened and dignified.[3] Nor does he object
to Spenser's eye-rhymes, those orthographical changes which
made the rhymes seem more precise.[4] Puttenham, he noted, had
given them his approval, and there were earlier precedents in
Chaucer and Lydgate. And lastly he defends Spenser's use of
allegory as a device characteristic of medieval poetry, which
had reached its consummation in the Faërie Queene.[5]

So far the work, we have seen, is mainly concerned with
submitting a corrected estimate of Spenser as a poet. In form,
however, it consists of a series of disjointed essays in which
Warton discusses by the way other matters of definite, if sub-
sidiary, interest. Thus, for instance, he rectifies and explains
readings and discusses Upton's earlier remarks on Spenser and
the Faërie Queene.[6] Elsewhere he has a word to say on Chaucer,
whose poems, he complains, were still regarded as 'venerable
relics, not beautiful compositions'. Yet apart from his humour,
which was generally conceded, Warton claims for him also
'pathos and sublimity'; while his vivid painting, his old-world
manners, his quaint and simple expression, are said 'to transport
one into fairyland'.[7] Then, too, of interest is the rough sketch
given of the rise and decline of allegory in English poetry;[8] its
medieval vogue, its culmination in Spenser, its subsequent
decline with the advent of the metaphysical poets, and the
ultimate rise of a new poetry 'in which imagination gave way
to correctness, majesty to conceits and epigrams'. Here is clearly

---

[1] *Observations*, ii. 268.   [2] *ibid*. i. 113 ff.   [3] *ibid*. i. 133.
[4] *ibid*. i. 117 ff.   [5] *ibid*. ii. 87 ff.
[6] *ibid*. ii. 71 ff.: cf. Upton, *Observations on Shakespeare* (1746), and his
letter to West.   [7] *ibid*. i. 197.   [8] *ibid*. ii. 101 ff.

15

seen the historical bias in his treatment of literature which later on was to produce his *History of English Poetry*; and for such treatment he puts up a defence.[1] He claims to have related Spenser's genius to his environment by bringing to light the books he had read; and he commends Theobald (despite Pope's ridicule) for his use of similar methods in connexion with Shakespeare. His own task he had performed with unprecedented thoroughness; and not without their interest are his frequent references to forgotten Elizabethan critics, including Puttenham and Jonson, Sidney, Daniel, 'E. K.', Harington and others.

The pioneering efforts and critical genius of the *Observations*, however, came to full fruition in his remarkable *History of English Poetry*, concerning which it has been truly said that 'the good which the book . . . must have done is something difficult to realise and almost impossible to exaggerate'. Now for the first time was recovered from the oblivion in which it had hitherto remained the pageant of English poetry as it had unfolded itself from the 13th to the 16th Century. Through some sixty profusely annotated chapters the narrative proceeds, bringing to light, not only a countless host of writers and their works, mostly unknown to 18th-Century readers, but in addition their themes and often their sources, and the various influences at work as well; all of which was accompanied by illustrative passages painfully gathered from obscure and neglected MSS. In the survey are included works great and small: accounts of metrical romances, chronicles and ballads, digressions on Provençal poetry, chivalry and minstrels, more detailed studies of Chaucer and his contemporaries, of Hawes, Skelton and Dunbar, and then in the succeeding generations the whole panorama of Tudor and Elizabethan achievement, the influences of the New Learning, the Reformation and Petrarch, the serried array of poets and poetasters, the numerous translations, the slow rise of the drama, the beginnings of criticism and the rest. In short, as a practically unaided effort at literary research, it is unrivalled, comparable only with Dr. Johnson's single-handed achievement in his famous *Dictionary*. Moreover, after this revelation of varied activities associated with what was commonly regarded as the twilight, if not the Dark Ages, of English literature, there could no longer be any illusions concerning the 'depth of Gothic ignorance and barbarity' and the like. Scattered hints had previously been given that English poetry had not really begun with Mr. Waller, and that Chaucer had not stood

[1] *Observations*, ii. 264.

alone in medieval times; but with this marshalling of facts and
the full picture thus presented, facile generalizations born of
ignorance were no longer possible.

Nor is it only the salvaging of a mass of forgotten writers that
has given this work its place in critical history. As a historical
document it has manifest defects which lesser scholars have since
pointed out. Some of his statements, for instance, have been
corrected by later investigations. His treatment of individuals
is often out of perspective, Lydgate for one receiving more
attention than either Spenser or Shakespeare; and in general
there is a lack of discrimination in assessing relative values.
Again, the loose chronological order adopted is not the most
effective; while an undisciplined indulgence in digression is
sometimes distracting. Nevertheless the work has a very definite
critical value of its own, and is something more than a mere
catalogue or a compilation of bare facts relating to certain
writers, their lives and works. It is true that there is little
appreciation of an aesthetic kind, a form of criticism which he
had previously discountenanced; though his remarks on the
'early blossoms' of Milton,[1] the long-neglected minor poems, are
worthy of note. On the other hand what is more generally aimed
at is the criticism that helps towards the understanding of
literary movements, their causes and effects; and in this critical
task he has amply succeeded. He adopts throughout the historical point of view; and tracing the development of native
poetry against a background of changing conditions, he suggests
that literature is no static affair but something in close relation
with the movement of contemporary life and thought. Occasionally, again, he makes use of the comparative method, as, for
instance, when he notes parallel developments in France and
elsewhere. His *History*, in short, like his *Observations on Spenser*,
marks a definite advance in critical aims and methods. In recalling the literary achievements of the Middle Ages he filled a
yawning gap in literary history, provided material which enlarged the current conception of literature, and opened up new
fields for critical adventure. And while by his methods he prepared the way for future workers in those same fields, he also
indirectly gave fresh impetus to the new 'romantic' movement.

There yet remains one outstanding performance in which the
efforts of Gray and the Wartons to arouse imaginative interest
in the literature of the past may be said to have culminated.
This was the famous *Letters on Chivalry and Romance* (1762) of

[1] cf. *Preface to Milton's Minor Poems* (1790).

Robert Hurd (1720–1808), Bishop of Worcester, a work which, together with its author, has been subject to some amount of disparagement in the past, but which has latterly been more justly regarded as one of the major contributions in English critical history. Hurd's other critical works included *Critical Dissertations* (1753) and *Moral and Political Dialogues* (1759), besides Commentaries on Horace (1753) and Addison (pub. 1811); and they all have points of interest, though lacking in the grasp and insight that went to the making of his *Letters*.

In the *Critical Dissertations*, to begin with, which consists of formal treatments of poetry in general, the drama and poetical imitation, what is of most value are the occasional remarks on contemporary literature which suggest that the writer is no slavish adherent of the neo-classical school. It is true that at this stage he maintains that the 'kinds' are fixed, 'founded in nature and the reason of things', and therefore 'not to be multiplied at pleasure'.[1] Elsewhere, however, he states that 'the practice of the ancient stage is of no further authority than as it accords to just criticism';[2] and for the rest he comments with an open mind on the developments of his time. Of interest, for example, are his tentative (if inconsistent) remarks on that new form, the modern novel.[3] He concedes that it provided pleasure by means of fiction, two of the main criteria of poetry; though lacking verse, he adds, 'it is no true epic'. But in view of its obvious success he cannot refrain from recognition, and concludes that in such case a mixture of the 'kinds' might be permitted.

Or again, he approves of recent extensions in modern drama, particularly in comedy, in which the conception of Greek comedy, described as the product of mere chance, had been improved by reflexion. Thus comedies of high life, as well as tragedies of low life, he defends as refinements of ancient conceptions, being the outcome of social conditions which differed from the classless society of ancient Greece.[4] Moreover he conceives of plays that were neither comedies nor tragedies according to ancient models; and in particular he approves of an 'intermediate species', 'the weeping comedy' or *la comédie larmoyante* advocated by Fontenelle.[5] Terence, he stated, had shown that ridicule was not the essence of comedy; and with the more intensive study of humanity and the vogue of the love-theme, the new form, he held, had justified itself by its success in affording pleasure and novelty to elegant minds even

---

[1] *Works* (1811 ed.), ii. 20   [2] *ibid*. ii. 71.
[3] *ibid*. ii. 19–20.   [4] *ibid*. ii. 86.   [5] *ibid*. ii. 75 ff.

if less effective with the general public. Nor must his occasional references to Shakespeare and Ben Jonson be overlooked. In one place, for instance, he notes that the art of Jonson had formerly been preferred to that of Shakespeare, though his own contemporaries had since been convinced of the mistake;[1] and this conviction he himself shared when he condemned Jonson's characters built up on abstract ideas as 'an unnatural delineation of passions unlike anything in real life'.[2] At the same time he utters a warning that the idolizing of Shakespeare with 'his divine raptures' should not be carried too far, to the detriment of recent poets of a more correct and polished kind.[3] Yet his reverence for Shakespeare was undoubted. 'Shakespeare', he claimed,[4] 'was the first that broke through the bondage of classical superstition'; and in reply to a current controversy, he added, 'that felicity he owed to his want of what is called the advantage of a learned education'.

Interest of another kind is attached to his *Moral and Political Dialogues*; and Dialogue III calls for special notice as being a preliminary study of matters discussed more fully in his later *Letters*. In that Dialogue the main object was to correct the prevailing estimate of Elizabethan times; and this was accomplished by means of an imaginary conversation in which Addison and Arbuthnot are represented as discussing their impressions received during a supposed visit to Kenilworth Castle. An attempt is first made to remove the prejudices commonly entertained concerning a yet earlier age, the age of chivalry. To Addison the ancient scene is said to recall merely the barbarous manners bound up with tournaments and the like; institutions, he maintained, which were the outcome of 'Gothic fierceness', but which had been happily 'laughed away' by the admirable Cervantes. To this Arbuthnot replied that Gothic tournaments in reality had been 'the best schools of civility and heroism', and indeed of all the virtues; and that what Cervantes had ridiculed were only the abuses of chivalry. Moreover, it was added, the influence of this code of chivalry, together with the revival of learning, had been mainly responsible for a wonderful efflorescence of poetry in Elizabethan times. That age, argued Arbuthnot, was for historical reasons well fitted for great literary achievements, since it had shed the earlier 'rude essays of uncorrected fancy' and was also free from the later 'refinements of reason and science'. Hence his bold assertion of the superiority of Elizabethan poetry over all that followed, in virtue of its noble

[1] *Works*, i. 277. [2] *ibid*. ii. 53. [3] *ibid*. i. 277. [4] *ibid*. i. 248.

thought, its picturesque language, and its clear and simple style, unaffected as yet by 'the prosaic genius' of a later age. Such then was Hurd's corrected estimate of the poetry of 'the golden age of Elizabeth'; and its 'manliness and elegance', he added, 'we might do well to imitate'.

It is in his *Letters of Chivalry and Romance* written three years later, however, that Hurd submits his considered judgment on the medieval chivalry and romance commonly ridiculed by condescending contemporaries as the products of a childish and 'barbarous' age. And now in extending his consideration back beyond Elizabethan times, he maintains that whereas the flame of medieval chivalry had soon burnt itself out, yet the spirit of romance kindled from that flame had proved to be an inspiring influence in later literature, embodying as it did elements conducive to the noblest poetry. He reminds his readers,[1] to begin with, that chivalry was a natural development of the feudal system with its jousts and tournaments; and that in its finer phases it had fostered the most noble of human qualities, martial prowess, generosity, gallantry, religious ardour and the like.[2] Indeed, he added, the code of conduct characteristic of knight-errantry was in no way inferior even to that of Homer's heroic age; and this he demonstrates from evidence supplied by old-world romances.[3] Thus, comparing the *Iliad* with medieval romances he points to certain close resemblances, and differences as well. In both, for instance, were to be found the same detailed accounts of martial exploits, the same stories of giants and dragons, of adventures and enchantments; but where differences existed the advantage, he claimed, lay with the 'Gothic' or medieval writings. Instead of the fierce passions of rage and revenge that disfigured the Homeric pages, the gentler emotions of love and friendship, he notes, characterized the romances, which thus acquired a beauty and pathos of their own. Moreover, the supernatural element of the Greek story with its 'rabble of pagan divinities' was less effective than that of the romances with their gracious forms of elves and fairies. In short, in the romances, he declared, 'we are on enchanted ground'; and he recalls the use made of this material by both Shakespeare and Milton. 'The fancies of our modern bards', he adds,[4] 'are more gallant, more sublime, more terrible . . . than those of the classic fablers. In a word, . . . the manners they paint and the superstitions they adopt are the more poetical for being Gothic.'

[1] *Letter ii.*   [2] *Letter iii.*   [3] *Letter iv.*   [4] *Letter vi.*

In thus suggesting the inherent value of medieval romances
Hurd, it might be noticed, had applied no rules but rather
Dryden's method of vindicating Chaucer, in comparing, much
to their advantage, those romances with a great and established masterpiece. And then in treating further of their beneficent influence on later poets he points out that both Spenser
and Milton, though inspired originally by classical tradition, had
nevertheless felt the charm of these 'Gothic fables of chivalry'.
Spenser, indeed, deliberately chose the age of chivalry and the
scene of fairyland for his theme, so that 'it was as a Gothic, not
a classical, poem that the *Faërie Queene* should be read and
criticized'.[1] And if Milton, preferring a classical to a 'Gothic'
model, thus avoided the structural faults of the old romances,
yet he too felt their charm, for it was with reluctance that he
abandoned the Arthurian story as the theme of his great epic,
while in *L'Allegro* and elsewhere in his poetry he showed himself
conscious of their magic spell.

So far Hurd had drawn freely on other writers for the views
thus formulated concerning the origin and the main features
of medieval chivalry and romance. He cannot have failed to
be influenced by the works of Gray and the Wartons, some
of whose ideas he obviously endorsed, while he also frankly
acknowledges his debt to certain French writings[2] for further
detailed information. From now on, however, the originality of
his treatment emerges when he considers as a natural corollary
the consequences in critical procedure and standards bound up
with this new estimate of medieval romance. He begins by submitting a revised judgment of the *Faërie Queene*, concerning
which he has something important to say.[3] Recalling his injunction that the poem should be read, not as a classical, but as a
'Gothic' or 'romantic', composition, he suggests that it should
accordingly be judged, as also Gothic architecture was to be
judged, not by standards of the ancients, but by those appropriate to its own nature. And his first contention is that as a
'romantic' poem, both its theme and its treatment were necessarily bound up with ideas of chivalry. Its theme, for instance,
was based on a custom common in days of knight-errantry,
when at a great feast knights were dispatched on sundry
adventures; and this subject-matter, he states, determined the

---

[1] *Letter vii.*
[2] *Histoire de l'Académie des Inscriptions et Belles-Lettres* and Saint-
Palaye's *Mémoires sur l'ancienne Chevalerie*, 1746, 1759.
[3] *Letter viii.*

plan or design of the poem—a principle, by the way, that with
some differences had determined the structure of Shakespeare's
plays. At the same time Hurd recognizes that every work of
art must have a unity of some sort; and he notes that, apart
from the unity afforded by the allegory, Spenser had attempted,
but without success (despite Thomas Warton's views to the
contrary), to give an appearance of unity to the poem by adopting a single hero, Prince Arthur. In spite of the several actions,
however, an effective unity, Hurd suggested, was nevertheless
achieved; and it was a unity of design or effect, that is, a unity
consisting, not of a single action, but of a number of actions
relating to a common purpose. And in thus enlarging the conception of artistic unity so as to embrace a unity of design or
effect, Hurd was not only throwing new light on Spenser's
achievement, he was also establishing a valuable principle of
modern critical theory.

But it was not only Spenser that had been unfairly judged
owing to the blindness of critics to the truths that the form of
a poem was largely determined by its subject-matter, and that
some other test than that of the classical unity of action was
needed for poetry of a 'Gothic' or 'romantic' kind. And Hurd
has in consequence some notable remarks to make on earlier
criticism in general.[1] He notes, for instance, that Ariosto on
account of his 'Gothic' elements had been dismissed by French
critics as 'a rude romancer'; and that, although Tasso had
received greater consideration as being more classical in his
treatment, yet he too had subsequently been denounced because
of his magic and enchantments. Whereupon Hurd decries in no
uncertain terms the French neo-classical system, and particularly its evil influence on 'our obsequious and over-modest'
critics at the Restoration. He recalls how Davenant and others
had introduced the pernicious French doctrine to English
readers, and how their theorizing had been slavishly adopted
by succeeding critics until 'with Rymer and the rest of that
school it grew into a sort of cant'.

Moreover to the same influence he attributed the contempt
and neglect into which Italian poetry had latterly fallen, and
which had been illustrated by Shaftesbury's arrogant remark
that 'the Italians were good for nothing but to corrupt the taste
of those who had no familiarity with the noble ancients'.[2] Or
again, there was Boileau's scornful reference to what he called
the *clinquant* (i.e. tinsel) *du Tasse*.[3] It was a phrase, added Hurd,

[1] *Letter ix.*   [2] *Advice to an Author*, III. ii.   [3] *Satire*, ix.

that was unhappily adopted by Addison[1] and thus became 'a sort of watch-word among critics', suggesting that Tasso was *clinquant* and nothing more. As Hurd shrewdly remarked, 'a lucky word which sounds well and everybody gets by heart goes farther than a volume of just criticism'. And not without their significance as bearing on the revival of interest in Italian literature at this date are his references to 'the golden dreams of Ariosto', 'the celestial visions of Tasso', as well as to the past glories of Italian poetry in general.

Not content, however, with these passing shots against neo-classicism, Hurd proceeds by reasoned argument to direct a frontal attack upon the whole system; and he begins by stating that 'the source of bad criticism . . . is the abuse of terms'.[2] His first objection therefore is to the limited sense attached to the word 'Nature' by neo-classical critics. That a poet should 'follow Nature', he states, is one of their basic axioms; but by Nature, they meant merely 'the known and experienced course of affairs in the world'. Yet to the poet, he protests, belongs a world of his own, where 'experience has less to do than consistent imagination', and which includes the world of the supernatural; so that with him 'all is marvellous and extraordinary, yet not unnatural'. In the second place he states that their 'trite maxim of following Nature' was wrongly held to apply indiscriminately to all forms of poetry. He grants that in those forms that dealt with men and their emotions a strict observance of the laws of human nature was indeed essential, since 'we must first believe before we can be affected'. But in the more sublime forms of poetry, the epic for example, strict verisimilitude was not called for. Such poetry, he maintained, was addressed primarily to the imagination and that was 'a young and credulous faculty which loves to admire and to be deceived'. Then, too, he explains further how the indiscriminate application of this maxim had come about. It was due, he states, to the careless extension of a particular precept relating originally to the drama into a maxim of a general kind. In the drama, he explains, verisimilitude was needed owing to its appeal to the eye; but in the epic narrative with its appeal to the imagination greater licence was permitted; and the dramatic principle was thus irrelevant and misleading when applied to poetry in general.

Having thus corrected false notions of chivalry and romance, and having disposed of current objections to Spenser and Tasso, together with the critical creed that had given rise to such false

[1] *Spectator*, Nos. 5 and 369.   [2] *Letter x*.

judgments, Hurd then proceeds to discuss 'Gothic' or 'romantic' poetry itself, and represents it to his readers in altogether a new light.[1] He first recalls the objections to such poetry raised by Davenant and Hobbes, noting also Addison's remark that in his day 'men of cold fancies and philosophical dispositions' had scorned 'the fairy way of writing' as lacking in probability.[2] Yet while he confesses that to many these tales were still but lies, 'fantastic and incredible and long exploded', he now boldly defends them (here following Aristotle) provided they were founded on popular beliefs. In the days of chivalry, he implies, men were convinced of the reality of these tales; and in order to appreciate them justly it was for modern readers 'to put themselves in the circumstances of those for whom the poet had written'. In other words the poems were to be read in the light of those earlier times and from the historical point of view. Nor is this all that he has to urge on their behalf; for he declares that he himself had been captivated by their charm and was deeply conscious of their appeal. To him the classical sections of Tasso's *Jerusalem Delivered* appeared but 'faint and cold and almost insipid', when compared with the glowing effects of the 'romantic' passages. 'We are all on fire', he states, 'with his magical feats and enchantments'; and for his own part Hurd protested that 'without them he would scarcely be disposed to give the poem a second reading'. And as for the so-called lies bound up with this 'romantic' fiction, to this charge he makes an interesting rejoinder, when he describes those fictions as 'creditable deceits'. It was an argument drawn from antiquity, from an utterance of the sophist Gorgias, preserved in Plutarch's pages,[3] which originally had been a defence of 'illusion' in tragedy. Hurd now recalls it in support of 'romantic' fiction; and not without effect. 'They who deceive', he writes, 'are honester than they who do not deceive, and they who are deceived, wiser than those who are not deceived.'

Hurd's statement on behalf of 'romantic' literature is now practically complete; but before concluding he cannot refrain from commenting on those causes that had led to the obloquy heaped upon it in the past. That early prejudice against it had been excited by the bad workmanship of some of the actual romances, more especially as compared with the masterpieces of antiquity, this, to begin with, he states, was one definite cause.[4] Then, too, he explains that by the time an improved

---

[1] *Letter x.*   [2] *Spectator*, No. 419.
[3] See Atkins, *Lit. Crit. in Antiquity*, i. 18.   [4] *Letter xi.*

poetic technique was available, the spirit of romance had already become faded and unfamiliar, and therefore unsuitable for serious poetic treatment. More than this, however, was the fact that genius in the person of Chaucer had at an early date apparently declared against it. It was true, he added, that in *Sir Thopas*—that 'prelude to the adventures of Don Quixote' —it was the defects, and the defects alone, that had been ridiculed. Yet the upshot was that 'these phantoms of chivalry had the misfortune to be laughed out of countenance before the substance of it had been . . . fairly represented by any capable writer'. Nor, again, he suggests, was romance subsequently re-established, despite the favour shown by the 'romantic Eliza-beth', when Spenser at length felt the charm of the old fairy world.[1] For, so Hurd maintained, he had handled his romantic material in apologetic fashion by throwing round it the mist of allegory, thus presenting stories of knights and giants as mere moral fictions, the reality of which should not be too closely scanned. And then, when the age of reason dawned, the taste for poetry took yet a new turn. Romance henceforth was scornfully rejected and the glamour of the chivalrous world no longer appealed to men of sense. As Hurd finally declared in his enthusiastic fashion:

Fancy, that had wantoned it so long in the world of fiction, was now constrained, against her will, to ally herself with strict truth, if she would gain admittance into reasonable company. What we have gotten by this revolution, you will say, is a great deal of good sense. What we have lost is a world of fine fabling.

It was a lament, but it was also a stirring challenge that in recalling past glories pointed the way with some confidence to future literary triumphs.

In now estimating the value of the critical work of Hurd what mainly strikes one is the skill with which he brings to a head the gradual widening of the critical outlook by his treatment of ideas and suggestions drawn from various sources. In a sense it might be said that he lacked originality. Gray, the Wartons, Saint-Palaye and others all furnished him with material facts; and he himself disclaims any merit as an independent investi-gator, confessing (with perhaps a touch of pride) that he had taken no part in the 'ungrateful task' of perusing 'barbarous volumes' or of working in the 'medieval quarry' of Warton and the like. As a result, therefore, his acquaintance with romances was largely of a second-hand kind, a fact which goes to explain

[1] *Letter xii.*

his flattering comparison of the romances with the *Iliad*. In his use moreover of the term 'imagination' he sees no farther than the rest of his generation; to him it is still, not a unifying and an organizing activity, but mere 'fancy', a credulous faculty that loves 'to admire and to be deceived'. Nor again do his judgments always mark an advance in aesthetic taste. He is attracted genuinely enough by the old romances, and he felt the charm of Elizabethan prose; but he has some doubts about the newly created novel, which he held would have been more effective in verse-form.

Yet in spite of all shortcomings his work represents something new in critical history as a clear and reasoned treatment of doctrines thrown out promiscuously by earlier writers, to which he adds something of his own. His concise and searching attack on the neo-classical creed, for instance, his timely reminder of the value of Italian poetry, and his uncompromising demand that romantic literature should not be judged solely by classical standards, all were matters that had been previously treated, but never in more convincing or persuasive fashion. And even more arresting are his original critical pronouncements, as when, for example, he points out that the theme in some measure dictates the form of a poem, or that there is such a thing as a unity of design as well as a unity of action; while in denouncing vague and ill-defined terminology as a source of bad criticism he brought to light for the first time a critical defect of all the ages. His most valuable performance, however, lay in arousing an imaginative interest in the past, and in reviving the historical sense where literature was concerned. For the true appreciation of earlier literature he insisted on the necessity for reading it in the light of the society and conditions of the time; and in his unequivocal defence of medieval literature he recalls the spirited plea put forward by Daniel in Elizabethan days. Thus he disposes once for all of the 'monkish barbarisms' long associated with medieval times; the term 'Gothic', no longer used in a disparaging sense, is displaced by the term 'romantic', which from now on was to acquire a world of new and suggestive meanings; and the idea that English poetry had begun with Mr. Waller had also become untenable. In thus redeeming from contempt the literature of medieval and Elizabethan times Hurd was completing in his own way the scholarly efforts of Gray and the Wartons. And in so doing he gave fresh impetus to that wider study of literature indispensable for a just understanding of the nature of the English literary genius.

CHAPTER VII

SHAKESPEARE CRITICISM: ROWE, POPE, THEOBALD, JOHNSON, KAMES, MRS. MONTAGU AND MORGANN

MEANWHILE the widening of the critical outlook which had fostered a more generous appreciation of literature in general had at the same time been accompanied by intensive studies of one particular author, the effects of which were equally significant in the critical development and the growing opposition to the neo-classical creed, and which therefore demand a chapter of their own. For the ever-increasing interest in Shakespeare at this date there were many reasons. From Elizabethan days there had been evident a definite, if more or less inarticulate, admiration for his plays. That admiration had successfully survived not only Rymer's foolish animadversions; but also the pedantic scruples of neo-classical purists, and even the mangled versions in which he was presented to 17th- and 18th-Century playgoers. And, now with newly awakened sensibilities where literature was concerned and in the light of what Dryden in particular had written, efforts were made by various writers to give reasons for the faith that was in them. It was a task rendered all the more urgent by Voltaire's gross misrepresentations after his brief stay in England (1726–9), and by the controversy regarding Shakespeare's merits that raged abroad in consequence. So that his plays were now for the first time submitted to careful editing. Attempts were made to decide what he had actually written, to explain obscurities in his text, as well as something of his artistic merits. And in addition to these editorial labours, further appreciations were forthcoming from a variety of sources, all of which marked an advance in critical methods and achievements.

For a just understanding of what was actually accomplished at this date by these Shakespeare studies, however, it is necessary to recall how things stood at the opening of the 18th Century. At no time during the previous century had Shakespeare's light been wholly extinguished. Occasional disparagements, it is true, had come from men like Prynne, Cartwright and Rymer; and perplexities had been caused by changes in taste and stage conventions, as well as by neo-classical doctrines newly acquired at the Restoration. Nevertheless a steady chorus of praise was maintained throughout the century; and in spite of the continued popularity of Jonson, Beaumont and Fletcher during the 17th Century, it was, significantly enough, the vogue for Shakespeare alone that had justified the publication at different intervals of four Folio versions of his plays, namely, in 1623, 1632, 1663–4 and 1685.

Nor were the tributes paid without their value, though couched for the most part in general terms. Jonson's well-known lines appended to the First Folio (1623) had led the way with their claims that Shakespeare had taken rank with the greatest of the ancients, and that his work was universal in its range and permanent in its appeal. Less striking, though also revealing, was the homage paid by young Milton in the first of his published poems, when in verses included in the Second Folio (1632) he held that Shakespeare had built for himself 'a live-long monument', and a tomb for which kings would wish to die. Most substantial of all, however, was the witness of Dryden, the third of the great 17th-Century poets, who provided not only what Dr. Johnson called 'a monument of encomiastic criticism' but also some searching and illuminating remarks of lasting value that were to give direction to later critics. Moreover, from quarters less distinguished came further evidence of Shakespeare's popularity. There was, for instance, the statement of Leonard Digges (1640)[1] that Jonson's plays in his day 'scarce defrayed the sea-coal fire and the doorkeepers', whereas Falstaff, Malvolio and the rest drew crowded houses. There was also Fuller's quaint reference in his *Worthies of England* (1662), wherein he described the lively wit-combats between the ponderous Ben Jonson and the quick-witted Shakespeare, and likened Shakespeare's plays to 'Cornish diamonds unpolished by any lapidary'. Or again, there was the spirited reply of the Duchess of Newcastle (1664)[2] to detractors, calling attention to Shakespeare's marvellous skill in depicting all sorts and conditions of men, and his power of 'piercing the souls' of his audiences. In the latter half of the century, moreover, references became yet more frequent; and the appearance of Sir Thomas Pope Blount's *De Re Poetica* (1694), in which current views concerning Shakespeare were collected, sufficiently indicates the ever-growing interest taken in the dramatist and his works.

By the close of the 17th Century, therefore, Shakespeare's

[1] Verses prefixed to an edition of Shakespeare's poems.
[2] *Letters*, cxxiii.

plays were generally, if instinctively, appreciated; and then followed an astonishing output of Shakespeare studies such as had not previously been devoted to any English writer. His works, to begin with, were edited in an unbroken stream by Rowe (1709), Pope (1725), Theobald (1733), Hanmer (1744), Warburton (1747), Johnson (1765), Capell (1768), Steevens (1773) and Malone (1790), each edition being introduced by a critical Preface. And, in addition, essays and comments of various kinds were forthcoming from Dennis (1711), Joseph Warton (1753–4), Lord Kames (1762), Richard Farmer (1767), Mrs. Montagu (1769), W. Richardson (1774), Maurice Morgann (1777) and Whateley (1785). The output was unprecedented and was not confined to *littérateurs* alone. All shared in the discussion, antiquarians, ecclesiastics, diplomatists and others. And the outstanding result of all these labours was, first, the gradual evolving of a text more nearly representative of what Shakespeare had written, and, secondly, a flood of new light thrown on the artistic values of the plays themselves.

The work of the editors, however, first calls for attention, though they vary in value. Neither Hanmer nor Warburton, for example, added much to the general enlightenment, the work of the former being little more than an *édition de luxe*, whereas Warburton's contribution was notable chiefly for its rash conjectures, its arrogant and quarrelsome tone. Besides, the later editions of Steevens, Capell and Malone were distinguished for sound textual scholarship rather than for criticism in the wider sense of the term. So that critical interest is mainly attached to the efforts of Rowe, Pope, Theobald and Johnson, all of whom contributed in their different ways to the critical advance. That advance, however, was not made without much petty and unedifying squabbling, in which Pope, Theobald and Warburton were chiefly concerned; and from Upton, Thomas Edwards and Zachary Grey [1] came periodical sniping at the various textual performances. Into this protracted warfare it is not proposed to enter; though it was sufficiently heated to draw from Johnson a striking comment, puzzled as he was with the age-long 'acrimony of scholiasts'. Variant readings and such-like, he protested, were after all but small matters, calculated to 'exercise the wit without engaging the passions'; yet in commentaries, he added, was often found

---

[1] cf. J. Upton, *Critical Observations on Shakespeare* (1746), Zachary Grey, *Critical, Historical and Explanatory Notes on Shakespeare* (1754), and Thomas Edwards, *Canons of Criticism* (1748).

more venomous invective than in the most furious of political controversies.

At the same time not the least valuable of the editorial activities were their attempts at textual criticism, which, besides being a necessary preliminary to a just artistic evaluation of the plays, also represented something new in English critical history, and therefore call here for more than passing notice. Now for the first time was realized the corrupt state in which Shakespeare had come down in the Folio and Quartos then available. And the immediate problem thus presented was two-fold; first, a determination of the most reliable of the existing versions, and, secondly, a correction of verbal and other errors that had crept into the texts. To these matters, as well as in a lesser degree to an appreciation of artistic qualities, editorial attention was therefore now directed. And the progress made, it should be noted, was largely due to the recognition of a principle to which notice had previously been called by more than one critic. That principle was that in treating of an earlier writer the conditions of his age should be taken into account. And by a recovery of the historical sense and an application of the historical critical method Shakespeare's texts and plays were now presented in a new and clearer light.

From the playwright Nicholas Rowe (1674–1718), to begin with, came the first new edition of Shakespeare's plays (1709), which however did little to improve the then accepted texts. Recognizing the total loss of the dramatist's original manuscript, he is content with the text of the Fourth, and latest, Folio (1685), the most incorrect of all the versions, though he has to his credit a few notable conjectural emendations;[1] while he also attempted to supply divisions of acts and scenes where they had hitherto been lacking. In his introductory *Account of Shakespeare*, however, he opens up new ground in supplying a coherent summary of the dramatist's life, at the same time recalling the sound doctrine that 'the knowledge of an author may sometimes conduce to a better understanding of his work'.[2] Occasional scraps of a biographical kind had previously come from Phillips, Langbaine, Pope Blount and others; but now Rowe, with the aid of the actor Betterton, compiled what was to prove the standard biography of the century, in spite of its mixture of fact and legend. Moreover, interested in the man

---

[1] e.g. 'Some are born great' (Folio, 'are become'), and 'the temple-haunting martlet' (Folio, 'bartlet').

[2] D. Nichol Smith, *18th-Century Essays on Shakespeare*, p. 1.

Shakespeare as well as in his works, he began the controversy which was to be continued for years to come regarding the extent of Shakespeare's acquaintance with the works of the ancients. Accepting, as Dryden had done, Jonson's statement of Shakespeare's 'small Latin and less Greek', he maintains that no traces of ancient learning were to be found in the plays;[1] though this, he protested, was no real disadvantage. Such acquaintance, he suggests, would have made Shakespeare more 'correct'; but would have also fettered his genius and detracted from the merits of his actual achievement.

It was in the same spirit that he attacked Rymer, denouncing his whole teaching and the imperfections of his play *Edgar*. Shakespeare, he asserted, was not to be judged by Aristotle or by laws that he knew not;[2] for, living in an age of 'universal licence and ignorance', he had written in the light of Nature alone. On the plays themselves he has less to say, though in general he regards their plotting as defective, their characterization as excellent. Apart from this, *The Merchant of Venice*, he suggests, was 'designed tragically' by Shakespeare though acted as a comedy; *Hamlet*, as compared with Sophocles' *Electra*, he held, inspired terror not horror; and not without its interest is his remark that *The Tempest* was no early play owing to the perfection of its workmanship in the matter of the Unities. Such then was Rowe's contribution to Shakespeare studies. It was naturally of a tentative character that ignored many vital matters including those of a textual kind. But, doubtless influenced by Dryden, he rejects for the most part neo-classical standards, and by means of biographical and other comments he prepared the way for a fuller investigation of Shakespearean problems.

With the appearance of Pope's edition (1725), however, came the first attempt at an historical approach to the textual problem in that poet's inquiries into the condition in which the plays had come down and the relative values of existing versions. Uncertain, as he states, whether any plays had been published by the dramatist himself, he recalls the existence of certain Quartos and Folios, and rightly directs attention to the earliest of those versions, explaining that the later Folios were based by 'impertinent editors' on the Folio of 1623. To the Quartos, however, he attached prime importance, as embodying plays printed separately during Shakespeare's life-time, sometimes in two or more forms, but unrevised by the dramatist

[1] Smith, *op. cit.* p. 2. [2] *ibid.* p. 15.

16

himself, as was suggested by faulty spellings and other defects. To the statement of Heminge and Condell that these Quartos were mostly 'stolen or surreptitious' copies he apparently attaches no value. Hence his description of the First Folio as, except in spelling, 'far worse than the Quartos'.[1] That first collection of the plays, he correctly states, had been printed from playhouse copies adapted for acting purposes, and in particular from 'prompters' books or piecemeal parts written out for the actors'. And, as a result, he added, cuts had been made, scenes deranged, speeches wrongly assigned, trifling and bombastic passages added; so that the version represented something far removed from the original texts. Yet while he thus throws light on the origin of the First Folio, his estimate of the Quartos was seriously at fault; as later investigators were to show, the Quartos had also laboured under certain disabilities.

Nevertheless with this imperfect conception of the relative values of the different versions in mind, he proposes to select for his text from the various readings those which seemed to him best. But while he thus recognizes the need for collation, in practice he has no settled principles regarding procedure. Scorning 'the dull duty of an editor', the drudgery involved in a systematic collation, he regards his own 'private sense' as the sole criterion of correctness; and his readings in consequence are often capricious and arbitrary, representing not what Shakespeare wrote but what Pope thought he ought to have written. In so doing he was but following current methods of 'improving' earlier works in the light of contemporary taste; but, as Theobald later remarked, by such treatment he 'frequently inflicted a wound where he intended a cure'. And this is seen, for instance, where his 'private sense' rejects some of Shakespeare's finest lines,[2] or again, when he offers verbal explanations that utterly destroy the original meaning.[3] At times, it is true, he consults the Quartos to good effect, as when he restores to *King Lear* more than a hundred lines not found in the Folio. Then, too, to his credit, he rejects the seven spurious plays first included in the Third Folio, plays previously rejected by Heminge and Condell, though, strangely enough, proclaimed much later as genuine by the German critics, Tieck

---

[1] Smith, *op. cit.* p. 57.
[2] e.g. 'Sleep that knits up the ravell'd sleave of care', and 'the multi-tudinous seas incarnadine'.
[3] e.g. 'unaneled' = no knell rung; 'disappointed' = unanointed.

and Schlegel. Yet in spite of some advance thus made by Pope in the historical treatment of the text, much still remained to be done before anything like the original text was attained.

In commending Shakespeare as a dramatist Pope in his *Preface* represents what was probably the critical attitude of the more cultured readers of his day. That the plays were not without their defects he readily concedes. 'As he has certainly written better,' states Pope, 'so perhaps he has written worse, than any other.' And from his 18th-Century eminence he remarks on the low life of Shakespeare's comedies, the unfounded traditions of his histories, and the far-fetched incidents, the bombast and thundering verse of his tragedies. Yet such defects, he suggests, were largely due to contemporary conditions: to the necessity for conforming to the popular taste and to the prevailing ignorance of the rules. For Shakespeare, he regretfully insists, wrote from first to last for the people, irrespective of cultured patrons, careless also of lasting fame and with no knowledge of ancient models. He therefore asserts, along with Rowe, that Aristotle's rules were not applicable to Shakespeare; that judgment thus formed would be 'like trying a man by laws of one country who acted under those of another'.[1] And here, it is not irrelevant to add, by adopting the historical point of view Pope incidentally recalls that important principle of Elizabethan dramatic art, namely, of aiming at pleasing 'not the cook's taste but the guests' '. Then, too, it should be noticed, he hesitates to accept Rowe's further statement that no traces of ancient learning were to be found in Shakespeare's works. He points, for instance, to the Roman spirit in *Julius Caesar*, to an acquaintance with Plutarch shown in *Coriolanus*, and to reminiscences elsewhere of Plautus and Ovid's fables. Such details, he points out, suggest wide knowledge however acquired; and he inclines to the opinion that Jonson's statement regarding Shakespeare's lack of classical learning was an exaggeration that had since been utilized by those desirous of exalting Jonson at Shakespeare's expense.

In positive appreciation of Shakespeare's art, however, Pope is by no means lacking, though it is mostly couched in general terms. He proclaims him, for instance, as 'a great original, . . . not so much an imitator, as an instrument, of Nature', and as one who knew the world and human nature by 'intuition'. What he admires most is Shakespeare's characterization. He points to the wonderful variety and consistency of his characters, each

[1] Smith, *op. cit.* p. 50.

being individually drawn, with no two alike; he comments also on Shakespeare's easy and natural handling of emotional effects and his abnormal skill in exciting laughter. In one place he explains that in spite of all faults 'a certain greatness and spirit now and then break out' revealing true mastery. But his general impression is most effectively revealed in his concluding remarks when he compares Shakespearean drama with works of a more orthodox kind. Shakespearean drama he likens to 'an ancient majestic piece of Gothic architecture', the more 'regular' drama to 'a neat modern building'.

> The latter [he explains] is more elegant and glaring, but the former is more strong and more solemn. . . . It has much the greater variety and much the nobler apartments; though we are often conducted to them by dark, odd and uncouth passages. Nor does the whole fail to strike us with greater reverence, though many of the parts are childish, ill-placed, and unequal to its grandeur.

The main defects of Pope's edition, however, were almost immediately brought to light by an unsuccessful man of letters, who, though savagely derided, whether fairly or unfairly, by his contemporaries, was nevertheless destined to rank among the foremost of English textual critics. In 1726 Lewis Theobald (1688–1744) produced his *Shakespeare Restored*, in 1733 his edition of the plays; and although in neither of these works is much light thrown on Shakespeare's dramatic art, in the clarifying of the text they are of unrivalled importance. In *Shakespeare Restored*, which he justly described as 'the first essay of literal criticism upon any author in the English tongue', he submits Pope's text to a close examination, treating mostly of *Hamlet* but of other plays as well; and in the rather clumsy *Preface* to his edition he explains his critical theory, which involved a more reasoned approach to textual problems. From Rowe and Pope he may have taken certain ideas; and on Shakespeare generally he has a few remarks to make. But his real work was done in improving Shakespeare's text, in throwing new light on the relative values of the Quartos and Folios, and, most important of all, in establishing more rational and convincing methods of emending existent versions.

Of interest, in the first place, is his correction of Pope's estimate of the Quarto and Folio versions, when he suggests that there was less to be said for the Quartos than Pope had implied. Recalling Heminge and Condell's evidence of 'stolen and surreptitious' copies among the Quartos, he states that many plays during the time of acting were 'taken down in shorthand and imperfectly copied by ear',[1] and were thus subject to glaring errors from which the First Folio was free. He therefore claims for that Folio a respect denied to it by Pope; but he also recognizes that both Quartos and Folio were defective in many respects, and that their errors had been multiplied and propagated in the later Folios. At the same time the Quartos and the First Folio, he maintained, stood nearest to what Shakespeare had written; and upon them should therefore be based the texts of the plays.

It is however his convincing methods of reconstructing his Shakespeare text that call for most praise. And, to begin with, he rightly objects to Pope's arbitrary method of clearing up all difficulties in the light of his own 'private sense'. That many passages in the available versions were 'desperate and irretrievable' he fully recognizes; but then that was no reason for neglecting all doubtful places. And, recalling that many classical texts had come down from antiquity in mutilated form, he now proposes to apply to Shakespeare the method of restoration adopted by classical textual critics. It was a task, he claimed, never before attempted in connexion with any modern author; for Bentley's version of Milton (1732), he cryptically remarked, was 'a performance of another species'. His plan is therefore to collate carefully the Quartos and the First Folio, adhering scrupulously to the actual texts, retaining 'low and trivial' readings provided the sense was clear, and emending only such passages as could be proved to be corrupt.

Not less praiseworthy, however, is his actual treatment of difficult readings, and his perception that some knowledge of Shakespeare and his times would frequently provide the key to their solution. Thus Shakespeare, he notes, sometimes followed closely the sources on which he drew; and in connexion with his History and Roman plays more especially, such sources, he explained, would often supply the genuine reading.[2] Then, too, words obscure to 18th-Century readers had often been current coin in Shakespeare's day; and he claims to have read widely in Elizabethan plays and romances for light as to their meaning. Moreover other verbal difficulties, he asserted, could sometimes be solved by referring to similar but clearer passages in Shakespeare's works themselves.[3] It was a device (according to a French critic) *plus sûr que tous les commentaires*; and also, it might be added, a practice of textual critics from the earliest

[1] Smith, *op. cit.* p. 79.   [2] *ibid.* p. 82.   [3] *ibid.* p. 83.

times.[1] Most valuable of all, however, are his conjectural emendations, which often reveal a touch of genius and have commended themselves to later generations by their ingenuity and their poetic quality alike. The most familiar of these emendations is of course the felicitous reading of 'a' babbled of green fields'[2] (for 'a table of green fields'), with its convincing blend of humour and pathos in the description of the passing of Falstaff. But there are many others of interest as well; for instance, the readings 'Alcides beaten by his page'[3] (for 'rage'), 'scotched the snake'[4] (for 'scorched'), or again, 'the vagabond flag (i.e. rush) . . . lackeying the varying tide'[5] (for 'lacking'). It was such happy conjectures as these, together with his historical approach to the whole textual problem, that enabled him to render unique service to Shakespeare studies and that won for him later the title of the Porson of English textual criticism.

Apart from this he has but little to say on Shakespeare's dramatic achievement, though he regards him clearly enough as 'a genius in possession of an everlasting name'. Unlike most of his contemporaries he is not greatly troubled by Shakespeare's occasional anachronisms. Hector's reference to Aristotle in *Troilus and Cressida*,[6] for instance, he attributes to poetic licence rather than to ignorance. And similarly with regard to departures from historic fact. These were due, he explains, to the workings of free creative activity, to 'the blaze of his imagination which carried all before it'. Nor does he find in occasional resemblances to ancient thought and expression any infallible proof of conscious borrowing or imitation. Such passages, he states, only go to show how happily Shakespeare expressed himself on the same topics. Of interest elsewhere is his suggestion that Shakespeare's experience as an actor enabled him to identify himself more effectively with the various characters depicted; or again, less certainly, that his 'sweetness of temper' contributed to his facility in writing. And finally, there were his remarks on Shakespeare's style and expression, when to him he applied, without any customary reservation, what Addison had written concerning Milton, namely, that 'our language sunk under him and was unequal to that greatness of soul which furnished him with such glorious conceptions'.[7]

---

[1] cf. Atkins, *Lit. Crit. in Antiquity*, i. 188: see also p. 81 *supra*.
[2] *Hen. V*, II. iii. 14.   [3] *M. of Ven.*, II. i. 35.
[4] *Macb.* III. ii. 13.   [5] *Ant. and Cl.*, I. iv. 45–6.
[6] II. ii. 166: cf. Dennis, p. 245 *infra*.   [7] *Spectator*, No. 297.

Such then was Theobald's contribution to Shakespeare criticism. It was something more substantial and lasting than the contemporary estimate of the man and his work would lead one to expect. Aggravated by the hostility and contempt of Pope, he had unwisely indulged in his edition of Shakespeare in frequent jeers at Pope's errors; and in consequence was censured by Johnson for what he called his 'contemptible ostentation', as well as for his lack of genius, though Johnson had to confess that 'what little he did was commonly right'. Moreover, his new method of emendation, and indeed his verbal criticism in general, was ridiculed by more than one writer, and notably by David Mallett in verses *On Verbal Criticism* (1733), published anonymously. So that altogether he was written down by many of his contemporaries as nothing more than 'a dull, muddling pedant'; an estimate which, backed by Pope's prestige, was maintained for some time to come. Yet nowadays his achievement is more justly appreciated. By reason of his sound critical methods and his ingenious conjectures he ranks among the foremost of English textual critics; and the results are visible in Shakespeare's text as we know it to-day.

Concerning Warburton's edition (1747) less need be said; though in his *Preface*, apart from violent censures of previous editors, he has a few remarks that are perhaps worthy of note. There was, for instance, his comment on Shakespeare's facility of expression. 'No one', he maintained,[1] 'thought clearer or argued more closely than Shakespeare', yet 'hurried on by the torrent of his matter', he adopted the first words that came in his way. Then, too, like his predecessors, Warburton is definite in proclaiming that neo-classical rules were not binding on Shakespeare. Shakespeare, he asserts,[2] was to be judged 'not by rules which Dacier, Rapin and Bossu had collected from antiquity', nor by superficial estimates couched in meaningless jargon, but only by 'the laws and principles on which he wrote, Nature and common sense'. Or again, not without its significance is his defence of textual criticism against current attacks.[3] Pointing out that a great need of the time was a standard grammar or dictionary, he holds that both should necessarily be based on the authority of established English writers. Such authority however could not be set up until their texts had been examined and settled; and that, he claims, was the function of textual criticism.

The most valuable of these editions, however, has yet to be

[1] Smith, *op. cit.* p. 103. [2] *ibid.* p. 105. [3] *ibid.* p. 110.

mentioned. It was Johnson's edition (1765) with its masterly *Preface*, though previous contributions had been his *Observations on Macbeth* (1745), certain papers in the *Rambler* (1750–2), and not least, his *Proposals for printing the Dramatic Works of Shakespeare* (1756). In general his best work was done, not so much perhaps in emending the text, though he corrects many rash conjectures of Pope and Warburton, as in providing a judicial estimate of the whole position, and in furthering a better understanding of Shakespeare by his original and illuminating treatment. Drawing, as he himself confesses, on all his predecessors, he concentrates on what was of value in their works, and their findings he presents in fresh and coherent fashion. More than this, however, is the skill with which he opens up new avenues of approach to Shakespeare study by his reasoned treatment and his appeal to first principles. At times he deals effectively with vexed questions concerning Shakespeare's art; but more suggestive still is the new light he sheds on the workings of Shakespeare's genius by means of his keen insight, his balanced judgment and historical sense. In the *Proposals* and the *Preface* his views find their most adequate expression; and his remarks on textual matters, and above all, on Shakespeare's art, represent something new in English critical history.

In the first place his pronouncements on the problems presented by the earlier Quartos and Folios are more judicial and comprehensive than the sporadic comments of preceding editors. He notes, as his predecessors had done, that much confusion had resulted from the way in which the texts had come down; and he refers to the errors caused by shorthand reporters, illiterate transcribers, actors and printers, as well as to other errors due to the compiling of texts patched together from fragments and acting versions. In the *Proposals*, however, he further explains that many difficulties were due to Shakespeare himself, writing careless of fame at a time when the language was unsettled, and making use not infrequently of unfamiliar colloquial expressions. Moreover other difficult readings, he states, were bound up with Shakespeare's style, which he describes as 'perplexed and obscure'; and he ascribes many difficulties to 'the fulness of Shakespeare's ideas', when 'the rapidity of his imagination hurried him to a second idea before he had fully expressed the first'. The truth was, he explained,[1] that Shakespeare regarded more 'the series of ideas than of words, and his language, not being designed for the reader's desk, was all

[1] Smith, *op. cit.* p. 146.

that he desired it to be if it conveyed his meaning to his audience'.

Not less suggestive were the methods he proposes for correcting the texts; and here he is obviously criticizing the work of earlier editors. To begin with, he advocates as essential a careful collation of the oldest copies; since, as he explained, the readings of the earliest versions were most likely to be true, and 'were not to be disturbed for the sake of elegance, perspicuity, or mere improvement of the sense'.[1] Then, too, where many alternative readings were possible it was necessary to select the reading most in keeping with Shakespeare's 'cast of thought and turn of expression'.[2] At times, however, all readings would seem corrupt; and then conjectures with all their dangers were inevitable. That such conjectural emendations had a dangerous fascination for critics, indeed, 'all the joy and all the pride of invention', this much he recognizes. On the other hand he allows that they had hitherto played a great part in restoring ancient classical texts; but such emendation, he suggests, had been easier in connexion with the settled languages of Greek and Latin. He therefore utters a warning against too arbitrary and capricious an employment of such means. 'As I practised conjecture more', he states,[3] 'I learned to trust it less'; and again, 'an emendation is wrong that cannot without much labour appear to be right'. He thus decries all 'wanton and licentious' emendations; urges that conjectures were more safely based on a knowledge, not only of the manners and traditions, but also (as Thomas Warton had shown) of the literature, of Shakespeare's day; and in the course of his edition he gives new meaning to many of the earlier mangled readings.

While however he thus presents the main causes of the corruption of the earlier texts and the best means of remedying them, equally illuminating for the most part are his remarks on Shakespeare's dramatic art in his *Preface*, where his originality and his critical acumen yet more clearly emerge. To begin with, nothing is more characteristic of his skill in penetrating to the heart of the matter than his establishment at the outset of Shakespeare's sound claims to supremacy in literature. And this he effects, not by an appeal to classical or neo-classical rules, for which, as he states elsewhere, he had much respect, but rather by applying the Longinian test of all great literature, namely, 'length of duration and continuance of esteem'.[4] The ancients, he explains, were valued, not because they were

---

[1] Smith, *op. cit.* p. 155.   [2] *ibid.* p. 144.   [3] *ibid.* p. 156.   [4] *ibid.* p. 113.

ancient, but because they had successfully endured the test of time. And Shakespeare, he maintains, had by then assumed the dignity of the ancients, his plays having survived more than a century of changing tastes and manners, and having won fresh honours from each succeeding generation.

Not content however with a bare general statement he points, with similar directness and certainty, to the supreme quality that had commended the dramatist to successive generations. And this he defines as the universality of his outlook, the faithful portrayal of the fundamental qualities of human nature common to all the ages. As he explains,[1] 'nothing can please many and please long but just representations of general (i.e. universal) nature'. Thus Shakespeare's characters, he states, are never unnatural; they are real men and women, true to actual life, acting and speaking under the influence of passions common to all humanity—a vivid contrast, he adds, to the abnormally good or abnormally depraved characters of other dramatists, characters conversing in language never heard, on topics never discussed, and with whom the one passion of love was falsely represented as dictating every action. And this universal treatment, he further asserts, marked Shakespeare's handling of extra-natural worlds; for, as he had previously stated,

> Each change of many-coloured life he drew,
> Exhausted worlds and then imagined new.[2]

Even then however things were said to happen in accordance with the laws of human nature. The event which he represents will not happen, wrote Johnson, but if it were possible, its effects would probably be such as he has assigned. In short, while Shakespeare in general revealed human nature as it acts in real crises, he also suggested how it would act in trials to which it could not be exposed. Moreover, it was in defence of this claim to universality of treatment that Johnson denounces the objections raised by Rymer, Dennis and Voltaire against Shakespeare's characterization as wanting in 'decorum'. Thus Rymer and Dennis had described Shakespeare's Romans as 'not sufficiently Roman', whereas Voltaire had objected to his representation of the usurping king in *Hamlet* as a drunkard. To these charges Johnson replies that Shakespeare, careless of minor details, had nevertheless preserved the essential human characters. 'His story', he explains, 'requires Romans or kings

---

[1] Smith, *op. cit.* p. 114.

[2] See *Prologue* at the opening of Drury Lane theatre (1747).

but he thinks only of men.'[1] And he curtly dismisses the objections as 'the petty cavils of petty minds'.

Having thus established Shakespeare's claims to greatness on grounds that could not be questioned, Johnson then brings to light further qualities which contributed to the magnitude of his achievement. He points, for instance, to Shakespeare's originality, suggesting that no one except Homer had invented so much as he, claiming also that the form, the characters and the language of the English drama were all due to his initiative. And in this connexion he approves of Dennis's earlier statement[2] that with Shakespeare had originated the harmony of dramatic blank verse, that form so well suited for action and dialogue. Then, too, he notes as the special excellence of Shakespeare's style its colloquial colouring which prevented that style from ever becoming stilted or obsolete. Free from affectations, from 'modish and learned innovations', added Johnson, it stood for a form of expression 'above grossness and below refinement, where propriety resides'.[3]

Apart from this, he holds that Shakespeare's real power is shown, not in detached passages, but in the development of his plots and his skill in dialogue. And it is in the comedies that he finds the clearest manifestation of Shakespeare's genius. His tragic scenes Johnson finds laboured, with 'something wanting', though they are said to please by means of incident and action; whereas his comedies, described as 'instinctive and unlaboured', are said to have suffered little from the lapse of time, being endowed with 'the simplicity of primitive qualities'. Like most of his contemporaries, Johnson finds Shakespeare's greatest merits in his characterization, for he has less to say about the structural details of his plots. His characters, however, he states, are clearly and convincingly drawn, successfully combining the particular with the universal, and presenting 'human sentiments in human language'. Moreover, scattered throughout his editorial notes are striking and lasting appreciations, as when, for instance, he describes the secret of the 'inimitable Falstaff' to be the quality of perpetual gaiety, his unfailing power of raising laughter, or again, when he states that 'the idea of dotage encroaching upon wisdom will solve all the phenomena of the character of Polonius'.

Johnson's admiration for Shakespeare, however, falls short of idolatry and he does not scruple to indicate what he regards

---

[1] Smith, op. cit. p. 118.   [2] ibid. p. 140: see p. 244 infra.
[3] ibid. p. 122.

as his faults. He remarks, for example, on the untidy endings
of some of his plots,[1] his weakness for gross jests and tiresome
quibbles, his tendency to amplify unduly his narratives and set
speeches, and to fall in his tragedies into bombast and obscurity,
despite 'scenes of passion often forceful and striking'. Such censures are not without some measure of justification. But there
is less to be said for his objections to Shakespeare's anachronisms
or his mingling of Greek and 'Gothic' mythologies; or again, for
his derision of Shakespeare's use of 'low' terms, as when in
Macbeth the avengers of guilt are to be prevented from 'peer-
ing through the *blanket* of the dark'.[2] Nor can his complaint
concerning Shakespeare's neglect of poetic justice be justly
endorsed. Shakespeare, he states, had written without moral
purpose, sacrificing virtue to convenience in his desire to please,
rather than to instruct; and whereas other faults, Johnson
allows, might be extenuated by the conditions under which he
wrote, a similar indulgence, he adds, was not possible here,
since 'it is always a writer's duty to make the world better'.

Yet among Shakespeare's faults, it is worth noting, he refuses
to include his practice of mingling tragic and comic elements,
or again, his neglect of the Unities of time and place—two
serious violations, as he recognizes, of the orthodox neo-classical
creed. In the first place he refutes the conventional objection
to this mingling of tears and laughter,[3] the objection being that
such procedure confused and impaired the emotional effects.
Such reasoning Johnson flatly declares to be not only specious,
but inconsistent as well with the actual experience of playgoers.
'All pleasure', he maintains, 'consists in variety'; and if the
practice complained of is 'contrary to the rules of criticism . . .
there is always an appeal open from criticism to nature'. The
truth was, he explained, that Shakespeare's plays were, strictly
speaking, neither tragedies nor comedies in the ancient sense,
and were therefore not subject to rules laid down in accordance
with those ancient traditions. Among the ancients, he stated,
had existed the dramatic convention of treating the crimes of
men and their absurdities in strict isolation; whereas Shakespeare, out of 'the chaos of mingled purposes' that made up life,
had originated a new type of play in which mourners and
revellers, wise men and foolish, all played their part. The aim
of all poetry, he declared, was 'to instruct by pleasing'; and
Shakespeare's 'mingled dramas', he claimed, did this effectively;

[1] Smith, *op. cit.* pp. 123 ff.   [2] *Rambler*, 168.
[3] Smith, *op. cit.* pp. 118 ff.

while there was also this to be said, that they had the further merit of being more nearly representative of actual life.

Even yet more significant are his comments on Shakespeare's non-observance of the Unities of time and place.[1] As he points out, Shakespeare in general had preserved the Unity of action in accordance with Aristotle's requirements, his plots having a beginning, a middle and an end, with events linked together, and conclusions resulting from what had gone before. In matters of time and place, however, he had directly challenged those laws 'established by the joint authority of poets and critics'; and with 'all due reverence' Johnson undertakes to defend him. He first presents the case for the Unities of time and place. They were necessary, so it was commonly said, to make a drama credible by dispensing with such absurdities as actions spread over years being represented in three hours, or a scene in Rome being subsequently treated as a scene in Alexandria. From such obvious impossibilities, it was argued, the mind revolted, and events thus presented could not but seem utterly unreal and unconvincing.

Yet, argued Johnson, surely the playgoer realizes from the first that the whole dramatic business is one of make-believe, and therefore finds no difficulty in imagining himself now in ancient Rome or later in Alexandria. But if this much be granted, added Johnson, to such imagining there can be no limitation. The playgoer, in 'a state of elevation above the reach of reason or of truth, and from the height of empyrean poetry', disregards all details of time and place; and by him a lapse of years is as easily conceived as a passage of hours. Nor does such imagining produce the effect of mere wild fancy; for the events represented are taken to be 'a just picture of a real original'. In other words, they are not mistaken for realities but they nevertheless 'bring realities to the mind'. And the delight of tragedy, added Johnson, comes from our consciousness of this very element of fiction or illusion,[2] and not, as Aristotle had suggested, from a realization of the dramatist's skill in presenting tragic themes.

Therefore Johnson finds Shakespeare justified in having neglected the Unities of time and place; though he recognizes that all the weight of authority was against him. Yet he states, and in no uncertain terms, that whereas Unity of action was essential, the Unities of time and place were unnecessary and rested on no sure foundation. They might sometimes conduce

---

[1] Smith, *op. cit.* pp. 126 ff.   [2] See pp. 329–30, 336.

to pleasure, he allows, though since Corneille's day they 'had given more trouble to the poet than pleasure to the auditor'; while plays written according to those rules were little more than 'elaborate curiosities, . . . the product of superfluous and ostentatious art'. In any case, such rules were always 'to be sacrificed to the nobler beauties of variety and instruction'; and it was high time to say so, and that, 'on the authority of Shakespeare'.

These then are Johnson's main comments on Shakespeare as a dramatist; though on one further point he is insistent, namely, on the need for forming an historical estimate of his work, since 'every man's performance', he holds,[1] 'to be rightly estimated must be compared with the state of the age in which he lived and with his particular opportunities'. He therefore recalls the disabilities under which Shakespeare had laboured and over which he had triumphed. He suggests, for example, that Shakespeare had written for uncultured audiences with the primitive tastes of a nation emerging from 'barbarity'; and his plays, he adds, are therefore full of exciting incidents and shows, as contrasted with the later, less effective, 'inactive declamations', however 'musical, elegant and impassioned' they might be. Then, too, he accepts Ben Jonson's statement that Shakespeare had been wanting in classical learning; but he also points out that Shakespeare had drawn much material from translations, popular novels and the like, enriching such stories with convincing motives and life. Or again, he notes that Shakespeare had written before human nature, thanks to Hobbes and Locke, had become the fashionable study; yet he had revealed an intimate and unrivalled knowledge of humanity as comprehensive as it was profound. And apart from all this, added Johnson, he had to do with a crude and ill-equipped stage, and was without any advantages of fortune or earlier technical guidance; yet all these encumbrances he is said to have flung aside as 'dew-drops from a lion's mane'.

The value of Johnson's contribution to Shakespeare criticism is therefore considerable. It must rank as one of the great works in English critical history. That he is short-sighted at times in his appreciation is apparent, as when he holds, for instance, that many of Shakespeare's tragedies are the worse for being acted,[2] or again, when he censures his non-observance of poetic justice and his corruption of the language by

---

[1] Smith, *op. cit.* p. 132.
[2] *ibid.* p. 130: cf. Lamb, *On the Tragedies of Shakespeare.*

'every mode of depravation'. Moreover he was doubtless indebted to his predecessors for some of his ideas; though his sane judgment is evident from the way in which he discriminates between what was valuable and what was not. Yet while later scholarship and heightened sensibilities were to lead to a fuller understanding of Shakespeare's art, his *Preface* remains one of historical and intrinsic interest, in virtue of his unerring skill in indicating essentials, his reasoned judicial methods, and the sound foundations he laid for future textual and aesthetic developments. Not least valuable are the fundamental principles he throws out from time to time; or again his recognition of the importance of some knowledge of Shakespeare and his conditions in forming an estimate of his achievement. And despite his reiterated reverence for the orthodox rules, nowhere are his sound sense and independent outlook more clearly seen than in his rejection of the rules as applied to Shakespeare. In general, he attributes to Shakespeare many graces, but many defects as well. To him Shakespeare is a forest of great oaks with its weeds and brambles, an inexhaustible mine of gold and diamonds with its impurities and meaner metals. But his final verdict is one of generous and well-founded admiration. 'The stream of time,' he states, 'which is continually washing the dissoluble fabrics of other poets, passes without injury by the adamant of Shakespeare.' And this judgment, handed on to later generations with the prestige of his great name, gave to Shakespeare criticism fresh impetus and new direction.

Such then was the contribution to Shakespeare criticism made by editors of his works, a contribution which may be said to have culminated in Johnson's *Preface* of 1765. No less important, however, though in a different way, were the writings which supplemented these editorial labours, and which, in the works of Lord Kames and Maurice Morgann more especially, represented studies of a yet more intensive kind; and these now call for notice. Before the publication of Johnson's edition the contributions of Dennis, Joseph Warton and Lord Kames had already appeared; and they in turn were followed by a series of critics, including Mrs. Montagu and Maurice Morgann, who discussed Shakespeare's art from various angles. By them, generally speaking, a more inward bias was given to Shakespeare study, earlier controversies being now for the most part disregarded. Thus neo-classical rules, including those of the Unities of time and place, had already been denounced in connexion with Shakespeare; and earlier discussions regarding

Shakespeare's learning were no longer burning questions. On the other hand, attempts at this later date were made at a more intimate and detailed study of Shakespeare's art; while Voltaire's savage attacks on Shakespeare now called for some reply. And meanwhile the main interest was being concentrated on Shakespeare's characterization, in which, all agreed, he stood supreme.

With Dennis had begun this occasional criticism in his letters *On the Genius and Writings of Shakespeare* (1711). And the chief interest of that early work lies in the direction he gave to later critical effort; for, owing possibly to his earlier repute, the points he raises were to be those discussed by the editors that followed. A profound admirer of Shakespeare, in the first place, he finds him to have been at his greatest in tragedy, 'his master passion', he explains, 'being terror'. For the rest he calls attention to Shakespeare's skilful characterization, which he describes as free from the predominant love-motive that vitiated so many of the later tragedies; and, in addition, he notes the abundance of noble and generous thoughts in his plays, as well as his manner of expression that had retained its power and charm after a hundred years. Yet more striking however is his recognition of the virtues of Shakespeare's blank verse, which he distinguishes from the blank verse used for epic purposes, explaining also those qualities that rendered it effective on the stage. Thus

Shakespeare [he stated][1] seems to have been the very original of our English tragical harmony; that is, blank verse diversified often by disyllable and trisyllable terminations. For that diversity distinguishes it from heroic harmony, and, bringing it nearer to common use, makes it more proper to gain attention and more fit for action and dialogue.

It was an original and illuminating comment, which Johnson subsequently saw fit to embody in his *Preface*.

These excellences, however, Dennis weighs, in accordance with current practice, against what he regards as Shakespeare's faults. And, the immediate occasion of his writing being an attempt to defend his own adaptation of *Coriolanus*, it is mainly to that work that he refers for illustration. Thus, for one thing, he finds Shakespeare guilty of indecorum in representing the worthy Menenius as little more than a buffoon; or again, in introducing a mob into both *Coriolanus* and *Julius Caesar*,

[1] Smith, *op. cit.* p. 25.

'against the dignity of tragedy'. Moreover Shakespeare, he states, is often inaccurate in his historical details. In *Troilus and Cressida*,[1] for instance, Hector is represented as speaking of Aristotle, who lived long after his day, while in *Julius Caesar* a wholly misleading portrait of the titular hero is presented. And, besides, Shakespeare is said to have been sadly wanting in failing to observe poetic justice. The Tribunes in *Coriolanus*, Dennis points out, were the cause of the tragic calamity; yet they were allowed to go unpunished, so that the play was without any moral value.

These charges, which witness to the influence of orthodox doctrine, were, as we have seen, refuted by later editors. And Dennis himself already modifies his censures by suggesting that such defects were not incompatible with an overwhelming admiration for Shakespeare. He had mentioned Shakespeare's faults, he states, in order to make his excellences more conspicuous; and this he does by pointing to extenuating circumstances and by viewing Shakespeare's performance in an historical light. Thus his faults, Dennis explains, were primarily due to the age in which he lived and to his lack of learning; though he adds that Shakespeare, besides being a busy actor with no time to polish or correct, had also no guide in artistic matters, since Ben Jonson, too, had defied the rules and had chosen for his tragic plots themes incapable of inspiring either pity or terror. It was true, he added, that some knowledge of Latin texts on Shakespeare's part was suggested by the fact that *The Comedy of Errors* was clearly an imitation of Plautus's *Menaechmi*. But he suspected that the actual source of the play was an English translation[2]—a suspicion later confirmed by the discovery of a translation (1595) due to W.W. (possibly William Warner)—and he therefore sees no reason for rejecting Jonson's testimony of Shakespeare's lack of acquaintance with the ancients. Declaring, with Dryden,[3] that such disabilities only redounded to the credit of Shakespeare's performance, he added that 'he who allows that Shakespeare had learning ought to be looked upon as a detractor from his extraordinary merit'. Hence the importance attached to this question by later critics; and in this, and in other details, Dennis may be said to have led the way in this first stage of Shakespeare criticism.

Interesting in a different sense were the occasional essays on Shakespeare contributed by Joseph Warton to *The Adventurer* (1753); for they mark the beginnings of those more intensive

[1] II. ii. 166.   [2] Smith, *op. cit.* p. 41.   [3] W. P. Ker, *op. cit.* i. 80.

17

methods of appreciation afterwards turned to good account by
Lord Kames and Maurice Morgann. There Warton already
declares that 'general criticism . . . is useless',[1] that only a
detailed study could reveal Shakespeare's real beauties; and
this critical principle, reaffirmed in his *Essay on Pope*, explains
the method employed in that particular work. As for the
Adventurer essays, though somewhat slight, they are yet significant on account of their more inward treatment, together
with the illustrations drawn from Shakespeare's pages. Here
Warton deals only with *The Tempest* and *King Lear*; but his
comments on plotting and characterization are all worthy of
attention.

With regard to plotting, in the first place, he points out the
skill with which Shakespeare had observed the Unities in *The
Tempest*; but concerning *King Lear* he has more to say. Of the
underplot in that play, it is true, he cannot approve, on the
ground that it destroyed the unity of the main story;[2] and
with greater justice he condemns the scene of the blinding of
Gloucester as creating effects beyond the legitimate range of
true tragedy. On the other hand, like most of his contemporaries, he notes with approval Shakespeare's choice here and
elsewhere in his tragedies of themes other than those bound up
with the love-motive, which, he added, had degraded recent
tragedies, reducing the stage to 'an academy of effeminacy'.[3]
And yet more original is his approval of the non-melodramatic
use of the storm in *King Lear*.[4] Addison had previously censured
the various artificial devices of contemporary playwrights; but
here, Warton explains, the raging elements on the bleak and
barren heath serve a definite dramatic purpose. In other hands,
he states, the daring quality of the scene would have resulted
in mere burlesque; but with Shakespeare this particular device
heightens the effects of Lear's distress and the pathos of his lot.

Of yet greater value are his remarks on Shakespeare's character-drawing; for not content with vague generalities concerning Shakespeare's lively creative imagination, or his masterly
delineation of human nature, Warton calls attention to certain
specific details in his treatment. With the help of illustrations,
for instance, he brings out the consistency of Ariel's character,
and incidentally, Pope's debt to Shakespeare in *The Rape of
the Lock*. But it is in connexion with Caliban that yet greater
penetration is shown. Recalling Horace's statement[5] concerning

---

[1] No. 116.   [2] No. 122.   [3] No. 113.
[4] No. 116.   [5] *Ars Poetica*, l. 128.

the difficulty of creating a really original character, he points
to the mastery with which Shakespeare had created in Caliban
a convincing personality outside the bounds of normal human
nature.[1] This had been accomplished, he states, by a shrewd
selection of relevant details whereby Caliban is endowed with
all the vices of his progenitors, with their savagery, malevolence
and ignorance, qualities which were however redeemed, without
inconsistency, by poetic touches of a charming human simplicity, when, for instance, enjoining silence on the drunken
Stephano, Caliban commands

> Pray you, tread softly, that the blind mole may not
> Hear a foot fall.[2]

It was a dramatic revelation of character, previously illustrated,
as Warton points out, by the significant fashion in which Caliban
is first brought on to the stage.[3] Nor does he fail to indicate
something of the greatness of Shakespeare's Lear, and the convincing treatment of the old king's madness, which, he claims,
surpassed that of Orestes' as drawn by Euripides. A perfect
picture, he maintains,[4] is presented of the workings of Lear's
mind and his changes of mood and passion. And this, he adds,
is achieved, not by long and laboured speeches, but by dramatic
representations of deep feelings suggested by 'a word, a look, a
short exclamation'. It was by such appreciations as these that
he opened up a new approach to Shakespeare for general readers.
His psychological studies, though cast appropriately in a popular
vein, were instrumental in calling attention to some of the
subtler beauties of Shakespeare's art and thus marked a definite
advance in contemporary Shakespeare criticism.

A yet more intensive appreciation of Shakespeare's plays,
however, came from Henry Home, Lord Kames (1696–1782), in
his *Elements of Criticism* (1762), a work primarily intended to
establish the principles of literary taste in general, but which in
the course of its treatment devoted to Shakespeare considerable
attention. Of the wider scope of the work something will be said
later;[5] but what the learned judge has to say on Shakespeare is
of the first importance and calls for notice here. From first to
last he approaches Shakespeare from the aesthetic point of view,
endeavouring to explain his merits and defects to rational minds.
Like Joseph Warton he has little use for vague and 'general'
criticism. His treatment consists of a keen examination of

---

[1] No. 97.   [2] IV. i. 194.   [3] I. ii. 312 ff.
[4] Nos. 113, 116.   [5] See pp. 337 ff. *infra*.

literary details and their effects on the human mind; and not least valuable are the abundant Shakespearean passages with which he clinches and illustrates his arguments. In this way he interprets Shakespeare on what were practically new lines, bringing to light many subtle beauties and giving fresh impetus to the psychological study of his plays. Much of his commentary is of an original kind; and despite occasional lapses his appreciation has been described as 'the best of his age'.

The main purpose that animates Kames's treatment of Shakespeare may briefly be described as the establishing of the fact that the essential greatness of his achievement lies in its faithful reflexion of the ways of men and the panorama of human life. Earlier critics, he complains,[1] had failed to understand the real nature of the genius that had produced his unrivalled performance. They had concerned themselves with what he called the 'mechanical' side of the plays—with structural matters, the Unities, historical accuracy, and the mingling of tragic and comic elements—and had thus missed those more vital qualities 'which could only be relished by those who dive deep into human nature'. It was in his profound knowledge of humanity and in the unfolding of even the most obscure and refined emotions, he maintained, that Shakespeare 'excelled all ancients and moderns'. And this, he added, was a rare faculty of the greatest importance in a dramatist, a faculty which enabled Shakespeare to surpass all other writers in the comic as well as the tragic vein. This then being Kames's main thesis, he emphasizes Shakespeare's intimate acquaintance with the intricacies of the nature of man, illustrating how that knowledge determined the quality of his character-drawing and expression alike, how, too, a disregard of human nature accounted for many of his faults; and in conclusion a few remarks are added on structural matters.

Of the first importance, therefore, is the new light now thrown on Shakespeare's skill in character-drawing. Earlier critics had noted in general terms that his characterization had been true to life; but Kames now enlarges on that generalization, presenting it anew in detailed and concrete fashion and claiming that Shakespeare had called into being men and women as real as in actual life. For one thing, he is the first to enlarge on Shakespeare's employment of the true dramatic method of revealing character, that is, by means of 'action and sentiment',[2] or, in other words, by what his characters do and say; and in

---

[1] Kames, *Elements of Criticism*, p. 221.   [2] *ibid.* p. 412.

this connexion he denounces the less effective and tiresome methods of declamation and description employed more especially by French dramatists. Not that Shakespeare was lacking in descriptive power; for, as Kames points out, nothing could exceed his pictorial effectiveness, as when, for instance, he depicts the crowds in *Julius Caesar* welcoming Pompey in his triumph, with all irrelevant details suppressed.[1] But in choosing instinctively the dramatic method Shakespeare, he maintains, was enabled to present a given character more convincingly and in the round, that is, with actions, feelings and thought all in keeping with his conception of that character.[2] And as instances of this he points to the skill with which Falstaff is revealed in his plausible account of the famous robbery,[3] or Shallow in his futile, rambling dialogue with Silence;[4] while Gratiano,[5] again, in the brief remark that 'he speaks an infinite deal of nothing' is 'painted more to the life than in many words'.

Besides this, however, Kames notes the wonderful accuracy with which such consistency was attained, particularly in Shakespeare's knowledge and subtle treatment of passion, which knowledge, Kames asserts, was greater than that of 'any of our philosophers'. And in scores of places Shakespeare's insight into the intricacies of human nature is duly indicated. Thus, for instance, anger is said to distort the vision; which would account for Richard II's indignation with his favourite steed for carrying proud Bolingbroke,[6] for Othello's too ready belief in his wife's infidelity, or for Lear's personification of the storm, associating it in a conspiracy along with his inhuman daughters.[7] Criminal passion, again, is said to dissemble as long as possible; whence the naturalness of King John's method of soliciting Hubert to murder young Arthur,[8] or of Antonio's subtle approach to Sebastian for a similar purpose.[9] Elsewhere it is stated that a given character may be agitated by different passions at one and the same time, of which phenomenon Othello provides illustrations in more than one of his speeches; and in any case, the language of passion should always be broken and interrupted, since 'no passion beats always with equal pulse'.[10] For illustrations of this Kames refers to Shakespeare's 'incomparable' soliloquies, explaining that a man when alone

---

[1] Kames, *op. cit.* p. 378: cf. *J.C.* I. i. 40 ff. [2] *ibid.* p. 220.
[3] *1 Hen. IV*, II. iv. 298 ff. [4] *2 Hen. IV*, III. ii. 39.
[5] *M. of V.* I, i. 114. [6] *Rich. II*, v. v. 86 ff.
[7] *K. Lear*, III. ii. 14 ff. [8] *K. John*, III. iii. 19 ff.
[9] *Temp.* II. i. 213 ff. [10] Kames, *op. cit.* p. 223.

gives impassioned utterance only by fits and starts, expressing strongest feelings at first, and acquiring gradually more coherence;[1] though he also adds that soliloquies uttered in calmer mood might assume more consecutive form, as, for example, Falstaff's reflexions on honour,[2] or Hamlet's serene meditation on life and immortality.[3]

But while the virtue of Shakespeare's characterization is said to lie in his convincing representation of the most subtle and refined of human emotions, hardly less notable, according to Kames, is his natural manner of expression, his skill in giving appropriate utterance to his characters, while employing means calculated to appeal to his audiences. In his plays in general, 'thought', states Kames,[4] 'is attuned to the passions displayed, and language to both'; and in this way consistency is attained in expression as well as in character-drawing. But over and above this, adds Kames, there are niceties of expression of psychological significance, which render his treatment still more natural and effective. Thus passions, whether painful or pleasant, are said to stimulate the fancy, giving rise to poetic flights and to figurative expressions of all kinds.[5] A simile, for instance, may be introduced merely to add beauty to a narrative,[6] or again, as in York's description of Bolingbroke's entry into London,[7] to place a scene in a stronger light; though violent passions, Kames adds, do not admit of such similes. Then, too, minds agitated by passion are said to be naturally prone to indulgence in personification;[8] and for instances of the pathetic fallacy Kames points to Antony's lament over Caesar's dead body,[9] and to Richard II's sentimental utterance on landing in Wales.[10]

Elsewhere attention is called to other features of Shakespeare's expression, to his general avoidance, for instance, of Miltonic inversions and of abstract and general terms, as being unnatural in dramatic dialogue. 'Homer', states Kames,[11] 'wrote before general terms were multiplied'; whereas 'the genius of Shakespeare displays itself in avoiding them after they were multiplied'. And in avoiding abstract terms Shakespeare is said to resort occasionally to personification,[12] as when Death and its

[1] *Ham.* I. ii. 129 ff.   [2] *1 Hen. IV*, v. i. 128 ff.
[3] *Ham.* III. i. 56 ff.   [4] Kames, *op. cit.* p. 220.
[5] *ibid.* p. 320.   [6] *A.Y.L.I.* II. i. 12 ff.
[7] *Rich. II*, v. ii. 27 ff.   [8] Kames, *op. cit.* p. 331.
[9] *J.C.* II. i. 255.   [10] *Rich. II*, II. ii. 6 ff.
[11] Kames, *op. cit.* p. 387.
[12] *ibid.* p. 335: cf. *Rich. II.* III. ii. 160 ff. and *2 Hen. IV*, III. i. 5 ff.

operations are described in concrete terms, or when life and action are given to Sleep. Nor does Kames fail to note the advantages that accrued from Shakespeare's adoption of blank verse as his medium, explaining that 'as a sort of measured prose' it was well suited for dialogue,[1] while with its greater freedom it fitly accompanied the dramatist in his boldest flights, providing 'a more extensive and complete melody' than was afforded by the heroic couplet. At the same time he remarks that its use was appropriate only in scenes of dignity and grandeur, since familiar thoughts and ordinary facts called for plain language. And Shakespeare, he shrewdly notes,[2] had discriminated accordingly, by making use of both verse and prose, and by employing prose for characters of the lower sort and for scenes that lacked elevation.

Not without their interest, however, are Kames's remarks on Shakespeare's lapses in expression, his tests, here as elsewhere, being of a psychological kind. What he censures mainly is the untimely use of fanciful sentiment that degenerated into mere 'point' or conceit, and therefore stood for no genuine emotion. He points, for instance, to the impropriety of imagery that clashed with agony of mind;[3] to similes unseasonably employed in scenes of terror or despair,[4] or by one engaged in a humdrum task;[5] or again, to strained hyperboles[6] and to a childish play upon words,[7] though the latter, he allows, might sometimes be of dramatic value, as employed in one place by Faulconbridge. All such devices he condemns as unnatural and something other than the language of the heart; though Corneille, he recalls, had countenanced such procedure in his *Examen* of the *Cid*.[8] There Corneille had defended the use of sentiment more ingenious and refined than was consistent with real passion, on the ground that it was only by such means that the necessary elevation would be obtained. But this, argued Kames, amounted to the suggestion that 'forced thoughts were more pleasing than natural ones'; and he, for his part, regarded such procedure as faulty and as mere indulgence in ill-timed flights of fancy. All the same, for these lapses on Shakespeare's part he finds excuses in the absence of earlier guidance, in his unbounded enjoyment

---

[1] Kames, *op. cit*. p. 301.   [2] *ibid.* p. 409.
[3] *ibid.* p. 209 ff.: cf. *Rich. III*, II. ii. 66 ff.; IV. iv. 9 ff.; and *K. John* III. iv. 93 ff.
[4] *3 Hen. VI*, I. iii. 12 ff.; v. ii. 11 ff.
[5] *Rich. II*, III. iv. 29 ff.   [6] *1 Hen. VI*. I. i. 8.
[7] *J.C.* III. i. 207.   [8] Kames, *op. cit*. p. 210.

of fine language, and the fertility of his fancy which led him
in less passionate scenes to give undue elevation to his dialogue.
Yet these faults, he notes, occur mostly in the earlier plays;
whereas in the later plays 'he has attained the purity and perfection of dialogue'.[1] This, Kames rightly adds, is a fact of some
significance, 'one that with greater certainty than tradition will
direct us to arrange his plays in order of time'; and here he is
the first to suggest the important part to be played later by
internal evidence in determining the chronological order of the
plays.

On structural matters he has less to say, though his few
comments are of an enlightened kind; and of interest, in the
first place, are his remarks on the Unities. Accepting, to begin
with, the need for an observance of the Unity of action, he
regards 'a plurality of unconnected fables as a capital deformity'.[2] Each play, he asserts, is a chain of connected facts,
with each scene advancing or retarding the action; while 'barren'
scenes, he suggests less certainly, are not justified even if they
reveal character. With regard to the Unities of time and place,
however, he has what he claims to be something new to offer,
something that would 'rescue modern poets from the despotism
of modern critics'.[3] These particular Unities, he states, had been
necessarily observed in Greece owing to stage conditions; but
although since proclaimed by French and other critics, they
were not really necessary for modern plays. The Greek drama,
he explains, with its Chorus ever-present, had dealt with an
unbroken action; but by omitting the Chorus it had become
possible latterly to divide the action by intervals of time during which the action was suspended. At each renewal of the
action, however, a lapse of time and a change of scene might
be arranged. And it was no more difficult for a spectator to
imagine a new place and a different time after each interval
than for him to imagine himself at first in Rome two thousand
years before. The spectator throughout, argued Kames, was
aware that the real time and place were not those of the
representation; the whole business in fact was merely 'a work
of reflection'.[4] So that while the observance of these Unities,
he allowed, might confer a certain artistic beauty, it was nevertheless a refinement that should give way to the more substantial excellences resulting from a greater freedom of action,
and was therefore no rule for modern plays. And this view, he

---

[1] Kames, *op. cit.* p. 221.   [2] *ibid.* p. 412.
[3] *ibid.* p. 414.   [4] *ibid.* p. 415.

held, was supported by the facts that an unbroken action was apt to be fatiguing, that absurd situations often arose from an observance of these Unities, while, with the limitations thus prescribed, no adequate development of the passions was possible.

Of interest also are his occasional remarks on other aspects of Shakespeare's plays: as when, first, on psychological grounds he insists on the need for a logical development of the tragic plot. *Romeo and Juliet*, for instance, he finds defective in this respect, since the catastrophe there is due to mere chance, to the late arrival of Friar Lawrence at the monument, thus giving an impression of anarchy and misrule.[1] Of *Othello* on the other hand he warmly approves, the fate of Desdemona being due to natural causes, to the jealousy of a barbarous husband, while the plot is developed in a 'regular chain of causes and effects'. Or again, there is his pronouncement on the part played by verisimilitude in tragedy.[2] That all characters should be true to life he readily concedes; but that the semblance of actuality should limit subject-matter by confining it to probable events (as Hobbes had proposed), this he flatly denies. 'To make verisimilitude in the sense of probability a governing rule in tragedy', he asserts, 'would exclude all extraordinary events in which the life of tragedy consists'; and here he was clearing up a difficulty that had exercised the minds of earlier critics. Then, too, of significance are his attempts to distinguish between wit and humour,[3] which he illustrates with frequent references to Falstaff, Beatrice and others. He notes that to define ridicule and laughter had puzzled all critics from Aristotle onwards; but his own efforts, if not final, mark a distinct advance in dealing with a perplexing subject. He makes at least a definite break with the traditional Jonsonian interpretation of 'humour', when he states that 'humour in writing is very different from humour in character'.[4] And, besides, he broadly distinguishes between the humorous writer and the wit. The former he describes as one who is quick to see improprieties, and who, 'affecting to be serious, paints his subjects in such colours as to provoke mirth and laughter'; while the latter was one who indulged in images that 'caused gaiety and gave a sudden flash which is extremely pleasant'.[5]

The freshness, ingenuity and general soundness of Kames's appreciation of Shakespeare are therefore apparent. It has its blind spots, but it is also full of suggestive and seminal ideas

---

[1] Kames, *op. cit.* p. 400.   [2] *ibid.* p. 407 f.n.
[3] *ibid.* p. 160 ff.   [4] *ibid.* p. 161.   [5] *ibid.* p. 167.

that opened up the way to more searching and subtle inquiries into Shakespeare's art. Free from all allegiance to neo-classical rules, as is shown by occasional replies to Corneille and Voltaire, he gave fresh impetus to psychological studies of Shakespeare; and his originality is shown, not only by his general treatment, but also by casual remarks thrown out here and there, as when, for example, he points to Shakespeare's dramatic method of revealing character and his effective use of both verse and prose, or again, when he suggests internal evidence as a test of date, and attempts to distinguish between wit and humour—all matters which were to be developed by 19th-Century critics. Apart from this, his influence on Shakespeare criticism must have been considerable; probably greater than is sometimes realized. His work, it is worth noting, was soon translated into German; and in England its popularity extended well into the following century, so that by the year 1840 no less than eleven editions had appeared. To him Maurice Morgann may possibly have owed some amount of inspiration; though Johnson, it would seem, was not indebted to him for his closely parallel treatment of the Unities; since that subject had been already debated in the earlier pages of *The Rambler*.[1]

Less important, though of definite interest, is the contribution of Richard Farmer (1735–97), Fellow, and later Master, of Emmanuel College, Cambridge, who, in his *Essay on the Learning of Shakespeare* (1767), replied more or less finally to those who, following Pope, had attributed to Shakespeare a wide knowledge of the ancient classics. Relying mainly on so-called parallel passages a group of pedants, including Gildon, Upton, Zachary Grey and Dodd, had maintained Shakespeare's indebtedness to the ancients; while Peter Whalley in his *Enquiry into the Learning of Shakespeare* (1748) had endorsed their views in yet more formal fashion. And now Farmer, recalling Dryden's contention that they who accused Shakespeare of wanting learning had in fact 'given him the greater commendation', endeavours for his part to establish the fact that Shakespeare had not needed 'the stilts of languages to raise him above all other men'. He therefore begins by ridiculing the rage for detecting parallel passages, refers, as *prima facie* evidence, not only to the well-known testimony of Ben Jonson, but also to the traditional views of Drayton, Suckling, Fuller and others, and then proceeds to show that Shakespeare was not necessarily, or even probably, indebted to ancient classics for his material. Hurd,

[1] See *The Rambler*, No. 156, and p. 278 *infra*.

as previously stated, had declared that 'Shakespeare's freedom
from the bondage of classical superstition was due to his want
of . . . a learned education'; and now Farmer supplies detailed
arguments in support of that view.

Writing throughout with the arguments of Upton and the rest
in mind, he allows, to begin with, that Shakespeare had scraps
of school-learning, besides some acquaintance with French and
Italian phrases picked up in conversation; but, for the rest,
he could find no evidence that his classical learning was other
than what he had gleaned from works written in English. For
instance, it was not necessary, Farmer explains, to infer a
knowledge of Greek from the borrowings from Plutarch visible
in *Antony and Cleopatra* and *Coriolanus*. Such material, he
points out,[1] might well have been acquired from a reading of
North's translation; and indeed, as he triumphantly adds, one
of Volumnia's speeches in *Coriolanus*[2] is 'little more than the
words of North thrown into blank verse'. Then, too, in *Timon
of Athens*[3] had been detected a passage reminiscent of one of
Anacreon's Odes. But here again, Shakespeare's source might
well have been an English work; for, as Farmer notes (here
quoting Puttenham), there had existed an English translation
by Southern (1584) of certain verses of Ronsard, which, themselves a translation of Anacreon, had embodied the very Ode
in question. Or again, the plot of *Timon* had frequently been
ascribed to the Greek version of Lucian. But then, as Farmer
points out, the story of the misanthrope was common knowledge in Elizabethan times, being found in Painter's *Palace of
Pleasure* and other popular collections; and some such source
had doubtless provided Shakespeare with the outline of his plot.

Nor was the evidence for a first-hand knowledge of Latin
literature any more convincing. An indebtedness to Ovid's
Metamorphoses, for instance, had been detected in Prospero's
address to his attendant spirits in *The Tempest*;[4] but here,
Farmer explains, the real source of the passage must have been,
not Ovid's text, but Golding's translation of that text, since
Golding's free translation had been closely followed by Shakespeare. And in like manner Farmer deals with a host of other
arguments adduced as proofs of Shakespeare's familiarity with
Latin texts, arguments based on nothing more than far-fetched
reminiscences of ideas, phrases and even words. Moreover, that
a resort to contemporary English works was Shakespeare's

---

[1] Smith, *op. cit.* pp. 172–3.   [2] v. iii. 94 ff.   [3] IV. iii. 42 ff.
[4] Smith, *op. cit.* pp. 190 ff.: *Metam.* vii. 197 ff.: *Temp.* v. i. 33 ff.

practice, he adds, was suggested by the use made of Holinshed (rather than Buchanan) in his treatment of the Macbeth story;[1] of the novel *The Historie of Hamblet*, rather than the version of the story due to Saxo Grammaticus;[2] or again, of W.W.'s translation of Plautus's *Menaechmi*, rather than the Latin original, as the source of his *Comedy of Errors*.[3]

On this much-vexed question of Shakespeare's acquaintance with ancient literature, therefore, Farmer's views are clear-cut and convincing. Shakespeare's intimate knowledge of life, he held, was due to the acquisitiveness of genius, while such book-learning as he possessed was drawn, not from classical texts, but from contemporary English works. The whole controversy, in short, he regarded as so much 'misapplied learning', devoted to a pedantic search for arguments in support of a hypothesis previously and arbitrarily adopted; though something must perhaps be attributed to the influence of neo-classical teaching, and to an inability to account for literary merit which seemed wholly at variance with classical tradition. Nor is the value of Farmer's work confined to its unmasking of a futile controversy. Its real merit lies in the fact that he directed attention anew to Shakespeare's background and to sources which were to lead to a sounder understanding of what Shakespeare had written. He himself had gone with Warton-like zeal into the highways and by-ways of earlier native literature, consulting long-forgotten plays, poems and novels of Shakespeare's own day, 'all such reading', as he puts it, 'as was never read'. And this, he maintains, was the necessary preliminary for a proper appreciation of Shakespeare's art; since those, he adds, who apply solely to the ancients for this purpose may with equal wisdom 'study the *Talmud* for an exposition of *Tristram Shandy*'. Moreover he has also a word of advice in parting for textual critics, urging that an acquaintance with these earlier writings, often worthless in themselves, would sometimes throw light on Shakespeare's text. 'The cant of the age,' he states, 'a colloquial expression, an obscure proverb, and obsolete custom', all are relevant for this purpose; and with this he gave new direction to Shakespeare studies, even though in the following century he was subject to some amount of misrepresentation by Maginn and others, who read his work as a presumptuous attack on the memory of Shakespeare.

Significant in yet another sense was the *Essay on the Writings and Genius of Shakespeare* (1769) of Mrs. Elizabeth Montagu

[1] Smith, *op. cit.* p. 196.   [2] *ibid.* p. 197.   [3] *ibid.* p. 200.

(1720–1800), a distinguished society hostess, whose 'English *salon*' was frequented by many of the intellectuals of the day. Subject from the first to prejudices of one kind and another, the *Essay* was highly praised by Reynolds, Thomas Warton, Cowper and others, though derided by Johnson, and it has since been disparaged by critics on grounds more concerned perhaps with minor inaccuracies and faults than with the real significance of the work. That significance lies in the fact that it was a direct attempt to defend Shakespeare against Voltaire's destructive criticism. Johnson, it is true, had spoken of Voltaire's 'minute and slender criticism', while Kames had commented on some of his doctrines; but Mrs. Montagu has throughout his delinquencies in mind, and her attack is forthright and detailed. Her work is not without many obvious defects; and among others, an inconsequent arrangement, a lack of historical knowledge, besides pretentious aims which unfulfilled give an air of superficiality to the work in general. Yet it has also definite critical interest in calling attention to an important phase of Shakespeare criticism at the time, while the remarks on Shakespeare, if rarely original, are nevertheless of no negligible kind.

The occasion of the work was thus the reactionary influence of one who, commanding universal attention at the time, had propounded views outrageous to many English readers. At first Voltaire had been instrumental in arousing interest in Shakespeare among French circles. His three years' stay in England (1726–9) had made him acquainted with something of Shakespeare's achievement; and until 1745 his admiration, if not whole-hearted, was at least apparent, not only in his *Lettres philosophiques* (1733), but also in the creation of several plays based on Shakespeare's tragedies. With the appearance of La Place's translation of Shakespeare's plays (1745), however, accompanied as it was by a liberal appreciation of the plays themselves, Voltaire's antagonism to Shakespeare, strangely enough, began, fired apparently by resentment at the challenge to his authority as an exponent of the English dramatist. Thereafter his earlier reservations assumed a new and more vicious form, embodying a bitter denunciation of Shakespeare's art as outraging all the tenets of the orthodox tradition. Nor was he deterred by the growing admiration of Shakespeare in France; for he tries to stem the tide by his frantic but unsuccessful *Appel à toutes les Nations de l'Europe* (1761) as well as by later utterances. At an earlier stage he had described Shakespeare's tragedies as 'monstrous farces', *Hamlet* as 'the fruit of the

imagination of a drunken savage';[1] and in a letter of 1776 he
still conceived of Shakespeare as 'a savage with sparks of
genius'. It was at the height of this abuse that Mrs. Montagu
wrote; and her retort with all its defects calls for more than
passing notice.

In her attempt to vindicate Shakespeare she is concerned
first with decrying Voltaire's qualifications as a critic of English
plays, as well as his standards of judgment. She ridicules, to
begin with, his knowledge of English in the light of various
translations which proved that he had not understood even
Shakespeare's meaning. And likewise in matters of taste he is
said to have been hopelessly at fault. Antony's funeral speech
in *Julius Caesar*, for instance, he had described as 'a monstrous
spectacle'; while the famous quarrel scene of Brutus and Cassius
was to him nothing more than a brawl of 'conspirators in a
tippling-house'.[2] Elsewhere he had objected to the presence of
the supernatural in *Macbeth*; whereas, Mrs. Montagu contended,[3]
the marvellous element had served definite dramatic purposes
in rendering the old story more credible and even sublime. Or
again, there were his strictures on Shakespeare's blank verse,
which he described as easy to write and therefore unfitted for
serious tragedy. To this Mrs. Montagu replied[4] that, so far from
this being true, blank verse was specially suited for providing
dramatic effects, now 'rising gracefully into the sublime, or
sliding happily into the familiar, hastening if impelled by
passion or pausing in doubt, . . . and ever capable of adapting
its harmony to sentiment and passion with all the power of
musical expression'.

Then, too, she refuses to accept his neo-classical conception of
dramatic work; and in consequence she makes an attack on
French plays in general, which, while pointing to defects, does
less than justice to their positive merits. Thus she calls attention
to their artificial diction, which she describes as 'jargon' based
on the usage of the French court; or again, to their characters,
all moulded in accordance with courtly standards; so that
courtiers, not men, are really depicted, as when, for instance,
the dissolute and ambitious Otho of Nero's reign was represented by Corneille as an effeminate Pastor Fido. Elsewhere she
complains that their plots, all 'regulated by Aristotle's clock',
are mechanical in their effects; that they are also marred by
passages of declamation into which the poet intrudes, thus

[1] Pref. to *Sémiramis* (1749).   [2] *Essay*, p. 220.
[3] *ibid.* pp. 168–9.   [4] *ibid.* p. 178.

detracting from the action, as well as by long descriptions ineffective in representing real passion. Nor again, she urges, does French tragedy purge by pity and terror. Its effects are said to be those of 'amorous ditties', characterized by false delicacies, by sentiments reminiscent of elegy and eclogue; so that its superiority lay in trivial beauties alone.

Apart from denying Voltaire's claims to pronounce finally on the merits of Shakespeare's plays, Mrs. Montagu, however, calls attention to some of Shakespeare's positive qualities. It is true that in her ignorance of the actual conditions under which he wrote, she concedes too much to hostile critics in lamenting his many indecorums and attributing them to 'paltry tavern, unlettered audiences' and the like. Yet despite this apologetic tone, of her genuine and well-founded admiration there can be no question. 'Approved by his own age and admired by the next,' she writes, 'he is revered, almost adored by the present refined age'; and while 'no great poet or critic', she adds, 'except Voltaire had disparaged him', she claims that he stood alone in characterization and expression, 'with faults true critics dare not mend'. Elsewhere again she reminds her readers that the 'boulders of Stonehenge can be admired without knowing by what law of mechanics they were raised'; and Shakespeare's art she compares with that of 'the dervish in the Arabian Nights, who could throw his soul into the body of another man and adopt his passions'.

Nor does she confine her defence to remarks of a general kind; for, regarding him notably as an explorer, she points to some of his innovations, and has besides some interesting comments to make on his dramatic art. Thus in his historical plays,[1] she claims, he had broken down barriers in defiance of the rules that had previously limited dramatic works to tragedy and comedy, and working on crude annals had created new dramas that revealed not only mysteries of state but also the manners of a people and the spirit of an age. Or again, in *Macbeth*[2] he had introduced into tragedy new sources of terror, of terror undefined, by the intervention of beings whose nature we do not understand. And concerning his original treatment of the supernatural here and elsewhere she has also more to say. She points out, for instance, that his ghosts and fairies are all based on national traditions which popular faith had consecrated and revered;[3] that to all such elements he had given an air of reality which induces 'our imaginations to adopt what our

[1] *Essay*, pp. 47 ff.   [2] *ibid*. pp. 147 ff.   [3] *ibid*. pp. 113 ff.

reasons would reject'; and that, so far from being merely ornamental, they contributed to the action, supplying motive, colour
and the like.

Equally suggestive, however, are her occasional remarks on
other aspects of Shakespeare's art, as when, for instance, she
describes 2 *Henry IV* as that rare thing, a successful sequel,
in which earlier characters are consistently maintained under
changed conditions, or when she points out that Shakespeare's
sententious utterances, so far from being excrescences, arise
naturally out of the various situations. Nor has she failed to
appreciate his skilful characterization. Falstaff, introduced to
give colour to Prince Hal's extravagances, is said to be distinguished for 'finesse of wit and drollery of humour',[1] a combination calculated to cause laughter free from all malice and
satire. Macbeth, again, passionate and ambitious, endowed
withal with the milk of human kindness, is described as a
character likely to be influenced by suggestions from without;
while attention is also drawn to the amazing revelation of his
various reactions, the checks of reason, the impulses of passion,
the fears that precede and the horrors that follow his monstrous
crime.[2] These are something more than the idle comments of
a fashionable society hostess; and the work cannot fairly be
dismissed as 'feeble and pretentious'. Least satisfactory is
the attempted comparison with Greek and French dramatists
announced on the title page; though the idea of comparing was
in itself commendable, as widening the approach to Shakespeare.
And, for the rest, something was doubtless owed to earlier
critics, notably to Thomas Warton and Hurd. Yet the *Essay*
has a positive value of its own in its timely reply to Voltaire and
to neo-classical ideals generally; and despite all defects, it makes
a contribution to Shakespeare criticism that cannot well be
overlooked.

What specially distinguished Shakespeare criticism at this
later stage, however, was not the vindication of the dramatist
despite neo-classical demands; though occasionally a defence
of Voltaire's position was forthcoming, as in Edward Taylor's
Cursory Remarks on Tragedy (1774), in which Shakespeare was
held to have failed as a tragic poet on account of flagrant
breaches of neo-classical rules. Nor was the best work done in
connexion with Shakespeare's sources; though the first collection of source-material had been made by Mrs. Lennox of *Female
Quixote* fame in her notable *Shakespear Illustrated* (1753), and

[1] *Essay*, p. 89.   [2] *ibid*. pp. 149 ff.

the scholarly discussions of Capell, Malone and others were to follow. The most striking feature at this date was however the profound impression made by Shakespeare's skill in character-ization and the growing interest of character-study as opposed to the study of formal matters. And this phase was illustrated, for instance, by Thomas Whateley's *Remarks on the Characters of Shakespeare* (1770). It was the first attempt to deal exclus-ively with Shakespeare's characters; the first also to illustrate the value of the comparative method in character-study, a task which he achieved by a minute analysis of the qualities of Richard III and Macbeth. Both, he points out, were placed in closely similar situations; but their different reactions threw light on their differing characters. Both, he maintained, were ambitious, courageous and ruthless; but while Richard was naturally vicious, without conscience, pity or remorse, Macbeth, on the other hand was possessed of some humane qualities, was led astray by supernatural and other influences, and suffered bitter remorse in consequence. Both characters, he concluded, were true to life, with Macbeth, the more intricate character, being the more subtly drawn. Then, too, in this connexion passing reference might be made to William Richardson's *Philo-sophical Analysis of Shakespeare's Characters* (1774), a work that witnesses in a curious way to the value attached to Shake-speare's characterization, though at the same time the author finds many blemishes due to a 'want of consummate taste'. Written with an ethical purpose, its author, a Professor of Humanity at Glasgow, takes for granted the fidelity of Shake-speare's character-drawing and endeavours to extract from the plays the guiding principles of human conduct.

The outstanding witness to this new tendency, however, was Maurice Morgann's *Essay on the Dramatic Character of Sir John Falstaff* (1777), one of the most original, acute and illuminating pieces of 18th-Century criticism. Of the author little is known except that, a one-time Under-Secretary of State, he rendered valuable diplomatic service in connexion with Canadian and American affairs. And the *Essay* is thus the product of scholarly leisure in which for his own amusement the writer attempted to refute the charge of cowardice commonly brought against Fal-staff. In this primary, and apparently trifling, aim he is emin-ently successful. But in so doing he had accomplished something very much more, in spite of the somewhat untidy form in which his argument is presented. For he inaugurated a new approach to Shakespeare, threw a vivid light on his creative processes

18

and employed methods which foreshadowed those of Coleridge and Hazlitt later. In his essay, as he himself recognized, 'Falstaff is the word but Shakespeare is the theme'; and within its limits it must be regarded as the most penetrating study of Shakespeare's genius and art that had yet appeared.

To begin with, he frankly states the particular problem with which he proposes to deal. Judged by the remarks of certain of Falstaff's companions, by his headlong flight at Gadshill, his ignominious feigning of death to escape from Douglas, and his never-failing lies and boastings, the case for branding him a coward, our author confesses, would seem unanswerable and the only conclusion possible for the 'logical understanding'. At the same time, cowardice, he suggests, is not really the final impression received from Shakespeare's Falstaff; and in dramatic works, he significantly adds, 'the impression is the fact',[1] that is, what really counts. But that final impression, he explains, is determined not merely by logical processes of the understanding but also by the mysterious workings of one's feelings and sensibilities; and the plain truth is, he insists, that 'we all like old Jack', in spite of apparent cowardice and manifest failings. That he is amusing and cheerful is true enough; but then those qualities would be insufficient to win all hearts. And that he really wins our affections is proved by the discomfort we all feel at the ingratitude of Prince Hal. How then to account for this intuitive sympathy felt by all? Can it be, asks our author, that Shakespeare has secretly impressed us with certain redeeming qualities, thus ridding us of the distaste we should otherwise feel? And to the solution of this problem he devotes a detailed inquiry 'hitherto unattempted', recalling that 'general criticism is as uninstructive as it is easy'.

Of importance, in the first place, are the methods applied by our author in order to arrive at a just conception of dramatic character. Kames had already pointed out Shakespeare's dramatic method of revealing character by what a given personage did and said; and Morgann now suggests that further evidence was provided by the remarks of other personages in the play giving their impressions of the character in question. Thus 'Shakespeare', he states,[2] 'seldom trusts to the apprehension of his audience; his characters interpret for one another continually and when we least expect such artful and secret management'. And such comments, he adds, act as a sort of Chorus shedding additional side-lights on character, as Enobarbus and Menenius

---

[1] Smith, *op. cit.* p. 219.   [2] *ibid.* p. 255.

had done. Of all three methods Morgann makes use in the course
of his discussion; and he is the first to suggest these cross-references in character-drawing. He has however one rider to add;
and that is, that in taking into account the evidence of other
characters their personalities and the attendant circumstances
should be carefully scanned. Thus, for example, Lancaster's
reproach to Falstaff for his late arrival on the scene of action
—'the only serious charge against his courage'—was clearly
to be discounted as being due to Lancaster's ill-will and the
insolence of power.[1]

It is in applying these three tests, however, that Morgann's
critical insight is most clearly displayed; for, examined in the
light of what he does, what he says and what others say about
him, Falstaff is shown, despite all appearances, to be something
other than the cowardly *miles gloriosus* of which Parolles and
Bobadil were examples. Thus his flight at Gadshill, it is
claimed, was more or less excusable on account of his age and
condition; his feigned death a trick which, inspired by despera-
tion, was one that appealed to his sense of humour; while, on
the other hand, it was highly significant that he led his raga-
muffins into battle and preserved his gaiety throughout.[2] Then,
too, his boastful speeches were sheer humour and not the
utterances of a coward.[3] They were lies 'gross as a mountain,
open, palpable', intended not to be believed but to raise a laugh;
for, as Morgann shrewdly notes, they were uttered after the
event, were directed to persons who like Prince Hal could not be
deceived and who relished his humour, whereas in the company
of the slow-witted Justices and his boon companions he indulges
in no such extravagances.

Or again, there was the evidence of other characters, none of
whom regards him in the light of a coward.[4] At his attempted
arrest, for instance, Mistress Quickly and others utter warnings
of his desperate courage; in a scuffle with Pistol the latter flees
from him 'like quicksilver'; Shallow tremulously recalls his
earlier dread exploits; and while Colville surrenders in sheer
awe of his name, there were also the facts that from the Prince
he received a military command and from the Chief Justice
warm praise for good work done at Shrewsbury. Nor is this all;
for Morgann dilates on Falstaff's noble origin,[5] together with
the corollary that good birth implied courage. Thus he points
to Falstaff's early acquaintance with John of Gaunt, his youthful

---

[1] Smith, *op. cit.* p. 262.   [2] *ibid.*   [3] *ibid.* pp. 255, 271.
[4] *ibid.* p. 231.   [5] *ibid.* pp. 239 ff.

dignity as a page in Norfolk's household, and his skill in back-sword 'when scarcely an eagle's talon in the waist'; or again, not without their significance were his possession of a crested family ring, his rank as a military knight, besides those vestiges of former splendour revealed in his shabby followers and his retention of a London apartment.

Such then is Morgann's analysis of the position; and this cumulative evidence, he argues, in dispelling the notion of Falstaff's cowardice, suggests that Shakespeare for some reason has 'obscured the better parts of Falstaff' instead of 'opening them fairly to our understandings'.[1] Indeed, the whole question, he maintains, had been solved by Falstaff himself in plain words, when, replying to the Prince, he stated, 'I am not John of Gaunt your grandfather, but yet no coward, Hal'.[2] And with this modi-fied view of Falstaff in mind Morgann presents his conception of the character as a whole and comments on Shakespeare's subtle art as seen therein.

The main clue to the interpretation of the character he finds in the incongruity inherent in the representation of one who, naturally courageous, is exhibited to all appearances as an arrant coward. And this element of incongruity, he suggests, is present throughout, so that Falstaff is essentially a bundle of opposites:

A man at once young and old, enterprizing and fat, a dupe and a wit, harmless and wicked, weak in principle and resolute by con-stitution, cowardly in appearance and brave in reality; a knave without malice, a liar without deceit, and a knight, a gentleman and a soldier without either dignity, decency or honour.[3]

As such he is described as a comic masterpice, since incongruity in a rational being is ever a source of laughter. Moreover, Morgann indicates something of the skill that had gone to the creation of Falstaff as opposed to the crude stage-fools of Shake-speare's day and later. For the latter some one folly 'with a dash of knave and coxcomb' had sufficed; but Shakespeare, greatly daring, aimed at effects more subtle and refined by creating a buffoon endowed, not only with wit and humour, but with good birth, dignity and courage as well.[4] These however were quali-ties productive of respect, not ridicule, which had consequently to be toned down; and Shakespeare therefore rendered him ridiculous in his 'figure, situation and equipage', while associat-ing with him loose principles and every vice and folly not

---

[1] Smith, *op. cit.* p. 245.   [2] *ibid.* p. 268.
[3] *ibid.* p. 286.   [4] *ibid.* p. 287.

destructive of his essential character. Nothing, states Morgann, could exceed the finesse with which Shakespeare has thus concealed for dramatic purposes those more respectable qualities of Falstaff of which we are made sensible by our feelings rather than our understandings; and the result is a triumph of Shakespeare's comic genius and art. In short, Falstaff, he adds, like other characters of Shakespeare, 'is struck out whole by some happy art which I cannot clearly comprehend'.

This masterly disquisition on Falstaff, however, does not exhaust the interest of this remarkable *Essay*; for Morgann's frequent digressions are full of good things, ideas and suggestions relating not only to Shakespeare but to literature and literary criticism in general. Of passing interest is his defence of Shakespeare's use of puns under certain circumstances;[1] as when Antonio, for instance, undertakes 'to pay the forfeiture with all his heart'.[2] As Morgann explains, often an affected gaiety under heavy misfortune reveals the gloom that is actually felt, and at the same time represents an effort of fortitude that is only partially successful and therefore most pathetic. Or again, there are his remarks on earlier critics: his derision of Rymer who 'with his constable's staff' had attacked Shakespeare in the name of Aristotle, his strictures on the 'foreign wit' (Voltaire) who had done his best to ridicule the work of the 'barbarian', as well as the less severe judgments on those earlier editors who had done little more than 'peck on the surface of things without entering into the soul of his compositions'.

Yet more striking however are the general remarks that emerge in the course of his inquiry. He has, in the first place, some shrewd comments on the subject of character-drawing generally. He claims, for instance, that Shakespeare's characters differ from those of any other writer in that they have 'a certain roundness and integrity',[3] so that characters seen only in part are yet capable of being understood as wholes. Moreover, he adds, his characters, acting from mingled motives of passion and reason, are all inwardly and individually drawn, characters of much the same sort having something peculiar and distinctive; and while all are represented as influenced by the conditions under which they lived, in not a few instances they are seen developing, as when 'Macbeth changes under our eyes'.

Nor does he fail to rise to the occasion when in more comprehensive fashion he attempts to express his admiration for

---

[1] Smith, *op. cit.* p. 267 n.   [2] *M. of V.*, IV. i. 280.
[3] Smith, *op. cit.* p. 246 n.

the greatness of Shakespeare's achievement as a whole. That
achievement he describes as unique, adding that 'there is nothing perishable about him except that very learning which he
is said so much to want'.[1] And continuing, he states that

Him we may profess rather to feel than to understand. . . . He
scatters the seeds of things, the principles of character and action
with so cunning a hand, yet with so careless an air . . . that all the
incidents, all the parts, look like chance, while we . . . are sensible
that the whole is design. . . . His characters . . . act and speak in
strict conformity to nature, . . . just so much is shewn as is requisite,
just so much is impressed; yet he commands every passage to our
heads and to our hearts, and moulds us as he pleases, and that with
so much ease that he never betrays his own exertions. . . . Everything is complicated, everything is plain, . . . He converts everything
into excellence: nothing is too great, nothing is too base; . . . action
produces one mode of excellence and inaction another. The Chronicle,
the novel or the ballad, the king or the beggar, the hero, the madman,
the sot or the fool; it is all one—nothing is worse, nothing is better.

Equally subtle and amazing, adds our author, is the skill which
dispenses with the Unities, when by 'subduing the understanding' we are rendered 'insensible to the shifting of place and
the lapse of time'. And rising to a yet higher note, he points
to Shakespeare's triumph in his occasional abandonment of
ordinary human nature and his treatment of the supernatural
world, that 'larger circle within which none durst walk but he'.
This venture he justifies by the arresting argument that 'true
poesy is magic, not nature;[2] an effect 'from causes hidden or
unknown'. And to the poet-magician he would prescribe no
laws; since 'means, whether apparent or hidden, are justified in
poesy by success, but then most perfect when most concealed'.
Such then is his masterly appreciation of Shakespeare's genius
and art; and it is no wonder that for the plays he confidently
prophesies a glorious future in lands remote. Impatient at the
imperfect appreciation of his contemporaries and with the extended vision of his diplomatic experiences in mind, he boldly
asserts, as Samuel Daniel had hinted before him, that

When the hand of time shall have brushed off his present editors
and commentators, and when the very name of Voltaire . . . shall be
no more, the Apalachian mountains, the banks of the Ohio, and the
plains of Sciota shall resound with the accents of this barbarian.[3]

For this most suggestive of essays, this study *aureus ac auro
magis aureus*, no praise can therefore be too high; and with it

[1] Smith, *op. cit.* pp. 249 ff.   [2] *ibid.* p. 252.   [3] *ibid.* p. 249.

the sound spade-work of earlier editors and critics may be said
to have culminated. That it represents the first intensive treatment of a single Shakespearean character, and that of one of
the most puzzling of his immortals, is doubtless part of its distinction. But in so doing it also opened up a new field of
Shakespeare criticism, suggesting new methods of interpreting
dramatic character which were to be developed by 19th-Century
critics. And it is these original and suggestive qualities that
render it unique at this particular date. Among the seminal
ideas scattered lavishly throughout its pages are the pronouncements that Shakespeare's characters are presented 'in the round',
that they undergo development and with them 'the impression
is the fact', that the plays themselves, apparently created with
so careless a hand, are in reality the result of 'cunning design',
and that Shakespearean drama, like all true poetry, is 'magic
not nature', in which the means adopted, 'whether apparent or
hidden, are justified by success'. And over and above all this is
the plea on which the whole treatment is based, namely, that
for a just appreciation of literature the exercise of some other
faculty than the prose understanding is needed.[1] What that
faculty actually is, Morgann is not clear; though he is convinced
that the prose understanding, confined to visible existence, and
taking cognizance in dramatic criticism of action alone, arrives
by logical processes at judgments inadequate in kind. On the
other hand, literature, he suggests, has secret effluences which
the mere understanding is unable to assess; it has an appeal
to human sensibilities and feelings which constitutes the real
aesthetic effect. Here in vague terms he is hinting at that
faculty of the imagination which Coleridge was soon to define.
And to have raised the question in practical fashion is not the
least valuable part of Morgann's critical achievement.

[1] Smith, *op. cit.* pp. 220 ff., 252.

CHAPTER VIII

THE GREAT CHAM OF LITERATURE: JOHNSON

s o far in tracing the main features of the critical movement in
18th-Century England we have noted the growing challenge to
that body of neo-classical doctrine which had originated in
France and was generally, if tacitly, accepted in England as the
orthodox literary creed. By none of the outstanding critics,
however, was that system embraced in anything like its entirety.
Signs of independence, already betrayed by Addison, Pope and
others, were succeeded by a widening outlook where literature
was concerned, a development inspired partly by the influence
of 'Longinus' and certain French writers, by an awakening to
the merits of earlier native literature, and not least, by a
notable advance in the appreciation of Shakespeare's art. And
it yet remains to realize the actual part played by Dr. Samuel
Johnson (1709–84) in this general development. His importance
as literary dictator of the age has since been freely and generally recognized; yet his critical work has been subjected to a
surprising and confusing variety of estimates. He has been
hailed, for instance, as a champion of established conventions,
as the high priest of classicism, or again, as mainly a hanging
judge with eccentric and antiquated ideas; while one scholar
seriously asks whether 'any critic so narrow, so mechanical, so
hostile to originality as Johnson, has ever achieved the dictator-
ship of English letters'—estimates formed on certain aspects of
his performance to the neglect of others more important. Yet
the shrewdest of present-day critics are those who pay greatest
tribute to his critical spirit and methods, and defer respectfully
to many of his pronouncements: so that for a right judgment
it is more necessary than ever to make a detailed examination
and to select and interpret what is significant in his criticism.
Of his work on Shakespeare something has already been said;
and some estimate of his critical achievement in general must
now be attempted.

For the main body of his criticism we must turn to works of
various kinds, apart from reviews and occasional judgments
preserved by Boswell in his biography. Not without its interest,
for instance, is the fact that already in 1734 he had contributed to *The Gentleman's Magazine* 'short literary dissertations

embodying critical remarks on authors ancient and modern'; and about the same date he put together his *Life of Savage* (1744). Of greater importance, however, were his more popular contributions to *The Rambler* (1750–2), a bi-weekly paper which revived the *Spectator* tradition with its essays, ethical, social and literary, all written with a view to educating the public in 'civility', since nothing he held was better fitted for that purpose than 'the frequent publication of short papers which we read not as study but amusement'. Notable also was a second series of essays written for *The Idler* (1758–60) with lighter touch; and then came his dissertation on poetry in *Rasselas* (1759), that *conte philosophique* written in haste to meet the expenses of his mother's funeral. Finally as the crown of his achievement was published *The Lives of the Poets* (1777–83), a work treating of some fifty-two poets and representing with its combination of biography and criticism something new in critical history.

In assessing the value of this critical output it will be found that the *Rambler* and the *Idler* papers, no less than the *Lives*, merit close attention. In those periodicals Johnson endeavoured to explain to the reading public of his day the basic doctrines which commended themselves to him during his earlier years; and as they represented doctrines which remained with him practically unchanged to the end they afford the key to many of his later pronouncements and judgments. The *Lives* we owe primarily to the business enterprise of London booksellers, who, in an effort to compete with the Edinburgh project of a collection of British poets, decided in 1777 to issue a rival collection for which Johnson was engaged to write 'little Lives and little Prefaces'. The poets were the choice of the booksellers themselves. Significantly passing over Chaucer and the Elizabethans, they limited their scope to the years between Cowley and Gray, and in so doing they included many versifiers whose names are now forgotten; though Johnson was permitted to add to the list the names of Blackmore, Thomson, Watts and a few of the unknown. The resulting accounts are therefore of varying value, ranging from brief notices to ample biographies and appreciations; but Johnson's labours throughout were characteristically immense. Freely ransacking the earlier works of Wood, Aubrey, Edward Phillips, and a host of others, he made use of Spence's *Anecdotes* to supplement his own first-hand knowledge of 18th-Century poets, and when his vigour flagged he accepted material from interested contemporaries and made use of his own earlier account of Savage. Work compiled in this casual and unsystematic fashion was naturally not without its defects of detail; but nothing comparable of the kind had appeared before. Besides being the most readable of Johnson's writings, it rescued from oblivion many material facts, embodied many wise reflexions on literature and life, and presented for the first time critical accounts of certain poets which in the main have stood the test of time.

When we turn to consider the significance of these critical works of Johnson nothing emerges more clearly than the fact that his aim throughout was to inculcate a sounder appreciation of literature by improving the standards and methods of criticism. The matter was one that had already engaged the attention of earlier critics as being what the age most urgently needed. Addison, it will be recalled, had striven to foster a sounder literary taste, while Pope had collected sundry advice from earlier authorities; and Johnson now raises the whole question anew but from a somewhat different angle. Treating the inquiry in more ample and reasoned fashion, he deals at length, first, with current critical abuses, and then supplies in addition certain positive views that demand attention. To the question of what was wrong with contemporary criticism he returns again and again, more especially in the *Rambler* and *Idler* papers. In one place, for instance, he briefly presents his views in allegorical form; in another he provides a highly significant satirical sketch of the fashionable critic; elsewhere he pillories definite faults in the critical practices of the time. And these remarks he further supplements by advice of a more positive kind, in submitting his conception of the true aims of criticism, its proper standards and methods.

A discussion of criticism in general is therefore one of the main objects of Johnson's critical writings; and his views in the first place are partially revealed in his allegory of Criticism and her torch.[1] The torch of Criticism, he suggests, had originally been created by Labour and lighted by Truth, having been designed to reveal 'all sophistries, absurdities, false rhetoric' and the like. Degraded, however, by Flattery and Malevolence, Criticism, he added, ultimately withdrew from among men, leaving judgment to Time, and content with the thought that 'Time passes his sentence at leisure' without any regard to contemporary estimates.

In yet more drastic and realistic fashion, however, does he

[1] *Rambler*, 3.

ridicule the shallow and hackneyed criticism of his day, declaring that criticism was 'the study by which men grow important and formidable at a very small expense';[1] and this contention he illustrates by a lively satirical account of one Dick Minim, sometime apprentice to a brewer, but one who ultimately attained distinction as a critic.[2] By frequenting coffee-houses, it is explained, this aspirant to critical fame became first acquainted with such terms as 'sentiments, unities and catastrophes', and subsequently with the doctrines that the business of art was to copy Nature, that the great art was the art of blotting, and that literary work should be kept for at least nine years. Fortified with such theories the said critic then ventured to treat of individual authors, confidently asserting that all had their beauties and defects, and adopting the conventional estimates of Spenser, Shakespeare, Jonson and the rest. Thus emboldened our critic then turned to deal with general problems; why, for instance, English comedy had decayed in spite of eccentric characters developed under English political liberties; while he also hinted that love played too great a part in contemporary tragedy. By now, however, he had become a recognized authority and was admitted to rehearsals where he would suggest many happy thoughts, revealing also many hidden beauties, as when sound echoed sense. After this, still increasing in mental stature, he recommended the establishment of an academy of criticism and presided over a critical society of his own, where he lamented that the best thoughts were mangled by being confined in couplets. Milton's blank verse he consequently praised; and becoming yet more subtle and mysterious he would point to the uncommon effects of Milton's treatment. He could shiver in a hot-house, he explained, when he read that

The ground
Burns frore, and cold performs the effect of fire;

while another passage, he pointed out, had 'he knows not how, something that strikes him with an obscure sensation like that which he fancies would be felt from the sound of darkness'. For the rest, he was content to commend only those with established reputations, and until an author had arrived he would 'entrench himself in general non-committal terms, employing epithets of whose meaning he was not sure, but which were usefully applied to books which he had not read or could not understand'. As a

[1] *Idler*, 60.   [2] *ibid.* 60–1.

detailed and scathing satire of contemporary criticism this sketch throws a vivid light on Johnson's position. He had evidently no use for the stock of trite theories then current, any more than for the vapourings of those who judged by an un-regulated 'taste', or for those who attached undue value to political or climatic conditions. His lash is directed against the shallow judgments and the critical humbug of his day,— themes with which Sheridan later on in his *Critic* (1781) made great play.

Even so, Johnson does not leave the matter there; for dis-carding allegory and satire, he points more seriously to what he regards as specific defects in the critical practices then current. He first makes plain his attitude to the criticism which resulted from the application of 'taste', and which dealt with aesthetic qualities ascribed to beauty of various sorts. Beauty, however, for him was no sure test of literary values. In one place he describes it as a quality 'vague and undefined, different in different minds and diversified by time and place',[1] adding that 'it has been a term hitherto used to signify that which pleases us we know not why, . . . and indeed so little subject to the examination of reason that Pascal supposes it to end where demonstration begins'. Like the nature of evil, beauty is to him something of a mystery, an insoluble problem. And just as in his review of Soame Jenyns's *Free Inquiry into the Nature and Origin of Evil* (1757) he condemned the discussion of so elusive a matter as evil, as being likely to 'encourage impious presumption or to stimulate idle curiosity', so in the treatment of literature he discountenances what had been advocated as judgment by 'taste'. Such procedure, he notes, was merely 'to impose words for ideas upon ourselves and others, and to imagine that we are going forward when we are only turning round'. In short, speculation concerning literary values in-soluble by the aid of reason had no sort of appeal to his mascu-line type of mind. His aim, however misguided in this particular, was here as elsewhere 'to clear the mind of cant'.

He is on firmer ground in dealing with other contemporary practices, as when he states, for instance, that critical judgments were often made with but a trifling acquaintance with the works discussed.[2] Rapin, he suggests, can scarcely have read all the works he either praised or censured; and elsewhere he comments shrewdly on Pope's tenuous knowledge of Petronius.[3] Then, too, critics, he adds, were often led astray by various

[1] *Rambler*, 92.   [2] *ibid.* 93.   [3] See p. 169 *supra*.

prejudices. It might be an exaggerated affection for the work in hand, a fault incident to editors; or the bias might be of a patriotic kind, illustrated by Scaliger in preferring Virgil to Homer; or again, excessive indulgence to living authors was also to be deprecated, since 'every writer', Johnson maintained, 'was a kind of general challenger whom everyone has the right to attack'. Apart from this, some critics, he points out, were wont to read with 'the microscope of criticism',[1] attaching undue importance to minutiae, to discordant syllables, recurrence of the same word, slight improprieties, all petty inaccuracies treated as enormities. Such critics, he contended, had but a distorted vision, neglecting as they did matters of greater import, such as an effective structure, the general spirit of a work, the harmony of the parts and the like. Others there were who employed the telescope in their critical activities. They saw clearly what was too remote for others to see, yet were blind to what was obvious to all. In every passage, explained Johnson, they discovered 'some secret meaning, some remote allusion, some occult imitation which no one ever suspected'; though they remained deaf to a cogent argument or to an emotional passage, blind also to verbal felicities or flowers of fancy. Such critics, it was added, 'pry into worlds of conjecture and amuse themselves with phantoms in the clouds'. This then is Johnson's arraignment of the critics of his day. It is altogether a shrewd performance, illustrative of his good sense and power of analysis; and if he himself was not exempt from some of the defects mentioned, from others present-day criticism is not entirely free.

Equally significant and of more positive value are the indications he gives of what he regards as sound principles to be observed in critical activities; for here he endeavours to establish criticism on a firm foundation likely to appeal to reasonable minds. And this he does in stating that the task of criticism[2] is

To distinguish those means of pleasing which depend on known causes and rational deduction from the nameless and inexplicable elegances which appeal wholly to the fancy, from which we feel delight but know not how they produce it, and which may well be termed the enchantresses of the soul.

In other words, the business of criticism was to free literary judgments from 'the anarchy of ignorance, the caprices of fancy and the tyranny of prescription'; and to assign values on

---

[1] *Rambler*, 176.   [2] *ibid.* 92.

rational grounds. This process however was to be freely and impartially applied. Whereas Addison, he noted, had asserted that your true critic pointed out beauties rather than faults, Johnson's contention was that the critic's duty was 'neither to depreciate nor dignify by partial representation but to hold out the light of reason whatever it might discover'.[1] And this tenet, as we have seen, Johnson signally observed in his treatment of Shakespeare.

At the same time he holds firmly to what after all is the final test of all great literature, namely, the requirement of *quod semper, quod ubique, quod ab omnibus*. At this doctrine he had hinted in his allegory of Criticism and her torch; and he enlarges on the idea in more than one place. Thus, with Boileau (and ultimately 'Longinus') as his authority, he states that the works which have stood the test of time have a claim to our regard because 'the long continuance of their reputation proves that they are adequate to our faculties and agreeable to Nature'.[2] This agreeableness to Nature, moreover, he further explains in the statement that 'the work of one who carefully studies nature and can well describe it is the kind of literature that can hope for a long continuance of fame'.[3] And as examples of such writings he refers to Bacon's *Essays*, which 'come home to men's business and bosoms', and would therefore 'last as long as books last'.

Then, too, in forming literary judgments, he suggests the importance of taking into account historical considerations.

To judge rightly of an author [he states] we must transport ourselves to his time and examine what were the wants of contemporaries and what were his means of supplying them. That which is easy at one time was difficult at another.[4]

And not without its interest in this connexion is Johnson's acknowledgement of indebtedness to Thomas Warton for having shown critics the way to a successful appreciation of earlier writers by directing them to the books which those authors had read.[5] Moreover, he also insists on the need for judging a literary work as a whole, and not by mere verbal tests.

It is not by comparing line with line [he notes] that the merit of great works is to be estimated; but by their general effect and ultimate result.[6]

[1] *Rambler*, 93.　　[2] *ibid*. 92.　　[3] *ibid*. 106.
[4] G. Birkbeck Hill, *Johnson's Lives*, i. 411.
[5] *ibid*. ii. 162 f.n.　　　　[6] *ibid*. i. 454.

And to these he adds that a work of imagination should provide delight of a permanent kind; it should either help us 'to enjoy life or to endure it'. It was this quality, he maintained, which 'in defiance of criticism continues Shakespeare the sovereign of the drama', noting further that 'that work is good in vain which the reader throws away'.

These remarks of Johnson censuring current abuses and submitting a few constructive ideas on criticism in general go some way towards revealing his attitude as a critic, and constitute part of his main achievement. Further light, however, as to his critical standards is derived from comments on literary theory scattered throughout his pages; and these too call for attention. One thing at least is clear; and that is, that he is no adherent of the neo-classical school,—a fact that emerges from what is perhaps the most searching examination of that particular creed. The neo-classical tradition, it will be recalled, had been founded on certain definite principles. It had required an imitation of the ancients, the recognition of certain fixed 'kinds' originated in antiquity, as well as an observance of rules ostensibly derived from the ancients; and Johnson will have nothing to do with these rigid requirements. What he has in mind is an entirely different approach to literature and literary values. And in thus discarding neo-classical doctrines and the restrictions they imposed he renews in a more determined form the challenge of Addison and the rest, and thus opened the way, however imperfectly, to a more rational, and ultimately a more enlightened, critical treatment.

Johnson's rejection of neo-classicism is therefore of considerable interest in critical history; and with regard to its fundamental doctrine of 'imitation', in the first place, his views are tolerably plain. In the field of knowledge, it is true, he recognizes the necessity for following in the steps of earlier workers and utilizing discoveries already made; but in the sphere of art, he holds, things are different. In literature, for instance, which 'claims fiction for her dominion', he sees

Boundless regions of possibility, a thousand recesses unexplored, a thousand flowers unplucked, a thousand fountains unexhausted, and combinations of imagery yet unobserved,[1] . . . whereas the imitator [he adds] treads but a beaten walk, and with all his diligence can only hope to find a few flowers . . . untouched by his predecessors, the refuse of contempt or the omissions of negligence.[2]

[1] *Rambler*, 121.   [2] *ibid.* 86.

The truth is, he flatly declares, 'no man ever yet became great by imitation';[1] a doctrine repeated by Imlac in *Rasselas*,[2] after having studied all the poets of Persia and Arabia. And on this point Johnson enlarges further:

> Whatever hopes [he states][3] for the veneration of mankind must have invention (i.e. originality) in the design or execution. . . . Either truths hitherto unknown must be discovered or those which are already known enforced by stronger evidence, facilitated by clearer methods or elucidated by brighter illustrations. . . . That which hopes to . . . stand firm against the attack of time must contain in itself some original principle of growth. The reputation which arises from the . . . transposition of borrowed sentiment may spread for a while like ivy on the rind of antiquity; but will be torn away by accident or contempt, and suffered to rot unheeded on the ground.

Nor again can he accept the doctrine that all literature could be conveniently classified under different species or 'kinds', and defined accordingly. Recalling that definitions in civil law were notoriously hazardous, he asserts that the creations of art are likewise too inconstant and uncertain to be reduced to any formula, more especially as the 'imagination' (i.e. the fancy), which played so great a part in artistic affairs, was a lawless faculty admitting of neither limitation nor restraint. His judgment on the matter is therefore unequivocal;

> There is . . . scarcely any species of writing [he states][4] of which we can tell what is its essence or what are its constituents; every new genius produces some innovation which . . . subverts the rules which the practice of foregoing authors had established.

And, in addition, he indicates how inadequate had been previous attempts at defining certain of the 'kinds'. Thus definitions of comedy, for instance, had been mainly concerned with the means by which comic writers attained their ends and had described that dramatic form as merely a representation of ignoble men or of trivial and fictitious action. Yet such elements, Johnson maintains, were far from comprising all the possible methods of causing laughter, which, he adds, 'were not limited by Nature'. A sounder definition would have concentrated on the psychological effects of comedy, which would then have been more adequately described as 'a dramatic representation of human life calculated to excite mirth'.

Yet more pointed are his comments on the rules prescribed

---

[1] *Rambler*, 154.   [2] ch. x.   [3] *Rambler*, 154.   [4] *ibid*. 125.

by neo-classical authorities. His chief objection is that their rules were 'seldom drawn from any settled principle . . . or adapted to the natural and invariable constitution of things'.[1] They were in fact nothing more than

The arbitrary edicts of legislators, authorised only by themselves, who, out of various means by which the same end may be attained, selected such as happened to occur to their own reflexion, . . . and who thus prohibited new experiments . . . and restrained fancy from . . . hazard and adventure.

In consequence, he argues, such rules were liable to serious error. It was not only that faults as well as excellences of earlier writers were often advocated. There were, besides, the errors due to the misunderstandings of critics, seen for example in the false teaching of 16th-Century Ciceronians; or again, in the rule requiring for the epic a plain and simple opening, whereas Horace's precept had referred only to the modest tone of Homer's exposition rather than to the manner of expression. Moreover, Johnson adds,[2] compiled in this arbitrary and haphazard fashion, these 'accidental prescriptions of authority when time had procured for them veneration, are . . . often confounded with the laws of Nature, and . . . are supposed coeval with reason'. In short, his main contention is that these neo-classical rules had been built up on shifting foundations; and he would have all literary laws dictated, not by mere precedent, but by an unchanging reason or Nature, thus directing attention anew to the psychological study of literature.

Not content, however, with these general statements Johnson elaborates his objections to the rules by asserting that all laws previously laid down were not of equal validity, some being 'fundamental and indispensable', others merely 'useful and convenient'.[3] The former, he explains, were dictated by reason or necessity, being in conformity 'to the order of Nature and the operations of the intellect'; whereas the latter, based merely on earlier precedent, were liable to question and modification. Of the fundamental and obligatory laws he mentions by way of illustration those involving unity of dramatic action, besides others requiring for the plot a strong central character upon whom interest might be concentrated. For the rest, he adds, a writer 'ought to distinguish Nature from custom, or that which is established because it is right from that which is right only because it is established'; and urges further that 'a poet may

---

[1] *Rambler*, 158.   [2] *ibid*. 156.   [3] *ibid*.

19

neither violate essential principles by a desire for novelty, nor
debar himself from the attainment of beauties . . . by a needless
fear of breaking rules which no literary dictator had authority
to enact'.

Of the non-essential neo-classical rules he has yet more to
say, pointing to the futility of not a few of them. There was,
first, the rule requiring that three speaking personages only
should appear at one time on the stage.[1] This he attributes
to mere accident, to the fact that tragedy, long a monody,
admitted subsequently of two, and then three, actors on the
stage; though such limitation had since proved impossible in
the more intricate modern plays. Or again, there was the
mysterious decree that required a play to consist of five acts.
Such a rule, he held, was not dictated by the nature of things,
since the intervals of time varied in different actions and were
not limited to five or any other number. Nor can he regard
an observance of the Unity of time as essential. Probability, he
allowed, required that the time of an action should approach
somewhat nearly to that of representation. But since some
amount of illusion was inevitable on the stage it was difficult
to see where a limit to such illusion should be placed. 'Minds
not prepossessed by mechanical criticism', he states,[2] 'are rarely
offended by a time-duration of more than one day; or again,
'he who can multiply three hours into twelve or twenty-four
might image with equal ease a greater number'—arguments
subsequently reproduced in his *Preface* to Shakespeare's works.
On the other hand, tragicomedy, frowned at by neo-classical
critics, he is inclined to defend as being justified by Nature,
reason and experience alike. What more natural, he asks, than
the mingling of great and trivial actions so common in life?
And the stage after all is but a mirror of life. Nor could the relief
afforded by comic elements in treating of tragic themes be said
to impair the emotional effect. 'Experience', he states, 'had
shown that this objection was subtle rather than just'; since
'no plays had oftener filled the eyes with tears . . . than those
variegated with interludes of mirth'. And as he notes elsewhere,
'tragicomedy may chance to please even when it is not critically
approved'.[3] At the same time he has doubts and some reservations to make. He 'does not think it safe to judge of works
of genius by the event',[4] and he hesitates to vindicate tragicomedy even in the light of Shakespeare's performance. Perhaps Shakespeare, he adds, would have been more effective had

[1] *Rambler*, 156.   [2] *ibid*.   [3] *ibid*. 107.   [4] *ibid*. 156.

he not indulged in such liberties. 'We might have been more interested in the distress of his heroes had we not been so frequently diverted by the jokes of his buffoons.'

Such then is Johnson's denunciation of neo-classicism; a pronouncement more reasoned and complete than that of any of his predecessors, and influential in virtue of his great prestige. With the discarding of neo-classical doctrine, however, the need for positive guidance to take its place became apparent, and Johnson therefore advocates an approach to literature based on Nature, the watchword and controlling idea of 18th-Century thought. The conception of Nature had coloured contemporary speculation in the fields of religion, philosophy, politics and to some extent literature;[1] since its laws, those of reason, were regarded as fixed and stable, the one sure foundation in an age of conflicting thought. And upon this foundation, this cosmic law which governed all material, as well as spiritual, things, Johnson now rests the framework of his doctrine as likely to appeal to all reasonable minds. So that the main structure of his doctrine was determined by principles intuitively discerned in Nature, namely, those of order, proportion, fitness, perspicuity and the like, as well as by others inherent in human nature, and embodying qualities satisfying to the mind of rational man. It is true that he nowhere expounds his theory in complete or systematic form; but its animating principles are clearly visible in remarks scattered throughout his various writings, in his comments on formal matters, for instance, and in the psychological reasons he gives for his judgments on this or that effect. And in these remarks he deals, first, with poetry in general, then with certain particular forms of poetry, and incidentally with other branches of literature as well.

Concerning poetry in general, to begin with, he has little to say relating to its more abstract qualities, its nature and function. The time had long gone by when an apology on those lines was needed; and he is content with defining it as 'an art of uniting pleasure with truth by calling imagination (i.e. fancy) to the help of reason';[2] while the equipment of the poet, like that of Cicero's orator, is said to embrace all available knowledge of man and Nature.[3] What he is mainly interested in explaining, however, is poetry in the concrete, its practice and technique, and notably matters of expression and verse; and

---

[1] See Basil Willey, *The 18th-Century Background*, for a full treatment of this development.

[2] Hill, *op. cit.* i. 170.   [3] *Rasselas*, ch. x.

here his guiding principles, he claims, are those of Nature and reason.

As regards poetic expression, in the first place, he stands definitely for clarity and simplicity, for 'natural thought expressed without violence to language',[1] so as to counteract those ornamental devices which he complains had accumulated since Dryden's day. Among such undesirable devices he includes colourless epithets and epithets employed merely to fill out a line, besides needless inversions and harsh and daring figures, all of which militated against natural utterance. 'It is less difficult', he asserts, 'to write a volume of lines swelled with epithets, brightened with figures and stiffened with inversions than to produce a few couplets graced only by naked elegance, . . . which require care and skill.' Of the value of one of the recognized devices, however, he seems somewhat uncertain; and he hesitates to approve of the findings of Dionysius of Halicarnassus long ago regarding Homer's successes in making sound echo sense by means of vocalic, consonantal and rhythmical arrangements.[2] Such onomatopoetic effects he is inclined to regard as fanciful. 'Nothing in the poetic art', he remarks, 'is more subject to the caprice of individual fancy.' Yet Virgil, he allows, was often successful in such efforts; and he leaves the matter an open question. 'It would be too daring', he adds,[3] 'to declare that all the celebrated adaptations of harmony are chimerical; that Homer had no extraordinary attention to the melody of his verse, . . . or that Milton in places did not intend to exemplify the harmony which he mentions.' And, again, it is in no dictatorial mood that he preserves an open mind on the use of the expletives *do* and *did*, as well as on rhymes formed of obsolete endings, such as *waxeth* and *affecteth*. He condemns Waller and others for resorting to such devices; but he cautiously adds, 'I know not whether it is not to the detriment of our language that we have rejected them.'

On the other hand his demand for the use of general terms in poetry is emphatic and unqualified. Temple and Joseph Warton had previously urged the superiority of particular images for poetic purposes; but Johnson now insists that the poet should always aim at general expressions, thus revealing 'general and transcendental truths'. Already in *The Rambler*[4] he had stated that 'poetry cannot dwell upon the minuter distinctions . . . without departing from that simplicity and grandeur which fills

[1] *Idler*, 77.   [2] *Rambler*, 92.
[3] *ibid*. 94.   [4] *ibid*. 36.

the imagination'. And yet more clearly is the principle enunciated in *Rasselas*[1] where it is laid down that

The business of the poet is to examine not the individual but the species, to remark general properties and large appearances. He does not number the streaks of the tulip or describe the different shades in the verdure of the forest; he is to exhibit in his portrait of nature such . . . features as recall the original to every mind.

Moreover in *The Idler*[2] he gives reasons for this theory, explaining that such generalization was essential if poetry was to have a universal appeal.

He that writes upon general principles or delivers universal truths [he states] may hope often to be read, because his work will be equally useful at all times and in every country. . . . Fugitive topics like those of *Hudibras* are soon forgotten.

And, again, elsewhere he points out by way of illustration how Cowley's neglect of the doctrine had made ridiculous what would otherwise have been great and forcible, when, investing Gabriel with the brightest colours of the sky, he relates whence Gabriel had first obtained his skin, then his mantle, lace and scarf, in terms reminiscent of 'the mercer and tailor'.[3] The truth was, so Johnson maintains, that the grandeur of general terms was lost by those 'who pursued their thoughts to their last ramifications'.[4] 'For', he adds, 'of the greatest things the parts are little; what is little can be but pretty, and by claiming dignity became ridiculous': so that all power of description is destroyed by a scrupulous enumeration of details. It would therefore seem that Johnson is here influenced by the Aristotelian doctrine relating to the presence of a universal element in all great poetry and accounting for its permanent appeal. But then Aristotle had also maintained that the poet represented the universal in and through the particular; and it is through the 'streaks of the tulip' that some of the greatest imaginative effects have been attained.

Yet more detailed are Johnson's comments on versification which he submits with the dictates of Nature—regularity, fitness and the like—primarily in mind, thus supplementing Addison's brief treatment of the subject, and providing his readers with explanations free from 'the dialect of the grammarians'. 'The essential constituents of metrical compositions' he defines as 'the recurrence of settled numbers';[5] and he

---

[1] ch. x.   [2] No. 59.   [3] Hill, *op. cit.* i. 53.
[4] *ibid.* i. 45.   [5] *ibid.* iii. 227.

concerns himself solely with the heroic measure, the line of ten syllables, the purest form of which he regards as the iambic, that in which the accent falls regularly on every second syllable. This, he categorically declares, 'provides the most complete harmony of which a single line is capable'.[1] To avoid the monotony inseparable, however, from an unbroken repetition of such lines in a long poem, he recognizes the need for some variety of effect; and this, he adds, was afforded by the occasional use of a 'mixed measure', that is, a line with irregular accents, in which slow iambic feet for instance were varied with more speedy trochaics. This, however, he described as so much licence though freely used by Milton, who, with his trisyllabic feet, spondees and the rest, 'had seldom two pure lines together'. The necessity for such liberties he somewhat grudgingly admits; for while the resulting harmony, he held, was technically defective, yet relief was provided, and occasional discord made one more sensible of the harmony of the normal line. Moreover, he added, 'where the senses are to judge, authority is not necessary'.

Then, too, in the treatment of the heroic measure the same qualities of Nature were to be observed in the use made of the caesura and verbal music. The caesura, in the first place, he states,[2] falls most fitly after the fourth or sixth syllable; and this was because the line was then divided into sections both of which were harmonious. A pause after the first or ninth syllable was ruled out since no harmony could be provided by a single word or syllable; and, in any case, a pause on a light syllable was unsatisfactory to the ear. But here too he concedes that some liberty should be allowed for the sake of variety; and Milton, he notes, had provided all in this kind that English would permit. Then, again, tonal quality or verbal music, he states,[3] was one of the factors that contributed to effective verse; and this was to be attained by 'a proper mixture of vowels and consonants and in tempering the mute consonants with liquids and semi-vowels' as Milton had done. Of that poet's elision of one vowel before another in the following word, however, he approves only in rare cases. He recognizes it as a device formerly accepted in English, and not without its charm in other languages both ancient and modern. Nevertheless to him it is merely a licence; and 'one language', he asserts, 'cannot communicate its rules to another'. In addition, he remarks on Milton's use of an extra syllable at the end of a line, though his

---

[1] *Rambler*, 86.   [2] *ibid.* 90.   [3] *ibid.* 88.

statement that instances occur 'almost in every page' was later on confuted by Coleridge. To this departure from the normal he does not object on musical grounds. Yet highly significant is his suggestion that the device should not be employed in epic poetry but should be confined to dramatic poetry, as bringing that verse nearer to prose and ordinary conversation.

Nor must his remarks on the relative merits of blank verse and the heroic rhyming couplet pass unnoticed.[1] Convinced as he was that the essential quality of all verse was 'the recurrence of settled numbers', he found in blank verse a disordered freedom which militated against that ideal. The ever-varying position of the caesura and the use of run-on lines, he claimed, led merely to metrical confusion; such verse 'seemed to be verse only to the eye'. And with the verse-pattern thus obscured so that there was 'neither the easiness of prose nor the melody of numbers', the very looseness of the verse conduced to loose and verbose expression, and blank verse was too often found to be 'in description exuberant, in argument loquacious, and in narration tiresome'.[2] Moreover it was unfitted for many themes; employed (as by some contemporaries) for familiar and commonplace subjects it could prove disastrous, resulting merely in 'absurd novelty', unnatural and transient.[3]

On the other hand, whereas poetry, he allows, might subsist without rhyme, he doubts whether English poets could safely dispense altogether with its use; and he holds in general that rhyme is necessary for the full music of the decasyllabic line, though he suggests in one place that perhaps the couplet form had latterly been too constantly employed.[4] 'The music of the English heroic line', he explains,[5] 'strikes the ear so faintly that it is easily lost unless all the syllables of every line co-operate together'; and this co-operation, he maintained, was obtained by the use of rhyme. Here Johnson, it is evident, does less than justice to blank verse. Deaf to the varied rhythm of the Miltonic line and to the majestic sweep of Milton's paragraphs, he stands for the ordered regularity of the heroic couplet. Milton, he oddly suggests, had found blank verse easier than rhyme and had tried to persuade himself that it was the better form. Yet 'all that reason could urge in defence of blank verse', so Johnson stated, 'had been confuted by the ear'; though characteristically enough, 'he would not wish that Milton had written in rhyme'.

[1] Hill, *op. cit.* i. 192–4.   [2] *ibid.* iii. 417.
[3] *ibid.* ii. 319.   [4] *ibid.* i. 81.   [5] *ibid.* i. 192.

Apart from these remarks on certain aspects of poetry in general, of equal significance are Johnson's occasional comments on particular forms of that art, which throw further light on his literary doctrine and judgments. In these places, it is worth noting, he does not treat of the conventional neoclassical 'kinds'. It is true that he shows his acquaintance with Bossu's doctrine in his discussion on *Paradise Lost*; and occasionally he touches on points of epic and dramatic theory, as when, for instance, he approves of Dryden's suggestion with regard to epic machinery as being 'the most reasonable scheme of celestial interposition',[1] superior to the intrigues of pagan deities, as well as to 'the enchantments of later Italians'; or again, when he refuses to regard 'poetic justice' as a necessary element in tragedy, on the ground that it was untrue to life.[2] What he concerns himself with, however, are immediate problems, those significant developments in English poetry—the nature of the school of poetry inaugurated by Donne, the respective values of the traditional pastoral, Pindarics, sacred poetry and the like—most of which were being cultivated at the time. All seemed to him to transgress those laws of poetry which commended themselves to reasonable minds, since in different ways such forms were lacking in naturalness and fitness, and thus failed in the poetic task of combining 'pleasure with truth'. And if his treatment of 'metaphysical' poetry stands alone in its originality, its keen analysis and suggestive value, not less revealing are his estimates of the other poetic forms.

Of interest, in the first place, is the fact that Johnson regarded his *Life of Cowley* as his best, on account of its dissertation on 'metaphysical' poetry. The term 'metaphysical', as applied to the school of poetry which flourished between Donne and Cowley, he took over from Dryden[3] as conforming with his own idea of that development, the term being interpreted, not in its modern, but in its ancient and more literal sense, as that which 'came after' the physical or natural (*meta physica*) in the field of studies. Such work, he held, represented no real imitation of Nature, but dealt rather with abstract ideas often bizarre and extravagant; and accordingly, their authors, he agrees with Dryden, were best regarded as 'wits' not poets.[4] Having thus endorsed Dryden's brief judgment, he enlarges on it to some purpose, pointing out, first, the nature of the 'wit' thus implied. It was not, he maintains, Pope's idea of that

---

[1] Hill, *op. cit.* i. 385. [2] *ibid.* ii. 135.
[3] See p. 139 *supra.* [4] Hill, *op. cit.* i. 19 ff.

quality—that 'which oft was thought but ne'er so well expressed'—for their thoughts were peculiarly their own and were often badly expressed; and, by the way, he condemns Pope's definition as faulty in thus reducing 'wit' to neat expression of commonplaces. Nor, again, was it that more adequate conception of 'wit' as a mode of expression natural and new, the meaning of which, not obvious at first, was found almost at once to have been subtly and happily conveyed; for the thoughts of these poets, he added, were seldom natural or just, more often merely perverse. On the other hand the 'wit' thus involved was of that philosophic kind known as *discordia concors*, consisting of a 'combination of dissimilar images or discovery of occult resemblances in things apparently unlike'. Of 'wit' of this kind, added Johnson, they have more than enough. And he proceeds to dilate on the artistic qualities of such poetry, illustrating his remarks by quotations from Donne, Cowley and Cleveland.

That poetry of this sort was wanting in emotional effect, this, he states,[1] would be readily seen. For the treatment of these poets throughout was impersonal and objective. 'Their courtship was void of fondness and their lamentation of sorrow. Their wish was only to say what they hoped had been never said before.' Then, too, they never attained the heights of sublimity with thoughts that filled the mind with rapture and astonishment. 'Great thoughts', Johnson recalled, 'are always general'; whereas

Their attempts were always analytic; they broke every image into fragments, and could no more represent by their slender conceits and laboured particularities the prospects of nature or the scenes of life, than he who dissects a sunbeam with a prism can exhibit the wide effulgence of a summer noon.

Moreover, what they lacked in greatness of thought they attempted to supply by means of hyperbole, which gave to the work an air of unreality and excess. 'They left', so stated Johnson, 'not only reason but fancy behind them, and produced combinations of confused magnificence that not only could not be credited but could not be imagined.' And these general remarks he supplements by revealing more particularly the fondness for conceits characteristic of this school of poetry. Many, he points out, were drawn from far-fetched thoughts and unfamiliar learning, remote and trifling ideas being brought together in reckless fashion, and with allusions and thoughts,

[1] Hill, *op. cit.* i. 20.

sometimes elegant, sometimes gross, abounding. Thus 'hetero-
geneous ideas', he explained, 'are yoked by violence together,
and nature and art are ransacked for illustration, comparison
and allusion'. Altogether such poetry was the product of men
'more desirous of being admired than understood', who, moreover, displayed their 'ingenious absurdities' in verse that was
often of an unmusical kind.

Yet nowhere is Johnson's scrupulous fairness more clearly
seen than in stating that, in this poetry which outraged his
conception of that art, there existed qualities of value, if not of a
strictly poetical kind. 'Great labour directed by great abilities',
he asserts, 'is never lost.' And he suggests that from these works
acute and unexpected truths and ingenious expressions would
occasionally emerge, while the mind of the reader was constantly 'exercised by recollection, reflection and inquiry'. That
he fails to appreciate the full significance of this new form of
poetry is of course true. His limited historical horizon where
English poetry was concerned prevented him from realizing
the audacious break-away from Elizabethan conventions, the
more masculine form of expression, and the subtle rhythms,
which, appreciated in part by Thomas Carew, had drawn from
Ben Jonson the enthusiastic statement that 'Donne was the first
poet of the world in some things'. Besides, Johnson's survey of
this form of poetry was coloured by its later developments.
With Cowley the innovations introduced had already degenerated into abuses; the fantastic conceit had taken control. But
while a more searching analysis was needed for a just appreciation, for that more adequate judgment Johnson had prepared
the way.

Not less significant, however, are his remarks on forms of
contemporary verse which were based on ancient models; and
these too he submits to his tests of reason and Nature.[1] In the
first place, in connexion with the conventional pastoral of the
ancients, he recognizes its original possibilities of affording
universal pleasure, since external Nature with its varied charms
was unchanging in order and beauty, and appealed to childhood
and manhood alike. Yet the tradition handed down from Theocritus, he states, had since become vitiated by an air of artificiality. It had become necessary to evoke on all occasions the
atmosphere of the Golden Age with its lilies and roses and
whispers of love, with the manners of Arcadia, and scenes in
which unlettered shepherds complained of corruptions in Church

[1] *Rambler*, 36–7.

and State, or else with Daphne and Thyrsis uttering laments on the death of some illustrious person. It was all in fact utterly incongruous and unreal. 'We grow weary', he exclaims, 'of the uniformity of Arcadia, regions where no wind is heard but the gentle zephyr and where no scenes are displayed but valleys enamelled with unfading flowers.' And elsewhere he reminds his readers of the reality of things—the matchless glories of the English country-side, with its ever-changing scenes and its un-failing appeal to the minds and hearts of men.[1]

For similar reasons he described as unsuitable for a modern age that form of lyric known as the Pindaric.[2] Originally the product of the vehement imagination of a Greek lyrical poet, it was designed, he explains, to appeal by means of striking thoughts, sudden transitions and exclamations, in which thought followed thought without any expression of the inter-mediate ideas. Free rein was thus given to the poet's wildest flights of fancy; yet 'confusion and irregularity', he states, 'produce no beauty'. Moreover, 'unconnected sentiments in quick succession', he adds, 'may for a time delight by their novelty, but they differ from systematic reasoning as glances of lightning from the radiance of the sun'. To Congreve[3] he attributed wrongly the cure of this 'Pindaric madness'. He is said to have first pointed out that Pindar's odes were regular, that 'enthusiasm has its rules', and that 'in mere confusion there is neither grace nor greatness'.

Then, too, Johnson has something to say on other forms of contemporary verse which, having developed under influences other than those of the ancients, had come to represent some-thing like new 'kinds' of poetry. And among these were notably the religious poetry attempted by Cowley, Waller and Black-more, 'Imitations' of Spenser by Thomson, Akenside and Shen-stone, as well as poetry of a burlesque sort by Butler, John Philips and others. Religious poetry, in the first place, he cannot away with, since it had obviously failed in its primary object, that of kindling piety.[4] Religious doctrine, he allows, might be defended in a didactic poem; but such argument did not neces-sarily foster a pious frame of mind. Nor could intercourse between God and the human soul be inspired by the poet's efforts; for 'man in prayer is already in a higher state than poetry can confer'. Moreover, the essence of poetry, he declares, is invention, the producing of something unexpected that causes

[1] *Rambler*, 80. [2] *ibid*. 158.
[3] Hill, *op. cit.* ii. 234: *cf.* however p. 94 *supra*. [4] *ibid*. i. 291 ff.

surprise and delight. Yet religious themes, he adds, are few and familiar; they could receive no added grace from novelty of expression.

> Omnipotence [he states] cannot be exalted; Infinity cannot be amplified; Perfection cannot be improved. . . . Of sentiments purely religious . . . the most simple expression is the most sublime. . . . The ideas of Christian theology are too simple for eloquence, and too majestic for ornament; to recommend them by tropes and figures is to magnify by a concave mirror the sidereal hemisphere.

And these sentiments he repeats in another place where he states that in such poetry

> All amplification is frivolous and vain. . . . The miracle of Creation though it may team with images is best described with little diffusion of language. 'He spake the word and they were made.'[1]

Nor, again, can he see any great virtue in the 'Imitations' of earlier poets then in vogue. To an imitation of Spenser, his stories and allegory, he has no objection; but he firmly opposes the use of that poet's diction and stanza.[2] His archaic style, Johnson notes, was condemned even in his own day; whereas his stanza he describes as difficult and unpleasing, an Italian form unsuited to the genius of the English language by reason of its length and intricate rhyming system, which often led to distortion in the matter of expression. Apart from this, Spenserians, argued Johnson, did not even imitate Spenser aright; for they did little more than introduce archaisms here and there, whereas a genuine imitation required the omission of all words introduced since Spenser's day. It might well be, wrote Johnson, that an adequate imitation might be attained by further labour. But then, he added, 'life is surely given us for higher purposes than to gather what our ancestors have wisely thrown away and to learn what is of no value but because it has been forgotten'. Furthermore, he protests, such 'Imitations' at their best had but little to recommend them, since they appealed to neither reason nor passion.[3] They might give evidence of industry and keen observation, he conceded; but they meant nothing to readers unacquainted with the originals. 'The noblest beauties of art', he asserted, 'are those of which the effect is co-extended with rational nature. . . . What is less than this can only be pretty, the plaything of fashion and the amusement of a day.'

And, lastly, he cannot approve of the new form of poetry

---

[1] Hill, *op. cit.* i. 49.   [2] *Rambler*, 121.
[3] Hill, *op. cit.* iii. 332.

known as burlesque and illustrated by *Hudibras*. His main objection lies in the nature of burlesque itself, which he describes as consisting of 'a disproportion between style and sentiments', and containing therefore 'an element of corruption, since all disproportion is unnatural'.[1] In other words, it is an exhibition of what is monstrous and grotesque. Admired at first, it may be, on account of its novelty; but when it is no longer strange its deformity becomes clearly apparent. In addition, he notes in its later developments, in Philips's *Splendid Shilling* and *Cyder*, for instance, the tendency to degrade the magnificent utterances of Milton by applying them to low and trivial themes.[2] And he comments briefly on the unfortunate choice of blank verse in *Cyder*, which dealt largely with the culture of trees.

Contending angels [he states] may shake the regions of heaven in blank verse; but the flow of equal measures and the embellishment of rhyme must recommend . . . the art of engrafting and decide the merit of the 'redstreak' and 'pearmain'.

These then are Johnson's major pronouncements on specific forms of poetry cultivated in his day; though among his minor comments there was for instance his general censure on the undue and 'unnatural' part played by the love-theme in poetry, in view of 'the multiplicity of human passions and wants'.[3] From time to time, however, he remarks also on contemporary prose writings; and these too are worthy of note. There are, for instance, his views on that new literary form, the 18th-Century novel;[4] and it is significant that, unlike many others, he treats this innovation seriously and with an open mind. To him it was a natural development of the 17th-Century romance; but embodying, like comedy, a realistic treatment of ordinary life, it was thus devoid of such elements as giants and magic castles; so that a suitable description for such work would seem to be that of 'the comedy of romance'. Moreover, written primarily for 'the young, the idle and the ignorant', this new form, he states, should be infused with some amount of moral teaching. It was a requirement that was recognized as unnecessary for those earlier romances, which, treating of the world of fancy, possessed an ethical code with no bearing on actual life—a point made later by Lamb in his defence of Restoration comedy. With this safeguard, however, Johnson recommends the novel to his

---

[1] Hill, *op. cit.* i. 218.   [2] *ibid.* i. 317–19.
[3] *ibid.* i. 287.   [4] *Rambler*, 4.

generation as providing reading of a more useful character than
that of volumes of 'professed morality'.

Of interest, too, are his remarks on the writing of biography;
and most biographies of his day he describes as 'barren and
futile'. The business of the biographer, he held,[1] was not mere
panegyric or the collecting of matter from public records. It
was rather 'to reveal character in the light of illuminating
details of daily life'; and 'rarely a life passed', he adds, 'but its
faithful account might be useful'. For such work, however, he
required an exercise of taste and discretion, an avoidance of
what has since become known as 'debunking'. 'It is much
better', he states,[2] 'that caprice, obstinacy, frolic or folly, however much they might delight in the description, should be
silently forgotten, than by wanton merriment or unseasonable
detection a pang should be given to widow or friend.' On letter-
writing, too, he has something to say[3]; though here his views
are obviously biased by his reading of Pope's *Letters*, which he
describes as artificial, affected and unreal. He therefore refuses
to endorse the age-long opinion that the true characters of men
are revealed in their letters. It may have been so, he allows, in
the simple friendships of the Golden Age; but 'no man', he
curtly remarks, 'sits down to depreciate by design his own character'. Nor should his comments on the affected prose of his day
be overlooked, comments in which he ridicules the writers who
'thought nothing so characteristic of genius as to do common
things in an uncommon way'.[4] There were, he states, those who
'diffused every thought through so many diversities of expression that it was lost like water in a mist'; others who 'showed
by examples and comparisons what was clearly seen at once';
others again who 'proved what no man disputed'; and yet others,
like many philosophers, with whom 'the most evident truths
were so obscured that they could no longer be perceived'. Johnson's demand is therefore for 'plain truth in plain language'; and
the affectations he ridicules did not cease with his day.

An attempt has now been made to recall Johnson's efforts to
inculcate sounder standards and methods of criticism; and it
remains to inquire what he himself contributed to literary
appreciation in his *Lives of the Poets*. In that work the choice
of poets, determined as it was by interested booksellers and by
the prevailing view that English poetry had begun with Waller
and Denham, was in consequence limited to those writing during

---

[1] *Rambler*, 60.   [2] Hill, *op. cit.* ii. 116.
[3] *ibid.* iii. 216.   [4] *Idler*, 36.

the century between Cowley and Gray, though some, like Herrick, Herbert and Vaughan, are strangely enough omitted. Yet nothing is more remarkable than the success with which, from the scattered accounts of some fifty-two poets, the main literary developments of a century are made to emerge. Catalogue *Lives* and a few notable monographs had appeared before; but nothing comparable, either in scope or treatment, to Johnson's wide and significant survey of literary performances, embracing in Cowley certain aspects of an earlier period, in Milton the closing triumph of the Renascence age, and then the new traditions of Dryden, Pope and Addison, with Gray and Collins opening up new vistas hitherto unappreciated. To-day the general picture thus presented has become familiar; but it was first indirectly outlined in Johnson's pages.

Not less remarkable, however, are the certainty and skill, though not without lapses, with which he recognizes the main qualities of a large variety of writers, whose achievements he estimates practically for the first time, thus submitting a body of fresh judgments which on the whole have stood the test of time. Some, it is true, are developed at greater lengths than others; but for a proper appreciation of Johnson's achievement some regard must be paid to the mere scope of his labours, comparable only to those involved in the making of his massive Dictionary. Moreover he enlarged his canvas by a frequent use of the biographical, historical and comparative methods, amassing in the process an abundance of new facts, together with anecdotes relevant and illuminating, and adding besides vigorous comments and valuable digressions of his own. The work has occasionally been inadequately and even patronizingly praised; but it marks a distinct advance on anything that had appeared before. It is in fact none other than a treasury of literary traditions, if not of antiquarian research, embodying material which, unsifted and unorganized previously, nevertheless gave new direction to critical studies in making the concern of critics from now on not so much the art of composing, as of appreciating, poetry.

Of considerable interest, in the first place, are the accounts of outstanding pre-Augustan poets—Cowley, Waller, Denham and Milton—all representing different forms of poetry, as well as literary ideals differing from his own. Thus Cowley, to begin with, is regarded as representative of those conditions of extravagance and obscurity from which the Augustans were held to have rescued English poetry. Passing mention is made of early inspiration derived from Spenser, but the poet is hailed primarily as 'almost the last of the school of Donne and undoubtedly the best';[1] though elsewhere Johnson briefly dismisses the first half of the 17th Century as a time of 'forced thoughts and rugged metres'. And in Cowley's poems he finds much of which he heartily disapproves. He condemns, for example, the artificial and unconvincing treatment of love in *The Mistress*; from the first he had no use for 'the phantoms of gallantry'. The tests of excellence, he states, must ever be the truth. And, besides, there was an excess of vapid conceits, each stanza being crowded with 'darts and flames, with wounds and death, with mingled souls and broken hearts', all of which was 'unnatural and wearisome'.[2] Then, too, in the *Pindarics* there was the same lack of fitness, the paraphrases of Pindar's majestic odes being marred by trifling conceits, ignoble epithets, and above all by lax and lawless verse. Such verse, Johnson allowed, was not without its chance felicities; but its very liberties, being misunderstood, he added, had since fostered a race of incompetent poetasters. Nor could he accept Sprat's suggestion that such free verse suited all sorts of subjects; though his retort that 'verse which is fit for every thing can fit nothing well'[3] is not wholly convincing. His real objection was based on his earlier theorizing; 'the great pleasure of verse', he reiterates, 'arises from the known measure of lines and uniform structure of the stanza'. Moreover, *The Davideis*, he maintains, was disfigured by a light and offensive treatment of sacred themes, a trick caught from Donne; and incidentally, he corrects Rymer's ill-founded praise of that particular poem.

At the same time his general comments are characteristically more judicial and even generous than the scathing innuendo of Pope—'who now reads Cowley?' Johnson finds in that poet, for instance, much learning, rich fancy and ingenious thought; and describes him as the first to impart to English verse 'the enthusiasm of the greater ode and the gaiety of the less'.[4] In addition he is credited along with others with having freed translation from slavish literal methods; and if his verse left much to be desired, the merits of his charming prose style, on the other hand, are rightly and generously recognized. As Johnson stated, 'in his *Essays* nothing is far-sought or hard-laboured; but all is easy without feebleness, and familiar without grossness'. In the main Cowley's defects as a poet are attributed to the fact that

---

[1] Hill, *op. cit.* i. 35.   [2] *ibid.* i. 40.
[3] *ibid.* i. 47.   [4] *ibid.* i. 64.

he paid court to the passing fashion instead of 'tracing intellectual pleasure to its natural sources in the mind of man'.[1] And
Johnson's final verdict, as opposed to that of Pope, is that 'too
much praised at one time' he was 'too much neglected at
another'.

New traditions, however, came in with Waller and Denham;
and Johnson pays them customary homage as 'the fathers of
English poetry', those who first led the way towards 'Nature
and harmony'. They had shown, he claimed, that rhyming verse
was more pleasing in couplet form, and that verse consisted not
only in the number but in the arrangement of syllables as well.
But as yet, he maintained, they had made only a beginning; and
he corrects the current notion that they had established that
particular verse-form in general use.[2] Their works, he argued,
were of too limited a range to commend their innovations for
adoption in all forms of poetry. And he shrewdly and rightly
questioned whether their influence alone would have sufficed
to overcome the long-standing evils of the former age, more
especially in view of the support given to those earlier conventions by the much-acclaimed Cowley. It was therefore Dryden,
he asserted, who established the new versification on a stable
foundation; and since Dryden wrote, he added, 'English poetry
has not reverted to its former savagery'.

With regard to the poets themselves he comments, first, on
the merits and limitations of Waller, prefacing his remarks with
a valuable and animated account of contemporary public affairs,
which directed attention to those French influences brought
back to England by Waller and other exiles from abroad. His
poetry in general is described as consisting of delicate trifles,
panegyrics and the like; elegant, lively and refined, distinguished
by unfailing good taste and by verses smooth and flowing. Yet
for such airy productions Johnson has but little sympathy.
'Genius now and then', he states,' produces a lucky trifle'; and
elsewhere he refers to Catullus as an example. But then, he
added, 'verses merely pretty are quitted in time for something
useful'. Concerning Denham he calls attention to that poet's
share in teaching 'the art of concluding the sense in couplets';
and commends especially the familiar couplet beginning 'Though
deep yet clear', not only on account of its smoothness and
majesty, but also for the skill with which much sense was confined in so few words. He notes also the encouragement given to
free translation by Denham's praise of Fanshawe's version of

<hr>

[1] Hill, *op. cit.* i. 18.   [2] *ibid.* i. 419.

Pastor Fido. But most interesting of all is Johnson's comment on *Cooper's Hill*,[1] which is said to have originated 'local poetry', that is, 'the description of some particular landscape, with such embellishments as may be supplied by historical, retrospective, or incidental meditation'. In Denham's treatment he finds certain defects; digressions too long, moralizing too frequent, and sentiments sometimes feeble. But he welcomes this innovation of 'local poetry', as providing a more sensible and realistic approach to external Nature than was present in the conventional and artificial pastoral, and as heralding later efforts in the same field made by Garth, Thomson, Dyer and others.

In treating next of Milton Johnson was faced with other and loftier traditions; and the poet's performance is fittingly presented on a somewhat larger scale. He introduces the poet with an interesting biography, no 'honeysuckle *Life*', as he himself confesses, but one in which the poet is described as 'an acrimonious and surly republican', one of those 'who most loudly clamour for liberty and yet do not most liberally grant it'. Nevertheless, neither here nor elsewhere are political or sectarian prejudices allowed to colour seriously Johnson's literary judgments. True, he dismisses Milton's earliest poems as worthless; but then he is merely voicing his dislike of short poems in general. Milton, he explains, 'never learned the art of doing little things with grace'; and, as he added elsewhere, 'he . . . could cut a Colossus from a rock but could not carve heads on cherry-stones'. *L'Allegro* and *Il Penseroso*, on the other hand, he admired greatly, describing them as two noble efforts of the imagination, natural and pleasing.

Nothing short of disconcerting however is his amazing and apparently insensate estimate of *Lycidas*,[2] which has come to be regarded as an outburst of political spleen and as the nadir of critical perversity. But here again his judgment is due to no sectarian animus. It is of a piece with literary views honestly held and previously expounded; for the poem was to him none other than an embodiment of much that he held to be vicious in poetry. For one thing, it was a poem in what he regarded as the artificial and outworn pastoral form, and hence devoid of real feeling; since 'passion', he protests, 'plucks no berries . . . nor calls upon Arethusa and Mincius'; and where 'there is no passion there is no Nature, no truth and therefore no art'. Moreover, he adds, there were passages at variance with the plain facts, for Milton 'never drove afield', nor had 'flocks to batten';

[1] Hill, *op. cit.* i. 77.   [2] *ibid.* i. 163.

and while secular matters were also impiously mingled with sacred themes, the verse, when judged by the 'complete harmony' of the heroic couplet, was unpleasing and the rhymes uncertain. For this judgment of a poem which has since been regarded as a touchstone of taste there can of course be no defence, since it ignores such things as the lively descriptions, the subtle music of the verse, and the pervading spirit of a gracious antiquity. Yet it is at least intelligible as something more than an unreasoned and capricious judgment. It reveals, plainly enough, defective standards and deficiencies of ear and temperament, seen also in his deafness to the charm of the songs in *Comus*, or his half-hearted tribute to Milton's sonnets, a form moreover which he declared had never succeeded in English. But it is possible to stress too strongly this particular lapse in his treatment of a subtle piece of poetry which lay outside his range of vision, especially when viewed against the background of his critical achievement as a whole.

It is in dealing with *Paradise Lost* that Johnson's critical genius, now on firmer ground, plainly asserts itself; and though he adopts Bossu's main lines in his analysis of the poem, and insists, as Bossu had done, on the necessary choice of a moral, yet his treatment gives ample evidence of original thought and just appreciation. The plot is first discussed along the usual lines.[1] It is represented as a great story, perpetually interesting and involving the fates of worlds, told with epic completeness, fit machinery and episodes, and with characters dignified, clearly distinguished, and in keeping with the main theme. Nor, despite Dryden's earlier contention, was there lacking an epic hero; for to Adam is assigned that particular function, since Satan is vanquished and Adam finally restored. It is when he enlarges on Milton's treatment of this epic structure, however, that Johnson's critical insight most clearly emerges. First and foremost he notes the uplifting power of the poet's imagination in representing supra-natural worlds wherein only the imagination could venture. Gifted beyond all others in his power of 'displaying the vast, illuminating the splendid, and enforcing the awful', Milton's chief characteristic is said to be sublimity, his 'natural port, gigantic loftiness', his aim being 'to raise the thoughts above sublunary cares or pleasures'.[2] Then, too, attention is called to the restraint and skill with which the poet has enlarged on the few facts provided by Scripture, in crowding the imagination with thoughts and fancies culled from ancient fable and

[1] Hill, *op. cit.* i. 170 ff.   [2] *ibid.* i. 177.

modern learning, with the help as well of similes ample, varied
and effective, thus giving to his theme yet more imposing dimen-
sions. 'Whatever be his subject', exclaims Johnson, 'he never
fails to fill the imagination'; and though (here agreeing with
Dryden) he allows that Milton viewed external Nature 'through
the spectacle of books', yet such allusions, he held, added
variety to the story and exercised the memory and fancy of
readers.

On the other hand he claims that the poem has its defects.
And among them he would include the lack of human interest,
together with the confusion of the spiritual and material in the
allegory of Sin and Death, or in the war in Heaven. Yet he
wisely refuses to follow Dryden in condemning the presence of
'flats among (Milton's) elevations',[1] arguing that 'a palace must
have passages and a poem . . . transitions'; and what is more, he
refrains from denouncing Milton's innovations in diction and
verse, even though they involved effects which ran counter to
his own cherished ideals. Milton's style, he held, was indeed
based on 'a perverse and pedantic principle',[2] English words
being used with a foreign idiom; so that, like Spenser, he wrote
no language, but 'a Babylonish dialect, harsh and barbarous'.
In his prose, added Johnson, such usage was naturally out of
place; but in his poetry things were different. What Milton, he
suggests, had here created was a new form of expression far
removed from common usage, but one which in the hands of
genius was made gracious in its deformity, so that 'criticism
sinks in admiration'. And in like manner with regard to Milton's
verse, Johnson reiterates his deep-seated preference for rhyming
verse, yet he cannot wish Milton to have written otherwise than
he did. These are no judgments of a hide-bound pedant per-
emptorily applying cut-and-dried theories to the work in hand.
Johnson had experienced aesthetically the elemental power of
Milton's great poem. 'What author', he exclaimed, 'ever soared
so high or sustained his flight so long?' To the poet he therefore accords the highest praise of genius, an originality that
triumphed over all adverse conditions. And his final and enthusiastic verdict is that 'Paradise Lost is not the greatest of heroic
poems only because it is not the first'.

For Johnson at his critical best, however, we must turn to
the large-scale Lives of Dryden and the Augustans, Pope and
Addison, to whom he stood closer in time and sympathy, and
whose literary ideals he in a large measure shared. And what he

---

[1] Hill, op. cit. i. 187: see p. 134 supra.   [2] ibid. i. 190.

thus provided have been fairly described as among the best
critical essays in English. In connexion with Dryden, in the
first place, a more intimate treatment is shown by his biographical remarks which bring out vividly, among other things,
the conditions under which the poet wrote, explaining how
poverty condemned him to write in order to live, and how the
quality of his work was thus affected in the hurried production
of works unrevised, and dictated originally either by the occasion or contemporary taste. Concerning Dryden's poetry, on
which the poet's fame then rested, Johnson has much to say,
though what he says is significantly lacking in the enthusiasm
displayed over *Paradise Lost*. The main facts relating to Dryden's varied activities are given, including accounts of his
panegyrics, his plays, his satires and translations; though, not
content with a bare recital of facts, Johnson also provides a
running commentary pointing out literary influences, borrowings and the like. But apart from this, as if intent on factual
matters, he is less concerned with aesthetic qualities, and his
appreciation is mostly on a lower note, sober, but informative
and always interesting. Occasionally, as in his comments on
Absalom and Achitophel,[1] he speaks with some warmth, but
here as always judicially. To him it is an unrivalled political
satire, with its effective characterization, its fierce invective, its
neat turns of language and pleasing verse. But then, he adds,
the allegory is incomplete; and the sudden conclusion is unsatisfactory, reminding him of 'an enchanted castle . . . which
vanishes into air when the destined knight blows his horn before
it'.

For the rest his critical comments relating to Dryden's
poetry are mostly of a general kind. In the first place he is
fully alive to the limitations of Dryden as a poet, and particularly as a dramatist. Thus he notes Dryden's wild extravagances and false magnificence in tragedy, his everlasting concern
with the 'turbulent effervescence of love', and his inability to
depict simple and elemental passions; or again, in comedy, his
resort to surprising incidents for his effects instead of to oddities
of character. The truth was, he adds, that Dryden was 'no rigid
judge of his own work', and that, as he had himself confessed,
he was often well aware at the time of writing that what he
wrote was 'bad enough to please'. Of his merits Johnson also
writes in the same general strain. In matters of verse and
expression he is said to have furnished a variety of models for

[1] Hill, *op. cit.* i. 436.

later writers, and to have prepared the way for later triumphs. His outstanding quality is described as 'strong reason rather than quick sensibility'; and he is credited with having taught men 'to think naturally and to express forcibly'. Moreover, he was the first, so it is more doubtfully claimed, to have joined argument with poetry; while in the matter of translation he is said to have pointed to a better way. It is therefore as a poet of good sense, original and sound technique that Dryden is mainly commended by Johnson. His great achievement, it was said, was to have 'refined the language, improved the sentiments and tuned the numbers of English poetry'.

It is in his treatment of Dryden's critical work, however, that Johnson's own greatness as a critic is forced upon us. And here, as a result of genuine admiration, amply testified by frequent references to the earlier critic elsewhere, Johnson now writes with an unwonted warmth of feeling, yet with keen insight and a just and balanced judgment, thus confuting by the way the prevailing opinion that Dryden's prose works were 'of accidental and secondary' value. To him Dryden is none other than 'the father of English criticism, the writer who first taught us to determine on principles the merit of composition';[1] though Johnson is aware of earlier contributions by Webbe and Puttenham, Jonson and Cowley. But when Dryden wrote, critical principles, he held, were known but to the learned few; and part of the merit of his achievement therefore lay in its historical value, in making current coin at that time the teaching of the ancients, of French and Italian authorities. This was illustrated, Johnson stated, in the *Essay of Dramatic Poesy*, where, writing with unwonted care and in dialogue form, Dryden had submitted their main doctrines in learned and lively fashion, and had supplied portraits of English dramatists that drew from Johnson one of his more animated judgments.

The account of Shakespeare [he writes] [2] may stand as a perpetual model of encomiastic criticism: exact without minuteness, and lofty without exaggeration. The praise lavished by Longinus on . . . Demosthenes fades away before it. In a few lines is exhibited a character, so extensive in its comprehension and so curious (i.e. careful) in its limitations, that nothing can be added, diminished, or reformed; nor can the editors . . . of Shakespeare boast of much more than of having diffused and paraphrased this epitome of excellence, of having changed Dryden's gold for baser metal, of lower value though of greater bulk.

[1] Hill, *op. cit*. i. 410.   [2] *ibid*. i. 412.

Such criticism, Johnson added, 'was a kind of learning almost new in England, by which popular judgment was much improved'.

Equally searching are his remarks on Dryden's critical work as a whole. He calls attention, for instance, to Dryden's prolific output, and its causes; how he was wont to add critical *Prefaces* to most of his published writings, in order to recommend his own or other plays, or to attack hostile critics, or else to increase the sales of his works by expositions of literary principles. Such criticism, stated Johnson, 'whether didactic or defensive, occupied almost all of his prose'; and 'none of his *Prefaces* was ever thought tedious'. On the nature of his criticism Johnson has also much to say. In the first place, Dryden's teaching, which 'depended on the nature of things and on the structure of the human mind',[1] he strongly commended as being psychologically sound. Besides, such criticism was 'often the criticism of a poet, not a dull collection of theorems, nor a rude detection of faults, but a gay and vigorous dissertation in which delight was mingled with instruction'. And this quality Johnson drives home by a happy comparison with the methods of Rymer.

With Dryden [states Johnson] [2] we are wandering in the quest of Truth, whom we find, if we find her at all, drest in the graces of elegance; and if we miss her, the labour of the pursuit rewards itself; we are led only through fragrance and flowers. Rymer . . . takes a rougher way; every step is to be made through thorns and brambles, and Truth, if we meet her, appears repulsive by her mien and ungraceful by her habit. Dryden's criticism has the majesty of a queen; Rymer's the ferocity of a tyrant.

On the other hand, less reliable were said to be Dryden's occasional judgments, which were sometimes biased, sometimes careless and capricious. Thus Johnson points to inconsistency in his attitude to rhyming plays, and his lack of scruple and even logic in refuting hostile critics, or again, in defending some licence of his own. In addition there were occasional inaccuracies in his statements, as when he referred to the tragedy of *Queen Gorboduc* or credited Chapman with employing Alexandrines in his *Homer*. The truth was, so Johnson explains, he was possessed of no very profound learning, despite appearances to the contrary, his critical doctrine being largely acquired in ordinary converse, and turned to account by a wise selection, shrewd thinking and experience. Yet in spite of all deficiencies, added Johnson, as a critic he stood alone in his good sense, his

[1] Hill, *op. cit.* i. 413.   [2] *ibid.*

keen insight and his wide acquaintance with both art and
Nature. Nor, finally, did Johnson fail to recognize the contribution made by Dryden's inimitable style to his effectiveness
as a critic; and an illuminating appreciation of his prose is
accordingly provided.

His *Prefaces* [states Johnson] [1] have not the formality of a settled
style, in which the first half of the sentence betrays the other. The
clauses are never balanced, nor the periods modelled; every word
seems to drop by chance, though it falls into its proper place.
Nothing is cold or languid; the whole is airy, animated and vigorous;
what is little is gay; what is great is splendid. He may be thought
to mention himself too frequently; but while he forces himself upon
our esteem, we cannot refuse him to stand in his own. Everything is
excused by the play of images and the spriteliness of expression.
Though all is easy, nothing is feeble; though all seems careless there
is nothing harsh; and though since his earlier works more than a
century has passed, they have nothing yet uncouth or obsolete.

In places such as these Johnson is perhaps at his best; though
it might perhaps be added that no apology nowadays is needed
for Dryden's frequent and endearing self-revelations.

In yet another of the large-scale *Lives*, that of Pope, are
Johnson's critical outlook and methods admirably illustrated.
The poet emerges from Johnson's pages, with his bodily in-
firmities and way of life, his friendships, his quarrels, his affectations and deceits, while with equal liveliness are represented
those intellectual qualities which determined the nature of his
literary output, namely, his ambitions, his good sense, his
artistic tact and 'poetical prudence'. At the same time an
illuminating background is provided by the light thrown on the
literary life of the period, more especially in the detailed
account of the conditions under which that 'poetical wonder',
Pope's *Homer*, appeared. That work, it is pointed out, was
printed by subscription, a practice previously employed in connexion with Dryden's *Virgil*, and one that for a time was
peculiarly English. References are also made to the jealousies
of contemporary writers, and to the arrogance of patrons
with their trifling criticisms and futile overtures of assistance—a matter with which Johnson dealt trenchantly in his
famous *Letter* to Lord Chesterfield. Moreover valuable insight
is afforded into Pope's methods of work when portions of the
original MSS. are supplied with all their variations and corrections; as if in reply to Waller's earlier remark that poets

[1] Hill, *op. cit.* i. 418.

often lost half their praise because readers knew not what they had blotted. And, again, Johnson gives some idea of the popularity of Pope's translation in stating that the poet's receipts from Tonson amounted to no less than £5,320, a sum which relieved him from financial anxieties.

Not less interesting, however, than the biographical section are the judgments pronounced on Pope as a poet; for, although we should not agree with his view that *The Temple of Fame* was an improvement on Chaucer, or that Pope's *Homer* is 'the noblest version of poetry the world has ever seen', yet on most of the other works Johnson has something suggestive to say. In *The Essay on Criticism*, for instance, he rightly admires the youthful poet's judicious selection from ancient and modern authorities; and in commending the well-known simile of the traveller in the Alps he takes the opportunity of defending the 'long-tailed' simile, then being derided in certain quarters. *The Rape of the Lock* is fairly described as 'the most exquisite example of ludicrous poetry'; and attention is called to the original and happy choice of machinery drawn from the Rosicrucians, whereby a new race of beings was called into existence, more effective for mock-heroic purposes than either the outworn classical deities or allegorical personages, those 'phantoms in motion', would ever have been. In the *Dunciad*, again, he notes the influence of Dryden's *MacFlecknoe*; and while he brushes aside Pope's claim to a moral motive, the treatment accorded to Theobald and other victims, he protests, was 'malignant but not very criminal', since 'an author solicits fame at the hazard of disgrace'. *The Ode for St. Cecilia's Day*, on the other hand, he regards as defective on account of its irregular Pindaric verse; the *Letters*, too, though something of a novelty, he decries as 'studied and artificial', written by one 'with his reputation in his head'. Nor is he unduly impressed with *The Essay on Man* in spite of its splendid imagery, its sparkling verse and seductive eloquence. The subject, he held, was unsuitable for poetry, and Pope was not master of his subject-matter; so that much of the poem was trite and commonplace.   In fact the poet is said to tell 'much of what every man knows and much that he does not know himself'; and Johnson's final verdict on the poem is that 'its flowers caught the eye which did not see what the gay foliage concealed'.

For the *Translation of Homer*, however, he puts up a special defence,[1] claiming that it supplied something that the Romans,

[1] Hill, *op. cit.* iii. 237 ff.

the Italians and the French had all failed to supply. To him it
was 'a treasure of poetical elegance which tuned the English
tongue'; but whereas its influence was undoubted, Coleridge's
estimate is probably nearer the truth when, while recognizing
its matchless art and ingenuity, he described it as 'the main
source of our pseudo-poetic diction'.[1] Johnson's chief concern,
however, is to defend it against current strictures, and especially against the alleged fault that it was not Homeric, that it
lacked the simplicity, the artless grandeur and majesty of
Homer. Such a charge he is in part prepared to concede; but
in estimating literary values, he recalls, differences of conditions should be taken into account. Many centuries, he notes,
had passed since Homer had written; and with a modern age
had come marked changes in language, verse, and habits of
thought. Virgil, writing some centuries nearer to Homer and in
a language and verse of the same general make-up, had already
responded to a demand for greater elegance; and Pope, writing
for 18th-Century readers, had likewise complied with the spirit
of his age in colouring his images and giving point to his expressions. In so doing, added Johnson, he had introduced many
'Ovidian graces' and beauties not found in Homer; but therein
lay his justification, even if something of Homer's sublimity had
thus been lost.

Most illuminating of all, however, in Johnson's treatment of
Pope is the masterly use made of the comparative method when
that poet is compared with Dryden,[2] and the qualities of each
are subtly analysed and thrown into relief. In the first place
both poets are credited with sound judgment and understanding, revealed by Dryden in his rejection of earlier doctrines, by
Pope in his meticulous craftsmanship from beginning to end.
But whereas Dryden was inconsistent in applying that judgment, writing merely to please and careless of perfection, Pope's
one aim was artistic excellence, as was shown by his numerous
corrections both before and after publication. In range of knowledge Dryden was held to be superior, being better acquainted
with human nature, gathering facts and fancies from a wider
field, and arriving at conclusions by free and bold speculation;
whereas Pope's scope was more limited, being confined mostly
to minute observations on contemporary life. In prose, again,
both poets are said to have excelled, but with qualities clearly
differentiated.

[1] *Biog. Lit.* i. 17, 39.
[2] Hill, *op. cit.* iii. pp. 220–3.

The style of Dryden [states Johnson] [1] is capricious and varied, that of Pope is cautious and uniform; Dryden obeys the motions of his own mind, Pope constrains his mind to his own rules of composition. Dryden is sometimes vehement and rapid; Pope is always smooth, uniform and gentle. Dryden's page is a natural field, rising into inequalities, and diversified by the varied exuberance of abundant vegetation; Pope's is a velvet lawn, shaven by the scythe and levelled by the roller.

Moreover, there was the test of poetic genius, defined by Johnson as 'that quality without which judgment is cold and knowledge is inert; that energy which collects, combines, amplifies and animates'. Here Johnson maintains, 'with some hesitation', it is true, that superiority must be assigned to Dryden, and remarks further that

It is not to be inferred that of this poetical vigour Pope had only a little, because Dryden had more, for every other writer since Milton must give place to Pope; and even of Dryden it must be said that if he has brighter paragraphs, he has not better poems. . . . If the flights of Dryden therefore are higher, Pope continues longer on the wing. If of Dryden's fire the blaze is brighter, of Pope's the heat is more regular and constant. Dryden often surpasses expectation, and Pope never falls below it. [2]

In thus awarding the primacy to Dryden Johnson adds in characteristic fashion that he is conscious of some 'partial fondness' for that poet which may have influenced his judgment. But, in conclusion, recalling Joseph Warton's earlier animadversions upon Pope, he triumphantly asks whether any reply was really needed. 'If Pope be not a poet', he exclaims, [3] 'where is poetry to be found?'

In treating of yet another of the great Augustans, namely, Addison, Johnson aims once more at displaying the general characteristics of a writer's work, and as a result Addison's contribution to poetry receives but slight notice, the main interest being concentrated on the significance of his works in prose. In general his poetry is said to possess no great excellence. Described as polished, the product of a fastidious mind, it is represented as lacking in life and vigour, while the poet is hailed as 'one of the earliest examples of correctness'. 'He thinks justly,' remarks Johnson, 'but he thinks faintly.' And these same qualities he finds in the much-discussed *Cato*, which he describes as a poem in dialogue form, lacking in dramatic qualities

---

[1] Hill, *op. cit.* iii. 222.   [2] *ibid.*   [3] *ibid.* iii. 251.

and emotional power alike, with characters lifeless and unconvincing, mere mouthpieces of sentiment and cold philosophy.
He also notes with approval Dennis's skill in detecting certain
faults in the play; but he refuses to accept that critic's demand
for 'poetic justice', though he agrees in condemning Addison's
observance of the Unities.

To Addison as a prose-writer, however, ample justice is done;
and much of what Johnson says has since become common
knowledge. To begin with, he points out what was original in
the scheme of the *Spectator* papers. Books on manners had been
written before; and Johnson recalls such works as Casa's *Il
Galateo*, Castiglione's *Courtier* and La Bruyère's *Caractères*.
But hitherto, he asserts, no *arbiter elegantiarum* had appeared
in England; and now Addison supplies the deficiency, adopting
their plans of regulating social conduct, but adding to those
plans the inculcating of a sound literary taste and the impart-
ing of truths by means of fiction and allegory. The results of
such work Johnson describes as 'having purified intellectual
pleasure, separating mirth from indecency and wit from
licentiousness, and of having taught a succession of writers to
bring elegance and gaiety to the aid of goodness'.[1] Moreover,
he points to Addison's oblique method of satire which was that
of flattering foolish opinions by acquiescence, thus rendering
their authors even yet more absurd.

It is with Addison's critical work, however, that Johnson
mainly deals; for whereas the popularity of the *Spectator* remained undiminished throughout the century, his work on
criticism was already being challenged, and Johnson undertakes to remove what seemed to him a grave injustice. The chief
objection to Addison's criticism was that it was 'tentative and
experimental rather than scientific',[2] deciding by 'taste rather
than by principles'. But, urges Johnson, such methods were
imposed upon him by the fact that he wrote for a public lacking
in the general knowledge common later in the century. Even
Dryden's critical teaching, he added, was 'too scholastic for
those who had their rudiments to learn'. And Addison's aim
was therefore to 'infuse literary curiosity by gentle and unsus-
pected conveyance', and 'to present knowledge in its most
alluring and familiar form'. Not that he was always successful;
though when Johnson demurs to Addison's estimate of *Chevy
Chase* he himself is at fault. For whereas Addison had rightly
detected in that poem certain beauties of feeling and expression,

[1] Hill, *op. cit.* ii. 126.   [2] *ibid.* ii. 145.

Johnson for his part saw little more than 'chill and lifeless imbecility'. Nevertheless Johnson is right in his main contention that Addison had provided the criticism that was needed in his day. He even went further and claimed that in his essays on *The Pleasures of the Imagination* he had employed 'scientific methods' in 'founding art on the base of Nature and drawing the principles of invention from dispositions inherent in the mind of man'.[1] In general, he allowed that Addison's judgments might be superficial, but then they were easily understood. *Paradise Lost* he had presented 'without the pomp of system or the severity of theory; but he had made Milton a universal favourite'; and in so doing he had aroused inquiry, improved the understanding and enlarged intellectual life. And this defence Johnson concludes with a few plain and caustic words to hostile critics. Addison's criticism, he maintained, was such as they would not easily attain; but then it 'was not uncommon for those who had grown wise by the labours of others, to add a little of their own, and overlook their masters'.

No account of Addison, however, would be complete without some reference to the distinguishing qualities of his prose works as a whole; and Johnson calls attention to his vivid descriptions of contemporary life and manners, his ripe wisdom embodied now in 'robes of fancy', now in 'the garb of reason', and above all to his rich vein of quiet humour, in which he stood alone. It was this peculiar humour, added Johnson, that gave the grace of novelty to his scenes of ordinary life. Never strained beyond 'the modesty of Nature', nor generated at the expense of truth, it gave an air of originality to his pictures of life that made them seem none other than products of the imagination. Nor does his unique prose style escape attention; and Johnson describes it at some length as the model of the middle style,[2] and as

Pure without scrupulosity and exact without apparent elaboration, always equable and always easy, without glowing words or pointed sentences. Addison [he continues] never deviates from his track to snatch a grace; he seeks no ambitious ornament and tries no hazardous innovation. . . . He is sometimes verbose in his transitions and connections, and sometimes descends too much to the language of conversation; yet if his language had been less idiomatical it might have lost something of its genuine Anglicism. What he attempted he performed; he is never feeble, and he did not wish to be energetic. . . . His sentences have neither studied amplitude, nor affected brevity; his periods, though not diligently rounded, are voluble and easy.

[1] Hill, *op. cit.* ii. 148.   [2] *ibid.* ii. 149.

And in the light of this analysis Johnson concludes with the well-known advice that 'whoever wishes to attain an English style, familiar but not coarse, and elegant but not ostentatious, must give his days and nights to the volumes of Addison'.

It is in these greater *Lives* that Johnson's more memorable judgments are pronounced; and to those already mentioned must be added his acute analysis of Swift's prose style distinguished for 'an equable tenour of easy language'.[1] But the minor *Lives*, too, have their critical value; and to pass over them in silence would be to lose sight of the immense range of Johnson's work, and to neglect significant side-lights on his critical outlook. Thus a readiness to recognize new literary values is revealed in his treatment of more than one writer. In Gay's *Beggar's Opera*, for example, originally written in ridicule of Italian musical plays, Johnson detects 'a new species of composition',[2] the ballad opera, which he praises for its novelty and gaiety. Experience had shown, he states, that it well suited popular audiences, and he describes it as likely to keep the stage. Again, a similar open-mindedness is shown by the welcome he gives to Congreve's new form of comedy, despite the fact that the characters are 'artificial, with very little of Nature and not much of life'. Yet he is alive to the new and effective comic element thus introduced, consisting in 'gay remarks and unexpected answers'.[3] Congreve's scenes, he allows, have but little humour or passion, while his characters are 'a kind of intellectual gladiators'; but his effects, he added, are obtained in original fashion by a sort of mental fireworks. 'Every sentence is to ward or strike; the contest is never intermitted; his wit is a meteor playing to and fro with alternate coruscations.'

Most notable in this connexion, however, is Johnson's appreciation of the originality and significance of Thomson's *Seasons*. In that poem he sees and commends not only new ways of thinking and new forms of expression, but also an original use of blank verse, unlike that of Milton, which, for the poet's purpose, was preferable to rhyme. But what most attracts him is Thomson's attitude to external Nature, so different from the studied artifice of pastoral poets. He had already commended the 'local poetry' of Denham, and now he approves yet more warmly of Thomson's ampler and more realistic treatment of the sights and sounds of the country-side. In his descriptions, Johnson points out, he deals with large and general effects, which bring out the magnificence of external Nature, 'the gaiety

[1] Hill, *op. cit.* iii. 51 ff.   [2] *ibid.* ii. 282.   [3] *ibid.* ii. 228.

of Spring, the splendour of Summer, the tranquillity of Autumn and the horror of Winter';[1] and in so doing, adds Johnson, 'his enthusiasm causes our thoughts to be expanded with his imagery and kindled with his sentiment'. One defect of the poem was said to be its want of ordered arrangement; but that, Johnson confessed, seemed unavoidable, since 'of many appearances subsisting all at once, no rule could be given why one should be mentioned before another'. And, for the rest, his praise of Thomson's achievement is couched almost in lyrical terms:

He looks round on Nature and on life [writes Johnson] with the eye which Nature bestows only on a poet, the eye that distinguishes in every thing . . . whatever there is on which imagination can delight, . . . and with a mind that at once comprehends the vast and attends to the minute. The reader of the *Seasons* wonders that he never saw before what Thomson shows him, and that he never yet has felt what Thomson impresses.[2]

Johnson was no hostile critic of innovations in the field of art, though as yet his conception of Nature poetry was limited to descriptions of 'pleasing scenes' accompanied by reflexions suggested by those scenes—the qualities which he commends, for instance, in Dyer's *Grongar Hill*.

Among other aspects of Johnson's criticism that emerge in the course of these minor *Lives*, there was, for instance, his independent judgment revealed by the corrected estimates he submits from time to time. Thus the earlier fame of Mulgrave he attributes to 'flattery and favour'; Roscommon is said to be 'elegant but not great'; while Johnson's own contemporary, Akenside, is censured for tedious and long-winded expression. 'After many turns in the labyrinth', exclaims Johnson, 'the reader comes out as he goes in.' On the other hand certain limitations appear in his failure to recognize subtle literary effects. Prior's poems, for example, are dismissed as 'tissues of common thought', his excellence in the familiar style passing unnoticed; while the devotional poetry of Watts, the author of many of our most majestic hymns, is described as simply 'unsatisfactory'. Elsewhere, too, Johnson's judgment is influenced by certain prejudices, as when he derides the short-lined verses of Ambrose Philips as such, adding that 'little things are not valued but when they are done by those who can do greater'; or again, when influenced by the piety of Blackmore he unduly

[1] Hill, *op. cit.* iii. 299.   [2] *ibid.* iii. 298–9.

commends his *Creation* as capable in itself of placing its author among the first of English poets.

Nowhere, however, are Johnson's shortcomings attended with more unfortunate results than in his treatment of Collins and Gray, those harbingers of a later spring whose lyrical flights he was unable to follow. Of Collins,[1] in the first place, he cherished some tender memories; and his consideration of that poet's work is accordingly of a sympathetic kind. He recognizes Collins's delight in flights of fancy 'beyond the bounds of Nature', his love of popular superstitions, fairies and the like, besides oriental fiction and allegorical imagery; and he notes the use made of the wild and the extravagant, which at times, he allowed, produced effects both splendid and sublime. But this exotic subject-matter, argued Johnson, detracted from the merit of his poetry; it was none other than 'a quest of mistaken beauties'. Moreover, his descriptions of external Nature were unaccompanied by the necessary reflexions; his diction is described as 'harsh and unskilfully laboured'; and he is said 'to have affected the obsolete when it was not worthy of revival', and 'to have put his words out of the common order, seeming to think that . . . not to write in prose is certainly to write poetry'. Yet all these departures from normal Augustan standards were but a foretaste of things to come; and there was much in Collins which Johnson failed to appreciate.

Even yet less adequate is Johnson's estimate of Gray as a poet; though despite, or perhaps because of, marked differences of temperament, he strove to present an unbiased judgment of Gray as a man. Johnson's own impression was that he was a dilettante, affected, fastidious and somewhat effeminate; so he generously submits the opinions of friends as a counterbalance, according to which Gray was represented as 'perhaps the most learned man in Europe',[2] one possessed of the widest culture in natural history and antiquarianism, and 'a man likely to love much when he loved at all'. In attempting a judgment of Gray's poetry, however, he limits his remarks to his own personal impressions; and it becomes clear that he is puzzled by Gray's departures from Augustan standards, by the strangeness of his subject-matter and the new idiom of his expression. He has a word of praise for the sentiments of *The Ode on Adversity*; but he inconsistently censures the *Eton Ode* for its treatment of pregnant commonplaces—the very element to which later he attributes the greatness of the *Elegy*.

[1] Hill, *op. cit.* iii. 337, 341.   [2] See p. 197 n. *supra*.

With the *Progress of Poetry* and the *Bard*, however, his perplexity increases; and he fails to understand either the themes
or the handling of the poems. Applying the test of common
sense he discusses mere verbal points, a type of criticism he had
formerly disparaged; and, for the rest, his general remarks only
witness to his lack of comprehension. His main judgment is that
Gray in striving for original effects had stepped beyond the
limits of what was possible in poetry. The *Progress of Poetry*
he describes as 'a high Pindaric on stilts'; the alliterations in
the *Bard*, he holds, are too trifling for a poem that aimed at
sublimity; and the *Odes* as a whole have 'a kind of cumbrous
splendour that we wish away'.

[They] are marked [he continues] by glittering accumulations of
ungraceful ornaments; they strike rather than please. . . . The mind
of the writer seems to work with unnatural violence. 'Double,
double, toil and trouble.' He has a kind of strutting dignity, and is
tall by walking on tiptoe. His art and his struggle are too visible, and
there is too little appearance of ease and Nature.[1]

Apart from this, the language of the poem, he declares, is
'laboured with harshness'; and, alluding to Gray's dictum concerning poetic diction, he remarks that 'Gray thought his
language more poetical as it was more remote from common
use'. Thus he denounces Gray's experiments in diction, parti-
ciples formed from nouns like 'cultured' and 'honied'; epithets
like '(Idalia's) velvet (green)' drawn from art and therefore
degrading to Nature; compounds like 'many-twinkling (feet)';
besides expressions such as 'buxom health' or the use of expletives 'do' and 'did' for metrical purposes; all of which were but
anticipations of a greater freedom of expression.

In the *Elegy* alone does he find elements of unquestioned
greatness, approved by the common sense of the plain man,
'uncorrupted with literary prejudices' or subtle refinements of
taste. Here the appeal of commonplaces enshrining great simple
truths proves irresistible. 'The *Churchyard*', he states, 'abounds
with images which find a mirror in every mind, and with sentiments to which every bosom returns an echo.' Moreover, many
of the thoughts, he suggests, were here uttered for the first time;
yet every reader is persuaded that they had always been his
own. 'Had Gray written often thus', added Johnson, 'it had
been vain to blame, and useless to praise him.' And a like
tribute, it might be said, would also hold true of Johnson
himself.

[1] Hill, *op. cit.* iii. 440.

21

With the varied critical activities of Johnson now in mind—
his scattered theorizing, his judgments on Shakespeare and a
whole array of poets—what is there to be said of his critical
achievement as a whole? As has already been hinted, since his
day he has been subjected to some surprising judgments, perhaps more so than any other of the great critics. If not actually
abused, he has been presented, more often than not, in apologetic fashion, with much confident explanation of his manifold
defects; the chief complaint being that he lacked the sympathetic imaginative temperament for revealing the finer literary
effects, and so failed to let us into the secrets of the poetic
appeal. But this is by no means the whole trouble; his criticism
has also been said to suffer from sundry prejudices, from a
narrow conception of what poetry really is, as well as from his
methods of forming and pronouncing judgment; while he has
also been denounced as a rigid moralist and a determined foe of
all innovation. Apart from this, further alleged defects have
been gathered from isolated fragments of his doctrine and
judgments, which, torn from their context and therefore distorted, have been accepted as a sound basis for a final evaluation.
Thus he has been grouped, for instance, among the neo-classical
critics; for did he not make use of Bossu's categories in his
treatment of Milton? Or again, that he was surely lacking in
the historical sense was held to be indicated by his references
to the 'savagery' of Elizabethan times, and his want of sympathy with yet earlier periods of English poetry. Then, too,
there were those unhappy comments on *Lycidas* and Gray; and
besides all this, to his judgments in general he brought as his
tests settled principles of his own, whereas the enlightened
critics of a later day sought the touchstone of excellence in the
work of the poet itself. So that, altogether, despite substantial
work in connexion with Shakespeare and other English poets,
he created in the minds of some the impression of an obtuse,
dogmatic, and ponderous critic, who hindered, for the time
being, an aesthetic appreciation of literature, and was in fact
little more than a prosaic critic in an age of prose.

Yet this after all is but a superficial and shallow judgment;
for his performance, to be rightly appreciated or even understood, must be viewed, not in the light of 19th-Century theory
and practice, but against an 18th-Century background with its
special problems and its shortened horizon where poetry was
concerned. That he had his defects must of course be granted.
It is true that he had prejudices, both personal and literary,

that he was blind to many of those 'nameless and inexplicable graces' that go to the making of great poetry, that he disliked irregular metres, elaborate rhyming systems, the pastoral convention, short poems, and the like, and that, despite his regard for the critical and historical work of the Wartons, he had but little sympathy with their liking for earlier poetry. Moreover he would limit the themes of literature to the known world of human society and experience; he frequently indulged in mere verbal fault-finding which at other times he denounced; while his robust, downright form of utterance was not calculated to win all readers. Over and above all this, however, was his reliance on Nature or reason as his main instrument for forming literary judgment, 'imagination' being to him mere 'fancy'. It was a test which was tantamount to the prose understanding or good sense, with its 'intuitive perception of what was fitting' and in accordance with the demands of human nature; but it was also one which, in the absence of an imaginative element, fell short of being the highest aesthetic touchstone, and could not but fail to sound the deeper mysteries of the literary art.

On the other hand when viewed in its proper setting Johnson's criticism will be found to possess many positive qualities of lasting value for his own and later generations. Not least significant was his settlement of a much-vexed question, when, refusing to accept neo-classicism as his creed, rejecting also the test of mere individual taste, he found in the law of Nature or reason his guide; and in thus making his main test the appeal to the mind of rational man, he gave direction to contemporary criticism, and prepared the way at least for reasoned psychological methods yet more effective, when the mind of man had been more fully explored. At the same time manifest critical abuses he successfully ridiculed, commending besides numerous precepts of lasting value, such as, the importance of the tests of time and universality of appeal as ultimate criteria of literary value, the necessity for judging a work of art as a whole, or again, the need for taking into account historical considerations in forming literary judgment. Moreover by his actual use of the biographical, historical and comparative methods in forming judgments, he emphasizes the value of such methods in throwing light on literary matters from various angles. As a thinker he is acute rather than profound; and many of his ideas he assimilated from preceding critics. But only after careful scrutiny; while his independence is shown by his fearless challenging of earlier writers, including Dryden, by whom, for the rest, he was definitely influenced. Moreover he was far from being the dogmatic, hide-bound critic he is sometimes made out to be. In his theorizing, for instance, he frequently gives expression to doubts and reservations in his desire for perfect accuracy; and in his appreciations he reveals a noteworthy open-mindedness in welcoming innovations for which a reasoned case could be made. Thus from him came an early recognition of the possibilities of poetry dealing realistically with external nature; and this interest, betrayed in the works of Denham, Thomson, Dyer and, later, Crabbe, not only accounts for his attack on the pastoral tradition, but also anticipates later notable developments in that field of literature.

As a result he has handed down a body of critical judgments up to then unsurpassed in their wide scope, their original biographical detail, their keen and dispassionate psychological analysis within certain limits, and their scorn of affectations, humbug and all excesses. More successful in dealing with the Augustans than with earlier or later poets, and with prose works rather than with poetry, he opened up new ground with what is in effect the history of a whole century of English poetry; and while many of his judgments hold good to-day, have indeed become accepted as final, they are presented in a style, rhetorical and antithetic it may be, yet always clear, forceful and often picturesque. But what most appeals to present-day readers is perhaps the essentially critical spirit, the sanity and ripe wisdom that inspire his generalizations on life and letters. 'Great popularity in one age', he states, 'is followed by neglect in the next.' 'In every activity of valuing, the mind discovers in the object that which is akin to itself.' 'About things on which the public thinks long it commonly attains to think right.' 'Pedantry is an unseasonable ostentation of learning.' 'Good humour is the balm of being.' These are critical commonplaces which every age has to learn or re-learn. Since his day the critical spirit, having left the region of pure intellect, has soared freely in the realm of the imagination, and has latterly, for better or for worse, explored tracts that lie beneath the level of the conscious. But Johnson reminds us that literature, whatever else it may be, is a vehicle of rational thought and articulate emotion, that it is subject to no rigid moral requirements, but is essentially an uplifting power enabling men 'to enjoy life or to endure it', thus making a contribution to the art of living. And these are welcome reminders in ages of perplexity. The unflattering reception which his critical work has sometimes since experienced was perhaps a natural reaction from an earlier adulation accorded to a dictator, though it may also have been due to excessive zeal for later 'romantic' doctrine; while the absorption of a critic's findings into the stock of common knowledge has not infrequently led to a forgetfulness of the ultimate source of those ideas. Yet it is as a master who helped in changing the current of critical ideas that he figures in critical history. Having made use of psychological tests and having revealed incidentally the limits of the prose understanding for critical purposes, he unconsciously prepared the way for the later triumphs of those who made imagination or the higher reason their criterion of poetic values. And for this and other reasons his claims to greatness as a critic admit of no dispute; even though he was one who, 'attaining his full purpose, lost himself in his own lustre'.

CHAPTER IX

CRITICAL CROSS-CURRENTS: FIELDING, SHERIDAN,
COWPER, SHAFTESBURY, HUME, BURKE, KAMES,
REYNOLDS AND BEATTIE

THE main track of the critical development has now been outlined but there yet remain those diverse contributions which
accompanied the main movement and which had come in ever-
increasing volume from various quarters, from literary men
themselves, from philosophers and writers of a specialist or
popular kind. Not all of these works were of course of equal
value. Yet all in their different ways go to fill in the picture,
and call for notice in a survey of what was accomplished
at this stage in artistic theory and judgment. Fresh light for
instance is thrown on the actual critical position by Fielding,
Goldsmith, Sheridan and Cowper, who in the course of their
creative work pronounced some interesting judgments on contemporary literature. Then, too, definite importance is attached
to the philosophical works of those who discussed art in general
and its psychological appeal in particular, with a view to
satisfying interests of an intellectual kind. Such writers included Shaftesbury, Hume, Burke and Kames, who treated,
among other things, of the meaning to be assigned to what was
known as 'taste'. Nor must the vogue for comparative studies
of the sister arts be overlooked, even if much of the work was
of a tentative and ineffectual kind. The contributions of Reynolds in this field, for instance, are of special interest; and so,
for different reasons, are the works of Percy and Tyrwhitt,
Beattie, Harris and others.

Among the more notable critical works of literary men, to
begin with, are those of Henry Fielding (1707–54), which appear
first in his burlesque play *The Tragedy of Tragedies, or the Life
and Death of Tom Thumb the Great* (1731), and, later, in his novel
Tom Jones (1749). The former is a lively and successful exposure
of the dramatic extravagances of his day; while in the latter he
casually submits his views on novel-writing in short chapters
inserted at intervals as a sort of Chorus to the story. *The Tragedy
of Tragedies*, in the first place, was obviously inspired by the
earlier *Rehearsal* in that the attack is mainly directed against
heroic plays, the absurdities of which were very much alive at

the time of writing. On the other hand it differs from the *Rehearsal* in being itself a sort of heroic drama, relating in mock-heroic style the astounding exploits of a diminutive hero 'round whose chariot-wheels giants crowded'; and, besides, the satire, is made to embrace the absurdities of specific dramatists up to 1730, among whom were Thomson, Nat Lee, Young and others. Then, too, there is the satire directed against dramatic critics, when, adopting the device of a Dr. Wagstaffe who had parodied Addison's remarks on *Chevy Chase* in what he called *A Comment upon the History of Tom Thumb* (1711), Fielding added to his play footnotes ridiculing the pedantic judgments, the insipid appreciations, the absurd emendations and needless quoting of parallel passages which (not always fairly) he associated with the critics Dennis, Bentley and Theobald. From the critical standpoint, however, the real value of the play lies above all in its ruthless revelation of what was wrong with play-writing at the time. The plot, with its amazing incidents and melodramatic effects, its ghost scene, its prophecy, its love-passages and final indiscriminate slaughter, was suitably matched with characters fantastic, crude and utterly impossible, as well as with the fashionable fustian, bathos and plagiarisms. Every incident and every line were more or less travesties of earlier passages all too familiar to contemporary playgoers; and as a parody of glaring dramatic abuses the play must be reckoned as one of the most successful in the language.

Interest of another kind is attached to Fielding's remarks on the novel, that new form which was already challenging the drama as a means of entertainment. At the outset he claims to be 'the founder of a new province of writing, and therefore at liberty to make what laws he pleases'.[1] And in virtue of this claim he had previously ridiculed in *Joseph Andrews* (1742) the sentimentality and 'hot-house' morality of Richardson's *Pamela* (1740). Of greater significance, however, are the positive ideas he now submits concerning the form and scope of the new development. It is true that he employs familiar terminology in defining it as 'a comic epic in prose'; but, for the rest, he flouts the epic rules laid down by latter-day theorists. 'The laws of writing', he complains,[2] 'were no longer founded on the practice of authors but on the dictates of critics', and in consequence, 'rules had been established which had not the least foundation in truth or Nature, and which merely curbed and restrained genius'. As an example he states that 'nothing is

[1] *Tom Jones*, II. i.   [2] *ibid.*

more cold than the invocation of a Muse by a modern writer'; and elsewhere he ridicules the rules in ironical fashion when he makes use of an impassioned invocation, introduces Sophia to his readers in magniloquent style, or employs grandiose similes to emphasize some striking situation.

At the same time he himself lays down no fixed code or system, but is content with suggesting some general principles. The novel, he held, was distinguished from earlier romances— 'those productions, not of Nature, but of distempered brains'— in treating solely of the actual life of men; and in such works, it followed, supernatural agents of the Homeric epic, as well as far-fetched fancies, were out of place.[1] Man, he insists, is the highest subject for any writer, and was above all to be treated in the novel in realistic and convincing fashion. Possibility was not enough; the action was to be rendered probable, 'brought within the compass of human agency and performed by agents whose characters made it possible'. And within these limits a free treatment of the wonderful was permitted. Apart from this he holds that characteristic types, not individuals, should be represented, and that a comic spirit should prevail throughout, since morals were better refined by wholesome laughter than by noisy indignation. At the same time, he added, passages of seriousness might be introduced by way of contrast, while truth, mingled with fiction, would be rendered more probable than history. He further vindicates pure and honest love as a suitable theme, since it contributed to human happiness, while also inculcating that 'goodness and innocence' at which the novel should aim. And as a final injunction to his readers he urges that 'every book ought to be read with the same spirit and in the same manner as it is writ'.[2]

Less substantial is the critical work of Oliver Goldsmith (1730–74), which consists merely of *An Inquiry into the Present State of Polite Learning in Europe* (1759), and certain essays in *The Bee* (1759) and elsewhere. The former has but little bearing on the critical development. Apart from a superficial treatment of earlier ages, together with discussions on such matters as the age-long hostility of critics and the recent decline of patronage, his own age he describes as decadent, and deplores the vogue of blank verse with its 'disgusting solemnity of manner'; and hailing Parnell as the last of the poets modelled on the ancients, he censures Gray's *Odes* on account of their obscurity, besides finding much in Shakespeare that he would wish away.

[1] *Tom Jones*, VIII. i.   [2] *ibid.* IV. i.

Nor does his essay *Of Eloquence* throw much fresh light on its subject. There are the usual commonplaces; that 'rules are useless, they only prevent faults but do not introduce beauties'; that clear expression follows clear ideas; and that eloquence needs variety. What he mainly discusses is the pulpit oratory of the period. Thus the crude 'enthusiasms' of Methodist preachers are commended with some reservations; whereas the more studied and intricate periods of Tillotson are said to be less effective. Goldsmith's ideals are therefore those of simplicity and naturalness. 'True declamation', he states, 'does not consist in flowery periods, delicate allusions or musical cadences, but rather in a plain, open and loose style.'

Of greater interest is his essay *On Sentimental Comedy* (1773) where he discusses one of the live questions of his day, namely, whether the *comédie larmoyante*, fashionable at the time, was worthy of survival. He describes it as a new species of drama, designed to exhibit the virtues, rather than the vices, of ordinary men, and one in which the interest was supplied by the distresses, and not the faults, of mankind. From earliest times, he notes, tragedy and comedy had been kept strictly apart; and writers of antiquity had been content to ridicule folly without 'exalting their characters with buskined pomp, or making what Voltaire called a tradesman's tragedy'. Yet the new drama, he confesses, had won much success, due partly to novelty, but partly also to the flattering of playgoers who beheld therein their own follies commended and had their emotions lightly touched. Thus comedy had invaded the field of tragedy, whereas tragedy itself was being neglected; and as a result, he exclaims, 'we are all the poorer'. Yet, he adds, it was not enough to claim that, since delight was afforded by weeping in comedy, such comedy was thereby justified; for true comedy would afford yet greater delight, and the new comedy after all was but a 'bastard tragedy'. The truth was, he states, that humour was apparently departing from the stage; that an art once lost was not easily recaptured; and that, with humour banished, we should deserve to lose the art of laughing. It was therefore in defence of humour, and not as an infringement of the neoclassical code, that he condemns sentimental comedy. And it was in support of these views that Tony Lumpkin and other estimable characters saw the light.

A similar attack on the contemporary stage forms the critical contribution of R. B. Sheridan (1751–1816) in *The Critic* (1779), another play inspired by Buckingham's *Rehearsal*, which it closely resembles. Like Goldsmith, Sheridan ridicules anew the 'insipid' sentimental comedy as having 'nothing ridiculous in it from beginning to end'; but his chief darts are reserved for the absurd methods of contemporary playwrights and critics, the former being represented by Sir Fretful Plagiary, who stood for Cumberland, the then popular author of sentimental plays, the latter by Puff and Sneer, characteristic 'practitioners in pane-gyric and censure'. And the result is one of the most brilliant of literary parodies, scintillating with wit and ruthless in its revelations of the manifest absurdities bound up with the ludicrous historical drama, *The Spanish Armada*, as an example. With special delight Sheridan points to the clumsiness of the prevailing dramatic technique: the naïve and obvious methods of conveying information to the audience, the use of double plots frankly unrelated, the thrusting of incongruous love-passages into stately historical scenes, and the clearing-up of complications and disguises with unconvincing crudity. Or again, it might be the hackneyed melodramatic effects then common: a clock chiming to 'beget an awful attention', the use of soft music or grandiloquent verse to usher in the heroine, or the inevitable prayer to Mars before a battle. And apart from these were the artificial devices that formed part of stage con-ventions: the mechanical use of 'small-sword logic' or one-word dialogue, portentous nods and silences calculated to convey profound thoughts, as well as asides, speeches from within and the like. All were an outrage on good sense and taste, and they are staged by Sheridan in delightful fashion. Nor does he fail to unmask some of the critical practices of the time in his account of the frauds and subtleties bound up with the art of theatrical advertisement, with the puff direct, the puff preliminary, the puffs collateral, collusive and oblique. Altogether it is a sound and acute judgment on the contemporary stage, a judgment kept alive by unfailing wit and humour.

Among the further contributions of creative artists at this date were certain *obiter dicta* of Sterne and Gibbon which are worth recalling, while Cowper demands more serious attention. Significant, for instance, is Sterne's derisive attack on neo-classicism in *Tristram Shandy*[1] (1760–7), an attack unreasoned, but made memorable by his use of picturesque, if whimsical, terms. Thus he speaks of critics as 'befetished with the bobs and trinkets of criticism', ridiculous judgments arrived at with the help of 'Bossu's rules', the 'stop-watch', or 'the rules and com-

[1] III. ch. 12.

passes'; and declares that 'of all cants . . . the cant of criticism is the most tormenting'. Interesting in another sense are the tributes of Edward Gibbon (1737–94) to 'our immortal Fielding', and again to 'Longinus'. Johnson in conversation had lightly alluded to Fielding as 'that barren rascal'; whereas Gibbon now boldly affirms that '*Tom Jones*, that exquisite picture of human nature will outlive the palace of the Escurial'.[1] Yet more important, however, are his comments on the work of 'Longinus'. He not only gives evidence of first-hand acquaintance with the text and an acute perception of its literary and critical qualities; he also notes its peculiar verbal difficulties, and is astonished at the excellence of a work then supposed to have been written in the 3rd Century A.D. And in a remarkable passage he describes one chapter (ch. ix.) as 'one of the finest monuments in antiquity'.

I was acquainted [he writes] [2] with only two ways of criticising a beautiful passage; the one, to shew, by an exact anatomy of it, the distinct beauties of it and whence they sprung; the other, an idle exclamation or a general encomium, which leaves nothing behind it. Longinus has shewn me that there is a third. He tells me his own feelings upon reading it; and tells them with such energy that he communicates them.

It was an isolated, but a striking, judgment at this date, not more remarkable for its penetrating insight than for its happy, if unconscious, suggestion of much that criticism at its best was ultimately to mean.

The century however does not close without some foretaste of this more illuminating criticism, represented in the literary impressions of the poet William Cowper (1731–1800), scattered mostly throughout his *Letters*, which, as the stray comments of a sensitive soul in correspondence with friends, are the unlaboured expression of artistic views and spiritual experiences conveyed with unfailing and infectious charm. Systematic theory, in the first place, is not his line; though his remarks are always of interest, and not least, those relating to his own poetic standards and methods. With regard to the respective values of rhyming and blank verse, for one thing, his views are definite. Rhyme, he conjectures, was first introduced to mark the 'measure' in modern languages since they were less metrical than those of the ancients; but, in general, he adds, rhyming verse in practice imposed heavy fetters on the poet, although

---

[1] *Autobiography* (1794), *ad init.*   [2] *Journal*, Oct. 3, 1762.

effective in short poems like *L'Allegro*, and necessary in more formal rondeaus, odes and the like. Blank verse, on the other hand, he held to be capable of greater variety of movement, and thus called for greater attention to caesura and cadence. It was in fact the most difficult of verse-forms, and was the only measure for works of translation. Here Cowper is reacting definitely against the traditional 'correctness' of Pope's rhyming verse, to which, he complains, men's ears had become unduly attuned. And he refuses to sacrifice the spirit or sense of a passage to its sound.

Readers to-day [he states][1] are squeamish; if a line do not run as smooth as quicksilver they are offended. . . . For this we may thank Pope; but unless we could imitate him in the closeness and compactness of his expression, as well as in the smoothness of his numbers, we had better drop the imitation which serves no other purpose than to emasculate and weaken all we write. . . . Give me a manly, rough line with a deal of meaning in it rather than a whole poem full of musical periods that have nothing but their oily smoothness to recommend them. . . . There is a roughness on a plum which nobody that understands fruit would rub off, though the plum would be more polished without it.

Of interest, again, are his remarks on the ballad, which he describes as 'a species of poetry peculiar to this country, equally adapted to the drollest and the most tragical subjects'.[2] What he has in mind are the then popular ballads, such as Gay's ''Twas when the seas were roaring'. Originally, however, he explains, it was a poetic form characterized by simplicity and ease, in which our earliest poets had excelled, though until recent years the secret had been lost. There existed, he added, but few good odes in English; but many ballads had recently appeared which rivalled some of the best odes of classical antiquity.

Then, too, there are those occasional remarks of his that throw light on his own poetic craft, as Wordsworth did later in his *Prelude*. Thus he claims to have striven for originality throughout, and to have 'stumbled upon some subjects that had never before been poetically treated'.[3] He confesses, for instance, to a religious cast in all his writings; points to descriptions all taken direct from Nature, and to his treatment of the human heart as based on his own experiences; while his blank verse, he adds, was also peculiar to himself.[4] Elsewhere hints are given

---

[1] *Letters*, Jan. 1791.   [2] *ibid*. Aug. 4, 1783.
[3] *ibid*. Oct. 19, 1781.   [4] *ibid*. Oct. 10, 1784.

of the sources from whence he drew inspiration. 'Winter,' he states, 'which generally pinches off the flowers of poetry, unfolds mine'; again, 'the most ludicrous lines I ever wrote have been written in the saddest mood'; and, writing in one place of impressions received from an all-embracing Nature, he adds that 'the sights and sounds of the ocean . . . have often composed my thoughts into a melancholy not unpleasing'.[1] In addition, his casual remarks on technique are also worth recalling. He insists, for instance, on careful workmanship. 'To touch and re-touch', he states, 'is the secret of almost all good writing'; and he claims to have observed this precept in the strictest sense. With earlier censures on the use of compounds he does not agree; such epithets as 'black-eyed' and 'nut-brown', he holds, are as agreeable to English, as to Greek, ears. And on methods of translation he has much to say, noting more especially that since 'no two languages furnish equipollent words' translation should therefore 'be close but not so close as to be servile, free but not so free as to be licentious'; and that, for translating Homer, blank verse was the only adequate verse-form. He also recalls his perplexity in his efforts to attain the native simplicity of Homer, and how, having first 'imitated the quaintness of 15th-Century writers', he finally discarded all obsolete expressions and adopted a purely modern idiom.

Most valuable of all, however, is the fresh air that blows freely through his literary judgments, opening up new views of literary values and clearing away the mists that had previously distorted the vision. No formal or full-length estimates are anywhere attempted; but all judgments alike are suggestive, illuminating, and often corrective in his 'divine chit-chat'. It was inevitable that Milton for one should receive attention; and Cowper touches lightly on that poet's art, alluding first to the grandeur of his style, then suggesting that in going beyond the language of his day he had 'taken a long stride forward', and that he was 'never quaint . . . but everywhere grand and elegant, without resorting to musty antiquity for his beauties'.[2] As for Milton's verse, 'its music', he maintained,[3] 'is like that of a fine organ', with 'the fullest and deepest tones of majesty', together with all 'the softness and elegance of the Dorian flute'; and, unending in its variety, it had 'never been equalled unless perhaps by Virgil'. Contemporary ears, Cowper explained,[4] were unfamiliar with his divine harmonies, and men complained

[1] *Letters*, Sept. 26, 1781. [2] *ibid.* March 1790.
[3] *ibid.* Oct. 31, 1779. [4] *ibid.* Aug. 31, 1786.

about his elisions though it was to such elisions that their majesty was largely due. Nor does he fail to deal faithfully with Johnson's unfortunate handling of Milton, pointing out the jaundiced treatment of Milton as a man, and charging the Doctor with having 'plucked one or two of the most beautiful feathers out of the poet's Muse's wing, and trampled them under his great foot'.[1] Here the reference is obviously to Johnson's abuse of *Lycidas*, which, despite 'the childish prattlement of pastoral compositions', is nevertheless for Cowper a charming poem, distinguished for 'the liveliness of its descriptions, the sweetness of its numbers and the classical spirit that prevails in it'. And with an irreverence secured by epistolary conditions Cowper indulges in the impious longing to 'thresh (the Doctor's) old jacket till he made his pension jingle in his pocket'.

Concerning Pope, too, he has some pertinent remarks to make, in which he challenges the position of the great Augustan. He grants that Pope had 'managed the bells of rhyme with more dexterity than any man'; he also credits him with a felicity of expression peculiar to himself; and he cannot hold with those who would not allow him to be a poet at all. But having said this, he refuses to accept the poetic tradition inaugurated by Pope, and agrees with Johnson in recognizing Dryden to have been the greater inspiration and force. Cowper's chief complaint is that Pope had made poetry 'a mere mechanic art', the fruit of sheer industry and labour. He is said to have worked with 'the unwearied application of a plodding Flemish painter who draws a shrimp with the most minute exactness;' and never, it is added, 'were such talents and drudgery united'.[2] Dryden, on the other hand, is held to have succeeded by 'mere dint of genius, and in spite of laziness and carelessness'. His faults are described as 'those of a great man, and his beauties . . . such as Pope with all his touching and re-touching could never equal'.

And this hostility to Pope is intensified when Cowper comes to deal in his later years with the task of translating Homer. Impressed, as others have been, with its peculiar difficulties, he attacks Pope's version with something like fury.[3] It was not only that Pope 'had tied the bells of rhyme about Homer's neck', and in some places had failed to understand what Homer had written. What was even more, he had grossly misrepresented the spirit of Homer, 'bedizening him with ornament', and distorting his sublime simplicity with effects tawdry and

[1] *Letters*, Oct. 31, 1779.   [2] *ibid*. Jan. 5, 1782.   [3] *ibid*. Dec. 7, 1785.

tumid. To Homer it was natural, so Cowper protests, 'to say great things and to say them well', and little ornaments were beneath his notice. By Pope, however, Homer's native simplicity was disfigured with 'puerile conceits, extravagant metaphors and strutting phrase'; while his characters were all 'reduced to the perfect standards of French good breeding'. 'The garden in all the gaiety of June', exclaimed Cowper, 'is less flowery than Pope's version.' And this revised estimate of what had long been regarded as one of the finest fruits of 18th-Century literary culture was not without its significance. Swift and others had hinted at the same things; but Cowper's more searching treatment was now a clear indication of radical changes in critical values soon to come.

Nor, it might be added, are these corrected impressions confined to Pope alone; for, free from neo-classical and other prejudices, Cowper presents in a new light poets who had hitherto received but scant justice. Recalling, for instance, Johnson's curt pronouncement on Watts as a poet, he finds in him, at his best, qualities of undoubted excellence; and he accordingly describes him as of true poetic metal, 'frequently sublime in his conceptions and masterly in his execution'[1]—a judgment with which many modern readers would agree, if wide and lasting appeal is any criterion. Or again, there was Prior, whose use of classical fable had been condemned as insincere by Johnson; while, more important still, that poet's most subtle quality had been entirely missed. Now Cowper however defends Prior's references to classical deities as a recognized convention of his day, pointing out that Tibullus, who had made great play with those old gods, no more believed in them than did modern readers, and yet was regarded as 'the prince of all poetical inamoratos'.[2] In addition, with exquisite taste Cowper also reveals Prior's distinguishing poetic quality, namely, the easy charm with which he makes use of 'the familiar style, of all styles the most difficult to succeed in'.[3] As Cowper added, 'to make verse speak the language of prose without being prosaic . . . is one of the most arduous tasks a poet can undertake'.

And similar exercises of fine taste are further shown in his notice of the outstanding merit of Gray as a letter-writer, as well as his instant recognition in 1787 of the possibilities of Burns as a poet. Puzzled by the Scots dialect and doubtful of some of the poet's themes, Cowper rashly wished him to be

[1] *Letters*, Sept. 18, 1781.   [2] *ibid.* Jan. 5, 1782.   [3] *ibid.* Jan. 17, 1782.

content with writing pure English. Yet he unerringly discerns the presence of genuine poetic qualities, and pronounces the work to be 'a very extraordinary production'. 'His candle is bright', he states,[1] 'but shut up in a dark lantern.' Altogether then Cowper's critical contribution is by no means negligible, but is full of significant pronouncements. Free in his judgments from all hampering systems and rules, he forms his estimates with a sensitive taste which responds to literary effects of various kinds, and is fearlessly and happily expressed in epistolary form. If in poetry he represents a link between 18th- and 19th-Century achievements, the same is also true of his critical work.

Meanwhile an approach to this critical business was being made from a somewhat different angle by philosophers, who came to the support of men of letters in their endeavours to establish criticism on a sound intellectual basis, their concern being mainly with general principles relating to 'taste' and the like, and with them a fresh critical cross-current was set in motion. Early in the century had appeared, for instance, the contribution of the first Earl of Shaftesbury (1671–1713) in his *Characteristics* (1711), a work consisting of remarks on 'Men, Manners, Opinions and Times', and embodying in random and discursive fashion his views on criticism, 'the coolest of all studies', as he terms it. The views thus expressed are unsystematic and at times inconsistent; they are submitted with the irritating, affected air of a superior person endeavouring to avoid pedantry; but they have the interest of throwing light on current tendencies and thought. To begin with, he would seem to advocate some system of rules. He ridicules, for instance, the attitude of those who held that 'we Englishmen are not to be tied up to such rigid rules as those of the ancient Grecians or modern French critics';[2] and Dryden, he added, had been incorrigible in defying critical authorities. He therefore recalls the teaching of ancient critics ranging from Isocrates to Pliny; and regrets that the best guidance in English had hitherto been provided by burlesques such as the *Rehearsal*. In similar vein he notes the English dislike of *limae labor*. 'An English author', he states,[3] 'would be all genius'; and to this cause he attributes the neglect of rules which had marred current literature.

At the same time all beauty he regarded as an expression of

---

[1] *Letters*, July 24, 1787.
[2] *Miscellaneous Reflections*, v. ch. 2.   [3] *ibid*. v. ch. 1.

the divine life of the world, and the animating principle of literature; and he shares in the growing tendency to attempt an appreciation of literature by means of 'taste'.[1] Such 'taste', however, was to be based, not on caprice or sensational appeals, but on a sound acquaintance with the best art, and a rejection of all extravagances and vulgarities.[2] Moreover, he is conscious of emotional values in literature. 'There is a power', he states,[3] 'in numbers, harmony, proportion and beauty of every kind, which naturally captivates the heart and raises imagination to a conceit of something majestic and divine.' And 'enthusiasm' he regards as the 'most natural' of passions, one from which not even Lucretius had been free. But control, he added, was necessary, lest it became licence and superstition, and good humour was the best security against its excessive use;[4] while the 'Gothic' manner above all excited his derision. Apart from this, it is worth noting, he points to the limits of time over which an action represented in painting may extend; and he is also alive to the influence of social and political conditions on literature.[5] Looking back on the achievements of the Elizabethans, he described their performances as youthful and raw products, which nevertheless provided later generations with the 'richest ore', in that they re-asserted the ancient liberty of poets in discarding 'the horrid discord of jingling rhyme'. And this he attributed to the political liberties they enjoyed, as contrasted with conditions in Imperial Rome when the loss of liberty led to the decay of oratory and letters.

Nor are his occasional remarks on current literature without their interest. Thus he ridicules, for example, the invocation of the ancient Muses by modern poets as artificial and absurd;[6] and enlarges more than once on that 'monstrous ornament, rhyme'. He laments that modern poets, with their 'metred prose' (i.e. blank verse) should not have attained more grace and harmony;[7] though he notes that there had been a partial reform in poetic expression, inasmuch as 'the gouty joints and darning-work of the whereby's and thereof's', so useful in pulpit and forensic oratory, had latterly been dispensed with. Elsewhere he regrets the craze of his generation for books of travel, with their accounts of 'monstrous men and manners', the counterpart of books of chivalry that had appealed to earlier

---

[1] *Misc. Refl.* iii. chs. 1 and 2.   [2] *Advice to an Author*, iii. sect. 3.
[3] *Misc. Refl.* ii. ch. 1.   [4] *Letter concerning Enthusiasm*, sect. 3.
[5] *Advice to an Author*, ii. sect. 1.
[6] *Letter concerning Enthusiasm*, sect. 1.   [7] *Misc. Refl.* v. ch. 1.

22

ages.[1] Or again, the taste for informal and irregular writings—essays, discourses and 'other small craft'—he denounces, as a taste generated by our unstable climate, with its sudden changes and surprises.[2] From all this it will be seen that his views on criticism are of a mixed and fluid kind. With a restless and open mind he discusses many of the current theories; and in that sense he may be said to reflect in his own peculiar way many of the critical tendencies of his time.

Of a more direct and substantial kind are the critical views put forward by the philosopher David Hume (1711–76), who in *His Own Life* (1777) described 'a passion for literature' as 'the ruling passion' of his life, and whose interest in that field was shown, not only by various essays and a *History of England* (1754–61), but also by the revision of his earlier philosophical opinions mainly with a view to improving their literary form. In his *Essays Literary, Moral and Political* (1741) he frankly faces some of the unsolved difficulties bound up with current critical standards, and attempts a solution based on the understanding, holding it a reproach that the foundations of criticism should not hitherto have been stabilized. With the 'easy philosophy' representing only the common sense of mankind expressed in graceful terms he is dissatisfied. 'The fame of Cicero flourishes at present,' he states,[3] 'but that of Aristotle is utterly decayed; . . . and Addison perhaps will be read with pleasure when Locke shall be entirely forgotten.' His endeavour is therefore to suggest doctrine of a more profound and accurate kind; and while his main effort is devoted to establishing a standard of 'taste' for the first time on a firm and rational basis, he has also some pertinent remarks to make on 'tragedy', oratory and the art of writing in general.

Concerning 'taste', in the first place, he concedes that it is a matter of great delicacy; and he alludes to Fontenelle's analogy drawn from the mechanism of a clock,[4] illustrating how ordinary devices suffice to indicate the hours, yet only the most elaborate can mark the smallest differences of time. Moreover he describes it as a matter involving much perplexity, seeing the various standards of art that had prevailed, not only amongst individuals, but in different ages and among different races as well. Besides, there remained the difficulty of agreeing on terms. Men might agree in commending grace and simplicity in art and in condemning fustian and all false brilliance; yet on

---

[1] *Advice to an Author*, iii. sect. 3. [2] *Misc. Refl*. iii. ch. 3.
[3] *Essays*, xxxix. sect. i. [4] *ibid*. 1.

what was meant by such terms there was no general agreement. It was therefore essential, he maintains, to arrive at a reasoned conception of what constituted 'good taste', a conception that would be free from individual, racial and other prepossessions.

According to common sense, he points out, such a standard of 'taste' was frankly impossible, owing to the part played by sentiment or feeling in forming judgment. All feelings excited by an object of art were in a sense justifiable, as being the result of real correspondence between the object and the mind of the observer. But then true judgment should be based, not on mere subjective feelings, but on qualities inherent in the object itself; and here lay the difficulty. For 'beauty', Hume maintains,[1] 'is no quality in things themselves; it exists merely in the mind which contemplates them; and each mind perceives a different beauty'. So that to seek the real inherent beauty of art was apparently a fruitless task; according to this reasoning there could be no disputing concerning tastes. Yet common sense, Hume argues, does not really sustain the principle of the natural equality of tastes, for it was obviously alive to the vast difference between Ogilby and Milton; and amidst all the confusion it realizes that there do exist certain general principles and tests for forming judgment. It recognizes in fact that there are rules of composition based on experience, and consisting of general observations on what had been found pleasing in all ages and countries. These rules of art approved of by Hume were, however, of no rigid kind. If certain poets, such as Ariosto, had pleased in spite of breaches of accepted rules, the pleasure, he explains, arose from conformity to new rules, since elements that 'are found to please . . . cannot be faults, let the pleasure . . . be ever so unexpected and unaccountable'. Moreover, the rules of art, thus founded on experience and an observation of human nature, could be tested and confirmed by the lasting quality of the works based on their precepts; for such works would be found to have survived all vicissitudes.

The same Homer [writes Hume][2] who pleased at Athens and Rome two thousand years ago, is still admired at Paris and at London. All the changes of climate, government, religion and language have not been able to obscure his glory. Authority or prejudice may give a temporary vogue to a bad poet or orator; but his reputation will never be durable or lasting.

Hume's ultimate tests are therefore those of 'Longinus',

[1] *Essays*, xxii. p. 136.   [2] *ibid*. xxii. p. 138.

namely, the universality and permanence of appeal. But then, he remarks, just judgments based on these principles are often hindered by various causes, by defects existing in the minds of men, and notably by a want of sensibility to the finer effects. For, as he explains, while beauty is not a quality in the objects themselves, there are yet in them elements calculated to produce the effect of beauty. Yet such disabilities might be overcome by various means. First, by refusing to form hasty judgment and by examining a piece of literature more than once and from different angles, so that the relation of the parts, the qualities of style, and such like, which had escaped a first reading, might be detected. And, besides, false beauties which pleased at first would then be found to pall and to be incompatible with reason. Moreover, comparison[1] might also be of great use, and even essential, in assigning praise or censure; while familiarity with great literature of other ages would enable a given work to be rightly placed among the productions of genius. The most vulgar ballads, he patronizingly adds, are not wholly destitute of harmony or nature; but a comparison with other and superior works would reveal their actual merit.

Apart from this he urges that criticism should be disinterested and free from all prejudices and preconceived opinions. Thus the critic of an ancient work should place himself in the circumstances of those for whom the work was originally written, and should take into account their interests, passions, and opinions.[2] Moreover, there were rational elements in every piece of art, and they too should be appreciated. For, as he explains, 'if reason be not an essential part of taste it is at least requisite to the operations of this latter faculty'. And among those rational elements he includes excellence of design and reasoning powers, as well as the adaptability of means to ends. 'Every work of art', he significantly notes,[3] 'has a certain end or purpose for which it is calculated; and it is to be deemed more or less perfect as it is more or less fitted to attain this end.' Hence for him a just taste implies a sound understanding. 'Strong sense, united to delicate feeling, improved by practice, perfected by comparison and cleared of all prejudice', these qualities alone, he declares, go to form the true critic, and 'the verdict of such . . . is the true standard of taste and beauty'. It was an arresting treatment of a difficult problem, and one which by its keen insight and generous outlook opened up a new conception of the critical process. Good taste, he demonstrates, was no

---

[1] *Essays*, xxii. p. 142.   [2] *ibid.*   [3] *ibid.* xxii. p. 143.

indeterminate faculty; it did not depend on any code handed
down by earlier theorists, nor was it the result of mere individual
impression or even of a vague common sense. It was rather a
combination of reason and feeling, making use of historical and
comparative methods, and recognizing as a sound test that of an
aim clearly conceived and consistently carried out, a test which
was to prove the touchstone of excellence with more than one
of the 19th-Century critics.

Yet another of the vexed questions upon which Hume comments was that relating to the enjoyment produced by tragedy
on the stage,[1] a problem that had exercised thinking minds
from the earliest times, and yet remained something of a
mystery. Plato's explanation had been that in man there were
emotions, such as anger, fear, pity and the like, which, though
painful in character, were not devoid of pleasure when freely
indulged, and that the pleasure arising out of the tragic spectacle was due to the existence of these 'mixed feelings' in
human nature.[2] Aristotle's implied solution was that such
pleasure was due mainly to the emotional balance or calm
resulting from the 'catharsis' or working-off of unhealthy
emotions; in part also, as in all other arts of imitation, to a
delight in the artistic skill revealed in the process of imitation.
This singular phenomenon had since caused perplexity to others
than St. Augustine; and Hume now raises the matter anew,
pointing out the strangeness of the position in that spectators
of stage-tragedy 'were pleased in proportion as they were
afflicted'.

He first recalls the suggestion of Abbé Du Bos in his *Réflexions
critiques sur la Poésie et la Peinture* (1719), that the pleasure of
tragedy arose from the fact that any sort of emotional excitement, however painful or unpleasant, was preferable to the
listless state of ennui from which tragedy aroused its spectators.
While acknowleding the partial truth of this explanation Hume
however declares it to be unsatisfying, on the ground that it
failed to take into account that the greater emotional excitement caused by a tragedy in actual life, so far from enlivening
a jaded mind, gave rise only to unmitigated distress. Rather
more was therefore to be said for Fontenelle's explanation in
his *Réflexions sur la Poétique*,[3] an explanation on the lines of
Plato's 'mixed feelings'. Thus pleasure and pain, he suggests,
are not essentially different. Tickling carried too far, he argues,
becomes painful, and pain when moderated provides some

[1] *Essays*, xxi.   [2] *Philebus*, 47d–48a.   [3] § 36.

degree of pleasure. So that he infers the existence of a psychological condition in which the heart is gratefully touched by an emotional appeal, while the pain caused by disastrous circumstances is effectively lessened by some means or other. And this mixed pleasure and pain, this sort of pleasing melancholy, Fontenelle conceives to be the effect of tragedy. As for the means by which the pain caused by a tragic spectacle is weakened and assuaged, this he ascribes to the fact that stage representation always falls short of reality, as well as to the consciousness that after all it was but fiction, not reality, that was being represented.

With Fontenelle's main principle Hume is in general agreement, but suggests that the assuaging factor is something other than the fictitious character of the material with which tragedy deals. He recalls, for example, that 'mixed feelings' of the tragic kind were evoked by Cicero in his moving account of the butchery of the Sicilians by Verres; and here the theme was obviously of no fictitious nature. Indignation and pity were primarily aroused by Cicero's narrative; but these and other painful emotions, he contended, 'received a new direction' from other and secondary influences. The minds of the hearers, so Hume explains, being deeply moved by the tragic story, were thereby rendered more susceptible to the influence of art; and Cicero's eloquence in its turn swept all before it, casting a veil of beauty over ugly facts and transforming distress into something like delight. Such a transformation, he allows, was not possible if the theme outraged common decency or consisted of 'the mere suffering of plaintive virtue'. But, for the rest, he maintains, the pleasure claimed for tragedy is not as paradoxical as it would seem. While agreeing with Aristotle that 'an imitation is always of itself agreeable', he holds that the peculiar pleasure of tragedy arises from the presence of 'mixed feelings', with the splendours of art transmuting distress into a tempered delight, just as in the elegy happiness is distilled from grief. It was a notable psychological inquiry making use of Platonic and Aristotelian doctrines; and if he did not bring to light the whole of the mystery, it is because art is ever reluctant to yield up all her secrets.

There yet remain his pronouncements on several other matters, including the development of art, and advice on oratory and prose writing. Concerning the development of art, in the first place, he has some remarks to make which bear on the use of the historical method in criticism. He is apparently convinced that the arts can only originate and flourish under a free government; and he definitely says so in one place,[1] thereby implying that social and political conditions were not unrelated to artistic achievement. 'Longinus', he recalls, held the same doctrine on the ground that the loss of liberty in Greece and Rome led to the decay of the arts; though on the other hand, he cannot refrain from noting the great achievements in later Florence and Rome while 'groaning under the tyranny' of the Medicis and others, as well as the more recent perfection attained under the absolute government of France.[2] At the same time he holds that critical concern with historical conditions might be abused. For a proper appreciation of an ancient work he requires that the circumstances under which the work was written should be taken into account.[3] But to employ the historical method to explain the causes of the rise and progress of literature, this he discountenances, as giving rise to much subtle ingenuity which had no foundation in fact. 'To inquire why Homer for instance existed in such a place and in such a time', he states,[4] 'could only lead to false subtleties and refinements.' Into such achievements, he added, chance and the inspiration of genius as incalculable factors entered; and his remarks here form an early commentary on what later became known as 'scientific' criticism, ushered in by Taine.

Then, too, like Goldsmith, he betrays an interest in the oratory of his day, at a time when men of letters were beginning to play an important part in political life. Compared with ancient oratory, the oratory of modern times, he maintained,[5] was vastly inferior; and England, more especially, had little to boast of, in spite of its popular government. Antiquity, he recalled, had produced in Demosthenes and Cicero two of the greatest orators of all time, conspicuous for their sublime and impassioned utterance which appealed irresistibly to the minds and emotions of men. Their ideals and standards, however, had since been abandoned as too ardent, and therefore lacking in appeal to the superior good sense of later days. In oratory of the law-courts, he conceded, it might be desirable to rest content with a colourless oratory, consisting of arguments drawn from laws and precedents, and eschewing all rhetorical and emotional effects. But in Parliament and other popular assemblies, he held, there was ample scope for a nobler eloquence, in which, as with Demosthenes, sublime and stirring effects would

---

[1] *Essays*, xiii.   [2] *ibid.* xi.   [3] See p. 274 *supra*.
[4] *Essays*, xiii.   [5] *ibid.* xii.

be obtained by expression that fired the imagination, by harmony and rhythm adapted to the sense, and by a stream of rational argument that brought conviction in its train. As things were, modern oratory, he pointed out, was of the Atticist kind, that of Lysias and Calvus of old, a style elegant and restrained, appealing solely to the reason, but never rising above the plane of ordinary discourse. It was a style, moreover, that had been eclipsed in antiquity by the more spacious and spirited Attic manner of Demosthenes and Cicero; and it was their grand style that Hume was here advocating—not altogether without success, if we may judge from Burke's large and majestic utterance in his great political speeches.

On prose style also he has something to say; and accepting Addison's definition of fine writing as 'consisting of sentiments which are natural without being obvious', he is careful to add that mere simple and natural expression is not enough. 'The chit-chat of the tea-table copied faithfully', he states,[1] 'would make but an insipid comedy'; and some modification of ordinary conversation, some heightening of expression were needed to give artistic pleasure. On the other hand the process of refinement could easily be carried too far; an immoderate use of wit, conceits, epigrams and the like would be equally fatal. And here, as elsewhere, he maintains, 'beauty lies in a medium', in a happy balance between simplicity and refinement. The greatest need, however was to guard against excess of ornamental devices, for this he held was the chief defect of contemporary prose. And alluding once more to ancient standards, he suggests that while modern oratory had degenerated from pure Attic to the bloodless Atticist manner, contemporary prose had acquired, not Attic standards, but those of the ornate Asiatic school. For the rest, he could supply no rules for attaining the necessary balance; though he notes that emotional passages called for a greater simplicity of expression than passages of reflexion or observation, and that the works most often read and loved the most were those which had the virtue of simplicity and of great simple truths suitably expressed. His ideals in this matter are therefore clear, and are indeed suggested by the polished clearness of his style in these *Essays*. 'It is with books as with women,' he adds, 'where a certain plainness of manner and of dress is more engaging than that glare of paint and airs and apparel which may dazzle the eye but reaches not the affections.'

[1] *Essays*, xix.

Such then is Hume's contribution to critical theory; and it is on the theoretical side that he claims attention. For in his occasional judgments on literature in the concrete he is singularly inept. He fails for instance to appreciate the old-world ballads; he derides Bunyan's simple but effective style compared with that of Addison; and he also maintains that whereas one reading of Cowley sufficed, Parnell's verse remained fresh after many readings. Elsewhere he commended Swift as the first writer of 'polite prose'; Sprat and Temple he decried as inelegant and lacking in art; while to the French he accorded the primacy in dramatic affairs, holding that 'they excelled even the Greeks, who far excelled the English'. On the other hand his theorizing added something of very great value to the critical output. Familiar with French critics, with many of the ancients, including 'Longinus' as well, he attempted to show that 'taste' could be something more than mere impression, or the result unaided of a vague good sense. With neo-classical doctrine he has nothing to do; but to his task he brought an acute and vigorous intellect, which revealed that true aesthetic judgment involved an exercise of both feeling and reason, and that specific tests were also available, in universality and permanence of appeal, or in an aim clearly perceived and successfully carried out. Inaccuracies of fact there were, as in his historical work; but his analysis was the most complete and illuminating up to date, with its indications of the uses of historical and comparative methods. In more than one respect his remarks on 'taste' cleared the way for those who followed; and they had the additional merit of being submitted with unphilosophical clarity.

Animated by the same desire to arrive at firm ideas on matters of 'taste', Edmund Burke (1729–97) next calls for notice; and in his youthful philosophical work, *The Origin of our Ideas of the Sublime and Beautiful* (1756), will be found his views on aesthetic matters. At the time increasing interest was being taken in such inquiries both at home and abroad. Apart from Addison's superficial discussion on 'The Pleasures of the Imagination' and Hume's more searching treatment in his *Essays*, there had latterly appeared in Germany, France and England a number of works treating of aesthetic problems, the nature of beauty, the relation between the arts, and kindred themes; and Burke's work was obviously influenced by this movement. His particular object was to discriminate between two critical terms then current but loosely used; and his recognition of the 'sublime' as something apart from the 'beautiful' pointed not only to the persisting influence of 'Longinus', but also to an increasing nicety in aesthetic appreciation and to the influence of Hume in particular. The plan he adopts is first to clear the ground by some discussion of what was meant by 'taste', after which the terms 'sublime' and 'beautiful' are submitted to detailed examination, though not least important are certain afterthoughts arising out of the discussion and relating to tragedy and the sister art of painting. Despite some crudities the work gives evidence of keen thought, is stimulating and suggestive; and although overshadowed by the greater political contributions of the author's maturer years it still has qualities that merit attention.

Of interest, in the first place, is his attempt to give definite meaning to the term 'taste'. He contends, for instance, that for forming critical judgment, no less than for artistic creation, some knowledge was required of that human nature to which all art made its appeal.[1] He realizes that many poets had succeeded without this conscious knowledge, and that critics had hitherto derived their rules from poems, pictures and the like. But these methods, both creative and critical, he maintained, rested on no sure foundation. 'Art', he asserted, 'could never give rules that make an art'; and such poets and critics had been merely 'imitators of one another'. It was therefore in the light of human nature that critics, he held, should approach literature; and 'taste' he accordingly defined as 'that faculty of the mind which, being affected with, and forming judgment of, works of imagination', enabled a correct approach to be made.[2] Moreover, the faculty of 'taste' he further described as no mere instinct, for into its workings reasoned judgment entered, and along with reason the imagination. Imagination, however, he limited to 'the creative power of representing or combining images received by the senses', though incapable of creating anything new; and here Locke's influence is perceptible. Such then was Burke's conception of this critical faculty which was to judge literature, not by applying rules but by considering its appeal to human nature, its emotions and passions; and the discussion, in spite of its psychological limitations, marked an advance in speculative power.

The main interest of the work, however, lies in what Burke has to say on the nature of the 'sublime'; for he brings out explicitly a point of considerable value which had been merely implied in Lowth's treatment, namely, a further aspect of that

[1] I. sect. xix.   [2] *Introduction.*

overwhelming force that 'strikes and overpowers the mind', and
was generally known as 'sublimity'. By Lowth such 'sublime'
effects had been mainly attributed to grandeur of conception
and simplicity of utterance. But by Burke attention was now
called to the effects of conceptions that were awe-inspiring, or
as he puts it, 'what was in any way terrible'. It was thus, he
maintained, that the strongest emotions of which the mind was
capable of feeling were produced;[1] and in enlarging on this
theme he submits the suggestive idea that in order to make
things awe-inspiring or terrible, obscurity seemed in general to
be necessary.[2] For illustrations he refers to Milton's 'judicious
obscurity' in his portrait of Death,[3] 'vague, confused and sublime to the last degree'; to the sublimity of that poet's description of Satan,[4] where 'the mind is hurried out of itself by a
crowd of great and confused images'; to the 'amazing' passage
in *Job*,[5] where the sublimity is due to 'the uncertainty of the
thing described'; or again, to the vague and awe-inspiring
descriptions of Divine power and majesty in the *Psalms* and the
prophetical writings. Moreover, other sources of the sublime he
describes as darkness, vastness, silence and the like; while the
conceptions of eternity and the infinite of which we have but
the vaguest notions, these, he asserts, are 'among the most
affecting we have'. In all such instances, he rightly remarks,
it is the vague and obscure presentation that produces the
sublime effect. But he is less convincing when he explains the
emotion excited to be that of a mixed feeling, a 'delightful
horror', intimately connected with pain and terror; whereas a
more probable explanation would be that by means of the
confused and imperfect representation a free rein is given to
the reader's imagination, with emotional results beyond the
power of clear and precise description. Elsewhere Burke himself
notes that 'the images raised by poets are always of an obscure
kind',[6] thus hinting at the oblique and suggestive methods of
poetry; while 'a clear idea', he maintained, 'is but a little idea'.
The device of springing the imagination by leaving something
to the reader had been commended by Theophrastus and others
in antiquity.[7] And in regarding a judicious vagueness as contributing to sublime effects Burke was on firm ground though
his explanation is not wholly acceptable.

Concerning the nature of 'beauty' he is less instructive; thus

[1] I. vii. [2] II. iii. [3] *P.L.* ii. 616 ff.
[4] *ibid.* i. 588 ff. [5] ch. iv. 13 ff. [6] II. iv.
[7] See Atkins, *Lit. Crit. in Antiquity*, i. 158; ii. 206.

'beauty', he asserts,[1] consists neither in proportion of parts (as Hogarth and others had held), nor yet in fitness and utility, seeing that many things, such as flowers, are beautiful which have yet no real utility, and that their effect is previous to any knowledge of their usefulness. In other words, 'beauty', he suggests, is no creation of our reason, it answers to no mathematical tests, but is rather a quality incapable of full explanation, that acts mechanically and mysteriously on the senses. When however he attempts a comparison between the 'sublime' and the 'beautiful' he is less convincing; for here, in keeping with current ideas, he associates aesthetic effects with physical phenomena. Thus 'sublime' objects, he declares,[2] are of vast proportion, rugged and formless, dark and gloomy; whereas 'beautiful' objects are of small dimension, smooth and polished in form, light and delicate in texture. It was a pronouncement that added little to aesthetic theory. Nor is his discussion elsewhere devoid sometimes of perverse ingenuities, as when, for instance, he distinguishes between 'delight' and 'pleasure', representing 'delight' as the sensation resulting from the removal of pain;[3] or again, when he argues for the agreeableness of even painful emotions.

It is in this connexion, however, that he expresses certain views on tragedy, and more particularly, on the old problem of the pleasure arising from the sight of painful events enacted on the stage.[4] With Aristotle's theory of 'catharsis' he agrees, conceding that all natural exercise of the emotions has a purgative effect, clearing away 'dangerous and troublesome encumbrances'. But for the pleasure afforded by tragedy he has an explanation of his own to offer. Whereas Aristotle had attributed that pleasure to the artistic representation of tragic detail, Burke (following Hume) now accounts for it by insisting on the existence of 'mixed feelings', and by asserting that all emotions, even painful emotions like the terror excited by tragedy, are in themselves delightful. Moreover he claims, in spite of difficulties raised by Fontenelle and Hume, that the more realistic the tragic spectacle, the more it fascinates and attracts. And this he suggests was proved by the fact that the grim announcement that a great criminal was about to be executed in a neighbouring square would immediately empty any theatre in which even the most sublime of tragedies was being performed.

Such then is this essay of Burke which followed new lines

[1] III. ii. ff.   [2] III. xxvii.   [3] I. iv.   [4] I. xv.

of critical inquiry; and it is in its suggestiveness, rather than in its positive teaching, that the merits of the work consist. And this is nowhere more clearly seen than when incidentally he discriminates between poetry and painting. 'Poetry', he explains,[1] 'does not succeed in exact description as well as painting does; its business is . . . to display rather the effect of things . . . than to present a clear idea of the things themselves.' And its workings he illustrates by the emotions excited by Homer's suggestion of Helen's beauty, when Priam and the Trojan elders exclaimed 'she moves a goddess and she looks a queen'.[2] Here, Burke points out, no details of her beauty are supplied. Nevertheless, he adds, we are more moved by the effects suggested than by a detailed description such as Spenser had given in his treatment of Belphoebe. This, he explains, was accounted for by the nature of the poet's medium, that is, words, which with their properties of sound and association could express all emotions and convey not only ideas but also their effect on the human mind. Here Burke was replying to Du Bos who, in his *Réflexions critiques sur la Poésie et la Peinture* (1719), had claimed that painting was the more effective in stirring the emotions because of its greater clearness in representing ideas. Dennis, for one, as already stated, had noted that 'neither painting nor sculpture can show local motion'.[3] But Burke's statement had an added importance in that it apparently suggested ideas to Reynolds and Lessing, the latter of whom not only undertook a translation of the essay, but also developed in his *Laokoon* Burke's illuminating pronouncement on the relation of the sister arts.

The last, and by no means the least influential, of these philosophical critics was Henry Home, Lord Kames, whose treatment of Shakespeare in his *Elements of Criticism* (1762) has already been noted. An appreciation of Shakespeare, however, was not the primary object of that work. It had a larger scope, aiming at establishing some of the main principles of literary taste in general; and Kames's further contribution to critical theory also calls for attention. Some measure of his quality has already been suggested; but to the freshness of outlook, the keen insight and sound judgment displayed in his remarks on Shakespeare, must now be added a wide acquaintance with literature, both native and foreign. English and French poets and dramatists he knew well, and what was more, he gave evidence of a detailed knowledge, not only of modern, but also

<hr/>
[1] v. v.   [2] v. iv.   [3] *Remarks on Pope's Homer* (1714), p. 56.

of ancient, critics, including Aristotle, 'Longinus', Quintilian,
Demetrius, Plutarch and others, and was thus unusually
well equipped for his particular task. The plan he adopted,
it is true, was not conspicuous for its clarity, while his treatment must be described as somewhat ponderous, revealing
obvious traces of the severity of a legal training. But his grasp
of critical principles is for the most part sure and manifest; and
it enabled him to dispel some of the vagueness of critical
terminology, and to discuss in convincing fashion many of the
current literary problems.

At the outset he states his dominant aim. It was to reveal
fundamental principles of the Fine Arts as drawn from human
nature—the true basis of criticism—and thus to improve contemporary taste. To this venture he had been drawn, he
explains, by his recognition of the fact that whereas reason in
recent times had triumphed over authority in intellectual matters,
yet criticism still remained a slave to earlier authoritative precepts. Thus Bossu, he added,[1] had supplied rules based on
ancient authority and practice, but had failed to consider those
rules in their relation to the mind of man. He could not have
thought, argued Kames, that ancient poets were entitled to
give laws to future ages; or again, since they themselves had
followed no rules why should they be imitated? On the other
hand, if those rules were after all in accordance with human
nature and thus embodied rational principles, why should not
those principles be made clear to modern readers? Hence Kames
proposes to arrive at his governing principles in the light of the
natural man, at the same time recognizing that some principles
there were that would elude detection. And in such case, he
asserted, 'time . . . was perhaps the only infallible touchstone of
taste'.[2]

His main plan was thus designed, first, to inculcate greater
definiteness in the use of critical terms and judgments, and,
secondly, to discuss certain aspects of literature in general. And,
in the first place, he attempts to clear up the critical terminology by means of a dispassionate psychological analysis, thus
enabling men to understand those excellences which otherwise
were blindly valued, and to give reasons for their impressions.
He first distinguishes, somewhat unnecessarily, between those
emotions and passions to which all literature made its appeal,
describing the former as 'feelings without desire for action', the
latter as 'emotions that led to a desire for action'. And then in

[1] *Intro.* p. xiv.   [2] *ibid.* p. xv.

view of those emotional effects he attempts to reveal the psychological principles underlying the various literary qualities, such
as beauty, sublimity, humour and the rest. At the same time he
remarks incidentally on the limitations of painting as compared
with poetry in producing those effects. 'Our emotions', he
states,[1] 'cannot be raised by painting to such a height as by
words', for 'a picture is confined to a single instant of time and
cannot take in a succession of incidents'. And here he was
confirming a principle previously noted by Dennis, Burke and
others.

Concerning 'beauty', in the first place, he has some remarks
to make, noting by the way that an object devoid of intrinsic
beauty might yet appear beautiful by reason of its utility.[2] An
old and ugly Gothic tower, for instance, might appeal in virtue
of its usefulness in matters of defence. And here he conceives
of beauty as a sort of by-product, holding with Cicero that
'Nature has contrived that things which have the greatest
utility have also the greatest dignity and beauty'.[3] In general,
however, intrinsic formal beauty, he holds, arises from the
qualities of regularity, uniformity, order and simplicity[4]—the
orthodox doctrine of the period—for, as he states, these are
qualities that respond to something in human nature, all contributing to clearness of understanding. At the same time he
adds that uniformity in excess might detract from beauty, that
true beauty consists of uniformity amidst variety, and that
there is also a place for novelty. Nevertheless, he continues,
beauty is not, strictly speaking, an inherent property of any
object. It is said to depend as much on the percipient as on the
object perceived. And Kames recalls with approval the saying
of the poet that 'beauty is not in the person beloved but in the
lover's eye'.[5]

On 'sublimity', too, he has some notable remarks, describing
the 'true sublime', to begin with, as 'the most delightful of
emotions, by which the reader is transported and raised to a
higher plane'. In the first place, 'Longinus', he states, had
pointed to the effect of greatness in giving rise to this emotion;[6]
and to that end, he added, a grandeur less regular than that
required for beauty was needed, as for instance that visible in
a Gothic cathedral. On the other hand he fails to convey 'Longinus's' real meaning when he states that the physical elevation
of an object—a tree on the edge of a precipice—affects us no

---

[1] p. 37.   [2] p. 84.   [3] *de. Orat.* iii. 178.   [4] p. 84.
[5] p. 88: cf. Hume, p. 327 *supra.*   [6] p. 89.

less than its magnitude; or again, when he demurs to 'Longinus's'
description of Sappho's famous ode as sublime, on the ground
that 'it depresses the mind instead of raising it'.[1] Apart from
this, however, he succeeds in recalling 'Longinus's' main precepts regarding the 'sublime'. Thus the effects of 'sublimity',
he states, were obtained by a judicious selection of significant
details, as in Homer's description of the storm;[2] or else by the
use of figures of speech, as in the reiterated expressions working
up to a climax in the Shakespearean passage of 'the cloud-capt
towers and gorgeous palaces'. Or again, it might be by means
of extreme simplicity, as in the oft-quoted passage in *Genesis*
describing the overwhelming effect of light breaking in on
primeval chaos.[3] There, Kames explains, 'the fewest words are
used to convey the infinite power of God'; though, he adds, the
sublime effect is but momentary, since the mind sinks at once
into humility and veneration. And, referring to the different
estimates of this passage formed by Boileau and Bishop Huet,[4]
he maintains that both were in a sense justified. One further
principle of his own he adds, and that is the injunction to avoid
as much as possible abstract and general terms;[5] and here he is at
variance with Johnson, Reynolds and others on a vital matter.
'Such terms,' he explains, 'similar to mathematical signs, are
contrived to express our thoughts in a concise manner; but
images, which are the life of poetry, cannot be raised in any
perfection but by introducing particular objects.' And, finally,
he utters the usual warning that a straining of the 'sublime'
could only result in 'bathos', when attempts are made to give
unwonted dignity to themes trite and ordinary.

Then, too, worthy of note are his attempts to assign definite
meanings to 'humour' and 'wit'. He agrees, to begin with, with
Shaftesbury in theory, and Addison in practice, that ridicule
was a touchstone of truth as applied to fashions, customs or
ideas; but of what ridicule or laughter really was he could find
no sound explanation, even in the attempts of Aristotle, Cicero
and Quintilian to deal with that subject. With undue compla-
cency he imagines that he himself had solved all difficulties in
distinguishing between the 'ludicrous' and the 'ridiculous', the
former producing laughter only, the latter, laughter coupled
with scorn. Yet what he has further to say is of considerable
interest, especially as his arguments are admirably illustrated,
here as elsewhere, by passages drawn from Shakespeare and a
host of other writers.

[1] p. 95 n.   [2] p. 99.   [3] p. 104.   [4] see p. 26 *supra*.   [5] p. 102.

With regard to 'humour', in the first place, he cannot accept the traditional idea that it consisted of 'a singular manner of doing or saying anything, peculiar . . . to one man only'.[1] This he regarded as inadequate, since a majestic air or a flood of eloquence would then be 'humour'. The truth was, he asserted, that humour in writing was very different from humour in character; and, among writers, he shrewdly refuses to recognize humour in one who wrote with the obvious and professed purpose of making his readers laugh. 'True humour', he maintained, 'belongs to an author who affects to be grave and serious, but paints his objects in such colours as to provide mirth and laughter'; and in Addison he finds humour of a most delicate and refined kind. In like fashion he disentangles the many meanings associated with the term 'wit',[2] and suggests for it something like its meaning of to-day. 'Wit' he describes as 'the most elegant of recreations, consisting of such thoughts and expressions as are ludicrous and cause surprise by their singularity and unexpectedness'. Its essence, he thus implies, is the element of surprise. The various images summoned are said to enter the mind with gaiety and to give a sudden flash which is extremely pleasant. Verbal wit, or a play upon words, he discountenances as a sort of 'bastard wit'.[3] He notes that it had proved a popular amusement among all nations in the earlier stages of their development, as indeed had been witnessed by Shakespeare and grave 17th-Century divines; but that with the growth of taste, it had gradually fallen into disrepute. Moreover, he explains that 'as language ripens, fine differences develop, and words held to be synonymous diminish daily', thus giving less scope for such play upon words. And this historical tendency to 'desynonymize' words, with the consequent growth of the power of expression, was later on noted by Coleridge.

These attempts at clearing up the critical terminology of his day are among the more significant sections of this work of Kames. But there are also other places, apart from those treating of Shakespeare, where in discussing literature in general he makes further interesting pronouncements. He repeats, for instance, a previous attack on the fundamental axiom of the neo-classical system, this time from another angle, when he ridicules 'the useless labour' of Bossu and others in their efforts to distinguish the epic by certain features, thus hunting, adds Kames, for what did not exist. With fixed 'kinds' and their distinctive qualities he will have nothing to do. 'Tragedy', he

[1] pp. 161 ff.   [2] pp. 166 ff.   [3] p. 167.

23

asserts, 'differs not from the epic in substance; in both the same
ends are present, . . . and in both the same means are employed; . . . they differ only in the manner of imitating.' And
this is followed by one of his most positive and striking pronouncements. 'Literary compositions', he states,[1] 'run into each
other precisely like colours; in their strong tints they are easily
distinguished, but are susceptible of so much variety . . . that
we can never say where one species ends and another begins.'   It
was a reasoned and final rejection of the neo-classical creed, and
an anticipation of the more complex conceptions of later days.

Apart from this there are also sundry views expressed on the
drama and epic; though what he has to say on dramatic method
—characterization, verse-form, the Unities and the like—has
already emerged to some extent in his treatment of Shakespeare.
Yet there still remain his further reflexions on the nature of
tragedy in general; and here he follows mainly the lines of
Aristotelian theory, modified however by French doctrine and
Shakespearean practice. Thus the ideal tragic hero he defines
as one who was himself the cause of his misfortunes,[2] owing, not
to an error of judgment as with Aristotle, but rather to a defect
of character as with Shakespeare. Such defect, moreover, should
be common to human nature, and therefore venial in kind, and
likely to appeal to the ordinary man. Hence it followed that
neither an innocent person nor a criminal character was a fit
subject for tragedy, since each failed to arouse the proper
tragic emotions; while victims of mere chance were also excluded as suggesting a world of sheer anarchy. As for the
emotions proper to tragedy, they were held to be the Aristotelian pity and terror, though with some slight differences.
For, according to Kames, the pity aroused was said to be on
behalf of the persons represented, whereas terror was excited in
and for the spectators themselves. Yet Kames's explanation of
the function of tragedy is not so very different from that of
Aristotle. For whereas to Aristotle it meant a working-off of
unhealthy emotions, with Kames it implied a healthy exercise
of sympathetic emotions, as a result of which those emotions
were improved and refined.

On epic poetry, too, he comments, treating more especially of
current practices. He condemns, for instance, for obvious reasons
the all too frequent use of redundant epithets,[3] as in the lines:

> When black-brow'd Night her dusky mantle spread,
> And wrapt in solemn gloom the sable sky.

[1] p. 395 n.   [2] pp. 397 ff.   [3] p. 386.

At yet greater length he censures the conventional use of epic machinery.[1] The interference of heathen gods, he points out, was originally dictated by the Greek religion; but to modern readers it gave but an air of gross unreality. Moreover, genuine emotion, he urged, could be aroused only by human action; and apart from this, even Christian machines, as had previously been argued, had merely the effect of weakening the catastrophe. Therefore he insists that such interposition of the gods should be confined to ludicrous subjects, and that it was most effective in such poems as *The Dispensary* and *The Rape of the Lock*. Nor was his attack on Voltaire's *Henriade*[2] without its significance; for therein he revealed something more of his views on epic theory. Thus he censures Voltaire's epic for adopting as its theme history as recent as that of Henry IV; for its incongruous and unconvincing mixture of historical and imaginary beings, such as the god of Sleep and demons of Discord and War; as well as for its use of rhyming verse incapable of rising to the height of a great argument. It was an attack that went home; and Voltaire fiercely replied in the *Gazette littéraire de l'Europe* (1764).

Turning now from these attempts of men of letters and philosophers to comment in their different ways on the theory and practice of literature, we find yet another and an important critical cross-current in the various efforts of art-critics to treat of the aesthetic sense and the appeal of art in general. It was a new development, characteristic at this date of England, of France and Germany as well; and if it bore but indirectly on literature itself, it led at least to a widening of the critical outlook and to a strengthening of the speculative and critical faculties. Up to the 18th Century no serious attempt had been made to discuss the general principles of art in its wider sense. Aesthetic consciousness was as yet inarticulate, though literary appreciation had by no means been wanting; and the problem of what constituted the appeal of art had not attracted earlier thinkers, more urgent matters having engaged their attention, matters relating to the nature of God, the nature of the mind, the extension of knowledge and the like. And now, as if by a concerted movement, efforts were made at home and abroad to arrive at the governing principles of art, thus inaugurating the study of aesthetics.

For these inquiries the way had doubtless been prepared by the psychological and analytical impulses fostered by Bacon,

[1] pp. 402 ff.   [2] pp. 378, 401.

Hobbes and Locke in England, by Descartes, Leibnitz and others abroad. But there were also other factors which diverted speculation at this date to a closer consideration of the arts; and among them was a newly awakened interest in classical archaeology and in the schools of Italian and Dutch painters. At the Renascence but an imperfect conception of classical literature had come down, and a still more imperfect idea of ancient formative art. Before the middle of the 17th Century, for instance, little was known of the golden age of Greek sculpture (5th Century B.C.), all the supposed examples of that art being associated with the Roman period. But with the discovery of genuine Greek antiquities at Herculaneum (1738) and Pompeii (1755), a new estimate of the monuments of ancient Greece became possible, and fresh impetus was given to their study, a work in which Englishmen shared, but which culminated in the writings of Lessing and Winckelmann. Meanwhile by the 18th Century fresh interest had also been aroused in the pictorial art; and in England more particularly men had become conscious of the slight contribution made by native genius in that field. Such pictures as were available were owed to foreigners, to the Italian school in the collection of Henry VIII, to Rubens and Vandyke in the additions made by Charles I; and while native activities had been hindered by the Civil War and by Puritan prejudices against art of all kinds, all that the Restoration had produced were the works of Lely and Kneller. With the 18th Century, however, a new and gifted school of painters had appeared in the persons of Hogarth, Gainsborough, Reynolds and Wilson; and the pictorial art became the subject of frequent discussion. Encouraged no doubt by such earlier ventures as Du Fresnoy's *De Arte Graphica*, and the *Parallels* between poetry and painting due to Junius, De Piles and Dryden, a large number of works were now devoted to aesthetic inquiries, and especially to comparisons between the sister arts.

Evidence of the vitality of this movement is supplied by the numerous treatises of varying value that appeared between Jonathan Richardson's *Two Discourses on the Art of Criticism as it relates to Painting* (1719) and Reynolds's more famous *Discourses* (1769–90). And among them were Hutcheson's *Ideas of Beauty and Virtue* (1725), Charles Lamotte's *Essay upon Poetry and Painting* (1730), James Harris's *Dialogue on Music, Painting and Poetry* (1744), Spence's *Polymetis* (1747) and *Crito, a Dialogue on Beauty* (1752), Hogarth's *Analysis of Beauty* (1753) and Beattie's *Essay on Poetry and Music as they affect the Mind*

(1762). Many, it is true, were concerned with technical and sometimes irrelevant details; but of positive interest for our present purpose were the pronouncements, here as elsewhere, on two main questions, first, the relations between poetry and painting, and, secondly, what were regarded as the essential elements of beauty in the several arts. The former had a bearing on the value to be attached to that descriptive poetry which flourished after Thomson had written, while the latter represented attempts at fixing the fluctuating standards of taste.

In the first place a consciousness of the limited scope of the plastic and pictorial arts as compared with that of poetry would seem to have been common among English men of letters at this date. As has been already stated, hints to that effect had come from Shaftesbury, Dennis, Burke and Kames; though Spence, following Du Bos, maintained that the range and power of sculpture were not inferior to those of poetry. The main general position however was confirmed by more than one of the art-critics. Jonathan Richardson, for one, recognizes differences of scope in the arts, asserting that painting spoke a universal language, was capable of revealing a whole scene at a glance, but could not speak as distinctly to the eye as poetry spoke to the ear. And similar points were made by Lamotte and Harris. Painting, it was stated, was limited to the description of a scene at a single moment; its appeal was immediate, since it displayed all the concurrent circumstances at once; but it was unable to represent the different stages of an action or to delineate character with any completeness. Poetry on the other hand was held to have a wider range, even though its effect was less immediate. Its primary object was that of representing action, and action throughout its progress; it depicted character and human passions fully and convincingly; and was therefore the most effective of the arts. Beyond thus discriminating between the functions of the arts—description being that of painting, action that of poetry—English critics did not go. It was left for Lessing to point to the significance of the facts, namely, that the difference of function was necessarily determined by the difference of medium. And in thus defining the boundaries of the arts he introduced, for the time being, a new principle into aesthetics, being actuated by the prevalence of descriptive poetry in England and Germany, which he regarded as poetry attempting to do what painting could do more effectively.

Of interest, again, are the various attempts to define that elusive quality of 'beauty' which gave vitality and charm to all the arts. Since Bacon had noted that there was 'no excellent beauty that hath not some strangeness in its proportions',[1] little or nothing had been done in England to clear up the mystery. Now, however, Berkeley, for instance, maintained the existence of some underlying principle, seeing that the beauty of long ago was still beauty; and Hutcheson held that there existed in man an innate sense of beauty antecedent to custom or education. Such explanations as were attempted were, however, largely concerned with formal and external features. Beauty was said, for instance, to result from an observance of uniformity, symmetry, variety and simplicity, with their appeal to the rational mind; or it might be qualities of smallness, smoothness and the like which also gave delight; or again, as Hogarth claimed for painting, it depended on 'the curving, flowing line', which gave play to the imagination and pleasure to the eye. Less definite but more suggestive were the remarks which witnessed to a sense of dissatisfaction with the theories propounded. Thus Hutcheson held that it was by 'an internal sense' that we perceive beauty, and that our pleasure is of a disinterested kind, due to no knowledge of 'the principles, causes, or usefulness of the object concerned'. For Berkeley, again, perfect beauty of architecture was attained when it answered the ends for which it was made; while others (like Hume and Kames) boldly stated that beauty was no quality in things themselves but lay in the eye of the beholder. The truth was that it was found easier to say what beauty was not than what it was; and Spence declared that he would 'as soon think of dissecting a rainbow as of forming grave and punctual notions of beauty'. The whole inquiry, not unnaturally, produced but little of lasting worth; for is not beauty one of the absolute and eternal values which do not admit of further analysis?

Of the greatest of these art-critics, however, more must be said; for the contribution of Sir Joshua Reynolds (1723–92), made up of certain *Idler* papers (1759) and his *Discourses* (1769–90), justly takes its place among the more substantial and illuminating of 18th-Century critical writings. Written primarily to inaugurate a new school of painting, in which the naturalism of Rubens and Vandyke was to be exchanged for the imaginative flights of Michael Angelo and Raphael, his *Discourses*, like 'Longinus's' great treatise, go beyond their ostensible aim, and become works of literary criticism in the widest sense of the term. 'There is no better way', he writes,[2]

---

[1] *Essays*, 43.   [2] *Discourse* xiii.

'of acquiring a knowledge of art than by comparing the arts'; since it was only by deducing the general principles of art from a consideration of all the arts that some idea might be gathered of 'the immutable and eternal nature of things'. And in discussing painting he has therefore in mind poetry and the sister arts throughout. Already in the *Idler* papers he foreshadows the main points of his later teaching, his attitude to the theory of the imitation of Nature, to the rules, and also to the parts played by genius and 'enthusiasm' in creative activities. But it is in his *Discourses* that his ripe wisdom most clearly appears, and that his doctrine is presented in its completeness, in masterly and attractive fashion.

And, first, there are his views on the nature of art in general. Its ultimate end he describes (here following Aristotle) as that of supplying the natural imperfections of things,[1] thus often embodying what never existed save in the imagination; whereas its immediate aim, he stresses, was to gratify the mind by an appeal to the imagination and feelings. This function, he added, was sometimes achieved by imitating Nature; but the real test was not whether the result was a true copy of Nature but whether a pleasing effect was actually attained. Then, too, he distinguishes between the arts. To poetry he ascribes 'a more extensive power' than to painting, since it affected many sides of human nature, working by gradual stages, exciting curiosity, arousing suspense, and finally surprising by an unexpected catastrophe.[2] Painting, on the other hand, was more limited in its effects, since what was done had to be done at one blow; though it had also its characteristic appeal, making use of variety, novelty and contrast to arouse and retain the attention. Moreover, he adds, 'no art can be grafted with success on another art'.[3] And here (writing in 1786) he was possibly influenced by Lessing, for his explanation is that each art has its own peculiar methods with which to accomplish its particular purposes.

Of more than passing interest, however, are his remarks on the methods of art in general; for herein lies the gist of his teaching, which, aiming primarily at diverting painting from Dutch realism to the inspired flights of the Italians, became ultimately in his hands a rousing summons to all arts (including poetry) to abandon the restricted world of fact for the free realms of the imagination. The main cause, he held, of the realistic bias that had hitherto prevailed had been submission

---

[1] *Disc.*, xiii.　　　[2] *ibid.* viii.　　　[3] *ibid.* xiii.

to false interpretations of the doctrine of Imitation, which, whether it was taken to mean an imitation of Nature or an imitation of earlier masters, had generally been applied in a narrow sense, thus hampering development. And it is against these two restrictive influences that he directs his attack.

In the first place he therefore calls for a larger and more liberal conception of what was meant by the imitation of Nature. Nature, he contended, should not be copied too closely; and in support he recalls Plato's saying in *Timaeus* (Bk. ii) that

He who takes for his model such forms as Nature produces and confines himself to an exact imitation will never attain to what is perfectly beautiful. For the works of Nature are full of disproportion and fall short of the true standard of beauty.[1]

Moreover, he points out how great artists had often attained their ends by being unnatural in the strict sense of the term. Shakespeare, for instance, had clearly recognized the need for a Nature modified, when he declared that 'in the very whirlwind of passion' one had to 'acquire a temperance' to soften the harsh tones of violent emotion.[2] And in so doing, added Reynolds, he overleapt the bounds of ordinary Nature the more effectively to achieve his purpose. But the same principle was also abundantly seen at work elsewhere; on the stage, for instance, where all was magnified beyond its natural state; or again in poetry generally where diction and style and metrical forms were all elements of expression never employed in actual life. The great end of all art, stated Reynolds, was to make an impression on the imagination and feelings; and here, too, the poet had attained his end by means none of which were representative of ordinary Nature.

But if a meticulous copying of Nature in all its particular details was not the business of art, yet Nature still remained the chief guide and inspiration. But it was Nature modified, not only by sundry devices that gave pleasure to the mind, but above all by a treatment of its general effects, by including only such details as contributed to those effects and omitting others that merely distracted the attention.[3] It was such treatment, Reynolds insisted, that resulted in the ideal beauty of art, thus 'getting above all singular forms, . . . particularities and details', and considering Nature in the abstract. And this ideal beauty, he explains, had gone to the making of 'the grand style' in painting. The Dutch school, aiming at literal truth and

---

[1] *Disc.* iii. [2] *ibid.* vii. [3] *Idler;* 79; *Disc.* iii.

a minute exactness, had attained the beauty of naturalness, a
lower order of beauty; whereas the Italian school, attending
only to 'the invariable, the great and the general, ideas which
were fixed in universal Nature', had achieved the 'grand style,
all genius and soul'. But what was true of painting was true of
all art, of poetry as well; for which, as compared with history,
was required something more than common observation and
mere understanding. For the highest art, he explains, both
'genius' and 'enthusiasm' were needed; though he confesses that
it was difficult to say the exact degree of 'enthusiasm' which
painting and poetry required. There may be, he states, too great
an indulgence, as well as too great a restraint, of the imagination; 'the one producing monsters, the other lifeless insipidity'.
He recommends, however, a freer rein in the matter of 'enthusiasm', since too much, he allows, was not the prevailing vice;
but, for the rest, he adds, 'good sense but not common sense'
must determine its limits. In thus insisting on the overwhelming
importance of general ideas in art Reynolds is reminiscent in
some measure of Aristotle's demand for a revelation of the
universal and ideal in poetry; though, like Johnson, in minimiz-
ing the effect of 'counting the streaks in the tulip' he fails to
recognize that the general might also be sought in and through
the particular.

At the same time he utters a warning against too slavish an
imitation of earlier masters; though their works, he allows,
having stood the test of ages, could provide most valuable
guidance and inspiration. Yet here, he urges, discretion was
necessary; for such models were to be studied merely to open
the mind and to shorten one's labour.

Copy not the details [he writes] but their conceptions only.
Instead of treading in their footsteps endeavour only to keep the
same road. Labour to invent on their general principles and ways
of thinking. Possess yourself with their spirit. . . . The true and
liberal ground of imitation is an open field in which you may always
propose to surpass your predecessors.[1]

And here, Reynolds, influenced it would seem by 'Longinus',
has recaptured the true meaning of that ancient classical
doctrine propounded by Isocrates, who first emphasized the
importance of example or imitation in matters of creation. The
doctrine had been sensibly and liberally amplified in antiquity
by Horace, Dionysius of Halicarnassus and Quintilian;[2] but was

---

[1] *Disc.* ii and vi.
[2] See Atkins, *Lit. Crit. in Antiquity*, ii. 348.

subsequently reduced to mere slavish and formal copying, first
by Bembo, Vida, and others, and then by the more rigid French
theorists of the neo-classical school. But Reynolds recalls its
true and vital significance as a spiritual process. He maintains,
as 'Longinus' before him had maintained, that the imitation of
earlier masters was an operation that aimed at recapturing
something of the ancient spirit, something of that creative force
which had gone to the making of earlier masterpieces; and its
effect he describes as that of illumination, guiding the mind in
some mysterious way to the lofty standards of the ideal.

While however Reynolds's efforts are thus mainly concerned
with fostering the pursuit of the ideal in art, he has also something to say about critical judgment and the formation of a
sound taste in artistic matters. In the first place, he would
discountenance mere judgment by rule.[1] The 'grand style', for
instance, could not be acquired by formula but by a kind of
felicity; and he warns against 'an unfounded distrust of the
imagination and feelings in favour of narrow rules' which took
no account of the actual aesthetic impression. With certain
fundamental rules to give mechanical skill he had no quarrel;
but they were not to fetter genius, which was subsequently free
'to play on the borders of the wildest enthusiasm'. Moreover,
many of the rules then current, he maintained, were palpably
false; and critics, obsessed with rules, could give no scope to
their imaginations. And in this connexion he derides Hogarth's
attempt to establish 'the flowing line' as the test of grace and
beauty. To suggest, he states, that the graceful form of the
swan, for instance, depended on 'the undulation of a curve' was
to take but a partial view of things, and to run counter to the
practices of 'the great Mother Nature'.

Of yet greater interest are his positive remarks concerning 'taste',[2] a term, he states, which had been 'enveloped in
mysterious and incomprehensible language', as if wholly capricious and irrational. He therefore insists, first, that reason
throughout must be our guide; it must even inform us when
reason itself as a test should give way to feeling. For the appeal
of art, he repeats, is directed above all to the imagination and
the emotions. Whatever pleases, he explains, has in it something analogous to the mind and therefore natural; and to
appreciate that appeal an intimate knowledge of human nature
was essential. Some there were, he added, who looked merely
to 'mathematical demonstration' for guidance, and were thus

[1] *Idler*, 79, 82; *Disc*. ii.   [2] *Disc*. vii and xiii.

unable to appreciate art addressed to the fancy. But this was to apply an inadequate test; and in such matters what he significantly calls 'a higher sense' or 'the greater reason' was to be followed. At the same time he notes that the sources of artistic pleasure were infinite and their principles unending; though as one reliable test he recalls the *quod semper* principle, since 'what has pleased and continues to please is likely to please again'. Apart from this he urges that the highest art will always reveal the ideal, the general truth of things; though in matters of ornament there may be some variation of taste. He notes, for instance, that in England the dispute as to whether blank verse or rhyme was to be preferred was not yet settled; or again, that in ancient oratory the Asiatic style, which to some appeared majestic and grand, to the Attic Greeks had seemed merely turgid and inflated. Moreover, not without their interest are certain *obiter dicta* which reveal his ripe wisdom and keen insight in aesthetic matters. In one place, for instance, he asserts that a rough sketch is often more effective than a finished picture, just as much of the beauty of Milton's description of Eve is due to his vague and suggestive expressions; for in such case the reader supplies the details by the workings of his own imagination.[1] And here Reynolds incidentally recalls the principle of artistic appreciation requiring an imaginative co-operation on the part of the reader, a principle enunciated in antiquity by Theophrastus and others. Or again, there is his shrewd hint regarding the proper approach to new and unfamiliar work, which, though great, may seem distasteful at first sight. Its unfamiliarity, urges Reynolds, should not lead to instant condemnation; but, quoting Hermes Harris, he advises that 'we should feign a relish till we find a relish come'.[2]

Of the vitalizing influence of Reynolds on his generation there can therefore be no doubt; and indeed it is not altogether fanciful to suggest that his influence extends also to a later generation and to the literary efflorescence that was soon to follow. Dealing primarily with a sister art he brings to light principles shared in common by both painting and poetry; and presenting a lofty notion of what art really stood for, he directs attention away from 18th-Century formalism, from narrow conceptions and restrictive practices, to the pursuit of the ideal and to the free play and inspiration of genius. For the proper appreciation of art he relies on no rules, finds common sense and the prose understanding alike inadequate; and claiming as his

[1] *Disc*. vi.   [2] *ibid*. xv.

touchstone 'the greater reason', he looks above all for universality of appeal and the effect on the imagination and the feelings.
Some blind spots he has; he fails, for instance, to do justice to
the virtues of realism and of counting the streaks in the tulip.
On the other hand, whether as a result of wide and judicious
reading, or as merely the fruit of his own experience, he revives
in timely fashion more than one of the great pronouncements of
classical antiquity, of Aristotle and 'Longinus' in particular, and
thus helped in putting an end to 18th-Century shibboleths and
to the reign of the neo-classical school. It is, in short, as a
liberating force, suggestive and compelling, that he figures at
this stage in critical history.

With this the tale of the more significant currents of 18th-
Century criticism is practically complete, though brief reference
must still be made to those lesser tributaries which, varying in
character and volume alike, swelled the main stream without
seriously disturbing its waters. A few, however, call for more
than passing notice; and of positive value, for instance, are the
works of Thomas Percy (1729–1811), later Bishop of Dromore,
and Thomas Tyrwhitt (1730–86), a distinguished Greek scholar,
Clerk to the House of Commons (1762–8), and chief detector of
Chatterton's forgeries, both of whom threw fresh light on earlier
native literature. Percy's *Reliques of Ancient English Poetry*
(1765) was the fruit of antiquarian rather than critical interests;
yet it restored to an unsympathetic generation something of
the glamour of the old ballads, with 'their heart-break and
bloodshed'. As a critic he had his defects. Unaware of the subtle
beauty of his material he adopts at times an apologetic tone, as
when he suggests, for instance, that 'the rust of antiquity had
obscured the style and expression' of the delightful *Nut-Brown
Maid*. Nor are his pioneering dissertations *On the Minstrels*, *On
the Ancient Metrical Romances*, and *On the Metre of Piers Plow-
man* free from error, as Ritson and others later pointed out.
Yet if the aim of criticism is to improve literary taste, the
work as a whole, judging from its widespread influence, was
of considerable critical value; and the judgments implicit in
the *Reliques* command for the work a place in the critical
development.

Likewise of importance was Tyrwhitt's critical edition of the
Canterbury Tales (1775–8), which restored something like the
original text by disposing of many of Urry's capricious emendations. Equally valuable was the introductory *Essay on the
Language and Versification of Chaucer*, in the course of which

he corrects some of Hickes's earlier observations on Old English verse, and presents a sketch of the main literary developments during the early medieval period. Most illuminating of all, however, is his appraisal of Chaucer's verse, the secret of which had hitherto been lost, but which he now revealed by scholarly acuteness, coupled with a wide knowledge of Old French, Provençal and Italian literatures. He points out, for instance, that Chaucer's verse was based, not on quantity, but on syllabic arrangement; that its music depended on a pronunciation different from the modern; and that final -e, as in French words, had syllabic value. Gray had previously made a similar pronouncement in connexion with 14th-Century verse; and now, in applying Gray's remarks to Chaucer's verse in particular, Tyrwhitt opened up a new phase in the appreciation of that poet's art.

Then, too, of interest, historical if not intrinsic, were James Beattie's *Essay on Laughter and Ludicrous Composition* (1764) and his *Dissertation on Fable and Romance*, works which, together with Clara Reeves's *Progress of Romance* (1785), represented a growing concern with that new phenomenon, the modern novel. As yet, the novel was regarded as a modified form of epic and romance, with certain realistic or comic features added; and Beattie's *Essay* is an attempt to justify the 'comic epopee' or 'comic romance' in the light of earlier theories. He therefore recalls theories of laughter propounded by various authorities, but rejects them all, including Aristotle's doctrine of laughter caused by 'a fault painless and not destructive', Hobbes's theory of 'a sudden glory', and Hutcheson's explanation that it arose from the contrast of 'dignity and meanness'. On the other hand he himself has not much to offer, though he suggests that it was due to a sense of incongruity, sudden and surprising; and in comic writing, he adds, the moderns surpassed the ancients. Nor are his judgments on Richardson, Fielding and Smollett of any great value; though for the 'inimitable Fielding' he expresses unbounded admiration, describing *Tom Jones* as an exquisite model, which with its perfect unity would have satisfied Aristotle himself, since every incident contributed to the plot by natural means, whereas Cervantes, he states, had to work a miracle for the cure of Don Quixote. At the same time he cannot refrain from uttering a warning against too great an indulgence in novel-reading. To him it seemed a 'dangerous recreation', filling the mind with extravagant thoughts and unfitting readers for more serious tasks—an opinion shared by many of his contemporaries.

Of greater value, despite its unalluring title, was James (Hermes) Harris's *Philological Inquiries* (1780), which provided for the first time a surprisingly accurate and exhaustive sketch of criticism from ancient days, thus definitely extending the critical vision. His survey includes not only early Greek and Hellenistic critics from Plato to Hermogenes, the Roman critics Cicero, Horace and Quintilian, but also later theorists and commentators, such as Donatus and Servius, and a fairly complete list of Italian, Dutch and French theorists, ranging from L. Valla and Robortello to Heinsius, Boileau and Bossu, with Bentley, Addison and Lowth as English representatives. And this background he supplements by accounts of Byzantine and Arabic literatures and cultures, recalling the names of Stobaeus, Planudes and others, and sketching literary developments in Western Europe from Bede to Chaucer. Of earlier English criticism he has little to say; his estimate of the native literature before Dryden was that the poetry was mostly turgid and bombastic, the prose pedantic and stiff. Nevertheless his main object was to call attention to the value of Greek critical doctrine, the universal bearing of which he illustrates by noting Shakespeare's conformity at his best with its governing principles; and in this task he is highly successful. It was a valuable service rendered at a time when England (with its Porson) was described by a foreign scholar as 'the most flourishing country in Europe in Greek literature'. And the work, which is distinguished for its wide scholarship rather than for any merits of speculation or style, has at least one striking utterance, when critics are described as 'a sort of masters of the ceremony in the court of letters through whose assistance we are introduced into some of the first and best company'.[1]

Of the remaining works which witnessed to widespread and varied critical activities without adding much to the critical advance, passing notice must here suffice. And among such works were John Mason's pamphlets, *The Principles of Harmony in Poetic Compositions* (1749) and *The Power and Harmony of Prosaic Numbers* (1749), Daniel Webb's *Beauties of Poetry* (1762), John Brown's *History of the Rise and Progress of Poetry* (1764), Shenstone's *Essays on Men and Manners* (1768), Robert Wood's *Essay on the original Genius and Writings of Homer* (1769), Vicesimus Knox's *Essays Moral and Literary* (1779), Hugh Blair's *Lectures on Rhetoric and Belles Lettres* (1783) and John Scott of Amwell's *Critical Essays* (1785). With them must

[1] Harris, *Works*, p. 398.

also be included sundry works that dealt with aesthetic questions. Thus Akenside's *Pleasures of the Imagination* (1744), an attempt to analyse the delights of poetry after the fashion of Addison, required for genuine imaginative effects the presence of the sublime, the beautiful and the wonderful, together with the workings of genius; but its treatment can only be described as frigid and uninspired. Nor can much be said for further efforts to arrive at principles of 'taste' by comparisons of poetry with the sister arts. The short but ponderous treatise of James Harris, *Concerning Art* (1744), for instance, and his dialogue *On Music, Painting and Poetry* (1744) have little that is new to offer. And this applies not only to Beattie's *Essay on Poetry and Music* (1762), and to similar essays by John Brown (1763) and Daniel Webb (1769), but also to more ambitious philosophical works *On Taste* by Alexander Gerard (1759) and A. Alison (1790), and to William Thomson's *Inquiry into the Elementary Principles of Beauty* (1798), most of which were discussions largely second-hand, wordy and often obscure.

At the same time contributions of some significance in this field were William Gilpin's three essays *On Picturesque Beauty* (1792), which were followed by Uvedale Price's *Essay on the Picturesque as compared with the Sublime and the Beautiful* (1794). Both works were inspired by the picturesque or 'romantic' qualities of external Nature, to which Gray for one had previously referred, and which now modified the conventional conception of beauty. Gilpin does little more than distinguish the beautiful from the picturesque by claiming for the former the quality of smoothness and for the latter roughness and ruggedness. Price, however, would distinguish the picturesque from both the sublime and the beautiful. He refuses to accept the ordered symmetry of the classical school as the main characteristic of the beautiful; while greatness of dimension and the infinity of the sublime, he holds, are no qualities of the picturesque. The essential features of picturesque beauty, he maintains, are surprising variety, intricacy and irregularity. The sublime, he adds, 'is austere whereas the picturesque captivates', thus 'filling up a vacancy between the sublime and the beautiful'. And the way was now prepared for a more reasoned appreciation of the irregular or 'romantic' beauties of Nature which were to be the theme of the later generation of poets.

CHAPTER X

CONCLUSION

WITH some idea of the various contributions of individual critics in mind an attempt must now be made to view the criticism of these two centuries as a whole and to get it into some sort of perspective, so as to realize the part it plays in the critical development. And in entering on that task one is reminded of Croce's timely remark that the only true history, the history which is philosophy, is that which sees the past as pressing towards a goal and consummation in the future. That progress, broadly speaking, had been made on what had gone before is for one thing abundantly clear. The main interests, for instance, were no longer confined to inculcating principles of good writing in prose by means of formal though re-vitalized Rhetorics, any more than to defending poetry against 'poet-haters', or to setting out in intelligible terms its nature and art. Besides, the theories now evolved were based on something more than fragmentary and often conflicting doctrines, indiscriminately gathered from classical, post-classical and medieval sources; while appreciations of literature in the concrete, comparatively lacking in the earlier period, formed now an outstanding feature of the critical activity. Apart from this, something of definite value had been achieved in the ultimate rejection of that systematic and coherent body of literary theory derived from France, which had seemed to promise an escape from earlier vague and confusing doctrines, but which had run counter to the innate predisposition of English minds to empiricism, and their suspicion of a closed system imposed by authority. Yet this rejection of what proved to be an ill-founded code was after all but a negative and transient performance; a clearing-away of error which in the course of discussion gave entry into wider fields where free speculation and more penetrating judgments were possible. The truth is therefore that the real progress, the positive and lasting significance of these two centuries in critical history, lies not in 'the dissolving of neo-classicism', but rather in the more enlightened conception of literary criticism that was gradually formed during that process, in its suggestive theories, its varied judicial methods and acute judgments, elements which, more effectively

356

than is sometimes supposed, prepared the way for the critical achievements of the 19th Century.

Yet the break with Renascence tradition and the acceptance of neo-classicism about the middle of the 17th Century, though but a passing phase, served nevertheless a useful purpose in giving fresh impetus and a new direction to critical inquiry. The truths of literature are often won through struggle and antagonism; and the development and decline of the movement in England are thus matters of historical interest and call for some notice. At first the advent of the new body of theory did little more than set men thinking on current problems of verse and drama, though before the close of the century the new creed was expounded in part by Rymer, Mulgrave and others. After 1674, however, counter-influences were already at work. Theories of a more liberal kind, drawn from Corneille, Saint-Evremond, and above all, from Boileau's translation of 'Longinus', were successful in casting doubts on the newly accepted creed, and in directing attention to more general and basic problems, which found expression in the works of Dryden and Temple. Then in the century that followed what would seem to have been a definite and concerted effort was made to establish criticism on sound and enlightened lines. Under the influence of 'Longinus', Dryden and writers such as La Bruyère and Bouhours, neo-classicism was forthwith challenged by Addison, Welsted and others; and this challenge was followed by persistent attacks due to various causes. A wider vision, in short, was being opened up by the newly awakened appreciation of Shakespeare and the earlier native literature, together with the speculations of philosophers, art-critics and literary men themselves; and this new phase witnessed the final rejection of the system. At no time, apart from translations and minor efforts by hack writers, had any adequate, or even serious, exposition of the creed been supplied, though lip-service throughout the century was paid to Bossu and the like. The orthodox code in fact was known but was generally defied. Certain dramatic works, it is true, were still being created on the prescribed models. Addison, for example, had produced his *Cato*, Johnson his *Irene*. But Johnson lived to describe plays in which the Unities were observed as mere 'elaborate curiosities, the product of superfluous and ostentatious art'. From him came also the most complete and convincing refutation of neo-classical doctrine; and from that series of critics ranging from Young to Reynolds came a united chorus on much the same lines.

24

Neo-classicism, however, with its essential precepts—'Imitation', the 'kinds' and the rules—was not disposed of without bringing to light some important critical truths. In the first place, mere formal 'imitation' of earlier masterpieces was strongly condemned as ill-founded and misleading. 'No man as yet ever became great by imitation' was Johnson's outspoken verdict; and the hard aesthetic fact that nothing is so unlike an original as a copy was being slowly grasped. In its place the Longinian conception of 'imitation' as a spiritual process, an imaginative stimulus derived from earlier masterpieces, was commended, notably by Dryden, Young and Reynolds. Furthermore, from Temple to Cowper the importance of originality, as opposed to 'imitation', was being constantly urged; and while Reynolds too condemned a slavish copying of earlier models, he also gave new meaning to the familiar term 'imitation of Nature', as involving, not a transcript, but a transformation, of Nature.

Similarly, the conception of fixed 'kinds' was also successfully combated; though Hurd in his early days still conceived of them as 'founded in Nature and the reason of things, and not to be multiplied at pleasure'. From the first, however, the orthodox classification was but lightly held. Davenant, for instance, conceived of an epic that should be dramatic in structure; and Dryden's defence of the heroic play was that it embodied features of the heroic poem or epic. Hobbes for his part set at naught the current tradition, and submitted a rational classification based on abstract divisions of mankind; while Lowth, having attempted to find in Hebrew poetry the neo-classical 'kinds', is forced to conclude that such classification was not of much use since 'there is scarcely a species of poem . . . which does not occasionally unite the different modes of expression'. On this point, moreover, both Kames and Johnson are explicit. To attempt to distinguish the epic from other forms was said by Kames to be lost labour. 'Literary compositions', he adds, 'run into each other precisely like colours, so that we can never say where one species ends and another begins.' And with this pronouncement Johnson is in entire agreement. To define the essence of any species of writing, he held, was practically impossible, seeing that 'every new genius produces some innovation' which subverts the established rules.

And equally determined was the opposition to the neo-classical rules. From the first, doubts had been expressed concerning their universal validity, since there were hidden graces and secret charms in poetry that no rules could teach. Moreover, the Unities of time and place when examined were found to be restrictive and unnecessary; and whereas Dryden suggested a modification of the conventional epic machinery, Kames would even discourage its use altogether in poems of a serious kind. That certain fundamental rules existed, this much is allowed by Johnson; and he endeavours to distinguish 'rules established because they were right from those which were right only because they were established'. At the same time it was contended by Hume, Burke and others that the rules of art were not to be arrived at by an analysis of earlier art; but that their only safe foundation was the laws of human nature. And this objection to what was one of the fundamental principles of neo-classicism was sustained by Kames, whose approach to critical questions was consistently of a psychological kind. Nor is it without its significance that but slight use was made of the rules in forming judgment. Dryden, for instance, even in his appreciation of Virgil, had commended him, not for his observance of this or that rule, but rather for aesthetic effects not covered by the rules.

In thus refusing to adopt neo-classicism and its rules as their basis English critics had indirectly prepared the way for what criticism was to mean to a later age; and it is therefore important to realize what of a positive kind was accomplished during this period and its ultimate significance. As we have seen, certain definite truths had emerged in disposing of the orthodox theory. But further and more substantial results followed from the attempts of 18th-Century critics to examine, and then to apply, their views on criticism as such, thus inaugurating a new aesthetic. And these efforts, both theoretical and practical, constitute the real and lasting advance made during this period. The inquiry had begun with Dryden and his suggestive remarks on critical aims and methods; for it was he, according to Johnson, who 'first taught us to determine on principle the merits of a composition'. He was followed by Pope, who was content however to recall merely what had been said on the subject by earlier authorities. But after this, throughout the century, writers of different sorts, from Addison to Cowper, discussed the critical process from various standpoints, and not without some success. Previously criticism had often been submerged by scholarship and scholarship by pedantry; it had also been more concerned with the art of composing literature than with appreciating it. But now less reliance was placed on *a priori* doctrines; critical efforts were directed primarily to literary appreciation; and the all-absorbing object became that of establishing on a sound basis the first principles of literary judgment. 'A blind admirer', wrote Dryden, 'is not a critic'; and from now on, critics strove to look with new eyes on literature and literary values.

Of considerable interest, in the first place, were the attempts now made to understand what poetry really was, not however as before for purposes of defence, but in order the better to appreciate literary merits. The conviction, to begin with, that there was more in poetry than a mere formal art was suggested by more than one critic; but the idea of something mysterious was most arrestingly voiced by Morgann when he declared that 'true poetry is magic, not Nature, an effect from causes hidden or unknown'. Moreover, it had been made clear by Dryden and Reynolds that poetry, like the rest of the arts, was not confined to a meticulous copying of things as they were, but that its aim might be a treatment of the ideal, thus supplying the deficiencies of Nature, the end to which, according to Aristotle, Nature herself was for ever striving. Most valuable of all, however, was the psychological inquiry which revealed the importance of the emotional element in poetry. Hobbes had first discussed the relation existing between the creative mind and poetry itself, thus opening up a host of new possibilities; and psychological analysis thus inaugurated came from now on into general use. Locke meanwhile had given fresh impetus to this line of inquiry in his studies of the mind of man. He had distinguished ideas due to sensory experience from those derived from reflective consciousness; and to contemporaries this distinction supplied a clue to the poetic process. Temple, for instance, had suggested that for poetic creation there were needed, first, 'an agitation of mind to invent', and then, 'a great calm to judge and correct'. This view was supported by Dennis, who held that the essential element in poetry was that 'enthusiastic' or heightened emotion which he defined as the 'fine frenzy' inspired by ideas in contemplation; and here we have an anticipation of Wordsworth's well-known conception of poetry as 'emotion recollected in tranquillity'. In the creation of poetry, it was suggested, both the sensibilities and the reason were concerned. Nor, further, should Gray's comment on what he regarded as the essence of poetry be overlooked. 'Sense', he maintained, 'is nothing in poetry, but according to the dress she wears'; and with the emphasis thus laid on the form and colour of poetry, as opposed to its meaning, many modern critics would agree; though it would perhaps be truer to say that the real essence lay in the happy blending of subject-matter and treatment.

In addition to these basic theories there were however numerous incidental remarks which in one way or another revealed a growing, if tentative, insight into the mysteries of poetry. With regard to the proper language of poetry, for instance, there was Gray's dictum that 'the language of the age is never the language of poetry', thereby inculcating the need for a heightening of poetic style and diction. By Johnson and others the use of general expressions was, less surely, required on the grounds that such terms added dignity, and that only by such means could 'general and transcendental truths' be revealed; whereas Kames, for his part, preferred to count the streaks in the tulip, and Joseph Warton insisted on the pleasing effects of common and familiar words. Elsewhere, again, Dryden hints at the importance of the choice and placing of words in poetry, pointing out how Virgil's magic immediately vanished on the slightest derangement of his word-order. And further statements were made on other aspects of poetic technique. Dryden, for instance, throws light on poetic truth in his treatment of Caliban, suggesting that a thing is true for a poet if it is true for the milieu in which a character is placed. Historical truth, or the strict observance of actual facts, on the other hand, he regards as non-essential, stating that 'chronology is a cobweb law', a mechanical rule to be ignored if necessary for the attaining of artistic effect; and elsewhere he defends the poet's use of borrowed material against the charge of plagiarism, justifying such procedure by the effective treatment of the material that resulted. Furthermore, Hurd in treating of Spenser points to the existence of a unity of design or effect in addition to the orthodox unity of action; while Gray decried the excessive use of description in poetry. Such descriptive element, he held, was an ornament, but as such, it ought never to be the main theme. And this comment, applied to the descriptive Nature poetry of the time, derived support from the newly discovered fact that whereas poetry dealt primarily with action, description was the particular province of the sister art, painting.

Passing reference might also here be made to the inadequate but noteworthy psychological attempts to solve the perennial but elusive problem of the pleasure afforded by tragedy. According to Johnson the tragic pleasure was due to an element of

fiction or illusion; but more often it was ascribed to the presence
of mixed feelings which were variously accounted for. To Hume,
for instance, the sadness of a tragic story was tempered and
transmuted into a species of pleasure by the magic of art; to
Burke all emotions, even painful emotions like the terror of
tragedy, had in them some measure of delight; and to Young
it was the sense of immunity from personal suffering that gave a
mixed pleasure to 'the movement of our melancholy passions'.
The problem was of course not solved; but such attempts point
to the vitality of psychological methods at this date. It was,
besides, to this conception of mixed feelings that the idea of an
emotion known as 'a pleasing melancholy' was due. Just as
Burke had insisted on the pleasing effects of the horrid and
terrible, so, it was maintained, 'agreeable sensations are produced not only by bright and lively objects, but sometimes by
such as are gloomy and solemn, . . . by the silent night, . . .
the melancholy grot, the dark wood and hanging precipice'[1]—a
theory that throws light on the contemporary vogue of 'grave-
yard' poems, such as Gray's *Elegy*, Young's *Night Thoughts* and
Akenside's *Pleasures of Melancholy*.

Nothing however is of greater significance than the co-
operative attempts now made to arrive at just notions of the
critical faculty and its workings. And in this connexion it should
first be noted that the break with the Renascence tradition was
not entirely complete; for 'Nature or reason', the instrument
of inquiry which had prevailed in antiquity, in medieval and
Renascence times, was still, nominally at least, the recognized
testing instrument in all fields of thought. Latterly, however,
the terms had been used (and were still used) in a somewhat
vague sense. 'Nature' had stood for the rule of law in the physical
world and in all human activities; whereas 'reason' was the
faculty which detected the workings of that universal law. And
now a more definite interpretation was sought for in connexion
with literature, one more in keeping with what was felt in the
presence of art, and with what an analysis of the judicial process
actually revealed. Tentative efforts were accordingly made,
inspired by the philosophical inquiries of Hobbes and Locke, to
define in psychological terms that critical process; and a new
and clearer light was gradually thrown on the critical faculty
and its activities.

The clue was found in the newly won conception of poetry
with its emotional element. At the time, in actual practice,

[1] Smith, *On the Sublime*, p. 34 n.

'Nature or reason' stood for the logical understanding, common sense, or the fitness of things. But now it was felt that intellectual faculties alone were inadequate tests of all that poetry had to offer, its appeal to the feelings, for instance, its impassioned utterances and aesthetic effects. And Dennis's timely suggestion that the faculties necessary for poetic creation were in the main those needed for critical appreciation came as a pointer to more fruitful doctrines. Addison was among the first to attach prime importance to what was called 'taste', a faculty of the soul capable of forming aesthetic impressions on its own by means of intuition or an innate sensibility, though such instinctive reactions were also to be guided by good sense. From other sources came also hints of the need for such emotional tests, as when, for example, statements were made regarding the appeal of poetry to the heart as well as to the head. At the same time Hume is careful to warn against mere impressions on the one hand and unaided good sense on the other. To him sound judgment resulted from the exercise of 'strong sense and delicate feelings', that is, from a balance of sensibilities and judgment. Then, too, the conviction that there was more in literature than the mere rationalist could perceive was otherwise gathering strength; and Welsted was not alone in suggesting that 'poetical reason' is not the same as 'mathematical reason'. Morgann for one claimed for the critic the exercise of 'the mysterious workings of feelings and sensibilities', in place of the logical understanding; and Reynolds, while insisting in general on the guidance of reason (even for deciding when reason was not to be the test), also emphasized the need in appreciating great art for resorting to 'a higher sense' and 'a greater reason'.

In the light of such evidence it cannot therefore be doubted that a clear and more generous idea of the critical process was slowly forming. The exercise of common sense and cold intellectualism was seen no longer to suffice; the appeal of literature was, in short, to the whole man. And literary judgment, it was increasingly felt, should be of a supra-rational kind, with sensibilities alive to aesthetic effects, and instinctive impressions subject to the dictates of good sense, as Hume had indicated. It was of course no absolute discovery of the 18th Century; for this balance of sensibilities and judgment had already been present with Dryden; it had also accounted for such things as Sidney's stirring comment on *Chevy Chase*, or for Jonson's glowing estimate of Shakespeare. But what had been instinctive and unconscious before was now rationally and

psychologically explained, at least in part; and it is not altogether fanciful to detect in Reynolds's suggestive references to
'a higher sense' and 'a greater reason' a significant groping
towards the faculty known later as the realizing imagination.

But equally important were the attempts now made to arrive
at stable ideas concerning critical standards and methods. And,
as regards standards, in the first place, with the neo-classical
rules rejected both in theory and practice, most notable is the
fact that by a surprising number of 18th-Century critics the
surest test of all, universality and permanence of appeal, is
already clearly recognized. That the test of the survival value
of all great literature suggested itself simultaneously and independently to a large body of critics is of course possible; but
a more likely hypothesis is that the pervasive influence of the
Longinian *quod semper* principle was here at work. This however was a test which required a lapse of time and therefore did
not apply to contemporary works. Efforts were accordingly
made by art-critics and others to establish 'beauty' as the test
of aesthetic value, on the ground that a consciousness of the
beautiful was felt by all men in the presence of art. But the
analyses of 'beauty' that resulted were not very enlightening.
With it were associated, for instance, the formal qualities of
regularity, uniformity and the like, qualities said to respond
to something in human nature and to contribute to clearness
of understanding. Elsewhere it was held to consist of uniformity
and symmetry blended with variety and novelty; a conception
which gave rise before the century closed to what was known as
picturesque or 'romantic' beauty, the predominant features of
which were a surprising variety, intricacy and irregularity.

Meanwhile the value of 'beauty' as a reliable test was somewhat shaken by Hume's contention that there was a subjective
element in our appreciation of the beautiful, that 'beauty' was
no quality in things themselves, but that it resided solely in the
mind of the spectator or reader. Johnson, too, pointed out the
difficulties of accepting so mysterious and elusive a concept as
a literary standard. Nevertheless, one, and that an important,
result was the outcome of it all, when Hume suggested (here
following Cicero[1]) that beauty was a sort of by-product, the
result of fitness, or, as he puts it, of 'an aim clearly conceived
and consistently carried out'. This conception was confirmed by
more than one 18th-Century writer; as when Adam Smith
declared that 'the fitness of objects for their intended ends is

[1] *De. Orat.* iii. 178.

the source of beauty, independent of custom'.[1] And it is of interest to note that this test of fitness, proposed by Hume, was in a modified form to be the touchstone of excellence for 19th-Century critics.

Of first-rate importance, too, was the light now thrown on judicial methods calculated to lead to more effective and discerning literary appreciation. And, to begin with, attention was now called to the different lines of approach to literary works open to critics. Thus Dryden, for instance, had been the first to commend the psychological method, in stating that it was necessary 'to enter into the causes and resorts of that which moves pleasure in a reader'. And this method of 'tracing the pleasure of literature to its natural sources in the mind of man', approved by Addison, Dennis, Johnson and Kames, became the common practice of other critics. Then, too, with the development of the historical sense it was increasingly recognized that all judgments of earlier literature should be made from the historical point of view, with the influence of environment and the possibility of relative standards ever in mind, so as to ensure the understanding and sympathy necessary for forming just and tolerant judgments. This method was successfully employed above all in the medieval studies of Thomas Warton and Hurd. At the same time the dangers bound up with this doctrine were already noted. Hume had pointed out that too much importance might be attached to the influence of environment to the exclusion of the part played by individual genius; and this caveat was renewed in the following century to discountenance the excessive application of what was known as 'scientific' criticism. Apart from this there was the comparative method, most effectively used by Dryden and Johnson. It involved a treatment that added to the refinement of critical perception and enabled literary nuances to be more clearly distinguished. Or again, of value was Rowe's suggestion of the biographical method, urging that some knowledge of an author would provide that insight and sympathy necessary for a sound appreciation of his work; a method that had been turned to excellent account, particularly by Johnson. And lastly, it might be noted that Dryden for greater precision had used with good effect the terminology of the sister art, painting, a device which was to become a marked feature of later criticism. All these methods in their different ways transformed the critical work of the time; and they represent a considerable advance in critical procedure.

[1] *Theory of Moral Sentiment* (1759), v. ch. I.

But this was not all that was put forward during this period for consideration in connexion with critical methods. From time to time a number of relevant if minor precepts were also submitted which gave further evidence of a widening conception of the critical activity. Thus Roscommon, for example, had incidentally revived the teaching of Aristarchus in noting that a poet is best interpreted by himself; a practice that was effectively employed by Shakespeare's editors. Wolseley, again, pleaded for aesthetic, in place of purely moral, judgments; and while Dryden pointed out that the influence of earlier writers should be taken into account, the influence of Chaucer on Spenser, for instance, Dennis shrewdly remarked that the talents for judging literature were the same as those that went to its creation. From more than one quarter besides came the advice that a piece of literature should be judged as a whole and not by petty or irrelevant details; and frequent warnings were issued against hasty judgments of new and unfamiliar works, lest, as Quintilian had pointed out, one should condemn what one did not understand. Moreover Joseph Warton decried the vagueness of 'general' criticism and required from the critic a detailed consideration of technique and the like. Johnson, again, deprecated the tendency of undue 'mining for meanings', when works were made to reveal secrets they never possessed; a frailty, it might be added, from which recent criticism is not entirely free. And finally, Gibbon noted from his reading of 'Longinus' that critical appreciation need not necessarily be submitted in objective and pedestrian fashion, but might consist of the lively and infectious praise of great literature. It was a discovery substantially made by Dryden at an earlier date when he detected in the best criticism 'a certain magnetism . . . which attracted others to their sense'; and in this magnetism Dryden himself had abundantly shared.

With this increased insight into the nature of the critical faculty and the further light that dawned on critical standards and methods came, not unnaturally, marked progress in critical judgment and in the appreciation of literature in the concrete. But, first, in view of Hurd's dictum that 'the abuse of terms was the source of bad criticism', something must here be said about the efforts made to give more precise meanings to critical terms then being loosely employed. Of these the terms 'wit' and 'humour' were among the most indeterminate and confusing. To the Elizabethans, for instance, 'wit' had stood for intelligence, ingenuity or fancy. In the 17th Century it was first distinguished from fanciful conceits or affected expression, being described as *discordia concors*, the discovery of occult resemblances in things apparently unlike; and while by Dryden it was defined as merely 'a propriety of thought and words', with Pope it was none other than the happy expression of commonplace truths. Addison, however, associated with it an element of surprise; but from Kames came perhaps the nearest approach to our modern meaning, when he described it as an amusing expression that with a sudden flash caused surprise and pleasure; though there was also shrewd wisdom in the remark of the unhappy Flecknoe that 'if I could tell you what it were it would not be what it is'. Then 'humour', too, long preserved the Jonsonian sense of a peculiarity of character; but Kames first distinguished between humour in writing and humour in character. Humorous writing he described as writing apparently serious and grave which nevertheless gave rise unexpectedly to laughter; and as an admirable exponent of this subtle quality he instances Addison.

Further examples of this clearing-up of terminology may also be traced in connexion with such terms as 'Gothic', 'sublime', 'imagination' and the like. Thus with the clearer conception of medieval literature attained, the term 'Gothic' with its associations of something barbaric became gradually identified with the term 'romantic', the irregular charms of which were latterly said to be more striking than those of the classical kind. Or again, there was the term 'sublime', which came to be associated with the most powerful of emotions; and, distinguished from the beautiful, it extended the scope of aesthetic appreciation. Vaguely used by Hobbes, it was a quality with which Lowth (following 'Longinus') connected great thoughts coupled with simplicity of expression, while Burke suggested as contributory a certain vagueness of utterance. The term 'imagination' however, still lacked clear definition. Throughout the whole period it stood for a mere wayward 'fancy', a source of mental aberration; and though Burke limited it to the faculty that represented and combined images received through the senses, Hurd, in identifying it with 'fancy', still described it as 'that credulous faculty that loved to admire and to be deceived'. Dryden, it is true, in one place regards it as something more than 'fancy', and as the faculty responsible for 'invention, fancy and judgment'. But no trace as yet was forthcoming of any estimate of it as a transcendental power, the creative force of poetry.

It is however when we consider finally the striking advance made in the appreciation of actual literature that we realize most forcibly the progress that accompanied all this theorizing, and the great change that in the meantime had come over the critical position. Of the detection of abuses, in the first place, that negative, if also necessary, side of criticism, there was no lack; and in this task good sense, as formerly, played its part. The defects of the contemporary stage, for instance, were handsomely dealt with, not only in *The Rehearsal* but also by Addison, Fielding and Sheridan. And the reigning melodramatic effects, the unreasoned thrills, the crude appeals to the emotions, the glaring absurdities and clumsy technique were all duly ridiculed. Then, too, it was not left for a later generation to deride the defects of style and expression in the wider field of poetry. Most critics were alive to the 'false wit' engendered by the distorted fancies of imitators of the earlier metaphysical poets; and whereas Pope in his *Art of Sinking* had dealt firmly with contemporaries guilty of the 'false sublime', Johnson also called attention to the debasing of Milton's glorious verse and style in burlesque poems, or in others, like *Cyder*, with their trivial and commonplace themes. Nor did the stilted and affected manner, together with what became known as 18th-Century diction, with its florid epithets, its windy periphrases and false elevations, escape unnoticed. Swift, for one, ridiculed those 'flat unnecessary epithets that cost nothing'; and Johnson also complained of 'colourless, redundant epithets' employed only to fill up a line. And yet another timely caveat was uttered when Gray decried the excessive use of allegorical figures in lyrical poetry.

Of greater significance, however, was the more constructive criticism that not only rectified earlier false judgments, but, what was more important, also opened men's eyes to the living quality and thrill of great poetry. Among the corrected estimates, in the first place, was that relating to the extent and value of the earlier native literature; for with the growth of the historical sense it could no longer be maintained that literature in England had begun with Mr. Waller. By Gray, Thomas Warton, Hurd and others fresh light was thrown on the manifold and long-lost achievements of the Middle Ages, on those days of chivalry which had produced their courtly romances and heart-warming ballads as well as tales of gramarye and fairyland; so that the period no longer appeared as a 'Gothic' twilight or an aftermath of the Dark Ages. Nor despite the animadversions of Rymer concerning 'savagery' and the like could Elizabethan literature be regarded as outmoded or wholly lacking in 'civility'. From now on, Shakespeare among the dramatists, and Spenser among the poets, assumed altogether a new status; and with Warton's *History* the achievements of the whole period were placed in a perspective of sorts. In connexion with contemporary poets, too, some revision of values went on. Though Milton's greatness in general had become fairly well established, there still remained certain censures that called for correction. And corrections were supplied by Johnson and Thomas Warton: the former, for instance, in refuting such things as Dryden's charge of 'flat passages' in the poet's great epic, the latter in affirming the value of his 'early blossoms', those minor poems which for a time had been so strangely depreciated and neglected. And notable in another sense was the revised estimate of Pope's *Homer* submitted before the century closed. To Johnson and many of his contemporaries the translation had seemed a miracle of art, in spite of stilted diction and non-Homeric qualities, which Johnson had defended as legitimate refinements demanded by current conventions. To Cowper, however, the version with its Ovidian ornament, 'its puerile conceits, extravagant metaphors and strutting phrase', was none other than a travesty of the original; and this, with some modification, was to be the verdict of later generations. But while such treatment of current abuses, together with the correction of earlier faulty estimates, provide ample evidence of a lively critical judgment at work, for the really great and substantial achievement of the period we must note the immense stride forward taken in the positive appreciation of literature, its subtle effects and varied appeal, and this with the help of new and illuminating methods already mentioned. There had been of course the perverse pronouncements of Rymer, as well as other wild judgments, due to wrong-headed theories or personal limitations. Yet altogether the light now thrown on literature from various angles was as suggestive as it was unprecedented. There had been little or nothing like it before. It constitutes an outstanding element in the critical performance at this date; and it prepared the way for 19th-Century triumphs in a measure not always appreciated.

Of this increasing sensitiveness to aesthetic effects the most striking witness was in connexion with Shakespeare. And one can but marvel at the sudden and effective awakening to those main problems, the elucidation of which from now on was to lead to a finer and ever-growing appreciation of his work. It was not only that Theobald and others, out of disordered and mutilated texts, gave to their generation versions corresponding more nearly to what Shakespeare had written. Nor was the wonder confined to such things as Dryden's early but comprehensive pronouncement on Shakespeare, any more than to his penetrating insight into the character of Caliban. Successful adventures in revealing characters were not uncommon at the time; and over them all Morgann's illuminating analysis of Falstaff stood supreme. But what was perhaps even more surprising was the intimate understanding of Shakespeare's technique that was now forthcoming, as if in reply to Voltaire's vicious denigration. Before the close of the century, for one thing, the main body of his source-material was known and its importance grasped; and in addition his subtle methods of depicting character were now for the first time analysed and clearly discerned. As Kames pointed out, he had distinguished characters mainly by means of action and speech, by what they did and said; while Morgann, even more subtly, noted also his use of cross-references for that same purpose, by means of which light was thrown on a given character by remarks of other characters in the play. Moreover, attention was now called to the 'roundness' of his characters, and to the skill with which character-development was contrived. Nor was this all; for Kames was the first to point out his discriminating use of verse and prose; and that defects in certain plays could be taken to indicate early work, thus providing internal evidence for arriving at a chronological order of the plays. Finally there was Morgann's insistence that for a just appreciation of dramatic qualities the logical understanding was not enough, that 'the impression was the fact', and that an exercise of the feelings and sensibilities was essential. So that altogether it is not too much to say that now were being prescribed the main lines along which future Shakespeare studies were to proceed. These 18th-Century principles were developed, but not originated, by 19th-Century critics.

Similarly it was now that a serious beginning was made in appreciating the work of a multitude of other writers; and the results represented the first drafts of later evaluations, the foundations on which the 19th Century was to build and refine. It was not only that the unfamiliar qualities of old romances and ballads had been brought to light; or that the account of Chaucer, bordering on the definitive, had revealed once for all the art underlying his characterization and verse, so that he could no longer be dismissed with a smile as a humorous old poet. Spenser, too, now placed in his proper background, was seen to possess qualities all his own, and was rescued from patronage and neglect. Milton's stature, again, was increased by the recognition of the cosmic sweep of his vision, the organ music of his verse, and the charm of his early poems. And while Pope's status as a poet had been surprisingly challenged, the key to the understanding of Donne's complex sensibilities had been found, though as yet his real significance remained unfathomed. Nor were the greater poets alone under review. Warton's *History* was the first attempt to cover the whole ground of earlier native literature. Johnson's survey extended from Cowley to Gray, a survey in which were included many minor poets from Waller and Denham onwards; and not least valuable were his eloquent and searching disquisitions on the prose styles of Addison and Dryden. It was thus that the wide and varied vista of English literature as it then existed was displayed to the view, and material provided for a coherent history of the national literature.

And the survey thus furnished was no cut-and-dried affair. It was characterized throughout by a growing freedom and alertness of judgment, which recognized on occasion subtle and original effects, while illustrating the value of new and hitherto untried critical methods. It was a refined taste, for instance, that detected the ease and charm of 'the familiar style' in Cowley's prose and Prior's verse, that style, according to Cowper, 'the most difficult of all styles to succeed in'; and equally penetrating was Joseph Warton's judgment in appreciating the exquisite delight of Thomson's *Seasons*, as that of opening men's eyes to unheeded beauties of external Nature, to 'the silence that preceded an April shower', or 'the murmurs of insects swarming on a summer's day'. Then, too, a marked acuteness of mind was responsible for Gray's comment on Chaucer's verse, and on the long-windedness of medieval narratives, which he explained as due to the slow-moving minds of contemporaries, who required some amount of tedious detail to give an air of reality to facts. And this was matched by Dryden's shrewd injunction to an age of gorgeous prose that 'a man should write only all he ought'; or again, by Morgann's profound thought that laughter was an admission that the object concerned had some good qualities, a truth that prompted his investigation of Falstaff.

In addition, the judgments now provided gave evidence also of an openness of mind and a readiness to recognize new literary values; critical qualities not always associated with the 18th Century. Thus, for example, not only were the merits of blank verse ultimately established, and its essence seen to be something more than prose cut into lengths, for Sprat also welcomed 'the new sort of writing' bound up with Cowley's Pindarics, as a kind of free verse with irregular and 'masculine' qualities, in contrast with the dull monotony of the heroic couplet. New and strange qualities were also made familiar by Lowth's appreciation of Biblical poetry; Gray, again, insisted on the superiority of lyrical poetry to every other kind, in opposition to the tradition which had regarded such poetry as of a lesser breed; and Hurd was not alone in commending 'the fairy way of writing', and the literature that dealt with themes other than those of the world of facts. It is worth noting, besides, that Johnson approved of Gay's *Beggar's Opera* as 'a new species of composition', despite current prejudices against that form of drama; or that Hurd defended the recent innovations of comedies of high life and tragedies of low life. The most notable example of this openness of mind, however, was in connexion with that new phenomenon, the modern novel. At first the term 'novel' was reserved for such works as the love-stories of Ariosto; and the new form was variously described in orthodox teminology as 'a comedy of romance', 'a comic epic in prose', and the like. Certain doubts were at first expressed as to its literary and social values; but it was welcomed by Johnson and warmly adopted by Fielding. To the latter it was primarily a realistic development of the 17th-Century romance, but devoid of its fanciful and fantastic elements. Its characters were said to be types of human nature; it was to be instinct with the comic spirit; and its theme was to be love treated in a vein of wholesome laughter.

Such then is the story of 17th- and 18th-Century criticism. It is a story, not so much of the repudiation of an unsuitable literary creed, as of a development from the study of literature *in vacuo* to the study of its relations to the mind of man and its external environment, from the correction of faults to an appreciation of beauties, and from a casual and ancillary activity to a definite quest for a new aesthetic. The development was the work of a whole society reflecting on the first principles of taste; and the chief contributors—men of letters, antiquarians, philosophers and art-critics—approached the main problem from different angles and drew their inspiration from various sources. Among the more pervasive influences was that of 'Longinus', who recalled to men's minds the spiritual side of literature; and not the least part of England's debt to Boileau was his introduction of that great critic to English readers. At the same time much was derived from the larger views suggested by certain French critics, from the revival of earlier native literature and a study of the sister arts. Dryden was perhaps the most active of native influences, though each of the greater critics in turn broke new ground in this or that direction. Hobbes and Locke, too, had set men thinking along fresh channels: while Hume suggested that aesthetic judgment involved an exercise of both feeling and reason. The results are seen in the theories and appreciations of critics ranging from Dryden to Cowper: and the intensive studies of the mid-18th Century in particular constitute one of the high-water marks of English criticism. Altogether the work done represents an integral and indispensable phase of English critical history, which at its best has rarely been surpassed in either initiative or insight. And if (according to Sainte-Beuve) the purpose of criticism is to inculcate the art of reading a book with judgment without ceasing to relish it, then the judicial criticism of this period had rendered invaluable service to its own and later generations.

Of the influence of this phase of criticism on 19th-Century activities there can be no question; and this, apart from the immense debt owed to 18th-Century Shakespearean and other studies; though the pedigree of ideas, it must be confessed, is often deceptive. Such influence, however, was surely present when occasional ideas characteristic of the 18th Century were adopted at this later date, ideas such as the definition of poetry as 'emotion recollected in tranquillity', or again, the commonplace that 'beauty lies in the eye of the beholder'. Besides, Lamb, for example, would seem to have been influenced by Johnson's views on Shakespeare's tragedies when he suggests that 'Lear was impossible to be represented on a stage'; and, still more clearly, when, in defending the amoral nature of Restoration comedy, he adopts Johnson's remark on the pardonable non-moral element in the fantastic 17th-Century romances.[1]

[1] cf. also Matthew Arnold's use of Reynolds's term, 'the grand style', and the reminiscence, in his matchless description of Oxford towers, of Gray's Burnham beeches 'ever dreaming out their old stories to the winds'.

25

More important than such sporadic reminiscences however was the influence of the general trend of 18th-Century criticism and its gropings for sound ideas on the critical process and standards. The 18th Century had revealed that for an aesthetic appreciation of a work of art its relation to the mind of man was fundamental, that intellectual faculties alone would not suffice; and while glimpses had been caught of higher levels of 'reason', it was felt that a synthesis of impressions and reason was the essential test. A more complete synthesis was to come with Coleridge's realization of 'the higher sense', and his exposition of the poetic imagination. But for this the 18th Century had prepared the way in suggesting that while reason was still to be the guide, yet 'the impression was the fact', that emotional as well as intellectual tests were to be applied, and that the first stage of the critic's duty, as Pater later on insisted, was 'to feel the virtue of the poet'.

Equally significant with the reaction from a sober rationalism and the value thus attached to the emotional side of literature was the emergence during the 18th Century, along with the Longinian test, of the first signs of what was to prove the prevailing standard of 19th-Century critics. Having realized that inadequate tests were provided by earlier theories, 18th-Century critics sought for standards more effective in the sense of the beautiful. But beauty being found to be an occult influence which defied analysis, the suggestion was made that the secret lay in an artistic aim clearly conceived and consistently carried out. Before the end of the century, it is worth noting, Herder had declared that 'the best way to judge an author is by the design of his own work'. Goethe, too, was to inquire what an author set out to do, whether his plan was reasonable and sensible, and how far he had succeeded in carrying it out. And this principle, which marked the transition from the old criticism to the new, was to govern the activities of English critics of the 19th Century. It put an end to all ideas of external and absolute standards. From now on, the touchstone of excellence was to be found in the work of the poet himself; and poets in consequence acquired greater dignity and freedom. It was a change indeed that was already reflected to some extent in 18th-Century conceptions of the critic's function. To Rymer he had been a sort of policeman; to Harris later, 'a master of ceremony in the court of letters'. And with this important transition already foreshadowed in the earlier century, the later triumphs were no sudden or unexplained development.

The truth was that under the superficial calm of the 'indispensable' 18th-Century subtle forces had been at work. Amidst much confusion efforts had been made to make literary judgment (in Plato's terminology) a matter of 'knowledge', not 'opinion'. The right questions had been asked if not as yet solved; and, in short, in the period represented by Dryden, Addison, Gray, the Wartons, Johnson and the rest, a new aesthetic was in the making and the foundations of 19th-Century criticism were being laid.

INDEX

Printed in Great Britain by
Butler & Tanner Ltd.,
Frome and London